Generalized Linear Models

To my parents,
To my daughter Laura,
To Marielle and Gaële

Series Editor
Nikolaos Limnios

Generalized Linear Models

Problems with Censored, Missing, and Zero-inflated Data

Jean-François Dupuy

ISTE

WILEY

First published 2025 in Great Britain and the United States by ISTE Ltd and John Wiley & Sons, Inc.

ISTE Ltd
27-37 St George's Road
London SW19 4EU
UK

www.iste.co.uk

John Wiley & Sons, Inc.
111 River Street
Hoboken, NJ 07030
USA

www.wiley.com

Library of Congress Control Number: 2025932421

British Library Cataloguing-in-Publication Data
A CIP record for this book is available from the British Library
ISBN 978-1-78630-702-6

Contents

Preface

Since their formulation by Nelder and Wedderburn in the *Journal of the Royal Statistical Society: Series A* in 1972, generalized linear models (GLMs) have become one of the cornerstones of statistical modeling. They have spawned – and continue to do so – an abundance of literature, powered by theoretical and methodological questions, or their links to applications. This work is dedicated to them. Of course, it does not have the aim of providing an exhaustive account of this literature. Several of the themes covered in the chapters deserve to be the subject of a work in their own right. This is the case for a question with missing data, or when a censored response needs to be taken into account. The aim of this work (and of the author) is therefore more modest, seeking to describe some problems that involve GLMs which have been recently studied (missing data, censored data and excess zeros) and to report, once again without claiming to be exhaustive, the solutions that arose with them.

The subjects covered in this work do not therefore cover the immense variety of contributions to the literature on GLMs. We will not find, for example, a chapter dedicated to questions regarding the validation of the models, or of variable selection in a high dimension. In fact, the choice of subjects covered involves some degree of subjectivity, and largely reflects the author's centers of interest. Another imperative guided the writing of this work and the choice of its content: the methods described there can, for the most part, be implemented using dedicated functions, immediately available within packages of the statistical and data analysis software R (a free and open-source software). Certain methods require a little programming work, and R code examples are provided throughout the book.

Equally, note that a majority of the problems described here (such as the problems with missing or censored data) do not only arise in GLMs. We have therefore tried to give a sufficiently general description of the solutions proposed here, so that the reader will understand the main principles and can either apply – or adapt – them in other contexts. Finally, this work has been written in such a way that it can be approached by those with different levels of understanding. It is thus possible to comprehend the content without dwelling on the theoretical proofs which are, for the most part, provided in appendices in each chapter. Although these chapters are written such that they can be read (almost) independently of one another, it is recommended nevertheless to go through them in the order given in the table of contents, as it follows an increasing progression with regard to the difficulty of the methods described. A data set (available under R) serves as a common thread throughout the book, and it is described in section 2.5, which should be read before moving onto the other sections that use this set of data.

My warmest thanks go to Nikolaos Limnios, for his constant encouragement since my thesis, for inviting me to write this work and for the additions he has suggested.

I would also like to sincerely thank Ben Brown, who did a tremendous job translating this book from French to English.

Jean-François Dupuy
March 2025

Notation and Acronyms

$\mathbb{E}(X)$, $\text{var}(X)$	Mean and variance of X
$\text{cov}(X, Y)$	Covariance of X and Y
$\bar{Y}_n$	Empirical mean of a sample $Y_1, \ldots, Y_n$
$\mathbb{P}_n$	Empirical measure
$\mathbb{G}_n$	Empirical process
$\xrightarrow{\mathcal{L}}$	Convergence in distribution
$\xrightarrow{\mathbb{P}}$	Convergence in probability
$\xrightarrow{a.s.}$	Almost sure convergence
$o_{\mathbb{P}}, O_{\mathbb{P}}$	Stochastic-order symbols
$\mathbb{R}, \mathbb{R}_+, \mathbb{R}_+^*$	Sets of the real numbers, positive reals, strictly positive reals
$\mathcal{B}(k, \pi), \mathcal{B}(\pi), \mathcal{NB}(k, \pi)$	Binomial, Bernoulli, negative binomial distributions
$\mathcal{P}(\mu)$, $\mathcal{GP}(\mu, \varphi)$	Poisson and generalized Poisson distributions
$\mathcal{N}(\mu, \Sigma)$, $\mathcal{T}_n$, χ^2_n, $F_{q,p}$	Normal, Student's t-, chi-squared, Fisher distributions
$G(\mu, \nu), \mathcal{E}(\lambda), IG(\mu, \sigma^2)$	Gamma, exponential, inverse-Gaussian distributions
u_α, $t_n(\alpha)$, $c_\alpha(q)$, $f_{q,p}(\alpha)$	Quantiles of order α of the $\mathcal{N}(0,1)$, $\mathcal{T}_n$, χ^2_q, $F_{q,p}$ distributions
Φ	Cumulative distribution function of the $\mathcal{N}(0,1)$ distribution
$1\{\cdot\}$	Indicator function
$A^\top$	Transpose of the matrix (or vector) A
AIC	Akaike's information criterion
AIPW	Augmented inverse probability weighted
BIC	Bayesian information criterion
EM	Expectation-maximization (algorithm)

GLM	Generalized linear models
i.i.d.	Independent and identically distributed (random variables)
IPW	Inverse probability weighted
LSE	Least-squares estimator
MAR	Missing at random
MCAR	Missing completely at random
MLE	Maximum likelihood estimator
MNAR	Missing not at random
MZINB	Marginal zero-inflated negative binomial
MZIP	Marginal zero-inflated Poisson
RSS	Residual sum of squares
s.e.	Standard error
ZIB	Zero-inflated binomial
ZIGP	Zero-inflated generalized Poisson
ZINB	Zero-inflated negative binomial
ZIP	Zero-inflated Poisson

1.2. Mean, variance, and variance function

Let Y be a random variable with density [1.1]. Additionally, set $\dot{a}(\theta) = \partial a(\theta)/\partial\theta$ and $\ddot{a}(\theta) = \partial^2 a(\theta)/\partial\theta^2$ (we will assume that a is infinitely differentiable; see Sundberg (2019)). We will now show the following result:

PROPOSITION 1.1.– *In the model [1.1], we have:*

$$\mathbb{E}(Y) = \dot{a}(\theta) \text{ and } \text{var}(Y) = \phi\,\ddot{a}(\theta)$$

REMARK.– Since the function $\dot{a}$ is continuous and strictly increasing on Θ (since $\ddot{a}(\theta) = \text{var}(Y)/\phi > 0$), it therefore admits a continuous inverse, $\dot{a}^{-1}$. ■

PROOF OF PROPOSITION 1.1.– Let us set $\dot{f} = \partial f/\partial\theta$, $\ddot{f} = \partial^2 f/\partial\theta^2$, and assume that we can interchange the integral and differential operators. To simplify the notation below, we will write $\int$ in the place of $\int_{\mathcal{Y}}$ and dy in the place of $d\mu(y)$.

Using this notation:

$$\int \dot{f}(y;\theta,\phi)dy = \frac{\partial}{\partial\theta}\int f(y;\theta,\phi)dy = 0$$

and:

$$\int \ddot{f}(y;\theta,\phi)dy = \frac{\partial^2}{\partial\theta^2}\int f(y;\theta,\phi)dy = 0$$

since $\int f(y;\theta,\phi)dy = 1$. Now, we differentiate [1.1] twice with respect to θ to obtain successively:

$$\dot{f}(y;\theta,\phi) = \frac{(y - \dot{a}(\theta))}{\phi} f(y;\theta,\phi)$$

and:

$$\ddot{f}(y;\theta,\phi) = \frac{(y - \dot{a}(\theta))^2}{\phi^2} f(y;\theta,\phi) - \frac{\ddot{a}(\theta)}{\phi} f(y;\theta,\phi)$$

Now, integrate these two expressions with respect to y. We obtain:

$$0 = \frac{\mathbb{E}(Y) - \dot{a}(\theta)}{\phi} \quad \text{and} \quad 0 = \frac{\mathbb{E}(Y - \dot{a}(\theta))^2}{\phi^2} - \frac{\ddot{a}(\theta)}{\phi}$$

From the first equation, we immediately deduce that $\mathbb{E}(Y) = \dot{a}(\theta)$ and, by observing that $\mathbb{E}(Y - \dot{a}(\theta))^2 = \mathbb{E}(Y - \mathbb{E}(Y))^2 = \text{var}(Y)$, we easily deduce from the second equation that $\text{var}(Y) = \phi\,\ddot{a}(\theta)$. ■

In the following, we will set $\mu := \mathbb{E}(Y)$, so that with this notation:

$$\begin{aligned}\text{var}(Y) &= \phi\,\ddot{a}(\theta)\\ &= \phi\,\frac{\partial}{\partial\theta}\dot{a}(\theta)\\ &= \phi\,\frac{\partial\mu}{\partial\theta}\\ &:= \phi\,v(\mu)\end{aligned}$$

where $v(\mu) := \frac{\partial\mu}{\partial\theta} = \ddot{a}(\theta)$. The function $v(\mu)$ is called the *variance function*. In the model [1.1], it describes the way in which the variance of Y varies as a function of its mean (this is said to be the mean-variance relation).

In the Gaussian model, we will see in section 1.3 that $v(\mu) = 1$. Therefore, $v(\mu)$ does not depend on μ: the variance and the mean vary independently from one another. For the Poisson distribution, $v(\mu) = \mu$: the variance varies like the expected value. For the gamma distribution, $v(\mu) = \mu^2$: the variance varies like the square of the expected value (the standard deviation varies like the expected value).

1.3. Examples of exponential families

Exponential families include many of the classical probability distributions. We will describe some examples below, though there exists a great deal more examples (Sundberg 2019).

EXAMPLE 1.1 (BINOMIAL DISTRIBUTION).– Let $k \in \mathbb{N}^*$ be fixed. The family $\{\mathcal{B}(k,\pi); \pi \in (0,1)\}$ of binomial distributions with parameter π is an exponential family. Indeed, with respect to the counting measure on $\{0,1,\ldots,k\}$, for the $\mathcal{B}(k,\pi)$ distribution, we have:

$$\begin{aligned}f(y) &= C_k^y \pi^y (1-\pi)^{k-y}, \quad y = 0,1,\ldots,k\\ &= \exp\left(y\ln\left(\frac{\pi}{1-\pi}\right) + k\ln(1-\pi) + \ln C_k^y\right)\end{aligned}$$

which can be identified with [1.1], if we set $\theta = \ln(\frac{\pi}{1-\pi})$, $\phi = 1$, $a(\theta) = -k\ln(1-\pi) = k\ln(1+e^\theta)$ and $b(y,\phi) = \ln C_k^y$.

We see that:

$$\mathbb{E}(Y) = \dot{a}(\theta) = k\frac{e^\theta}{1+e^\theta} = k\pi$$

and:

$$\text{var}(Y) = \phi\,\ddot{a}(\theta) = k\frac{e^\theta}{(1+e^\theta)^2} = k\pi(1-\pi)$$

Denoting $\mu = \mathbb{E}(Y)$, then the variance function is equal to: $v(\mu) = \mu(k-\mu)/k$.

REMARK.– The particular case when $k = 1$ corresponds to the Bernoulli distribution. We will denote it by $\mathcal{B}(\pi)$. ■

EXAMPLE 1.2 (POISSON DISTRIBUTION).– The family $\{\mathcal{P}(\mu); \mu \in \mathbb{R}_+^*\}$ of Poisson distributions with parameter μ is an exponential family. The density on $\mathbb{N}$ for the $\mathcal{P}(\mu)$ distribution is written as:

$$\begin{aligned} f(y) &= \exp(-\mu)\frac{\mu^y}{y!}, \quad y = 0, 1, 2, \ldots \\ &= \exp\left(y \ln \mu - \mu - \ln y!\right) \end{aligned}$$

We identify it with [1.1] by setting $\theta = \ln \mu$, $\phi = 1$, $a(\theta) = \mu = e^\theta$ and $b(y, \phi) = -\ln y!$. We see that:

$$\mathbb{E}(Y) = \dot{a}(\theta) = e^\theta = \mu \quad \text{and} \quad \text{var}(Y) = \phi\,\ddot{a}(\theta) = e^\theta = \mu$$

We recover the equality property (called *equidispersion*) of the mean and variance from the Poisson distribution. Finally, the variance function $v(\mu)$ is simply equal to $v(\mu) = \mu$.

EXAMPLE 1.3 (NEGATIVE BINOMIAL DISTRIBUTION).– Let us consider a series of independent events in which a "success" occurs with constant probability π (so that "failure" occurs with complementary probability $1 - \pi$). We repeat the events until a given number of k successes (with $k \in \{1, 2, \ldots\}$) have occurred. The negative binomial distribution $\mathcal{BN}(k, \pi)$ is the probability distribution of the random variable Y that counts the number of failures, which have occurred before obtaining k successes.

Its probability density is written as:

$$f(y) = C_{y+k-1}^{y}\pi^k\,(1-\pi)^y\,, \quad y = 0, 1, 2, \ldots$$

REMARK.– The particular case when $k = 1$ corresponds to the geometric distribution. ■

For each integer n, recall that $\Gamma(n+1) = n!$, and set $\kappa = 1/k$ and $\mu = k\left(\frac{1-\pi}{\pi}\right)$. We can then rewrite f as follows:

$$f(y) = \frac{\Gamma(y+\frac{1}{\kappa})}{y!\Gamma(\frac{1}{\kappa})}\left(\frac{\kappa\mu}{1+\kappa\mu}\right)^{y}\left(\frac{1}{1+\kappa\mu}\right)^{\frac{1}{\kappa}}, \quad y = 0, 1, 2, \ldots \qquad [1.3]$$

and then again, after some simple calculations:

$$f(y) = \exp\left(y\ln\left(\frac{\kappa\mu}{1+\kappa\mu}\right) - \frac{1}{\kappa}\ln(1+\kappa\mu) + \ln\Gamma\left(y+\frac{1}{\kappa}\right) - \ln\left(y!\Gamma\left(\frac{1}{\kappa}\right)\right)\right)$$

We identify f with [1.1] by setting $\theta = \ln\left(\frac{\kappa\mu}{1+\kappa\mu}\right)$, $\phi = 1$, $a(\theta) = \frac{1}{\kappa}\ln(1+\kappa\mu) = -\frac{1}{\kappa}\ln(1-e^{\theta})$ and $b(y,\phi) = \ln\Gamma\left(y+\frac{1}{\kappa}\right) - \ln\left(y!\Gamma\left(\frac{1}{\kappa}\right)\right)$. The negative binomial distributions therefore form an exponential family. We see that:

$$\mathbb{E}(Y) = \dot{a}(\theta) = \frac{1}{\kappa}\frac{e^{\theta}}{1-e^{\theta}} = \mu$$

and:

$$\mathrm{var}(Y) = \phi\,\ddot{a}(\theta) = \frac{1}{\kappa}\frac{e^{\theta}}{(1-e^{\theta})^2} = \mu(1+\kappa\mu)$$

The variance function is equal to:

$$v(\mu) = \mu(1+\kappa\mu) = \mu + \kappa\mu^2$$

The mean-variance relation is thus quadratic, from which comes the name "NB2 distribution" which is sometimes given to this distribution (the "2" refers to the power of μ in the variance function) (Cameron and Trivedi 1998; Hilbe 2011).

There exists another parameterization of the negative binomial distribution, in which the variance is a linear function of the mean. The corresponding distribution is hence called the "NB1 distribution".

The NB2 distribution can be obtained as a Poisson–gamma mixture (we show this in the technical appendix to this chapter; see section 1.5). This interpretation, along with the fact that $\mathrm{var}(Y) = \mu + \kappa\mu^2 > \mathbb{E}(Y) = \mu$, make the negative binomial distribution a very useful model for overdispersed count data.

EXAMPLE 1.4 (NORMAL DISTRIBUTION).– The family $\{\mathcal{N}(\mu, \sigma^2); \mu \in \mathbb{R}, \sigma \in \mathbb{R}_+^*\}$ of normal distributions with mean μ and variance σ^2 form an exponential family. The distribution $\mathcal{N}(\mu, \sigma^2)$ has the following density on $\mathbb{R}$:

$$\begin{aligned} f(y) &= \frac{1}{\sqrt{2\pi\sigma^2}} \exp\left(-\frac{1}{2\sigma^2}(y-\mu)^2\right), \quad y \in \mathbb{R} \\ &= \exp\left(\frac{y\mu - \frac{\mu^2}{2}}{\sigma^2} - \frac{1}{2}\left[\ln(2\pi\sigma^2) + \frac{y^2}{\sigma^2}\right]\right) \end{aligned}$$

which can be identified with [1.1] if we set $\theta = \mu$, $\phi = \sigma^2$, $a(\theta) = \frac{\mu^2}{2} = \frac{\theta^2}{2}$ and $b(y, \phi) = -\frac{1}{2}\left[\ln(2\pi\sigma^2) + \frac{y^2}{\sigma^2}\right]$. We see that:

$$\mathbb{E}(Y) = \dot{a}(\theta) = \theta = \mu \text{ and } \operatorname{var}(Y) = \phi\,\ddot{a}(\theta) = \sigma^2$$

The variance function is equal to $v(\mu) = 1$.

EXAMPLE 1.5 (GAMMA DISTRIBUTION).– The family $\{G(\mu, \nu); \mu \in \mathbb{R}_+^*, \nu \in \mathbb{R}_+^*\}$ of gamma distributions form an exponential family. There exist several parameterizations of the gamma distribution. The one that we use here is such that μ coincides with the expected value of $G(\mu, \nu)$. For this parameterization, the distribution $G(\mu, \nu)$ has the following density on $\mathbb{R}_+$:

$$\begin{aligned} f(y) &= y^{\nu-1} \exp\left(-\frac{y\nu}{\mu}\right)\left(\frac{\nu}{\mu}\right)^{\nu} \frac{1}{\Gamma(\nu)}, \quad y \in \mathbb{R}_+ \\ &= \exp\left(\frac{y(-\mu^{-1}) - \ln\mu}{\nu^{-1}} + (\nu - 1)\ln y + \nu \ln \nu - \ln\Gamma(\nu)\right) \end{aligned}$$

where $\Gamma(x) = \int_0^\infty e^{-t} t^{x-1}\, dt$ (the function $\Gamma(\cdot)$ is called the gamma function). We can identify f with [1.1] by setting $\theta = -1/\mu$, $\phi = 1/\nu$, $a(\theta) = \ln\mu = -\ln(-\theta)$ and $b(y, \phi) = (\nu - 1)\ln y + \nu\ln\nu - \ln\Gamma(\nu)$. We see that:

$$\mathbb{E}(Y) = \dot{a}(\theta) = -\frac{1}{\theta} = \mu \quad \text{and} \quad \operatorname{var}(Y) = \phi\,\ddot{a}(\theta) = \frac{\phi}{\theta^2} = \frac{\mu^2}{\nu}$$

The variance function $v(\mu)$ is equal to $v(\mu) = \mu^2$.

REMARK.– The gamma distribution $G(\nu, \nu/2)$ (with $\nu \in \mathbb{N}^*$) has the density:

$$f(y) = \frac{1}{2^{\frac{\nu}{2}}\Gamma\left(\frac{\nu}{2}\right)} y^{\frac{\nu}{2}-1} \exp\left(-\frac{y}{2}\right), \quad y \in \mathbb{R}_+$$

We recognize it as the probability density of the χ^2-distribution with ν degrees of freedom (with mean $\mathbb{E}(Y) = \nu$ and variance $\text{var}(Y) = 2\nu$). The χ^2-distributions also therefore form an exponential family. ■

EXAMPLE 1.6 (INVERSE-GAUSSIAN DISTRIBUTION).– The family $\{IG(\mu, \sigma^2); \mu \in \mathbb{R}_+^*, \sigma \in \mathbb{R}_+^*\}$ of inverse-Gaussian distributions is an exponential family. The density of $IG(\mu, \sigma^2)$ on $\mathbb{R}_+^*$ is given by:

$$\begin{aligned} f(y) &= \frac{1}{\sigma\sqrt{2\pi y^3}} \exp\left(-\frac{(y-\mu)^2}{2y(\mu\sigma)^2}\right), \quad y \in \mathbb{R}_+^* \\ &= \exp\left(\frac{y\left(-\frac{1}{2\mu^2}\right) + \frac{1}{\mu}}{\sigma^2} - \frac{1}{2y\sigma^2} - \frac{1}{2}\ln(2\pi y^3 \sigma^2)\right) \end{aligned}$$

It can be identified with [1.1] by setting $\theta = -1/(2\mu^2)$, $\phi = \sigma^2$, $a(\theta) = -1/\mu = -\sqrt{-2\theta}$ and $b(y, \phi) = -\frac{1}{2y\sigma^2} - \frac{1}{2}\ln(2\pi y^3\sigma^2)$. We check that:

$$\mathbb{E}(Y) = \dot{a}(\theta) = \frac{1}{\sqrt{-2\theta}} = \mu \quad \text{and} \quad \text{var}(Y) = \phi\, \ddot{a}(\theta) = \frac{\sigma^2}{(-2\theta)^{\frac{3}{2}}} = \sigma^2\mu^3$$

The variance function $v(\mu)$ is equal to $v(\mu) = \mu^3$.

REMARK.– It follows from expressions [1.1] and [1.2] that the distributions whose support depends upon a parameter are excluded from the exponential families (such as the uniform distribution on the interval $[0, \theta]$, since its support varies with θ). ■

Table 1.1 summarizes the principal elements for each exponential family described above (for the $\mathcal{B}(k, \pi)$ distribution; recall that we had set $\mu = k\pi$ and, for the $\mathcal{BN}(k, \pi)$ distribution, we had set $\mu = k\left(\frac{1-\pi}{\pi}\right)$).

In each of the preceding examples, we identified a function (let us denote it by g) that connects the mean $\mu = \mathbb{E}(Y)$ of the considered distribution to the canonical parameter θ, namely:

$$\theta = g(\mu)$$

Law	Support	$\mathbb{E}(Y)$	var(Y)	θ	ϕ	$v(\mu)$
$\mathcal{B}(k,\pi)$	$\{0,1,\ldots,k\}$	$k\pi$	$k\pi(1-\pi)$	$\ln\left(\frac{\pi}{1-\pi}\right)$	1	$\mu\left(1-\frac{\mu}{k}\right)$
$\mathcal{P}(\mu)$	$\mathbb{N}$	μ	μ	$\ln\mu$	1	μ
$\mathcal{BN}(k,\pi)$	$\mathbb{N}$	μ	$\mu\left(1+\frac{\mu}{k}\right)$	$\ln(1-\pi)$	1	$\mu\left(1+\frac{\mu}{k}\right)$
$\mathcal{N}(\mu,\sigma^2)$	$\mathbb{R}$	μ	σ^2	μ	σ^2	1
$G(\mu,\nu)$	$\mathbb{R}_+$	μ	$\frac{\mu^2}{\nu}$	$-\frac{1}{\mu}$	$\frac{1}{\nu}$	μ^2
$IG(\mu,\sigma^2)$	$\mathbb{R}_+^*$	μ	$\sigma^2\mu^3$	$-\frac{1}{2\mu^2}$	σ^2	μ^3

Table 1.1. *Characteristics of the classical exponential families*

This function is called the *canonical link function*. Recall that $\mu = \mathbb{E}(Y) = \dot{a}(\theta)$ from proposition 1.1. From this, we have $\theta = g(\mu) = g(\dot{a}(\theta))$ and thus $g = \dot{a}^{-1}$.

For the binomial distribution $Y \sim \mathcal{B}(k,\pi)$, $\theta = \ln(\frac{\pi}{1-\pi}) = \ln(\frac{\mu}{k-\mu})$. The function $\pi \mapsto \ln(\frac{\pi}{1-\pi})$ is called the logit function; we denote $\theta = \ln(\frac{\pi}{1-\pi}) = \text{logit}(\pi)$ ("logit" link). For the Poisson distribution $Y \sim \mathcal{P}(\mu)$, $\theta = \ln\mu$ ("log" link). For the negative binomial distribution, $\theta = \ln(\frac{\kappa\mu}{1+\kappa\mu})$. The canonical link function for the normal distribution $Y \sim \mathcal{N}(\mu,\sigma^2)$ is just the identity function. Indeed, $\theta = \text{id}(\mu)$. For the gamma distribution $Y \sim G(\mu,\nu)$, $\theta = -\frac{1}{\mu}$. For the inverse-Gaussian distribution $IG(\mu,\sigma^2)$, $\theta = -\frac{1}{2\mu^2}$.

Let us represent the densities of the binomial, Poisson, negative-binomial, normal, gamma and inverse-Gaussian distributions for various values of their respective parameters. The R code (R Core Team 2020) below was used to obtain Figure 1.1. It can be easily adapted to produce the other figures.

```
pi=c(0.1,0.5,0.9)
par(mfrow=c(1,3))
for (j in 1:3){
        barplot(dbinom(0:20,size=20,prob=pi[j]),
            names.arg=0:20,col='lightblue')}
```

1.4. Maximum likelihood estimation

Maximum likelihood estimation is a general estimation method used in parametric models.

Let us briefly write down the principle. Then we can apply it to estimate the parameter θ in the exponential model [1.1] (estimation of the dispersion parameter ϕ – when it is unknown – will be discussed in Chapter 2). Here again, we introduce just the notions necessary to understand the material presented in this book, and we refer the reader interested in more detailed treatments to van der Vaart (1998) and Sundberg (2019).

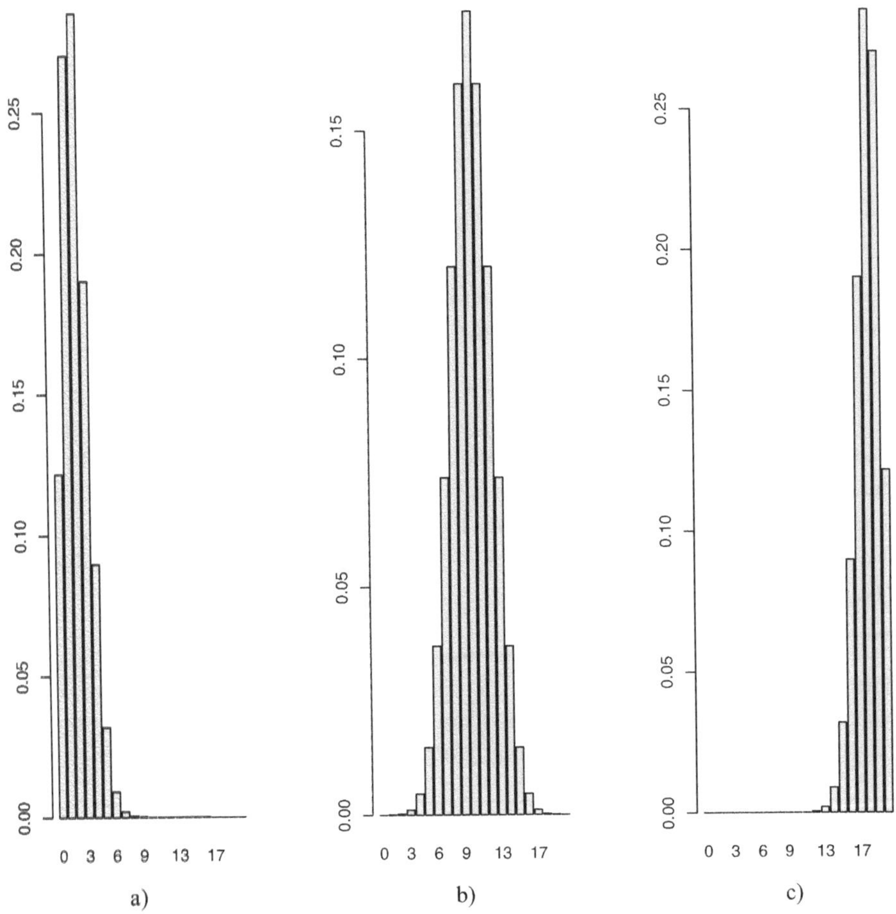

Figure 1.1. *Binomial distribution* $\mathcal{B}(k, \pi)$ *for* $k = 20$ *and* $\pi = 0.1$ *(a),* $\pi = 0.5$ *(b) and* $\pi = 0.9$ *(c)*

Consider a parametric statistical model $\{P_\theta; \theta \in \Theta \subseteq \mathbb{R}^p\}$, and denote by f_θ the density of P_θ with respect to an appropriate measure: the Lebesgue measure or the counting measure. Suppose that we observe a sample $\mathbf{Y} = (Y_1, \ldots, Y_n)$ of the distribution P_θ, where the value of θ is unknown. The quantities:

$$L_n(\theta) = f_\theta(\mathbf{Y}) \quad \text{and} \quad \ell_n(\theta) = \ln L_n(\theta) = \ln f_\theta(\mathbf{Y})$$

are called the likelihood and the log-likelihood of the parameter θ (with respect to the observation $\mathbf{Y}$), respectively. Subject to its existence, the maximum likelihood estimator (MLE) of θ is an element $\hat{\theta}_n$ of Θ, which maximizes the likelihood, or equivalently, the log-likelihood. Let us denote:

$$\hat{\theta}_n = \arg\max_{\theta \in \Theta} L_n(\theta) = \arg\max_{\theta \in \Theta} \ell_n(\theta)$$

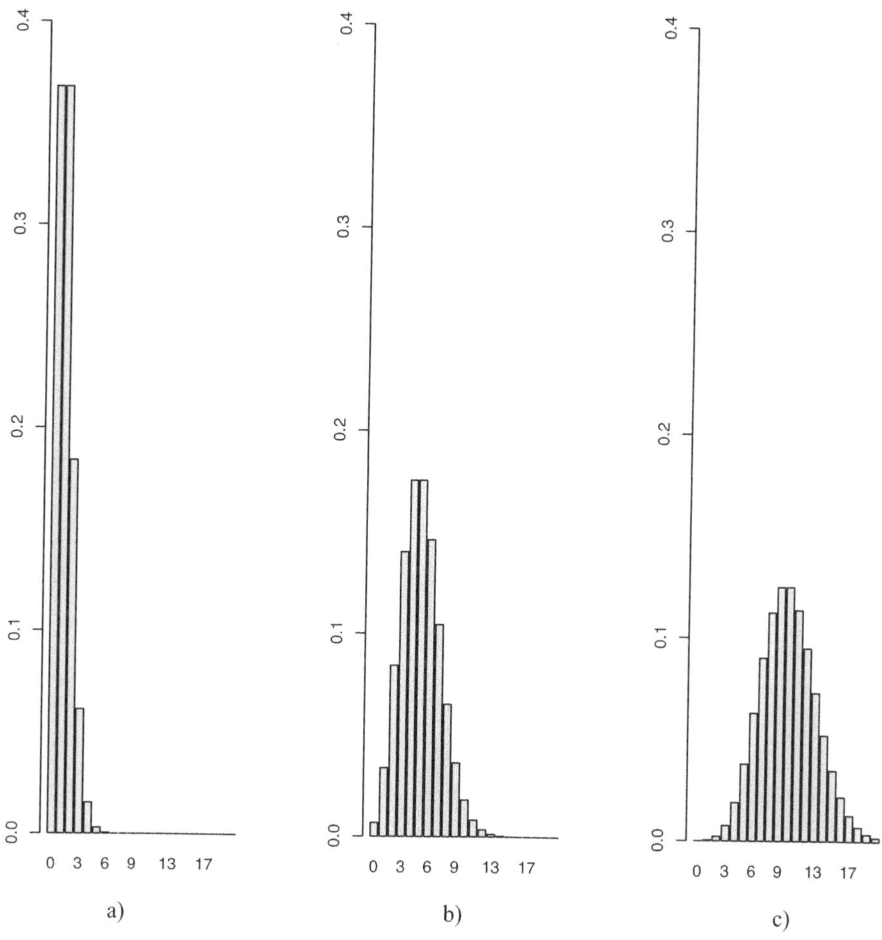

Figure 1.2. *Poisson distribution $\mathcal{P}(\mu)$ for $\mu = 1$ (a), $\mu = 5$ (b) and $\mu = 10$ (c)*

If it exists and is unique, then intuitively, the MLE is the value of the parameter which maximizes the probability of observing the available data. We can see this as being the most probable value (the most "likely") for the parameter, with respect to the sample $\mathbf{Y} = (Y_1, \ldots, Y_n)$. In the case where the observations $Y_1, \ldots, Y_n$ are independent and have the same density[1] f_θ:

$$\hat{\theta}_n = \arg\max_{\theta \in \Theta} \prod_{i=1}^{n} f_\theta(Y_i) = \arg\max_{\theta \in \Theta} \sum_{i=1}^{n} \ln f_\theta(Y_i)$$

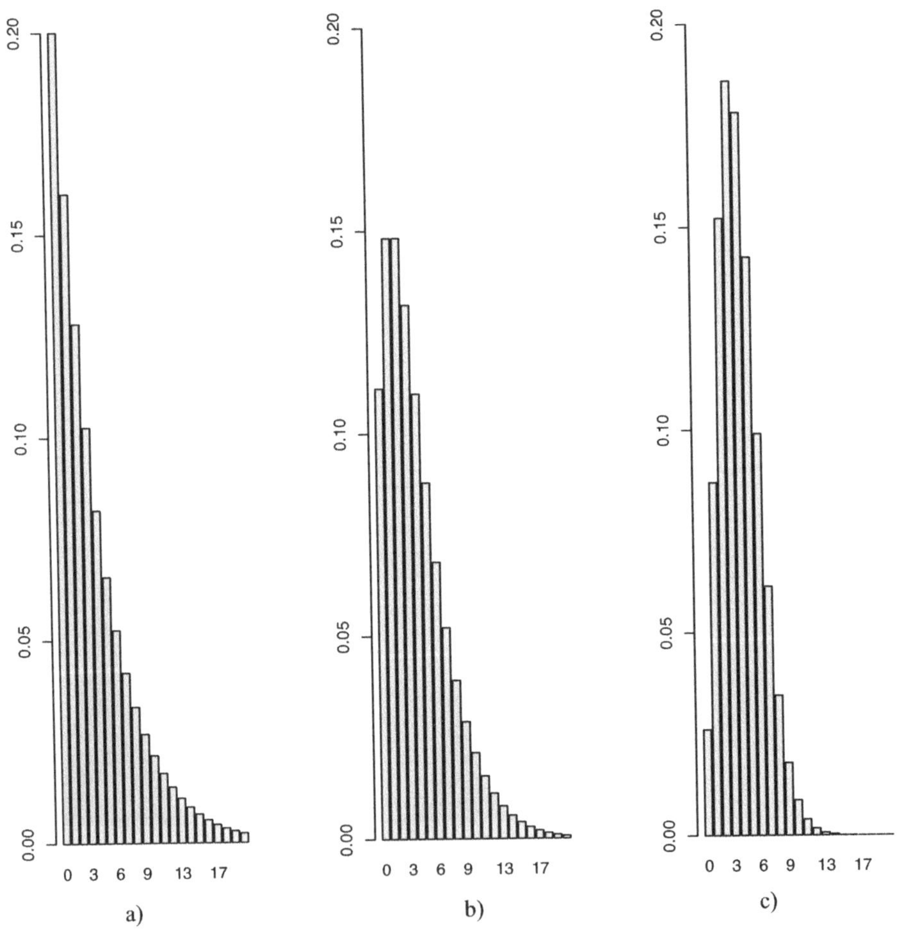

Figure 1.3. *Negative binomial distribution for* $\mu = 3$ *and* $\kappa = 1$ *(a),* $\kappa = 0.5$ *(b) and* $\kappa = 0.05$ *(c)*

1 We say then that $Y_1, \ldots, Y_n$ is an i.i.d. (independent and identically distributed) sample.

The MLE is a random variable, since it is a function of the random sample. Determining it consists of finding the global maximum of the likelihood. This can be achieved by directly searching for it or by differentiating the log-likelihood and solving the corresponding equation (called the score equation, the likelihood equation or the estimating equation):

$$\frac{\partial \ell_n(\theta)}{\partial \theta} = 0$$

(provided that the derivative exists). From the MLE, we can construct confidence intervals for θ, as well as decision rules for hypothesis testing problems involving θ.

This requires us to know the distribution of $\hat{\theta}_n$. This is only accessible in a few particular cases. Therefore, we will typically use the *asymptotic*[2] distribution of the MLE.

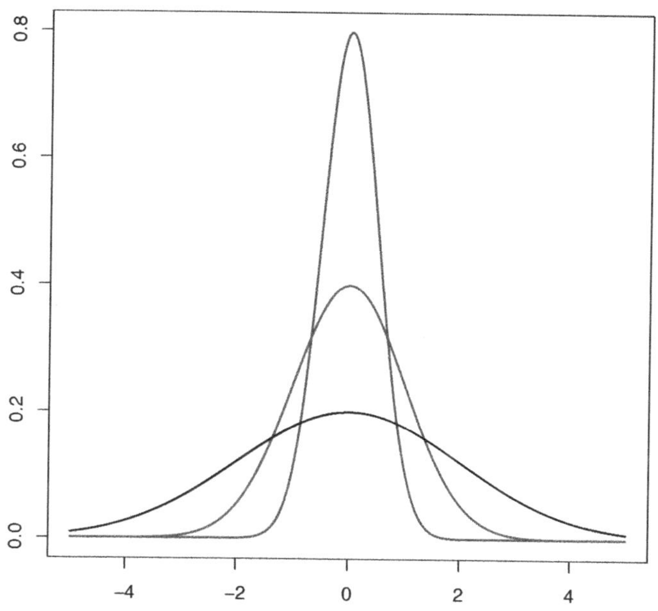

Figure 1.4. *Normal distribution $\mathcal{N}(\mu, \sigma^2)$ for $\mu = 0$ and $\sigma^2 = 0.25$ (blue), $\sigma^2 = 1$ (red) and $\sigma^2 = 4$ (black). For a color version of this figure, see www.iste.co.uk/dupuy/linearmodels.zip*

2 We use the term *asymptotic* when studying properties of the estimators, of test statistics, when the size n of the sample is made to go toward infinity.

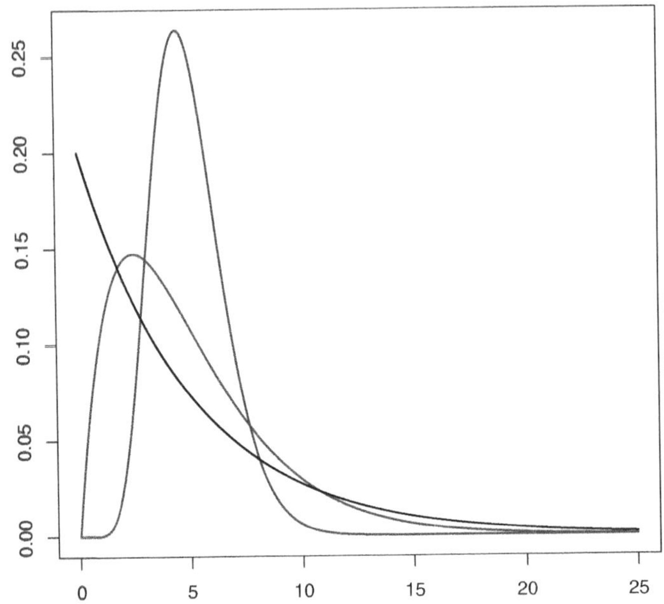

Figure 1.5. *Gamma distribution $G(\mu, \nu)$ for $\mu = 5$ and $\nu = 1$ (black), $\nu = 2$ (red), $\nu = 10$ (blue). For a color version of this figure, see www.iste.co.uk/dupuy/linearmodels.zip*

The asymptotic properties (consistency and asymptotic normality) of the MLE are established easily enough in the case of exponential models. We state them in proposition 1.2 (see van der Vaart (1998) for a detailed treatment in the case of general parametric models).

In this proposition and in the rest of this work, we will denote by $\xrightarrow[n\to\infty]{p.s.}$, $\xrightarrow[n\to\infty]{\mathbb{P}}$ and $\xrightarrow[n\to\infty]{\mathcal{L}}$ the almost sure (a.s.), in probability, and in distribution convergences (these convergences are to be understood when the size n of the sample tends toward infinity).

PROPOSITION 1.2.– *Let us denote by $(Y_1, \ldots, Y_n)$ an i.i.d. sample of the density [1.1], with $\theta \in \Theta$ an interval of $\mathbb{R}$. Assume that the true value of θ, which is unknown, lies within the interior of Θ. Then, the MLE $\hat{\theta}_n$ is consistent:*

$$\hat{\theta}_n \xrightarrow[n\to\infty]{p.s.} \theta$$

and asymptotically Gaussian:

$$\sqrt{n}(\hat{\theta}_n - \theta) \xrightarrow[n\to\infty]{\mathcal{L}} \mathcal{N}\left(0, \frac{\phi^2}{\mathrm{var}(Y)}\right)$$

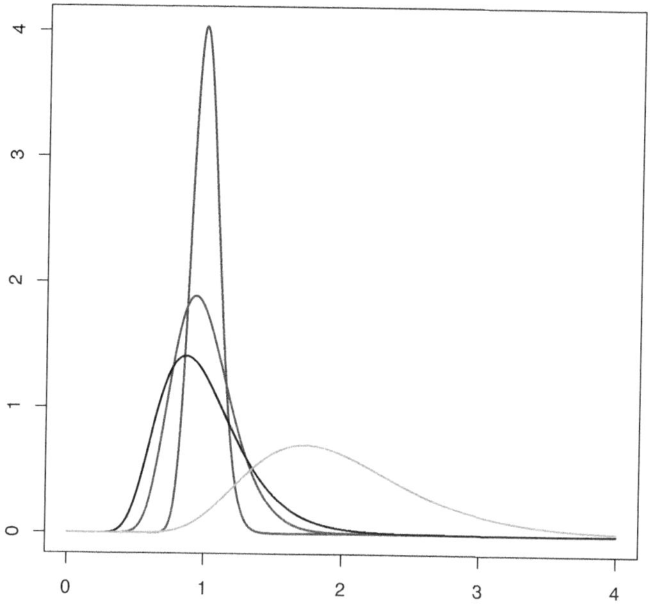

Figure 1.6. *Inverse-Gaussian distribution* $IG(\mu, \sigma^2)$ *for* $(\mu, \sigma^2) = (1, 0.01)$ *(blue),* $(\mu, \sigma^2) = (1, 0.05)$ *(red),* $(\mu, \sigma^2) = (1, 0.1)$ *(black) and* $(\mu, \sigma^2) = (2, 0.05)$ *(green). For a color version of this figure, see www.iste.co.uk/dupuy/linearmodels.zip*

PROOF OF PROPOSITION 1.2.– Since the observations are independent, the likelihood of (θ, ϕ) can be written as:

$$\begin{aligned} L_n(\theta, \phi) &= \prod_{i=1}^{n} \exp\left(\frac{Y_i\theta - a(\theta)}{\phi} + b(Y_i, \phi)\right) \\ &= \exp\left(\frac{n(\bar{Y}_n\theta - a(\theta))}{\phi} + \sum_{i=1}^{n} b(Y_i, \phi)\right) \end{aligned}$$

where $\bar{Y}_n = n^{-1}\sum_{i=1}^{n} Y_i$ denotes the empirical mean of the Y_i. From this, we obtain the log-likelihood $\ell_n(\theta, \phi) = \ln L_n(\theta, \phi)$:

$$\ell_n(\theta, \phi) = \frac{n(\bar{Y}_n\theta - a(\theta))}{\phi} + \sum_{i=1}^{n} b(Y_i, \phi)$$

of which the first two derivatives with respect to θ are:

$$\frac{\partial \ell_n(\theta, \phi)}{\partial \theta} = \frac{n(\bar{Y}_n - \dot{a}(\theta))}{\phi} \quad \text{and} \quad \frac{\partial^2 \ell_n(\theta, \phi)}{\partial \theta^2} = -\frac{n\ddot{a}(\theta)}{\phi}$$

The MLE of θ is obtained by solving the equation $\partial \ell_n(\theta, \phi)/\partial \theta = 0$, which amounts to solving:

$$n(\bar{Y}_n - \dot{a}(\hat{\theta}_n)) = 0$$

We obtain:

$$\dot{a}(\hat{\theta}_n) = \bar{Y}_n \qquad [1.4]$$

REMARK.– Since equation [1.4] does not depend on ϕ, the MLE of θ does not therefore depend on it either. ϕ can be estimated in a second step. Note also that at a fixed ϕ, ℓ_n is a strictly concave function of θ (since $\ddot{a}(\theta) > 0$, and therefore $\partial^2 \ell_n(\theta, \phi)/\partial \theta^2 < 0$), ensuring the uniqueness of the MLE. ■

The strong law of large numbers implies that:

$$\dot{a}(\hat{\theta}_n) = \bar{Y}_n \xrightarrow[n \to \infty]{a.s.} \mathbb{E}(Y) = \dot{a}(\theta)$$

As the function $\dot{a}^{-1}$ is continuous, we can hence apply the continuous mapping theorem (theorem 1.1, section 1.5) to obtain:

$$\hat{\theta}_n = \dot{a}^{-1}(\dot{a}(\hat{\theta}_n)) \xrightarrow[n \to \infty]{p.s.} \dot{a}^{-1}(\dot{a}(\theta)) = \theta$$

To show the asymptotic normality of $\hat{\theta}_n$, we begin by applying the central limit theorem to $\bar{Y}_n$:

$$\sqrt{n}\left(\bar{Y}_n - \mathbb{E}(Y)\right) = \sqrt{n}(\dot{a}(\hat{\theta}_n) - \dot{a}(\theta)) \xrightarrow[n \to \infty]{\mathcal{L}} \mathcal{N}(0, \text{var}(Y)) = \mathcal{N}(0, \phi\, \ddot{a}(\theta))$$

Then, we use the delta method (theorem 1.2, section 1.5) with $\varphi = \dot{a}^{-1}$ (we denote the derivative of $\dot{a}^{-1}$ by $(\dot{a}^{-1})'$), which gives us:

$$\sqrt{n}\left(\dot{a}^{-1}(\dot{a}(\hat{\theta}_n)) - \dot{a}^{-1}(\dot{a}(\theta))\right) \xrightarrow[n \to \infty]{\mathcal{L}} \mathcal{N}\left(0, \phi\, \ddot{a}(\theta)\{(\dot{a}^{-1})'(\dot{a}(\theta))\}^2\right)$$

However:

$$(\dot{a}^{-1})'(x) = \frac{1}{\ddot{a}(\dot{a}^{-1}(x))}$$

and thus:

$$(\dot{a}^{-1})'(\dot{a}(\theta)) = \frac{1}{\ddot{a}(\dot{a}^{-1}(\dot{a}(\theta)))} = \frac{1}{\ddot{a}(\theta)}$$

Furthermore, $\sqrt{n}(\dot{a}^{-1}(\dot{a}(\hat{\theta}_n)) - \dot{a}^{-1}(\dot{a}(\theta))) = \sqrt{n}(\hat{\theta}_n - \theta)$. And so, we finally obtain:

$$\sqrt{n}(\hat{\theta}_n - \theta) \xrightarrow[n\to\infty]{\mathcal{L}} \mathcal{N}\left(0, \frac{\phi}{\ddot{a}(\theta)}\right) = \mathcal{N}\left(0, \frac{\phi^2}{\text{var}(Y)}\right)$$ ■

REMARK.– Let us denote by $\hat{\mu}_n = g^{-1}(\hat{\theta}_n)$ the MLE of $\mu = \mathbb{E}(Y) = g^{-1}(\theta)$. We have: $\hat{\mu}_n = g^{-1}(\hat{\theta}_n) = g^{-1}(\dot{a}^{-1}(\bar{Y}_n))$ (from [1.4]). Therefore, $\hat{\mu}_n = g^{-1}(g(\bar{Y}_n)) = \bar{Y}_n$. From the central limit theorem, $\sqrt{n}(\hat{\mu}_n - \mu) \xrightarrow[n\to\infty]{\mathcal{L}} \mathcal{N}(0, \text{var}(Y))$. The Gaussian case is a particular case in which the results are exact for each n. If $Y_1, \ldots, Y_n$ is an i.i.d. sample of the distribution $\mathcal{N}(\mu, \sigma^2)$, then, for each n, $\bar{Y}_n \sim \mathcal{N}(\mu, \sigma^2/n)$. ■

EXAMPLE 1.7. (BINOMIAL DISTRIBUTION, CONTINUED).– Let $Y_1, Y_2, \ldots$ be an i.i.d. sequence of the distribution $\mathcal{B}(k, \pi)$. We have: $\mu = \mathbb{E}(Y) = k\pi$, $\theta = \ln(\frac{\mu}{k-\mu})$ and $\phi = 1$ (see Table 1.1). Then:

$$\sqrt{n}(\hat{\theta}_n - \theta) \xrightarrow[n\to\infty]{\mathcal{L}} \mathcal{N}\left(0, \frac{1}{k\pi(1-\pi)}\right)$$

and:

$$\sqrt{n}(\hat{\mu}_n - \mu) \xrightarrow[n\to\infty]{\mathcal{L}} \mathcal{N}(0, k\pi(1-\pi))$$

From equation [1.4], the MLE $\hat{\theta}_n$ is also a moment-type estimator. The method of moments is a simple method used to construct estimators. It takes advantage of the fact that empirical moments are "good" estimators of theoretical moments. Its principle is the following.

Consider a statistical model $\{P_\theta; \theta \in \Theta \subseteq \mathbb{R}^k\}$ such that the distribution P_θ admits a kth order moment, denoted by $\mu_k(\theta)$ (if $Y_1, \ldots, Y_n \sim P_\theta$, then $\mu_k(\theta) = \mathbb{E}(Y_i^k)$). For each $1 \leq j \leq k$, the jth order moment of P_θ is a function $\mu_j(\theta)$ of θ.

The method of moments consists of estimating θ by the solution $\hat{\theta}_n$ to the system of k equations:

$$\begin{cases} \frac{1}{n}\sum_{i=1}^n Y_i = \mu_1(\theta) \\ \frac{1}{n}\sum_{i=1}^n Y_i^2 = \mu_2(\theta) \\ \quad\vdots \\ \frac{1}{n}\sum_{i=1}^n Y_i^k = \mu_k(\theta) \end{cases}$$

which associates to each jth order moment its corresponding empirical moment.

A moment estimator of (θ, ϕ) in the model [1.1] is therefore a solution of:

$$\begin{cases} \frac{1}{n}\sum_{i=1}^n Y_i = \mathbb{E}(Y) \\ \frac{1}{n}\sum_{i=1}^n Y_i^2 = \text{var}(Y) + \mathbb{E}(Y)^2 \end{cases} \quad \text{or, alternatively:} \quad \begin{cases} \bar{Y}_n = \dot{a}(\theta) \\ S_n^2 = \phi\,\ddot{a}(\theta) \end{cases}$$

where $S_n^2 = \frac{1}{n}\sum_{i=1}^n Y_i^2 - (\frac{1}{n}\sum_{i=1}^n Y_i)^2$ denotes the empirical variance of the Y_i. If ϕ is known (binomial distribution, Poisson distribution, etc.), the moment estimator $\hat{\theta}_n$ of θ is the solution to the equation $\bar{Y}_n = \dot{a}(\hat{\theta}_n)$, which coincides with [1.4]. If ϕ is unknown, a moment estimator $(\hat{\theta}_n, \hat{\phi}_n)$ of (θ, ϕ) is the solution to the system:

$$\begin{cases} \bar{Y}_n = \dot{a}(\hat{\theta}_n) \\ S_n^2 = \hat{\phi}_n\,\ddot{a}(\hat{\theta}_n) \end{cases}$$

For example, if $Y_1, \ldots, Y_n \sim \mathcal{N}(\mu, \sigma^2)$, then, after setting $\theta = \mu$, $a(\theta) = \frac{\theta^2}{2}$ and $\phi = \sigma^2$ (see example 1.4), the moment estimator of (θ, ϕ) is given by the system:

$$\begin{cases} \hat{\theta}_n = \bar{Y}_n \\ \hat{\phi}_n = S_n^2 \end{cases}$$

since $\dot{a}(\theta) = \theta$ and $\ddot{a}(\theta) = 1$. As $(\theta, \phi) = (\mu, \sigma^2)$, we clearly recover the estimator which would have been obtained by applying the method of moments directly to the pair (μ, σ^2), without any reference to exponential families.

1.5. Technical appendix

1.5.1. *Some useful results from probability*

Below, we present two results that are useful in the proof of proposition 1.2.

THEOREM 1.1 (CONTINUOUS MAPPING THEOREM).– *Let g be a function whose set of discontinuous points is denoted by $\mathcal{D}_g$, (X_n) be a sequence of random vectors and X be a random vector. Suppose that $\mathbb{P}(X \in \mathcal{D}_g) = 0$. If the sequence (X_n) converges a.s. (respectively, in probability, in distribution) to X, then the sequence $(g(X_n))$ converges a.s. (respectively, in probability, in distribution) to $g(X)$.*

The reader can refer to van der Vaart (1998) for a proof of this result.

Let T_n be an estimator for a parameter θ. Suppose that we would like to estimate $\varphi(\theta)$, where φ is a known function. A natural estimator is $\varphi(T_n)$. We can therefore ask ourselves how the asymptotic properties of T_n are transferred onto $\varphi(T_n)$. If φ is continuous, then the continuous mapping theorem provides a first result. However, it does not answer the following question: if $\sqrt{n}(T_n - \theta) \xrightarrow[n\to\infty]{\mathcal{L}} T$, does the sequence $(\sqrt{n}(\varphi(T_n) - \varphi(\theta)))$ converge and, if so, toward what limit? If φ is linear, then $\sqrt{n}(\varphi(T_n) - \varphi(\theta)) \xrightarrow[n\to\infty]{\mathcal{L}} \varphi(T)$. The *delta method* answers the question provided that φ is differentiable (see van der Vaart (1998) for a proof).

THEOREM 1.2 (DELTA METHOD).– *Let (T_n) be a sequence of random variables such that $\sqrt{n}(T_n - \theta) \xrightarrow[n\to\infty]{\mathcal{L}} \mathcal{N}(0, \sigma^2)$, and let φ be a differentiable function with respect to θ, whose derivative $\dot{\varphi}(\theta)$ satisfies $\dot{\varphi}(\theta) \neq 0$. Then:*

$$\sqrt{n}(\varphi(T_n) - \varphi(\theta)) \xrightarrow[n\to\infty]{\mathcal{L}} \mathcal{N}(0, \sigma^2\{\dot{\varphi}(\theta)\}^2)$$

1.5.2. *Negative binomial distribution and Poisson-gamma mixtures*

Let U be a random variable of the gamma distribution $G(1, \nu)$. Let Y be a random variable which, conditionally on U, follows a Poisson distribution with parameter μU, where $\mu \in \mathbb{R}_+^*$. Denote $Y|U \sim \mathcal{P}(\mu U)$. We are going to determine the marginal distribution of Y. For each $y \in \mathbb{N}$, we calculate:

$$\begin{aligned}\mathbb{P}(Y = y) &= \int_0^\infty e^{-\mu u} \frac{(\mu u)^y}{y!} \frac{\nu^\nu}{\Gamma(\nu)} u^{\nu-1} e^{-u\nu}\, du \\ &= \frac{\nu^\nu \mu^y}{\Gamma(\nu) y!} \int_0^\infty e^{-(\mu+\nu)u} u^{y+\nu-1}\, du\end{aligned}$$

and make the change of variable $t = (\mu + \nu)u$. Then:

$$\begin{aligned}\mathbb{P}(Y = y) &= \frac{\nu^\nu \mu^y}{\Gamma(\nu) y!} \frac{\Gamma(y+\nu)}{(\mu+\nu)^{y+\nu}} \\ &= \frac{\Gamma(y+\nu)}{\Gamma(\nu) y!} \left(\frac{\mu}{\nu+\mu}\right)^y \left(\frac{\nu}{\nu+\mu}\right)^\nu\end{aligned}$$

Up to reparameterization (that is to say, in setting $\kappa = 1/\nu$), we recognize the density [1.3] of the negative binomial distribution.

REMARK.– We can arrive at the same result by setting $U \sim G(\mu, \nu)$ and $Y|U \sim \mathcal{P}(U)$. ■

1.6. Exercises

Exercise 1 – Two exponential models

1) Let $\pi \in (0,1)$. The geometric distribution $\mathcal{G}(\pi)$ has $f(y) = \pi(1-\pi)^y$ as its density for $y = 0, 1, 2, \ldots$. Show that the family $\{\mathcal{G}(\pi); \pi \in (0,1)\}$ is an exponential family. Identify $a(\cdot), b(\cdot,\cdot)$ and ϕ; then, from this, deduce the mean and the variance of the distribution $\mathcal{G}(\pi)$.

2) Repeat question 1 for the exponential distribution, with density $f(y) = \lambda \exp(-\lambda y)$, for $y \geq 0$ and $\lambda > 0$.

REMARK.– The geometric and exponential distributions are particular cases of the negative binomial and the gamma distributions, respectively. The fact that they form exponential families is thus also a consequence of the results from section 1.3. ■

Exercise 2 – Conway–Maxwell–Poisson distribution

The Conway–Maxwell–Poisson (CMP) distribution (Shmueli et al. 2005) has the probability density:

$$f(y) = \frac{\lambda^y}{Z(\lambda,\nu)(y!)^\nu}, \quad y = 0, 1, 2, \ldots$$

where $\lambda > 0$, $\nu \geq 0$ and $Z(\lambda,\nu) = \sum_{k=0}^{\infty} \lambda^k/(k!)^\nu$ (when $\nu = 0$, the probability density is defined using additional constraint $\lambda < 1$).

1) Some particular cases of the CMP distribution:

a) if $\nu = 1$, show that the CMP distribution reduces to the Poisson distribution $\mathcal{P}(\lambda)$;

b) if $\nu = 0$, show that the CMP distribution reduces to the geometric distribution, and identify its parameter.

2) Suppose that ν is known. Show that the family of CMP distributions (for $\lambda > 0$) is an exponential family. Identify $a(\cdot), b(\cdot,\cdot)$ and ϕ.

3) Denote by Y a random variable of the CMP distribution. By using proposition 1.1, show that:

$$\mu = \mathbb{E}(Y) = \frac{1}{Z(\lambda,\nu)} \sum_{y=0}^{\infty} \frac{y\lambda^y}{(y!)^\nu} \quad \text{and} \quad \text{var}(Y) = \frac{1}{Z(\lambda,\nu)} \sum_{y=0}^{\infty} \frac{y^2\lambda^y}{(y!)^\nu} - \mu^2$$

Exercise 3 – Moment-generating function

The moment-generating function (mgf) of a random variable Y is the function of $t \in \mathbb{R}$ defined by: $M_Y(t) = \mathbb{E}(e^{tY})$. In the following, denote $M_Y^{(1)}(t) = \partial M_Y(t)/\partial t$ and $M_Y^{(2)}(t) = \partial^2 M_Y(t)/\partial t^2$.

1) Suppose that Y admits a second-order moment. Show that $\mathbb{E}(Y) = M_Y^{(1)}(0)$ and $\text{var}(Y) = M_Y^{(2)}(0) - (M_Y^{(1)}(0))^2$ (e.g. treat the case when Y is a continuous variable).

2) If $Y \sim \mathcal{N}(\mu, \sigma^2)$, show that:

$$M_Y(t) = \exp\left(\mu t + \frac{1}{2}\sigma^2 t^2\right)$$

3) If $Y \sim \mathcal{P}(\mu)$, show that:

$$M_Y(t) = \exp\left(\mu(e^t - 1)\right)$$

4) Let Y be a random variable with density [1.1]. Show that its mgf can be written as:

$$M_Y(t) = \exp\left(\frac{a(\theta + t\phi) - a(\theta)}{\phi}\right) \qquad [1.5]$$

From this expression, obtain the formulas $\mathbb{E}(Y) = \dot{a}(\theta)$ and $\text{var}(Y) = \phi\,\ddot{a}(\theta)$. By using the elements from Table 1.1, if $Y \sim \mathcal{N}(\mu, \sigma^2)$, check that expression [1.5] does indeed agree with the expression found in question 2 (same question if $Y \sim \mathcal{P}(\mu)$).

5) Let $Y_1, \dots, Y_n$ be an i.i.d. sample of an exponential family with density [1.1]. Show that the distribution of the sample mean $\bar{Y}_n = n^{-1}\sum_{i=1}^n Y_i$ also belongs to an exponential family.

HINT.– Calculate $M_{\bar{Y}_n}(t)$ and use the fact that two random variables having the same mgf also have the same distribution.

Exercise 4 (taken from McCullagh and Nelder (1989))

Let f_0 be a probability density and let M be its corresponding moment-generating function (mgf). Suppose that M has the form:

$$M(t) = \exp(a(t))$$

where $a(\cdot)$ is a certain function. Let Y be a random variable with density:

$$f(y;\theta) = c_1 \cdot e^{\theta y} f_0(y)$$

where c_1 denotes a normalization constant.

1) Determine c_1 and show that $f(y;\theta)$ is of the form [1.1] (in particular, identify ϕ and $b(\cdot,\cdot)$).

2) Suppose now that f_0 is of the form $f_0(y) = c_2/(y!)$, where $y \in \mathbb{N}$ and c_2 is a normalization constant.

a) Identify c_2. To which distribution does f_0 correspond to? From this, deduce the expression for $a(\cdot)$.

HINT.– If $Y \sim \mathcal{P}(\mu)$, its mgf is given by $M_Y(t) = \exp\left(\mu(e^t - 1)\right)$.

b) From this, deduce $f(y;\theta)$ and identify the distribution of Y.

Exercise 5 – Truncated distributions

1) Let Y be a random variable of the Poisson distribution $\mathcal{P}(\mu)$. Denote by f its density. Consider the zero-truncated Poisson distribution, with density $g(y) = f(y|Y>0)$. Show that:

$$g(y) = \frac{\mu^y}{y!}\frac{\exp(-\mu)}{1-\exp(-\mu)}, \quad y = 1, 2, \ldots$$

Show that g is of the form [1.1] and identify $a(\cdot)$, $b(\cdot,\cdot)$ and ϕ. From this, deduce that:

$$\mathbb{E}(Y|Y>0) = \frac{\mu}{1-e^{-\mu}}$$

Show that:

$$\frac{\mathbb{E}(Y|Y>0)}{\mathbb{E}(Y)} \xrightarrow[\mu\to\infty]{} 1$$

Could this result have been expected? How could it be interpreted?

2) Let $Y \sim \mathcal{B}(k,\pi)$ (with $\pi \in (0,1)$) and let f be its density. Consider the zero-truncated binomial distribution, with density $g(y) = f(y|Y>0)$.

a) Determine g, show that it is of the form [1.1] and identify $a(\cdot)$, $b(\cdot,\cdot)$ and ϕ. From this, deduce $\mathbb{E}(Y|Y>0)$.

b) Show that:

$$\frac{\mathbb{E}(Y|Y>0)}{k\pi} \xrightarrow[k\to\infty]{} 1$$

Interpret this result. Could we have expected it?

3) Let Y be a random variable with density:

$$f(x;\theta) = \exp\left(x\theta - a(\theta) + b(x)\right), \quad x \in \mathbb{R}$$

Let $y \in \mathbb{R}$. Show that the density of the truncated distribution $Y|Y > y$ is also of the form [1.1]. From this, deduce that:

$$\mathbb{E}(Y|Y > y) = \frac{1}{1 - F(y;\theta)} \int_y^{\infty} x f(x;\theta)\, dx$$

where F denotes the cumulative distribution function of Y.

Exercise 6 – Logistic regression model (taken from Agresti (2015))

Consider a pair of random variables (X, Y), where $Y \sim \mathcal{B}(p)$ and $X|Y = y$ follows a normal distribution $\mathcal{N}(\mu_y, \sigma^2)$, $y = 0, 1$. Set $q = 1 - p$.

1) With the help of Bayes' theorem, show that the probability $\mathbb{P}(Y = 1|X = x)$ satisfies:

$$\text{logit}(\mathbb{P}(Y = 1|X = x)) = \beta_0 + \beta_1 x \qquad [1.6]$$

where $\text{logit}(p) = \ln(\frac{p}{1-p})$, and β_0 and β_1 are given by:

$$\beta_0 = \ln\left(\frac{p}{q}\right) + \frac{\mu_0^2 - \mu_1^2}{2\sigma^2} \quad \text{and} \quad \beta_1 = \frac{\mu_1 - \mu_0}{\sigma^2}$$

Expression [1.6] defines a *logistic regression model* (this model is the subject of section 2.4.1).

REMARK.– If the variances of $X|Y = 0$ and $X|Y = 1$ are not equal, that is to say, if $X|Y = y \sim \mathcal{N}(\mu_y, \sigma_y^2)$ with $\sigma_0^2 \neq \sigma_1^2$, in the same way, we can show that:

$$\text{logit}(\mathbb{P}(Y = 1|X = x)) = \beta_0 + \beta_1 x + \beta_2 x^2$$

with β_0, β_1 and β_2 coefficients which are expressed as functions of $\mu_0, \mu_1, \sigma_0, \sigma_1, p$ and q.

■

2) Now consider a pair of random variables (X, Y) such that $Y \sim \mathcal{B}(p)$ and $X|Y = y$ has for its density:

$$f(x, \theta_y, \phi) = \exp\left(\frac{x\theta_y - a(\theta_y)}{\phi} + b(x, \phi)\right), \quad y = 0, 1$$

Show that $\text{logit}(\mathbb{P}(Y = 1|X = x))$ is of the form:

$$\text{logit}(\mathbb{P}(Y = 1|X = x)) = \beta_0 + \beta_1 x$$

where:

$$\beta_0 = \ln\left(\frac{p}{q}\right) + \frac{a(\theta_0) - a(\theta_1)}{\phi} \quad \text{and} \quad \beta_1 = \frac{\theta_1 - \theta_0}{\phi}$$

In the case when $X|Y = y \sim \mathcal{N}(\mu_y, \sigma^2)$, check that β_0 and β_1 coincide with the expressions found in question 1.

2

From Linear Models to GLMs

This chapter is dedicated to generalized linear regression models, the formalization of which dates back to the work of Nelder and Wedderburn (1972). Since then, numerous other works have been dedicated to them. Without attempting to be exhaustive, we cite McCullagh and Nelder (1989) and Dobson (1990), which are two historic references, in addition to de Jong and Heller (2008); Hardin and Hilbe (2018); Sundberg (2019), and lastly Droesbeke et al. (2005) for a French reference.

In general, the aim of a regression model is to describe a variable Y (called the response, or outcome, variable) using a set of p explanatory variables $X_1, \ldots, X_p$ (also called covariates, regressors, or predictors). These explanatory variables can either be quantitative and/or qualitative.

Modeling the relationship between Y and the X_j, $j = 1, \ldots, p$ can serve several objectives. The first consists of searching for which variables, among the X_j, have a significant influence on the response variable. A second objective, related to the first, consists of numerically evaluating (we speak of *estimating*) the influence that the X_j have on the response variable (and testing whether this influence can be considered as being significant or not). This allows us to interpret the relationships between the X_j and Y and understand more about the underlying phenomena. A third objective, complementary to the first two, consists of using the obtained model to predict the response variable for different values of the X_j.

To accomplish these objectives in a statistical setting, we make observations on individuals or subjects (these individuals do not have to be physical people; in general, the term *individual* refers to the elementary units on which measurements or observations are performed). In the setting of regression, observations are presented in the form of a pair:

For a color version of the code in this chapter, see www.iste.co.uk/dupuy/linearmodels.zip.

$$(Y_i, \mathbf{X}_i), \quad i = 1, \ldots, n$$

where Y_i represents the response variable observed for the individual i, and $\mathbf{X}_i$ denotes the set of values $(X_{i1}, \ldots, X_{ip})$ for the $X_1, \ldots, X_p$ that are observed for the same individual. The set $\{(Y_i, \mathbf{X}_i), i = 1, \ldots, n\}$ forms the *sample* of observations. In the following, we will assume that each observation is independent from one individual to another.

The linear Gaussian regression model, or more simply the linear Gaussian model, is one of the most well-known regression models. It is used when the Y_i are real values (or have positive values, as in example 2.3, when their logarithm $\ln Y_i$ is modeled), and it is written as follows:

$$\begin{aligned} Y_i &= \beta_1 X_{i1} + \beta_2 X_{i2} + \ldots + \beta_p X_{ip} + \varepsilon_i, \quad i = 1, \ldots, n \\ &= \beta^\top \mathbf{X}_i + \varepsilon_i \end{aligned}$$

where $\beta = (\beta_1, \ldots, \beta_p)^\top$ is the vector[1] of regression coefficients, and $\mathbf{X}_i = (X_{i1}, \ldots, X_{ip})^\top$ is the vector of explanatory variables for individual i. By convention, in general, we set $X_{i1} = 1$ in order to introduce an ordinate – or constant – β_1 at the origin in the *linear predictor* $\beta^\top \mathbf{X}_i$. The other explanatory variables may either be random or fixed (for example, in the case of a controlled experiment).

The ε_i, $i = 1, \ldots, n$, denote i.i.d. random variables from the $\mathcal{N}(0, \sigma^2)$ distribution. Under these conditions, the observations Y_i are independent and come from the $\mathcal{N}(\beta^\top \mathbf{X}_i, \sigma^2)$ distribution, $i = 1, \ldots, n$.

The quantities β and σ^2 are called the *parameters* of the model, and these parameters are unknown. The statistical problem consists of estimating them, based upon observations (we say that we adjust the model to the data).

REMARK.– The linearity emphasized in the term "linear model" refers to the linearity of $\mathbb{E}(Y_i|\mathbf{X}_i)$ with respect to β (indeed, we have $\mathbb{E}(Y_i|\mathbf{X}_i) = \beta^\top \mathbf{X}_i$). The model:

$$Y_i = \beta_1 + \beta_2 X_i + \beta_3 X_i^2 + \beta_4 X_i^3 + \beta_5 X_i^4 + \varepsilon_i, \quad i = 1, \ldots, n$$

in which the regressors are successive powers of the explanatory variable, is a polynomial in the X_i and yet it is linear with respect to the parameters $\beta_1, \ldots, \beta_5$. It is therefore indeed a "linear model". ■

The linear Gaussian model is a generalized linear model. In fact, it is a very particular case of one since, in general, should statistical inference in the generalized

1 By convention, every vector that we define in this book will be a column vector. The $\top$ symbol denotes the transpose of a vector or matrix.

linear models depend upon asymptotic arguments (see section 2.3.2), then inference in the linear Gaussian model is exact (that is to say that it is characterized by properties which hold true for each n, including small values).

Generalized linear models take on the structure of a linear Gaussian model and they extend to cases in which the distribution of the Y_i is not Gaussian, and the mean of Y_i is nonlinear in β. It will therefore be easier to understand generalized linear models by beginning with the structure of the linear model, which is the model that the first section of this chapter is dedicated to.

2.1. Reminders on the linear model

In this section, we provide a brief overview on the linear model. We limit ourselves to the question of estimating β and the corresponding inferences (construction of confidence intervals and test statistics). The interested reader who wishes to learn more would benefit from the complete works of Guyon (2001); Cornillon and Matzner-Løber (2007) and Azaïs and Bardet (2012). In fact, there exists a considerable number of works dedicated (at least partially) to the linear model, and the reader should not have any difficulties in finding one meeting their expectations, whether they be theoretical, applied or have a particular software in mind.

Suppose that we have a sample $\{(Y_i, \mathbf{X}_i), i = 1, \ldots, n\}$ of observations of a real response variable Y_i and a vector of explanatory variables $\mathbf{X}_i = (X_{i1}, \ldots, X_{ip})^\top \in \mathbb{R}^p$ (with $X_{i1} = 1$). In the following, we will assume that $n > p$. As stated above, the linear model expresses a *linear* relation between the mean of Y_i and the parameter $\beta = (\beta_1, \ldots, \beta_p)^\top \in \mathbb{R}^p$:

$$Y_i = \beta^\top \mathbf{X}_i + \varepsilon_i, \quad i = 1, \ldots, n \qquad [2.1]$$

The statistical problem consists of estimating β with respect to the observations. The ε_i are noise or error terms, and are not observed. In general, we place the following hypotheses on the ε_i, $i = 1, \ldots, n$:

$$\mathcal{H}_1 : \mathbb{E}(\varepsilon_i) = 0, \quad \text{var}(\varepsilon_i) = \sigma^2 \quad \text{and} \quad \text{cov}(\varepsilon_i, \varepsilon_j) = 0 \text{ if } i \neq j$$

The ε_i are therefore centered, have constant variance (the homoscedastic hypothesis) and are uncorrelated (if the explanatory variables are random, these hypotheses must be understood conditionally on $\mathbf{X}_i$; in the following, to avoid overburdening the notation, we will assume that $\mathbf{X}_i$ is fixed). To begin with, we will not assume any particular distribution for the ε_i (the normality hypothesis will be introduced in section 2.1.5).

The model [2.1] can also be written in a matrix form which is very useful, as we will see next.

2.1.1. *Matrix form of the linear model*

We denote by $\mathbf{Y} = (Y_1, \dots, Y_n)^\top \in \mathbb{R}^n$ the vector of observations of the response variable and by $\mathbf{E} = (\varepsilon_1, \dots, \varepsilon_n)^\top \in \mathbb{R}^n$ the error terms. Define the $(n \times p)$-matrix $\mathbb{X}$ by:

$$\mathbb{X} = \begin{pmatrix} 1 & X_{12} & \dots & X_{1p} \\ 1 & X_{22} & \dots & X_{2p} \\ \vdots & \vdots & \ddots & \vdots \\ 1 & X_{n2} & \dots & X_{np} \end{pmatrix} \qquad [2.2]$$

The ith row of $\mathbb{X}$ is $\mathbf{X}_i^\top = (1, X_{i2}, \dots, X_{ip})$. It contains the values of the p explanatory variables for individual i. The jth column of $\mathbb{X}$ contains the values $X_{1j}, \dots, X_{nj}$ for the jth explanatory variable for each of the n individuals that make up the sample. The matrix $\mathbb{X}$ is called the design matrix and, with this notation, the model [2.1] can be written in matrix format as:

$$\mathbf{Y} = \mathbb{X}\beta + \mathbf{E} \qquad [2.3]$$

and the hypothesis $\mathcal{H}_1$ can be written as:

$$\mathcal{H}_1 : \mathbb{E}(\mathbf{E}) = 0 \quad \text{and} \quad \text{var}(\mathbf{E}) = \sigma^2 I_n$$

where I_n denotes the nth order identity matrix and var($\mathbf{E}$) is the variance–covariance matrix of $\mathbf{E}$ (that is to say, the $(n \times n)$-matrix whose (i, j)-th term is given by $\text{cov}(\varepsilon_i, \varepsilon_j)$). From the $\mathcal{H}_1$ hypothesis, we have:

$$\mathbb{E}(\mathbf{Y}) = \mathbb{X}\beta \quad \text{and} \quad \text{var}(\mathbf{Y}) = \sigma^2 I_n$$

since $\mathbb{E}(\mathbf{Y}) = \mathbb{E}(\mathbb{X}\beta + \mathbf{E}) = \mathbb{X}\beta + \mathbb{E}(\mathbf{E}) = \mathbb{X}\beta$ and $\text{var}(\mathbf{Y}) = \text{var}(\mathbb{X}\beta + \mathbf{E}) = \text{var}(\mathbf{E})$.

The model [2.3] is said to be *identifiable* if there exists a unique vector $\beta \in \mathbb{R}^p$ such that $\mathbb{E}(\mathbf{Y}) = \mathbb{X}\beta$. If this were not that case, then β could neither be estimated nor interpreted.

This identifiability condition is equivalent to saying that if β and γ are two vectors in $\mathbb{R}^p$ such that $\mathbb{E}(\mathbf{Y}) = \mathbb{X}\beta$ and $\mathbb{E}(\mathbf{Y}) = \mathbb{X}\gamma$, then we must necessarily have that $\beta = \gamma$. In other words, if $\mathbb{X}(\beta - \gamma) = 0$, then $\beta - \gamma = 0$. This is the same as assuming that the columns of the matrix $\mathbb{X}$ (and hence the explanatory variables) are linearly independent in $\mathbb{R}^n$, or equivalently, that $\mathbb{X}$ is of full rank equal to p (recall that we have assumed $n > p$). From here on, we will denote this hypothesis by $\mathcal{H}_2$ and we will assume that it is satisfied.

REMARK.– With the identifiability condition, the matrix $\mathbb{X}^\top\mathbb{X}$ is invertible, which will be a very useful result later on. To prove it, let us show that $\mathbb{X}^\top\mathbb{X}$ is positive definite. Recall that a symmetric real $(p \times p)$-matrix M is positive definite if $u^\top M u > 0$ for every non-zero vector u in $\mathbb{R}^p$.

So let u be a non-zero vector in $\mathbb{R}^p$ (and let $\|u\|$ denote its Euclidean norm). Then $u^\top(\mathbb{X}^\top\mathbb{X})u = \|\mathbb{X}u\|^2 \geq 0$. Suppose that $\|\mathbb{X}u\|^2 = 0$. Then $\mathbb{X}u = 0$. However, by hypothesis, $\mathbb{X}$ has a full rank, hence $u = 0$, which is a contradiction. We see therefore that $u^\top(\mathbb{X}^\top\mathbb{X})u > 0$, which implies that the matrix $\mathbb{X}^\top\mathbb{X}$ is positive definite and thus invertible. ■

2.1.2. *Some examples of linear models*

EXAMPLE 2.1 (SIMPLE LINEAR MODEL).– Suppose that we have a single explanatory variable X_i. Then the model [2.1] becomes:

$$Y_i = \beta_1 + \beta_2 X_i + \varepsilon_i, \quad i = 1, \ldots, n$$

where β_1 is the intercept and β_2 is the slope. This model carries the name of simple linear regression.

Let $\mathbf{1}$ denote the column vector of $\mathbb{R}^n$ whose components are all equal to 1, and also denote $\mathbf{X} = (X_1, \ldots, X_n)^\top$. The design matrix is formed by augmenting these two vectors with one another, an operation often denoted by $\mathbb{X} = [\mathbf{1}|\mathbf{X}]$. The model can be written in matrix form as $\mathbf{Y} = \mathbb{X}\beta + \mathbf{E}$, with $\beta = (\beta_1, \beta_2)^\top$. It is identifiable if there exist two values of X_i and X_j that are distinct.

EXAMPLE 2.2 (MULTIPLE LINEAR MODEL).– The multiple linear model is the model that was presented in the preamble to this chapter:

$$Y_i = \beta_1 + \beta_2 X_{i2} + \ldots + \beta_p X_{ip} + \varepsilon_i, \quad i = 1, \ldots, n \qquad [2.4]$$

It can be written in the matrix form [2.3], with the design matrix given by [2.2]. The multiple linear model reduces to the simple linear model when there is a single explanatory variable.

EXAMPLE 2.3 (COBB–DOUGLAS MODEL).– In economics, a production function allows one to express the relation between the production ("output") of a business and the means utilized ("input") to obtain this production. In the Cobb–Douglas model[2], the inputs are the capital and labor.

2 Named after the economist Paul Douglas and mathematician Charles Cobb (both American), who formalized this model in 1928.

Suppose that K_i and L_i are, respectively, the values of the capital and labor available for use and V_i ($i = 1, \ldots, n$) is the total production level for n businesses. Then, the Cobb–Douglas production function, denoted here by F, is written as:

$$F(K_i, L_i) = \mu L_i^{\beta_1} K_i^{\beta_2}$$

where μ, β_1 and β_2 are positive constants determined by the available technology. If we denote $V_i = F(K_i, L_i)$, then, after passing to the logarithm, we obtain $\ln V_i = \alpha + \beta_1 \ln L_i + \beta_2 \ln K_i$, where $\alpha = \ln \mu$. We can hence form the multiple linear model:

$$\ln V_i = \alpha + \beta_1 \ln L_i + \beta_2 \ln K_i + \varepsilon_i$$

to estimate the parameters μ, β_1 and β_2. We see that this model is of the form [2.4], with $Y_i = \ln V_i$, $X_{i2} = \ln L_i$ and $X_{i3} = \ln K_i$.

EXAMPLE 2.4 (ONE-WAY ANALYSIS OF VARIANCE).– Suppose that we have a single explanatory variable available, which is qualitative (such a variable is equivalently called a *factor*). The values taken on by a factor are called *modalities*; they can represent sex, age bands, degree level, treatment groups, etc. Suppose that we have n_i observations for the ith modality, where $i = 1, \ldots, p$. The total number of observations is $n = \sum_{i=1}^{p} n_i$. The *one-way analysis of variance* model is then written as:

$$Y_{ij} = \mu_i + \varepsilon_{ij} \qquad [2.5]$$

where Y_{ij} denotes the response variable of individual j ($j = 1, \ldots, n_i$) for the ith modality, and ε_{ij} are error terms which are assumed to be independent, centered and each having the same variance σ^2.

If the ε_{ij} are centered, then $\mathbb{E}(Y_{ij}) = \mu_i$. Thus, μ_i represents the mean level of the response variable for the ith modality, and ε_{ij} represents the variability of the jth individual with respect to this mean level. The parameters of interest in the model are the $\mu_1, \ldots, \mu_p$ (σ^2 is often called a nuisance parameter).

The model [2.5] can be written in matrix form as $\mathbf{Y} = \mathbb{X}\beta + \mathbf{E}$, where $\mathbf{Y} = (Y_{11}, \ldots, Y_{1n_1}, \ldots, Y_{p1}, \ldots, Y_{pn_p})^\top$, $\mathbf{E} = (\varepsilon_{11}, \ldots, \varepsilon_{1n_1}, \ldots, \varepsilon_{p1}, \ldots, \varepsilon_{pn_p})^\top$, $\beta = (\mu_1, \ldots, \mu_p)^\top$ and:

$$\mathbb{X} = \begin{pmatrix} \mathbf{1}_{n_1} & \mathbf{0} & \dots & \mathbf{0} \\ \mathbf{0} & \mathbf{1}_{n_2} & \dots & \mathbf{0} \\ \vdots & \vdots & \ddots & \vdots \\ \mathbf{0} & \dots & \mathbf{0} & \mathbf{1}_{n_p} \end{pmatrix} \quad [2.6]$$

where $\mathbf{1}_{n_j}$ denotes the n_j-dimensional column vector whose components are all equal to 1 ($\mathbf{0}$ denotes the column vector whose components are all 0, with its dimension varying according to which row of $\mathbb{X}$ is being considered; we do not represent it to avoid overburdening the notation). The matrix $\mathbb{X}$ has dimension $n \times p$, and it is uniquely made up of 0's and 1's. We see that the model it defines is indeed identifiable. Moreover, its specific structure leads to a particularly simple solution to the estimating problem of β.

The model [2.5] can be generalized to cases involving more than two factors, and interactions between factors can be introduced. When certain explanatory variables are quantitative and others are qualitative, we speak of *covariance analysis*. It is equally possible to express such a model in the form $\mathbf{Y} = \mathbb{X}\beta + \mathbf{E}$. The interested reader can find a complete treatment of variance and covariance analysis in Azaïs and Bardet (2012).

2.1.3. *Least-squares approximation*

Without any hypotheses placed upon the distribution of the ε_i, β is estimated using the least-squares method, which consists of searching for a value $\hat{\beta}_n$ of β by minimizing the residual sum of squares (RSS):

$$RSS(\beta) = \|\mathbf{Y} - \mathbb{X}\beta\|^2 = \sum_{i=1}^{n}(Y_i - \beta^\top \mathbf{X}_i)^2$$

To do so, we differentiate $RSS(\beta)$ and solve $\frac{\partial RSS(\hat{\beta}_n)}{\partial \beta} = 0$.

This gives us:

$$\frac{\partial RSS(\beta)}{\partial \beta} = -2\mathbb{X}^\top \mathbf{Y} + 2\mathbb{X}^\top \mathbb{X}\beta$$

The least-squares estimator (LSE) of β therefore satisfies: $\mathbb{X}^\top \mathbb{X}\hat{\beta}_n = \mathbb{X}^\top \mathbf{Y}$. If $\mathbb{X}$ is of full rank ($\mathcal{H}_2$ hypothesis), then $\mathbb{X}^\top \mathbb{X}$ is invertible, and furthermore:

$$\hat{\beta}_n = (\mathbb{X}^\top \mathbb{X})^{-1}\mathbb{X}^\top \mathbf{Y} \quad [2.7]$$

The matrix:

$$\frac{\partial^2 RSS(\beta)}{\partial\beta\partial\beta^\top} = 2\mathbb{X}^\top\mathbb{X}$$

of second derivatives of $RSS(\beta)$ is positive definite under $\mathcal{H}_2$ (see the remark on the invertibility of $\mathbb{X}^\top\mathbb{X}$), so $\hat{\beta}_n$ is therefore the unique value of β that minimizes the $RSS(\beta)$ function.

REMARK (GEOMETRIC INTERPRETATION OF THE LSE).– The set $\mathcal{E}_\mathbb{X} = \{\mathbb{X}\beta : \beta \in \mathbb{R}^p\}$ is a p-dimensional vector subspace of $\mathbb{R}^n$ (it is generated by the p column vectors of the matrix $\mathbb{X}$, which are linearly independent under the $\mathcal{H}_2$ hypothesis). Minimizing $RSS(\beta) = \|\mathbf{Y} - \mathbb{X}\beta\|^2$ therefore amounts to looking for an element of $\mathcal{E}_\mathbb{X}$ that is the closest to $\mathbf{Y} \in \mathbb{R}^n$ with respect to the usual Euclidean norm. This element is the orthogonal projection of $\mathbf{Y}$ onto $\mathcal{E}_\mathbb{X}$. It is determined as follows.

We denote by P the orthogonal projection onto $\mathcal{E}_\mathbb{X}$ and by $\langle\cdot,\cdot\rangle$ the standard scalar product on $\mathbb{R}^n$. Every vector $\mathbb{X}\beta \in \mathcal{E}_\mathbb{X}$ is orthogonal to $\mathbf{Y} - P\mathbf{Y}$, which means that:

$$\begin{aligned} 0 &= \langle\mathbb{X}\beta, \mathbf{Y} - P\mathbf{Y}\rangle \\ &= \beta^\top\mathbb{X}^\top(\mathbf{Y} - P\mathbf{Y}) \\ &= \beta^\top\mathbb{X}^\top\mathbf{Y} - \beta^\top\mathbb{X}^\top P\mathbf{Y} \end{aligned}$$

or equivalently: $\beta^\top(\mathbb{X}^\top\mathbf{Y} - \mathbb{X}^\top P\mathbf{Y}) = 0$. This equality holds true for every $\beta \in \mathbb{R}^p$. From this, we deduce that $\mathbb{X}^\top\mathbf{Y} = \mathbb{X}^\top P\mathbf{Y}$. However, $P\mathbf{Y} \in \mathcal{E}_\mathbb{X}$, thus there exists a $\hat{\beta}_n \in \mathbb{R}^p$ such that $P\mathbf{Y} = \mathbb{X}\hat{\beta}_n$, implying that $\mathbb{X}^\top\mathbf{Y} = \mathbb{X}^\top\mathbb{X}\hat{\beta}_n$. Finally, given that $\mathbb{X}^\top\mathbb{X}$ is invertible, we obtain the expression [2.7]. ■

From the remark above, we can deduce the expression of the matrix P (the orthogonal projection onto the vector subspace $\mathcal{E}_\mathbb{X}$). Indeed:

$$P\mathbf{Y} = \mathbb{X}\hat{\beta}_n = \mathbb{X}(\mathbb{X}^\top\mathbb{X})^{-1}\mathbb{X}^\top\mathbf{Y}$$

from which we see that $P = \mathbb{X}(\mathbb{X}^\top\mathbb{X})^{-1}\mathbb{X}^\top$. This matrix is sometimes called the *hat matrix* and is denoted by H, since the orthogonal projection of $\mathbf{Y}$ onto $\mathcal{E}_\mathbb{X}$ is generally denoted by $\hat{\mathbf{Y}} = P\mathbf{Y}$. Thus, the matrix P associates $\hat{\mathbf{Y}}$ (pronounced, "**Y** hat") with $\mathbf{Y}$.

EXAMPLE 2.5 (SIMPLE LINEAR MODEL, CONTINUED).– We saw that the simple linear model $Y_i = \beta_1 + \beta_2 X_i + \varepsilon_i$ $(i = 1, \ldots, n)$ can be written in matrix form as $\mathbf{Y} = \mathbb{X}\beta + \mathbf{E}$, where $\beta = (\beta_1, \beta_2)^\top$ and $\mathbb{X} = [\mathbf{1}|\mathbf{X}]$.

We denote by $\bar{X}_n = n^{-1}\sum_{i=1}^n X_i$ and $\bar{Y}_n = n^{-1}\sum_{i=1}^n Y_i$ the sample means of X_i and Y_i, by $S^2_{n,X} = \frac{1}{n}\sum_{i=1}^n X_i^2 - \bar{X}_n^2$ the sample variance of X_i and by $S^2_{n,XY} = \frac{1}{n}\sum_{i=1}^n X_iY_i - \bar{X}_n\bar{Y}_n$ the sample covariance of X_i and Y_i.

If we calculate [2.7], then we can easily verify that the LSEs of β_1 and β_2 are given by:

$$\hat{\beta}_{n,2} = \frac{S^2_{n,XY}}{S^2_{n,X}} \quad \text{and} \quad \hat{\beta}_{n,1} = \bar{Y}_n - \hat{\beta}_{n,2}\bar{X}_n$$

The estimated regression line, or the least squares line, is given by the equation $y = \hat{\beta}_{n,1} + \hat{\beta}_{n,2}x$, namely:

$$y = \bar{Y}_n + \frac{S^2_{n,XY}}{S^2_{n,X}}(x - \bar{X}_n)$$

EXAMPLE 2.6 (ONE-WAY ANALYSIS OF VARIANCE, CONTINUED).– The analysis of variance model $Y_{ij} = \mu_i + \varepsilon_{ij}$ $(j = 1, \dots, n_i, i = 1, \dots, p)$ admits the matrix form $\mathbf{Y} = \mathbb{X}\beta + \mathbf{E}$, where $\beta = (\mu_1, \dots, \mu_p)^\top$ and $\mathbb{X}$ is given by [2.6].

The LSE $\hat{\mu}_i$ of μ_i is easily obtained from [2.7]:

$$\hat{\mu}_i = \frac{1}{n_i}\sum_{j=1}^{n_i} Y_{ij}, \quad i = 1, \dots, p$$

The LSE of μ_i is therefore given by the sample mean of the observations Y_{ij} for the ith modality.

Let us return to the linear model [2.3]. The LSE is an unbiased estimator; indeed, we see that:

$$\begin{aligned}\mathbb{E}(\hat{\beta}_n) &= (\mathbb{X}^\top\mathbb{X})^{-1}\mathbb{X}^\top\mathbb{E}(\mathbf{Y}) \\ &= (\mathbb{X}^\top\mathbb{X})^{-1}\mathbb{X}^\top\mathbb{X}\beta \\ &= \beta\end{aligned}$$

Its variance can also be calculated easily enough:

$$\begin{aligned}\mathrm{var}(\hat{\beta}_n) &= (\mathbb{X}^\top\mathbb{X})^{-1}\mathbb{X}^\top \mathrm{var}(\mathbf{Y})\mathbb{X}(\mathbb{X}^\top\mathbb{X})^{-1}\\ &= \sigma^2(\mathbb{X}^\top\mathbb{X})^{-1}\mathbb{X}^\top\mathbb{X}(\mathbb{X}^\top\mathbb{X})^{-1}\\ &= \sigma^2(\mathbb{X}^\top\mathbb{X})^{-1}\end{aligned}$$

Beyond these moment calculations, we need to know the distribution of $\hat{\beta}_n$ in order to construct confidence intervals or test hypotheses on the components of β. In complete generality, this distribution is unknown. On the other hand, for each n, it can be perfectly determined if we assume that the ε_i follows a normal distribution (see section 2.1.5).

Without any hypothesis placed upon the distribution of errors then, under certain conditions, we have access to the limit – or the asymptotic – distribution of $\hat{\beta}_n$ (by a limit distribution, we mean the approximate distribution of $\hat{\beta}_n$ when we let the size of the sample, n, tend toward infinity). This will allow us to construct asymptotic confidence intervals and tests, which we will now describe.

2.1.4. *Asymptotics of the LSE*

Let us consider the linear model $Y_i = \beta^\top \mathbf{X}_i + \varepsilon_i$, $i = 1, \ldots, n$, or equivalently in the matrix form: $\mathbf{Y} = \mathbb{X}\beta + \mathbf{E}$. The matrix $\mathbb{X}$ depends on n (it has size $n \times p$). Up until now, we have not expressed this dependence in the notation but, in this section, it will be convenient to use to notation $\mathbf{Y} = \mathbb{X}_n\beta + \mathbf{E}$.

Furthermore, we denote by $H_n = \mathbb{X}_n(\mathbb{X}_n^\top\mathbb{X}_n)^{-1}\mathbb{X}_n^\top$ the orthogonal projection onto the vector subspace of $\mathbb{R}^n$ generated by the columns of $\mathbb{X}_n$, and by $\|H_n\| = \max_{1\leq i\leq n} | H_{n,ii}|$ its matrix norm ($H_{n,ii}$ denotes the ith diagonal element of H_n). Our first result states the consistency of the LSE.

THEOREM 2.1.– *Suppose that the $\mathcal{H}_1$ and $\mathcal{H}_2$ hypotheses are satisfied, and $(\mathbb{X}_n^\top\mathbb{X}_n)^{-1} \longrightarrow 0$ when $n \longrightarrow \infty$. Then $\hat{\beta}_n \xrightarrow[n\to\infty]{\mathbb{P}} \beta$.*

PROOF OF THEOREM 2.1.– The LSE is unbiased and its variance equals $\sigma^2(\mathbb{X}_n^\top\mathbb{X}_n)^{-1}$. If $(\mathbb{X}_n^\top\mathbb{X}_n)^{-1} \longrightarrow 0$, then $\mathrm{var}(\hat{\beta}_n) \longrightarrow 0$, and the LSE converges in mean square to β, and hence it also converges in probability. ■

Now, let us state the asymptotic normality property of the LSE.

THEOREM 2.2.– *Suppose that the $\mathcal{H}_1$ and $\mathcal{H}_2$ hypotheses are satisfied, the ε_i are i.i.d. and, when $n \longrightarrow \infty$, $\|H_n\| \longrightarrow 0$ and $\frac{1}{n}(\mathbb{X}_n^\top \mathbb{X}_n) \longrightarrow Q$, where Q is a positive–definite matrix. Then:*

$$\sqrt{n}(\hat{\beta}_n - \beta) \xrightarrow[n\to\infty]{\mathcal{L}} \mathcal{N}\left(0, \sigma^2 Q^{-1}\right)$$

The reader will find a proof of this theorem in Azaïs and Bardet (2012), along with a discussion on its hypotheses.

In these two theorems, note that we have not made any particular assumption on the distribution of the ε_i (in particular, we have not assumed that it is Gaussian).

REMARK.– In the one-way analysis of variance case with p modalities, we can easily check that $\frac{1}{n}(\mathbb{X}_n^\top \mathbb{X}_n)$ is a diagonal $(p \times p)$-matrix whose diagonal terms are given by the proportions $n_1/n, \ldots, n_p/n$ of the p classes. If $n_i/n \longrightarrow c_i \in (0,1)$ (with $\sum_{i=1}^p c_i = 1$), then the condition on $\frac{1}{n}(\mathbb{X}_n^\top \mathbb{X}_n)$ is satisfied.

In the multiple regression case, assume that each column j of $\mathbb{X}_n$ is made up of n independent realizations of a square-integrable (and, without loss of generality, centered) variable X_j. Furthermore, assume that the X_j, $j = 1, \ldots, p$ are independent from one another. By the law of large numbers, $\frac{1}{n}(\mathbb{X}_n^\top \mathbb{X}_n)$ converges to a diagonal matrix Q, whose diagonal terms are given by $\mathbb{E}(X_j^2)$. The condition on $\frac{1}{n}(\mathbb{X}_n^\top \mathbb{X}_n)$ in theorem 2.2 is again satisfied. ■

The asymptotic variance $\sigma^2 Q^{-1}$ of $\hat{\beta}_n$ involves σ^2, the (unknown) variance of the ε_i. To calculate confidence intervals and hypothesis tests for β, it is necessary to estimate σ^2.

If the ε_i were known, it would be natural to estimate σ^2 using their sample variance. However, the ε_i are not observed, so we form the approximations:

$$\hat{\varepsilon}_i = Y_i - \hat{Y}_i, \quad i = 1, \ldots, n$$

which are called *residuals*, where $\hat{Y}_i = \hat{\beta}_n^\top \mathbf{X}_i$ is the estimated value of the response variable for individual i. We therefore estimate σ^2 by:

$$\hat{\sigma}_n^2 = \frac{1}{n-p} \sum_{i=1}^n \hat{\varepsilon}_i^2$$

Using the notation introduced previously, $\hat{\sigma}_n^2$ can equivalently be rewritten as:

$$\begin{aligned}\hat{\sigma}_n^2 &= \frac{1}{n-p} \|\mathbf{Y} - \hat{\mathbf{Y}}\|^2 \\ &= \frac{1}{n-p} \|\mathbf{Y} - \Pi_n \mathbf{Y}\|^2\end{aligned}$$

The denominator $n - p$ corresponds to the difference between the number of observations and the number of components to be estimated in β. This normalization allows us to obtain an unbiased estimator of σ^2, which is to say that: $\mathbb{E}(\hat{\sigma}_n^2) = \sigma^2$.

The following theorem states the asymptotic properties of $\hat{\sigma}_n^2$ (see either Guyon (2001) or Azaïs and Bardet (2012) for a proof).

THEOREM 2.3.– *Suppose that $\mathcal{H}_1$ and $\mathcal{H}_2$ are satisfied and the ε_i are i.i.d. Then $\hat{\sigma}_n^2 \xrightarrow[n\to\infty]{\mathbb{P}} \sigma^2$. Furthermore, if $\mathrm{var}(\varepsilon_1^2) < \infty$, then:*

$$\sqrt{n}(\hat{\sigma}_n^2 - \sigma^2) \xrightarrow[n\to\infty]{\mathcal{L}} \mathcal{N}\left(0, \mathrm{var}(\varepsilon_1^2)\right)$$

Theorems 2.2 and 2.3 imply that, when n is sufficiently large, the distribution of the LSE can be approximated by the p-dimensional Gaussian vector $\mathcal{N}(\beta, \hat{\sigma}_n^2(\mathbb{X}_n^\top \mathbb{X}_n)^{-1})$. We denote:

$$\hat{\beta}_n \approx \mathcal{N}\left(\beta, \hat{\sigma}_n^2(\mathbb{X}_n^\top \mathbb{X}_n)^{-1}\right) \qquad [2.8]$$

From this result, we can construct a *two-sided* asymptotic confidence interval at the confidence level $1 - \alpha$ (where $0 < \alpha < 1$) for the jth component – denoted by β_j – of β:

$$\left[\hat{\beta}_{n,j} - u_{1-\frac{\alpha}{2}} \times \hat{\sigma}_n\sqrt{[(\mathbb{X}_n^\top \mathbb{X}_n)^{-1}]_{jj}}, \hat{\beta}_{n,j} + u_{1-\frac{\alpha}{2}} \times \hat{\sigma}_n\sqrt{[(\mathbb{X}_n^\top \mathbb{X}_n)^{-1}]_{jj}}\right]$$

where $[(\mathbb{X}_n^\top \mathbb{X}_n)^{-1}]_{jj}$ denotes the jth diagonal element of the matrix $(\mathbb{X}_n^\top \mathbb{X}_n)^{-1}$, and where $u_{1-\frac{\alpha}{2}}$ is the quantile of order $1 - \frac{\alpha}{2}$ of the normal distribution $\mathcal{N}(0,1)$, defined by $\mathbb{P}(\mathcal{N}(0,1) \leq u_{1-\frac{\alpha}{2}}) = 1 - \frac{\alpha}{2}$.

We can equally test the *null* hypothesis $\mathcal{H}_0 : \beta_j = 0$ against the *alternative* hypothesis $\mathcal{H}_1 : \beta_j \neq 0$ (we call this a (non-)significance test for the explanatory variable X_j). Under $\mathcal{H}_0$, the Wald test statistic:

$$\mathcal{W}_{n,j} = \frac{\hat{\beta}_{n,j}}{\hat{\sigma}_n\sqrt{[(\mathbb{X}_n^\top \mathbb{X}_n)^{-1}]_{jj}}}$$

converges in distribution to the normal distribution $\mathcal{N}(0,1)$. A decision rule at the asymptotic level α (where $0 < \alpha < 1$) therefore consists of rejecting $\mathcal{H}_0$ when $|\mathcal{W}_{n,j}| \geq u_{1-\frac{\alpha}{2}}$.

EXAMPLE 2.7. (COBB–DOUGLAS MODEL, CONTINUED).– A production function F is said to be constant returns to scale if, for every $\theta \in \mathbb{R}_+$, $F(\theta K, \theta L) = \theta F(K, L)$. That is to say, the output production value varies proportionally with the input production factors. The cost of production therefore remains constant (the returns to scale increases when the output variation is more important than the input production factors; in this case, the unit production costs decrease).

Let us reuse the notation from example 2.3. The equality $F(\theta K, \theta L) = \theta F(K, L)$ implies the following constraint on the parameters: $\theta^{\beta_1+\beta_2-1} = 1$. We can therefore test the hypothesis that F is constant returns to scale against the alternative hypothesis which states that it is not so, by testing:

$$\mathcal{H}_0 : \beta_1 + \beta_2 = 1 \text{ against } \mathcal{H}_1 : \beta_1 + \beta_2 \neq 1 \qquad [2.9]$$

Now set $\beta = (\alpha, \beta_1, \beta_2)^\top$ and $\mathbf{u} = (0, 1, 1)^\top$, so we have: $\mathbf{u}^\top\beta = \beta_1 + \beta_2$. Testing [2.9] therefore comes down to testing:

$$\mathcal{H}_0 : \mathbf{u}^\top\beta = 1 \text{ against } \mathcal{H}_1 : \mathbf{u}^\top\beta \neq 1$$

From [2.8], and when n is large, $\mathbf{u}^\top\hat{\beta}_n$ is distributed approximately as following the normal distribution $\mathcal{N}\left(\mathbf{u}^\top\beta, \hat{\sigma}_n^2\mathbf{u}^\top(\mathbb{X}_n^\top\mathbb{X}_n)^{-1}\mathbf{u}\right)$ and, under the null hypothesis $\mathcal{H}_0$:

$$\mathcal{W}_n = \frac{\mathbf{u}^\top\hat{\beta}_n - 1}{\hat{\sigma}_n\sqrt{\mathbf{u}^\top(\mathbb{X}_n^\top\mathbb{X}_n)^{-1}\mathbf{u}}}$$

approximately follows the $\mathcal{N}(0, 1)$ distribution. Similar to before, a decision rule at the asymptotic level α consists of rejecting $\mathcal{H}_0$ when $|\mathcal{W}_n| \geq u_{1-\frac{\alpha}{2}}$.

2.1.5. *Linear Gaussian model*

When the size of the sample is sufficiently large, it is no longer necessary to assume that the ε_i follow any particular distribution for inferences to be made on β. The (Gaussian) limit distribution of the LSE effectively allows us to calculate the *asymptotic* confidence intervals and hypothesis tests (see section 2.1.4). Note that there does not exist an absolute rule to decide when n is "sufficiently large". In practice, one considers this to be the case when n is of the order of a few dozen. When n is small, it is customary to assume the normality of ε_i. In this case, the distributions of the estimators and test statistics are known for each n. There exist tools to judge, at least empirically, the validity of the Gaussian hypothesis (as an example, we cite the QQ-plot, see Cornillon and Matzner-Løber (2007); Azaïs and Bardet (2012)). In practice, however, this is usually assumed without any further consideration.

In the following, we will explain how to construct the maximum likelihood estimator, confidence intervals and hypothesis tests in the linear Gaussian model. This will allow us to shine a light upon the very particular nature of this model among generalized linear models.

2.1.5.1. *Maximum likelihood estimator*

In the linear Gaussian model, the $\mathcal{H}_1 : \mathbb{E}(\mathbf{E}) = 0$ and $\text{var}(\mathbf{E}) = \sigma^2 I_n$ hypothesis is replaced with the hypothesis:

$$\mathcal{H}_3 : \mathbf{E} \sim \mathcal{N}(0, \sigma^2 I_n)$$

Note that $\mathcal{H}_3$ implies $\mathcal{H}_1$. Under $\mathcal{H}_3$:

$$\mathbf{Y} \sim \mathcal{N}(\mathbb{X}\beta, \sigma^2 I_n) \tag{2.10}$$

From this, we deduce that the observation Y_i follows a normal distribution $\mathcal{N}(\beta^\top \mathbf{X}_i, \sigma^2)$ for each $i = 1, \ldots, n$, and that the Y_i are independent (indeed, in the Gaussian case, non-correlation of the observations leads to their independence). We can therefore look for the LSEs of β and σ^2, since we know the distributions of each observation. The likelihood of (β, σ^2) based upon an independent sample $\{(Y_i, \mathbf{X}_i), i = 1, \ldots, n\}$ can be written as:

$$\begin{aligned} L_n(\beta, \sigma^2) &= \prod_{i=1}^{n} \frac{1}{\sqrt{2\pi\sigma^2}} \exp\left(-\frac{1}{2\sigma^2}\left(Y_i - \beta^\top \mathbf{X}_i\right)^2\right) \\ &= \frac{1}{(2\pi\sigma^2)^{n/2}} \exp\left(-\frac{1}{2\sigma^2}\sum_{i=1}^{n}\left(Y_i - \beta^\top \mathbf{X}_i\right)^2\right) \\ &= \frac{1}{(2\pi\sigma^2)^{n/2}} \exp\left(-\frac{1}{2\sigma^2} RSS(\beta)\right) \end{aligned}$$

From here, we deduce the log-likelihood:

$$\ell_n(\beta, \sigma^2) = -\frac{n}{2}\ln(2\pi\sigma^2) - \frac{1}{2\sigma^2} RSS(\beta)$$

Maximizing $\ell_n(\beta, \sigma^2)$ with respect to β amounts to minimizing the $RSS(\beta)$ (this operation does not depend on σ^2). The MLE of β in the linear Gaussian model [2.10] therefore coincides with the LSE of β in the model [2.3] under the hypothesis $\mathcal{H}_1$, and is given by $\hat{\beta}_n = (\mathbb{X}^\top \mathbb{X})^{-1}\mathbb{X}^\top \mathbf{Y}$. The MLE clearly inherits the unbiasedness property of the LSE, namely, $\mathbb{E}(\hat{\beta}_n) = \beta$, and its variance is the same as that for the LSE, namely, $\text{var}(\hat{\beta}_n) = \sigma^2(\mathbb{X}^\top \mathbb{X})^{-1}$.

By differentiating $\ell_n(\beta, \sigma^2)$ with respect to σ^2, we obtain the MLE $\hat{\sigma}^2_{MLE}$ of σ^2:

$$\begin{aligned}\hat{\sigma}^2_{MLE} &= \frac{1}{n} RSS(\hat{\beta}_n)\\ &= \frac{n-p}{n}\hat{\sigma}^2_n\end{aligned}$$

This estimator is biased, since:

$$\begin{aligned}\mathbb{E}(\hat{\sigma}^2_{MLE}) &= \frac{n-p}{n}\mathbb{E}(\hat{\sigma}^2_n)\\ &= \frac{n-p}{n}\sigma^2\end{aligned}$$

but its bias tends toward 0 as $n \longrightarrow \infty$ (we say that $\hat{\sigma}^2_{MLE}$ is asymptotically unbiased).

2.1.5.2. *Distributions of the MLEs*

In the linear Gaussian model, the distributions of $\hat{\beta}_n$ and $\hat{\sigma}^2_n$ are known for each n. They make up the content of the following proposition.

PROPOSITION 2.1 (DISTRIBUTIONS OF $\hat{\beta}_n$ AND $\hat{\sigma}^2_n$).– *In the linear Gaussian model, we have that:*

1) $\hat{\beta}_n \sim \mathcal{N}(\beta, \sigma^2(\mathbb{X}^\top\mathbb{X})^{-1})$;

2) $(n-p)\hat{\sigma}^2_n/\sigma^2 \sim \chi^2_{n-p}$;

3) $\hat{\beta}_n$ *and* $\hat{\sigma}^2_n$ *are independent.*

The definition of the χ^2-distribution (and of some other probability distributions, which all play a role in the Gaussian context) is recalled in the technical appendix to this chapter (section 2.6).

PROOF OF PROPOSITION 2.1.–

1) $\hat{\beta}_n$ is of the form $\mathbb{A}\mathbf{Y}$, where $\mathbb{A} = (\mathbb{X}^\top\mathbb{X})^{-1}\mathbb{X}^\top$. However, as $\mathbf{Y} \sim \mathcal{N}(\mathbb{X}\beta, \sigma^2 I_n)$, then $\hat{\beta}_n$ is also a Gaussian vector. We have already shown that $\mathbb{E}(\hat{\beta}_n) = \beta$ and $\text{var}(\hat{\beta}_n) = \sigma^2(\mathbb{X}^\top\mathbb{X})^{-1}$.

2) Recall that P denotes the orthogonal projection from $\mathbb{R}^n$ onto the vector subspace $\mathcal{E}_\mathbb{X}$ that is generated by the p columns of $\mathbb{X}$. We have $P\mathbf{Y} = \mathbb{X}\beta + P\mathbf{E}$, therefore, $\mathbf{Y} - P\mathbf{Y} = \mathbf{E} - P\mathbf{E}$ and:

$$\begin{aligned}(n-p)\frac{\hat{\sigma}^2_n}{\sigma^2} &= \frac{\|\mathbf{Y} - P\mathbf{Y}\|^2}{\sigma^2}\\ &= \frac{\|\mathbf{E} - P\mathbf{E}\|^2}{\sigma^2}\end{aligned}$$

We can write $\mathbf{E} - P\mathbf{E} = P_\perp \mathbf{E}$, where $P_\perp$ denotes the orthogonal projection onto the orthogonal complement of $\mathcal{E}_\mathbb{X}$ (it is an $(n-p)$-dimensional vector subspace of $\mathbb{R}^n$). Hence, we have:

$$(n-p)\frac{\hat{\sigma}_n^2}{\sigma^2} = \frac{\|P_\perp \mathbf{E}\|^2}{\sigma^2}$$

From Cochran's theorem (recalled in section 2.6), $\|P_\perp \mathbf{E}\|^2/\sigma^2 \sim \chi^2_{n-p}$.

3) $\hat{\sigma}_n^2$ is a function of $\mathbf{Y} - P\mathbf{Y}$, and $\hat{\beta}_n$ is a function of $P\mathbf{Y}$ (we recall that $\hat{\beta}_n = (\mathbb{X}^\top\mathbb{X})^{-1}\mathbb{X}^\top P\mathbf{Y}$). From Cochran's theorem, $P\mathbf{Y}$ and $\mathbf{Y} - P\mathbf{Y}$ are independent, so $\hat{\beta}_n$ and $\hat{\sigma}_n^2$ are equal. ■

From this proposition, and from the definition of Student's t-distribution (see section 2.6), we see that the random variable:

$$T_{n,j} = \frac{\hat{\beta}_{n,j} - \beta_j}{\hat{\sigma}_n \sqrt{[(\mathbb{X}^\top\mathbb{X})^{-1}]_{jj}}}$$

follows Student's t-distribution with $n-p$ degrees of freedom for each $j = 1, \dots, p$ (we use the notation $T_{n,j} \sim \mathcal{T}_{n-p}$). Starting from this result, we can construct some confidence intervals and hypothesis tests for β_j. Since the distribution of $T_{n,j}$ is known for each n, their level will be exact, even when n is small.

2.1.5.3. *Confidence intervals for a coefficient* β_j

Let $0 < \alpha < 1$. A two-sided confidence interval at the confidence level $1-\alpha$ for β_j is given by:

$$\Big[\hat{\beta}_{n,j} - t_{n-p}(1-\alpha/2) \times \hat{\sigma}_n \sqrt{[(\mathbb{X}^\top\mathbb{X})^{-1}]_{jj}},\\ \hat{\beta}_{n,j} + t_{n-p}(1-\alpha/2) \times \hat{\sigma}_n \sqrt{[(\mathbb{X}^\top\mathbb{X})^{-1}]_{jj}}\Big]$$

where $t_{n-p}(1-\alpha/2)$ denotes the quantile of order $1-\frac{\alpha}{2}$ of the $\mathcal{T}_{n-p}$ distribution, which is defined by $\mathbb{P}(\mathcal{T}_{n-p} \leq t_{n-p}(1-\alpha/2)) = 1 - \frac{\alpha}{2}$.

2.1.5.4. *Student's t-test on the nullity of a coefficient* β_j

We can equally test the null hypothesis $\mathcal{H}_0 : \beta_j = 0$ against the alternative $\mathcal{H}_1 : \beta_j \neq 0$, namely, we test the (non-)significance of the explanatory variable X_j. Under $\mathcal{H}_0$:

$$T_{n,j} = \frac{\hat{\beta}_{n,j}}{\hat{\sigma}_n \sqrt{[(\mathbb{X}^\top\mathbb{X})^{-1}]_{jj}}} \sim \mathcal{T}_{n-p}$$

A decision rule at the level α therefore consists of rejecting $\mathcal{H}_0$ when $|T_{n,j}| \geq t_{n-p}(1-\alpha/2)$. This test is known as "Student's t-test".

REMARK.– Note that $T_{n,j}$ coincides with the Wald test statistic $\mathcal{W}_{n,j}$ described in section 2.1.4. When n tends toward infinity, Student's t-distribution with n degrees of freedom can be approximated by the normal distribution, $\mathcal{N}(0,1)$ (in practice, $n > 30$ is considered to be sufficient). Therefore, if n is sufficiently large, $T_{n,j}$ is approximately distributed according to the $\mathcal{N}(0,1)$ distribution. We thus recover the limit distribution of $\mathcal{W}_{n,j}$. ■

More generally, we can apply the test to a linear combination of the components of β.

2.1.5.5. *Student's t-test on a linear combination of the β_j*

Let $\mathbf{u} \in \mathbb{R}^p$ and let $v \in \mathbb{R}$ be given. Suppose we want to test $\mathcal{H}_0 : \mathbf{u}^\top\beta = v$ against $\mathcal{H}_1 : \mathbf{u}^\top\beta \neq v$. Student's t-test described above is a particular case of this test, which is obtained when $v = 0$ and each component of $\mathbf{u}$ vanishes with the exception of the jth component, which equals 1. Under $\mathcal{H}_0$:

$$T_n = \frac{\mathbf{u}^\top\hat{\beta}_n - v}{\hat{\sigma}_n\sqrt{\mathbf{u}^\top(\mathbb{X}^\top\mathbb{X})^{-1}\mathbf{u}}} \sim \mathcal{T}_{n-p}$$

A decision rule at the level α therefore consists of rejecting $\mathcal{H}_0$ when $|T_n| \geq t_{n-p}(1-\alpha/2)$.

For example, in the Cobb–Douglas model, if we suppose that the ε_i are i.i.d. following $\mathcal{N}(0,\sigma^2)$, then the statistic $\mathcal{W}_n$ in example 2.7, which was calculated to test the hypotheses of a constant returns to scale production function, will follow Student's t-distribution, $\mathcal{T}_{n-3}$. The decision rule which consists of rejecting $\mathcal{H}_0$ when $|\mathcal{W}_n| \geq t_{n-3}(1-\alpha/2)$ will be exactly of level α for each n. When n is sufficiently large, this rule coincides with that described in example 2.7, since then, the $\mathcal{T}_{n-3}$ distribution will be "close enough" to the $\mathcal{N}(0,1)$ distribution.

2.1.5.6. *Tests between nested models (Fisher's test)*

Let us again consider the model:

$$\mathbf{Y} = \mathbb{X}\beta + \mathbf{E} \qquad [2.11]$$

under the $\mathcal{H}_2$ (that the $(n \times p)$-matrix $\mathbb{X}$ is of rank p) and $\mathcal{H}_3 : \mathbf{E} \sim \mathcal{N}(0, \sigma^2 I_n)$ hypotheses. Suppose that we want to test the null hypothesis that q of the components of β are simultaneously equal to 0. Without loss of generality and to simplify the notation, let us test the nullity of the last q components, namely:

$$\mathcal{H}_0 : \beta_{p-q+1} = \ldots = \beta_p = 0$$

against the alternative:

$$\mathcal{H}_1 : \text{ there exists } j \in \{p-q+1, \ldots, p\} \text{ such that } \beta_j \neq 0$$

The $\mathcal{H}_0$ hypothesis defines the model:

$$\mathbf{Y} = \mathbb{X}^{(0)}\beta^{(0)} + \mathbf{E} \qquad [2.12]$$

where:

– $\mathbb{X}^{(0)}$ is the matrix of dimension $n \times (p-q)$ obtained by dropping the last q columns from $\mathbb{X}$;

– $\beta^{(0)}$ is a $(p-q)$-dimensional vector of regression coefficients.

The vector subspace of $\mathbb{R}^n$ generated by the columns of $\mathbb{X}^{(0)}$ is $(p-q)$-dimensional, and it lies within the vector subspace generated by the columns of $\mathbb{X}$. We say that the model [2.12] is a *submodel* of [2.11], or equivalently that the model [2.12] is *nested* within [2.11].

To test $\mathcal{H}_0$, we can use Fisher's test. Its expression is natural enough: for each model [2.11] and [2.12], estimate $\mathbf{Y}$ using $\hat{\mathbf{Y}} = \hat{\beta}_n\mathbb{X}$ and $\hat{\mathbf{Y}}^{(0)} = \hat{\beta}_n^{(0)}\mathbb{X}^{(0)}$ ($\hat{\beta}_n$ and $\hat{\beta}_n^{(0)}$ denote the MLEs of β in each model [2.11] and [2.12]) respectively, and then calculate their difference $\|\hat{\mathbf{Y}} - \hat{\mathbf{Y}}^{(0)}\|^2$. Intuitively, if this difference is "small", then model [2.12] works "almost as well" as model [2.11], albeit with fewer explanatory variables (we say that it is more *parsimonious*). We will therefore prefer to conserve the submodel [2.12]; that is to say, we will keep $\mathcal{H}_0$. Fisher's test statistic can be written as:

$$F = \frac{\|\hat{\mathbf{Y}} - \hat{\mathbf{Y}}^{(0)}\|^2/q}{\|\mathbf{Y} - \hat{\mathbf{Y}}\|^2/(n-p)}$$

REMARK.– The quantity $\|\hat{\mathbf{Y}} - \hat{\mathbf{Y}}^{(0)}\|^2$ depends on the unit of measure used. Dividing through by $\|\mathbf{Y} - \hat{\mathbf{Y}}\|^2$ can be viewed as a normalization, which eliminates this effect. Furthermore, the quantities $\hat{\mathbf{Y}} - \hat{\mathbf{Y}}^{(0)}$ and $\mathbf{Y} - \hat{\mathbf{Y}}$, which belong to spaces of different dimensions, are further normalized by their respective degrees of freedom. ■

Under $\mathcal{H}_0$, the statistic F follows the Fisher distribution with $(q, n-p)$ degrees of freedom (see, for example, Azaïs and Bardet (2012) for a proof). A decision rule at the level α consists of rejecting $\mathcal{H}_0$ when $F \geq f_{q,n-p}(1-\alpha)$, where $f_{q,n-p}(1-\alpha)$ denotes the quantile of order $1-\alpha$ of the $F_{q,n-p}$ distribution.

REMARK.– Suppose that we want to test $\mathcal{H}_0 : \beta_j = 0$ against $\mathcal{H}_1 : \beta_j \neq 0$. The $\mathcal{H}_0$ hypothesis defines a submodel of the model [2.11] (this submodel is obtained by dropping the jth explanatory variable from $\mathbb{X}$). We can therefore use Fisher's test, which rejects $\mathcal{H}_0$ when $F \geq f_{1,n-p}(1-\alpha)$. It can be shown that this test is equivalent to Student's t-test of the nullity of β_j described above. ■

Proposition 2.1 also allows us to construct *confidence regions* for multiple parameters that are considered simultaneously (a confidence interval is a confidence region for a scalar parameter), confidence intervals for predictions, or for the variance σ^2. The interested reader can consult (Cornillon and Matzner-Løber 2007; Azaïs and Bardet 2012) for further details.

As mentioned in the preamble to this chapter, the linear Gaussian model is a generalized linear model. In fact, it is a very particular case of one, in terms of its formulation and the exact inference based upon the known probability distributions for each n, which we have just described. The following section defines generalized linear models in complete generality.

2.2. Three components of a generalized linear model

The specification of a generalized linear model is formed from three key elements, which are described below: a random component, a linear predictor and a link function.

2.2.1. *The random component*

The random component specifies the probability distribution of the response variable (its conditional distribution given the X_j, when explanatory variables are present). In generalized linear models, this distribution is chosen from one of the exponential families. Hence, we will assume that the density of the observation Y_i (with respect to an appropriate measure: the Lebesgue or counting measure) is of the form [1.1]:

$$f(y; \theta_i, \phi) = \exp\left(\frac{y\theta_i - a(\theta_i)}{\phi} + b(y, \phi)\right) \qquad [2.13]$$

where $i = 1, \ldots, n$. The canonical parameter of the model is allowed to depend on the individual. In certain situations, the parameter ϕ (dispersion parameter) further depends on the individual (see example 2.8). Nevertheless, to keep the notation simple, in this book, we will limit ourselves to the case where ϕ is constant across the individuals. This case includes the most typical ones.

EXAMPLE 2.8 (DOSE–RESPONSE RELATION).– Consider an experiment that consists of repeating a success/failure experiment n_i times in an independent manner, with a success occurring with probability π_i. The index i refers to the experimental conditions, of which there are n in total (that is to say, i cycles through the set $\{1,\ldots,n\}$). We denote by Y_i the proportion of successes obtained for the ith condition.

This setup is, for example, the one used in the analysis of the dose–response relationship, where the aim is to model the proportion of a population which is affected, depending on the concentration of a certain exposure (mortality of an animal or plant species depending on the quantity of pollutants in the environment, or the production of antibodies depending on the dose of a vaccine candidate).

Note that $Y_i = \frac{S_i}{n_i}$, where $S_i \sim \mathcal{B}(n_i, \pi_i)$. From this, we get the density of Y_i:

$$\begin{aligned} f(y) &= C_{n_i}^{n_i y} \pi_i^{n_i y} (1-\pi_i)^{n_i(1-y)}, \quad y \in [0,1] \\ &= \exp\left(\frac{y \ln\left(\frac{\pi_i}{1-\pi_i}\right) + \ln(1-\pi_i)}{1/n_i} + \ln C_{n_i}^{n_i y} \right) \end{aligned}$$

which can then be identified with [2.13], once we set $\theta_i = \ln(\frac{\pi_i}{1-\pi_i})$, $a(\theta_i) = -\ln(1-\pi_i)$, $\phi_i = 1/n_i$, and $b(y,\phi_i) = \ln C_{n_i}^{n_i y}$. Here, ϕ depends on i and is of the form ϕ/ω_i as mentioned in section 1.1, where $\phi = 1$ and $\omega_i = n_i$.

2.2.2. *The linear predictor*

The linear predictor, which is also called the systematic component, consists of a linear combination of the $X_{i1},\ldots,X_{ip}$. We denote it by:

$$\beta^\top \mathbf{X}_i$$

where $\beta = (\beta_1,\ldots,\beta_p)^\top$ denotes a p-dimensional vector of unknown regression coefficients that are to be estimated. The linear predictor can include transformations of the initial variables (such as X_{ij}^2 and $\ln X_{ij}$) or interaction terms (such as $X_{ij} \times X_{ik}$). These transformations can be identified in a validation step of the model (in particular, based upon the residuals, which measure the difference between the model and observations). The question of model validation will not be addressed here. The interested reader can consult, for example, Hardin and Hilbe (2018).

In the following, we will denote the linear predictor by $\beta^\top \mathbf{X}_i$, all while keeping in mind that $\mathbf{X}_i$ can be adapted to contain the prior transformations of the X_{ij}, as well as any interactions.

2.2.3. *The link function*

The third component of a generalized linear model, the link function (which we will denote by g), allows for the response variable to be linked to the linear predictor. To be precise, g links the conditional expectation $\mu_i = \mathbb{E}(Y_i|\mathbf{X}_i)$ of Y_i given $\mathbf{X}_i$ to $\beta^\top\mathbf{X}_i$. We set:

$$g(\mu_i) = \beta^\top\mathbf{X}_i$$

where g is a monotonic and differentiable function. However, in the model [2.13], $\mu_i = \dot{a}(\theta_i)$ (proposition 1.1). Therefore, we have that:

$$g(\dot{a}(\theta_i)) = \beta^\top\mathbf{X}_i$$

If we choose the canonical link function of the model for g, namely $g = \dot{a}^{-1}$, then the relationship above can be simplified to become $\theta_i = \beta^\top\mathbf{X}_i$.

REMARK.– In a general way, the linear predictor $\beta^\top\mathbf{X}_i$ takes its values in $\mathbb{R}$. The domain of variation of $\mu_i = \mathbb{E}(Y_i|\mathbf{X}_i)$ can be more restricted and depends on the distribution of Y_i (e.g. $\mu_i > 0$ if $Y_i \sim \mathcal{P}(\mu_i)$, whereas $\mu_i \in [0, k]$ if $Y_i \sim \mathcal{B}(k, \pi_i)$). The function g allows us to "form a link" between these two quantities despite the fact that they belong to two different spaces.In the particular case of the linear Gaussian model, where $Y_i \sim \mathcal{N}(\beta^\top\mathbf{X}_i, \sigma^2)$, the mean of Y_i coincides with the linear predictor, so that $\mu_i = \mathbb{E}(Y_i|\mathbf{X}_i) = \beta^\top\mathbf{X}_i$. The link function does not explicitly appear in the model: it is the identity function. ■

In many cases, generalized linear models are constructed using the canonical link function. Nevertheless, this choice is not always the most relevant. For example, if Y_i follows the gamma distribution $G(\mu_i, \nu)$, then $\mu_i = \mathbb{E}(Y_i|\mathbf{X}_i) \geq 0$. If g is the canonical link function, then we have (see Table 1.1):

$$g(\mu_i) = -\frac{1}{\mu_i} = \beta^\top\mathbf{X}_i$$

and thus $\mu_i = -1/\beta^\top\mathbf{X}_i$. Consequently, we see that $\beta^\top\mathbf{X}_i < 0$, which imposes a constraint on the estimation of β. For this reason, in general, we prefer to use the log link function by setting:

$$\ln\mu_i = \beta^\top\mathbf{X}_i$$

so that $\mu_i = \exp(\beta^\top\mathbf{X}_i)$, which allows for β to be estimated without any constraint, all while ensuring the positivity of μ_i.

2.3. Estimation in generalized linear models

2.3.1. *Maximum likelihood*

Let us consider the model [2.13]:

$$f(y;\theta_i,\phi) = \exp\left(\frac{y\theta_i - a(\theta_i)}{\phi} + b(y,\phi)\right)$$

where $g(\mu_i) = \beta^\top \mathbf{X}_i$, $\mu_i = \mathbb{E}(Y_i|\mathbf{X}_i)$, and g denotes the link function. In order to keep the notation simple, we limit ourselves to the case in which g is the canonical link function (the case of an arbitrary link function is the topic of Exercise 1, section 2.7). In this case, $\theta_i = \beta^\top \mathbf{X}_i$.

The dispersion parameter ϕ can either be known (as in the binomial or Poisson models) or unknown (as in the gamma model). Below, we denote the likelihood by $L_n(\beta,\phi)$, where ϕ can either be known or unknown. Suppose that we have a sample of independent observations $\{(Y_i, \mathbf{X}_i), i = 1,\ldots,n\}$ of the pair $(Y,\mathbf{X})$. As before, we assume that $\mathbf{X}$ is p-dimensional with $p < n$. The parameter β is estimated by maximizing the likelihood:

$$\begin{aligned} L_n(\beta,\phi) &= \prod_{i=1}^{n} \exp\left(\frac{Y_i\theta_i - a(\theta_i)}{\phi} + b(Y_i,\phi)\right) \\ &= \prod_{i=1}^{n} \exp\left(\frac{Y_i\beta^\top \mathbf{X}_i - a(\beta^\top \mathbf{X}_i)}{\phi} + b(Y_i,\phi)\right) \end{aligned}$$

or, equivalently, the log-likelihood $\ell_n(\beta,\phi) = \ln L_n(\beta,\phi)$:

$$\ell_n(\beta,\phi) = \frac{1}{\phi}\sum_{i=1}^{n} (Y_i\beta^\top \mathbf{X}_i - a(\beta^\top \mathbf{X}_i)) + \sum_{i=1}^{n} b(Y_i,\phi)$$

The maximum likelihood estimator (denoted by $\hat{\beta}_n$ in the following) is then the solution of the system:

$$\frac{\partial \ell_n(\beta,\phi)}{\partial \beta} = 0 \qquad [2.14]$$

We have:

$$\begin{aligned} \frac{\partial \ell_n(\beta,\phi)}{\partial \beta} &= \frac{1}{\phi}\sum_{i=1}^{n} \mathbf{X}_i \left(Y_i - \dot{a}(\beta^\top \mathbf{X}_i)\right) \\ &= \frac{1}{\phi}\sum_{i=1}^{n} \mathbf{X}_i(Y_i - \mu_i) \end{aligned}$$

Hence, the estimating equation is given as follows:

$$\sum_{i=1}^{n} \mathbf{X}_i (Y_i - \mu_i) = 0 \qquad [2.15]$$

It does not depend on ϕ; we can therefore estimate β without concerning ourselves with ϕ, even when it is unknown (it will be estimated in a second step).

If we set $\mu = (\mu_1, \ldots, \mu_n)^\top$, then [2.15] can be rewritten in matrix form as:

$$\mathbb{X}^\top (\mathbf{Y} - \mu) = 0 \qquad [2.16]$$

where $\mathbb{X}$ denotes the design matrix [2.2].

EXAMPLE 2.9 (LINEAR GAUSSIAN MODEL).– In the linear Gaussian model $Y_i \sim \mathcal{N}(\beta^\top \mathbf{X}_i, \sigma^2)$, we have $\mu_i = \mathbb{E}(Y_i|\mathbf{X}_i) = \beta^\top \mathbf{X}_i$ and $\mu = \mathbb{X}\beta$.

Equation [2.16] then becomes:

$$\mathbb{X}^\top (\mathbf{Y} - \mathbb{X}\beta) = 0$$

If $\mathbb{X}^\top\mathbb{X}$ is invertible, then its solution is $\hat{\beta}_n = (\mathbb{X}^\top\mathbb{X})^{-1}\mathbb{X}^\top \mathbf{Y}$, and we recover the MLE of β obtained previously in section 2.1.5.

EXAMPLE 2.10 (LOGISTIC REGRESSION MODEL).– Suppose that $Y_i \sim \mathcal{B}(k_i, \pi_i)$. The canonical link function is the logistic function. Let us set $\ln(\frac{\mu_i}{k_i - \mu_i}) = \beta^\top \mathbf{X}_i$, where $\mu_i = \mathbb{E}(Y_i|\mathbf{X}_i) = k_i \pi_i$, so that $\pi_i = \frac{e^{\beta^\top \mathbf{X}_i}}{1+e^{\beta^\top \mathbf{X}_i}}$.

The estimating equation [2.15] becomes:

$$\sum_{i=1}^{n} \mathbf{X}_i \left(Y_i - k_i \frac{e^{\beta^\top \mathbf{X}_i}}{1 + e^{\beta^\top \mathbf{X}_i}} \right) = 0 \qquad [2.17]$$

or, in matrix form, $\mathbb{X}^\top (\mathbf{Y} - \mu) = 0$, where $\mu = (k_1\pi_1, \ldots, k_n\pi_n)^\top$.

EXAMPLE 2.11 (POISSON REGRESSION).– Suppose that $Y_i \sim \mathcal{P}(\mu_i)$. The canonical link function is the logarithm function. Let us set $\ln \mu_i = \beta^\top \mathbf{X}_i$, where $\mu_i = \mathbb{E}(Y_i|\mathbf{X}_i)$, so that $\mu_i = e^{\beta^\top \mathbf{X}_i}$.

The estimating equation [2.15] becomes:

$$\sum_{i=1}^{n} \mathbf{X}_i \left(Y_i - e^{\beta^\top \mathbf{X}_i} \right) = 0 \qquad [2.18]$$

In matrix form, it can be rewritten as $\mathbb{X}^\top(\mathbf{Y} - \mu) = 0$, where $\mu = (e^{\beta^\top \mathbf{X}_1}, \dots, e^{\beta^\top \mathbf{X}_n})^\top$.

In these two last examples, the MLE does not admit an explicit expression. Iterative optimization algorithms must therefore be used in order to approximate its value (classical statistical softwares, such as SAS and R, utilize Newton–Raphson type algorithms).

2.3.2. *Asymptotic properties and inference*

In the linear Gaussian model, the distribution of the MLE is known for each n, allowing us to construct exact confidence intervals and hypothesis tests for each component β_j of β and for σ^2. This is a special case because, in general, the distribution of the MLE in generalized linear models is unknown. Under certain conditions, we nevertheless have access to its limit distribution, allowing us to construct *asymptotic* confidence intervals and *asymptotic* hypothesis tests.

The asymptotic properties of the MLE in generalized linear models (with either the canonical link function and any other link function) have been proven in Fahrmeir and Kaufmann (1985). In the particular case of the logistic regression model, they were established a few years prior in Gourieroux and Monfort (1981). We can find a summary of these results in Antoniadis et al. (1992) and additionally Guyon (2001). The work of Dunn and Smyth (2018), which is less theoretical, describes the different hypothesis tests which can be constructed in generalized linear models.

Theorem 2.4 states the consistency and asymptotic normality of the MLE $\hat{\beta}_n$ in a generalized linear model with its canonical link function (to simplify the notation, we assume that the dispersion parameter ϕ is known). It furthermore provides a consistent estimator of its asymptotic variance. Let us set $\mathcal{I}_n(\beta) = -\partial^2 \ell_n(\beta, \phi)/\partial\beta\partial\beta^\top$, $\Sigma = -\mathbb{E}[\partial^2 \ell_1(\beta, \phi)/\partial\beta\partial\beta^\top]$ and let $\lambda(\mathbb{X}^\top\mathbb{X})$ be the smallest eigenvalue of the matrix $\mathbb{X}^\top\mathbb{X}$.

THEOREM 2.4.– *Suppose that the explanatory variables $X_{ij}, j = 1, \dots, p$ are bounded and $\lambda(\mathbb{X}^\top\mathbb{X}) \to \infty$ when n tends toward infinity. Then $\hat{\beta}_n \xrightarrow[n\to\infty]{\mathbb{P}} \beta$, and:*

$$\sqrt{n}(\hat{\beta}_n - \beta) \xrightarrow[n\to\infty]{\mathcal{L}} \mathcal{N}(0, \Sigma^{-1})$$

Moreover, $n^{-1}\mathcal{I}_n(\hat{\beta}_n) \xrightarrow[n\to\infty]{\mathbb{P}} \Sigma$.

We can express this result again by saying that, for a "sufficiently large n", $\hat{\beta}_n$ is approximately distributed like a Gaussian vector $\mathcal{N}(\beta, \mathcal{I}_n(\hat{\beta}_n)^{-1})$. Each component

$\hat{\beta}_{n,j}$ of $\hat{\beta}_n$ is therefore approximately distributed according to the normal distribution $\mathcal{N}(\beta_j, [\mathcal{I}_n(\hat{\beta}_n)^{-1}]_{jj})$, where $[\mathcal{I}_n(\hat{\beta}_n)^{-1}]_{jj}$ denotes the jth diagonal term of the matrix $\mathcal{I}_n(\hat{\beta}_n)^{-1}$. We write this as:

$$\hat{\beta}_{n,j} \approx \mathcal{N}(\beta_j, [\mathcal{I}_n(\hat{\beta}_n)^{-1}]_{jj})$$

The quantity $\sqrt{[\mathcal{I}_n(\hat{\beta}_n)^{-1}]_{jj}}$ is called the *standard error* of $\hat{\beta}_{n,j}$ and is typically denoted by $\text{se}(\hat{\beta}_{n,j})$. We also have that:

$$\frac{\hat{\beta}_{n,j} - \beta_j}{\text{se}(\hat{\beta}_{n,j})} \approx \mathcal{N}(0,1) \qquad [2.19]$$

Starting from this result, we can construct asymptotic confidence intervals and hypothesis tests for the β_j, as we did with the linear model starting from the LSE (section 2.1.4).

2.3.2.1. *Confidence intervals, Wald and likelihood ratio tests*

A two-sided asymptotic confidence interval at the confidence level $1 - \alpha$ for β_j is given by:

$$\left[\hat{\beta}_{n,j} - u_{1-\frac{\alpha}{2}} \times \text{se}(\hat{\beta}_{n,j}), \hat{\beta}_{n,j} + u_{1-\frac{\alpha}{2}} \times \text{se}(\hat{\beta}_{n,j})\right]$$

where $u_{1-\frac{\alpha}{2}}$ is the quantile of order $1 - \frac{\alpha}{2}$ of the $\mathcal{N}(0,1)$ distribution.

We can furthermore use [2.19] to test the null hypothesis $\mathcal{H}_0 : \beta_j = \beta_j^0$ against the alternative $\mathcal{H}_1 : \beta_j \neq \beta_j^0$ for a fixed value β_j^0. In practice, this value will often be set to 0, allowing us to test the (non-)significance of the explanatory variable X_j. A decision rule at the asymptotic level α for the test problem of:

$$\mathcal{H}_0 : \beta_j = 0 \text{ against } \mathcal{H}_1 : \beta_j \neq 0$$

will consist of rejecting $\mathcal{H}_0$ when $|\hat{\beta}_{n,j}/\text{se}(\hat{\beta}_{n,j})| \geq u_{1-\frac{\alpha}{2}}$. This test, as we have seen previously, is known as the Wald test.

We may also want to carry out tests between nested models. Let us consider two models, denoted A and B, that share the same distribution [2.13] but have different linear predictors; that is to say that $g(\mu_i)$ is given by:

$$\text{model A: } g(\mu_i^A) = \beta^\top \mathbf{X}_i$$
$$\text{model B: } g(\mu_i^B) = \beta^{(0)\top} \mathbf{X}_i^{(0)}$$

where β is a p-dimensional vector and $\beta^{(0)}$ is a $(p-q)$-dimensional subvector of β. To simplify the notation and without loss of generality, let us assume that $\beta^{(0)}$ contains the first $p-q$ components of β. We have that model B is nested inside of model A (it is obtained by omitting the last q explanatory variables of $\mathbf{X}_i$). Then determining between either model A or B amounts to testing the null hypothesis:

$$\mathcal{H}_0 : \beta_{p-q+1} = \ldots = \beta_p = 0$$

against the alternative:

$$\mathcal{H}_1 : \text{ there exists } j \in \{p-q+1, \ldots, p\} \text{ such that } \beta_j \neq 0$$

We denote by $\hat{\beta}_n$ and $\hat{\beta}_n^{(0)}$ the MLEs of β and $\beta^{(0)}$, respectively. Then the test statistic, called the *likelihood ratio*, is calculated as follows:

$$\begin{aligned} R_n &= 2(\ell_n(\hat{\beta}_n, \phi) - \ell_n(\hat{\beta}_n^{(0)}, \phi)) \\ &= 2\ln\left(\frac{L_n(\hat{\beta}_n, \phi)}{L_n(\hat{\beta}_n^{(0)}, \phi)}\right) \end{aligned}$$

If $\mathcal{H}_0$ is true, which is to say, if model B fits the data correctly, then R_n follows approximately a χ^2-distribution with q degrees of freedom when n tends toward infinity.

A decision rule at the asymptotic level α therefore consists of rejecting $\mathcal{H}_0$ (and hence model A is chosen) when $R_n \geq c_{1-\alpha}(q)$, where $c_{1-\alpha}(q)$ denotes the quantile of order $1-\alpha$ of the χ^2_q-distribution. When this does not hold, then model B is chosen.

REMARK.– Intuitively, R_n measures an adjustment gap between the two models A and B. If R_n is "small", then model B does "almost as well" as model A, yet with fewer explanatory variables. In this case, it is preferable to use model B as it would be more parsimonious. ■

When ϕ is unknown, these results still hold when ϕ is replaced by a consistent estimator, such as the Pearson estimator, which will be described in the following section.

2.3.3. *Estimating the dispersion parameter*

We have remarked that it is not necessary to know ϕ in order to estimate β. However, ϕ plays a role when calculating confidence intervals and hypothesis tests (through $\mathcal{I}_n(\beta)$). For certain models, ϕ is known (e.g. $\phi = 1$ in the binomial and

Poisson models). However, when it is not known, it is necessary to estimate it, and there exist several estimation methods to do so. The first method begins with the relationship:

$$\phi = \frac{\mathrm{var}(Y_i)}{v(\mu_i)}$$

which is valid in the model [2.13]. Recall that $\mu_i = \mathbb{E}(Y_i|\mathbf{X}_i)$, $v(\mu_i)$ is the variance function, and $g(\mu_i) = \beta^\top \mathbf{X}_i$ (with $\beta \in \mathbb{R}^p$).

It is natural to estimate ϕ by estimating μ_i by $\hat{\mu}_i = g^{-1}(\hat{\beta}_n^\top \mathbf{X}_i)$, $\mathrm{var}(Y_i)$ by using the empirical variance:

$$\frac{1}{n-p}\sum_{i=1}^{n}(Y_i - \hat{\mu}_i)^2$$

and $v(\mu_i)$ by $v(\hat{\mu}_i)$. We obtain the moment-type estimator for ϕ:

$$\hat{\phi} = \frac{1}{n-p}\sum_{i=1}^{n}\frac{(Y_i - \hat{\mu}_i)^2}{v(\hat{\mu}_i)} \qquad [2.20]$$

This is *Pearson's* χ^2 *statistic* (the quantities $(Y_i - \hat{\mu}_i)/\sqrt{v(\hat{\mu}_i)}$ are called the Pearson residuals).

Consider the example of the linear Gaussian model:

$$Y_i \sim \mathcal{N}(\mu_i, \sigma^2), \quad i = 1, \ldots, n$$

where $\mu_i = \beta^\top \mathbf{X}_i$, $v(\mu_i) = 1$ and $\phi = \sigma^2$. In the notation of section 2.1.4, we have $\hat{\mu}_i = \hat{\beta}_n^\top \mathbf{X}_i = \hat{Y}_i$. The estimator [2.20] therefore becomes:

$$\hat{\phi} = \frac{1}{n-p}\sum_{i=1}^{n}(Y_i - \hat{Y}_i)^2 \qquad [2.21]$$

We recognize this as being the estimator $\hat{\sigma}_n^2$ given in section 2.1.4.

We can furthermore estimate ϕ using the maximum likelihood method. In the linear Gaussian model, for example, we saw that the MLE of σ^2 (and hence of ϕ, since $\phi = \sigma^2$) is:

$$\hat{\sigma}^2_{MLE} = \frac{1}{n}\sum_{i=1}^{n}(Y_i - \hat{Y}_i)^2$$

This estimator is biased (see section 2.1.5), hence we prefer to use the unbiased [2.21]. More generally, the Pearson estimator is the most commonly used one in practice, notably due to the fact that it is more robust than the MLE: it depends solely on the hypotheses of the first two moments of the distribution of Y_i. The MLE, in addition to being biased, will be more sensitive to the choice of distribution for the Y_i.

The interested reader will find a detailed discussion on how ϕ can be estimated in Dunn and Smyth (2018) (and many other estimators described there too).

2.4. Some examples

2.4.1. *Logistic regression model*

Logistic regression is the most commonly used regression model when the response variable is binary (that is to say, when Y_i can be encoded as either 0 or 1). For example, a binary variable could represent a patient's state of health after their treatment has ended (1: recovered; 0: not recovered), the possible failure of a borrower to make a monthly repayment (1: default; 0: no default), the presence of bacteria in a blood sample (1: present; 0: absent), etc. In the following, the event $\{Y_i = 1\}$ is said to be a "success".

We model Y_i using a Bernoulli distribution with parameter π_i. Let us denote $Y_i \sim \mathcal{B}(\pi_i)$; then, we have: $\mu_i = \mathbb{E}(Y_i|\mathbf{X}_i) = \pi_i$. The linear predictor $\beta^\top \mathbf{X}_i$ belongs to $\mathbb{R}$, whereas π_i belongs to the interval $[0, 1]$. To link these two quantities together, set:

$$\pi_i = h(\beta^\top \mathbf{X}_i)$$

where h is a function from $\mathbb{R}$ into $[0, 1]$. Cumulative distribution functions (cdf) provide a large class of functions from $\mathbb{R}$ into $[0, 1]$. If, for h, we choose the cdf of the *logistic distribution*, whose expression is:

$$F(u) = \frac{e^u}{1 + e^u}$$

then we obtain the logistic regression model. The inverse of $F(u)$ is the logistic function $u \mapsto \text{logit}(u) := \ln(\frac{u}{1-u})$. The density of the logistic distribution is:

$$f(u) = \frac{e^u}{(1 + e^u)^2}$$

The logistic distribution is symmetric, centered and has variance $\pi^2/3$. Figure 2.1 represents the logistic function as well as the cdf and density of the logistic distribution.

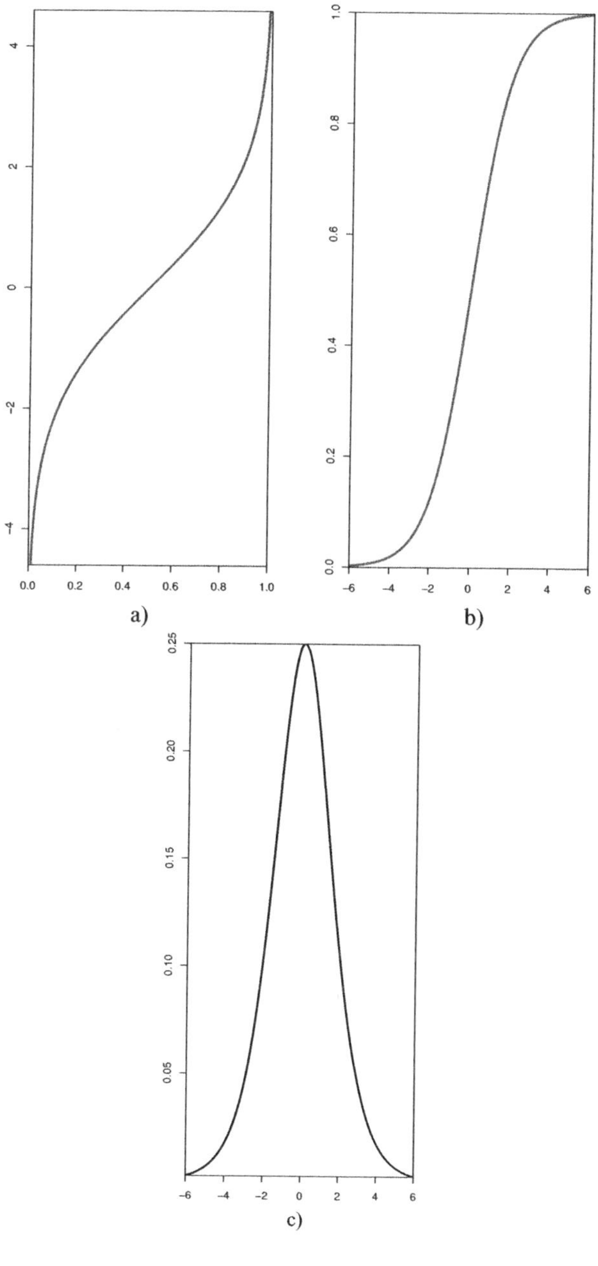

Figure 2.1. *Logistic function logit*$(u) = \ln(\frac{u}{1-u})$ *(a); cdf* $F(u) = \frac{e^u}{1+e^u}$ *of the logistic distribution (b); density* $f(u) = \frac{e^u}{(1+e^u)^2}$ *of the logistic distribution (c)*

The logistic regression model can therefore be written as:

$$\pi_i = \frac{e^{\beta^\top \mathbf{X}_i}}{1 + e^{\beta^\top \mathbf{X}_i}}$$

or, in an equivalent way:

$$\text{logit}(\pi_i) := \ln\left(\frac{\pi_i}{1 - \pi_i}\right) = \beta^\top \mathbf{X}_i \qquad [2.22]$$

Note that the link function, which here is the logistic function, is the canonical link function of the binomial model.

REMARK (THE PROBIT MODEL).– If, for h, we choose the cdf of the normal distribution $\mathcal{N}(0, 1)$, namely:

$$\Phi(u) = \int_{-\infty}^{u} \frac{1}{\sqrt{2\pi}} e^{-\frac{1}{2}t^2}\, dt$$

then we obtain the *probit* model, which is denoted by:

$$\pi_i = \Phi(\beta^\top \mathbf{X}_i)$$

Its link function is the inverse of Φ:

$$\Phi^{-1}(\pi_i) = \beta^\top \mathbf{X}_i$$

This choice of h can be justified as follows. Consider a quantitative variable Y_i^*, for example, the concentration of a particular pollutant in the air on day i. Then define the variable Y_i by $Y_i = 1\{Y_i^* \leq s\}$, where s denotes a fixed critical threshold and $1\{A\}$ is the indicator function for an event A (namely, $1\{A\}$ equals 1 if A is realized, and 0 otherwise). Hence, Y_i equals 1 if the pollutant concentration remains below the alert threshold, and $Y_i = 0$ otherwise. Suppose now that Y_i^* follows a linear Gaussian model. Then Y_i follows a probit model.

Indeed, suppose that $Y_i^* = \gamma^\top \mathbf{X}_i^* + \varepsilon_i$, where $\varepsilon_i \sim \mathcal{N}(0, \sigma^2)$ (to simplify the notation below, we will assume that $\gamma^\top \mathbf{X}_i^*$ does not contain an intercept term). Then we have:

$$\begin{aligned}
\pi_i = \mathbb{P}(Y_i = 1|\mathbf{X}_i^*) &= \mathbb{P}(Y_i^* \leq s|\mathbf{X}_i^*) \\
&= \mathbb{P}\left(\frac{Y_i^* - \gamma^\top \mathbf{X}_i^*}{\sigma} \leq \frac{s - \gamma^\top \mathbf{X}_i^*}{\sigma}|\mathbf{X}_i^*\right) \\
&= \Phi\left(\frac{s - \gamma^\top \mathbf{X}_i^*}{\sigma}\right) \\
&:= \Phi\left(\beta^\top \mathbf{X}_i\right)
\end{aligned}$$

where:

$$\beta = \left(\frac{s}{\sigma}, -\frac{\gamma^\top}{\sigma}\right)^\top \text{and} \mathbf{X}_i = (1, \mathbf{X}_i^{*\top})^\top$$

if the threshold s is unknown, and:

$$\beta = \left(\frac{1}{\sigma}, -\frac{\gamma^\top}{\sigma}\right)^\top \text{and} \mathbf{X}_i = (s, \mathbf{X}_i^{*\top})^\top$$

if the threshold s is known.

By introducing a threshold for Y_i^*, we have consequently obtained a probit model for Y_i.

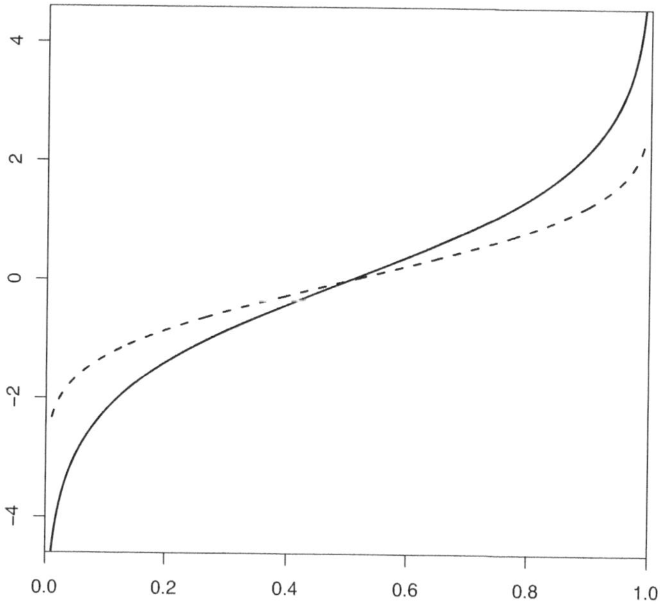

Figure 2.2. *Link functions for the logistic (filled line) and probit (dashed line) models*

The logit link function and Φ^{-1} are presented in Figure 2.2, whereas the cdfs F and Φ for the logistic and probit models are presented in Figure 2.3. These functions are very similar and are essentially only distinguished when π_i is close to either 0 or 1. In fact, we have (see Guyon (2001)):

$$\sup_{x \in \mathbb{R}} \left| \Phi(x) - F\left(\frac{\pi}{\sqrt{3}} x\right) \right| \approx 0.0227$$

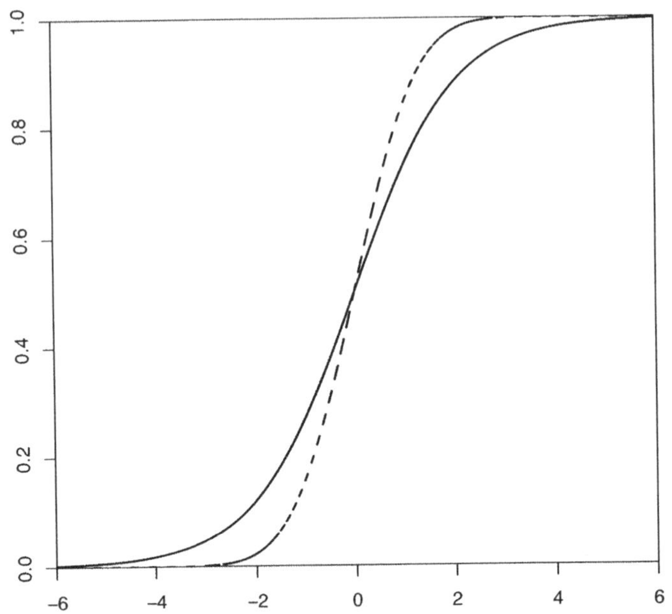

Figure 2.3. *Distribution functions for the logistic (filled line) and probit (dashed line) models*

Therefore, if we were to adjust the models $\pi_i = F(\beta^\top \mathbf{X}_i)$ and $\pi_i = \Phi(\gamma^\top \mathbf{X}_i)$ to the same data set, then their respective MLEs will be close to one another, and we would have $\hat{\beta}_n \approx \frac{\pi}{\sqrt{3}}\hat{\gamma}_n$.

The logistic model is more commonly used in statistical analyses, which is largely due to the fact that its coefficients can be interpreted in terms of *odds ratios*. ■

2.4.1.1. *Odds and odds ratio*

The ratio:

$$\frac{\pi_i}{1-\pi_i} = \frac{\mathbb{P}(Y_i = 1|\mathbf{X}_i)}{\mathbb{P}(Y_i = 0|\mathbf{X}_i)}$$

is called the *odds*. In the logistic regression model, this ratio is equal to $e^{\beta^\top \mathbf{X}_i}$.

The coefficients β_j can be interpreted in the following manner: if the explanatory variable X_j increases by one unit, with all other explanatory variables remaining unchanged (we say "all other things being equal"), then the odds of success are multiplied by the factor e^{β_j}. To see this, denote by π_i and π_i^+ the probabilities of the event $\{Y_i = 1\}$ when $X_{ij} = x$ and $X_{ij} = x + 1$, respectively, with all other things being equal. Then:

$$\frac{\pi_i^+}{1-\pi_i^+} \Big/ \frac{\pi_i}{1-\pi_i} = e^{\beta_j}$$

This quantity e^{β_j} is then called the *odds ratio*.

2.4.1.2. *Maximum likelihood*

The score equation in the logistic model can be obtained as a particular case from equations [2.15] and [2.16] (see example 2.10, section 2.3.1). Now, we will obtain it using the likelihood of the logistic model.

Suppose that we have a sample $\{(Y_i, \mathbf{X}_i), i = 1, \ldots, n\}$ of independent observations of the model [2.22], namely:

$$Y_i \sim \mathcal{B}(\pi_i) \quad \text{with} \quad \pi_i = \frac{e^{\beta^\top \mathbf{X}_i}}{1 + e^{\beta^\top \mathbf{X}_i}}$$

In the following, it will often be useful to state explicitly the dependence of π_i on β in our notation. We will therefore denote $\pi_i(\beta)$.

REMARK.– If the design matrix of an experiment is of full rank, then the logistic model is identifiable (this condition was encountered previously in the linear model). Indeed, suppose that $\pi_i(\beta) = \pi_i(\beta^*)$ for each i. Then $\beta^\top \mathbf{X}_i = \beta^{*\top} \mathbf{X}_i$ for each i, and consequently $\mathbb{X}(\beta - \beta^*) = 0$. If $\mathbb{X}$ is of full rank, then $\beta = \beta^*$, and the model is clearly identifiable.

The same argument applies to the model $\pi_i(\beta) = h(\beta^\top \mathbf{X}_i)$ if h is a strictly increasing function. Therefore, if $\mathbb{X}$ is of full rank, then the probit model is also identifiable. ■

In the logistic model, the likelihood of β can be written as:

$$\begin{aligned} L_n(\beta) &= \prod_{i=1}^n \pi_i^{Y_i}(1-\pi_i)^{1-Y_i} \\ &= \prod_{i=1}^n \left(\frac{e^{\beta^\top \mathbf{X}_i}}{1 + e^{\beta^\top \mathbf{X}_i}}\right)^{Y_i} \left(\frac{1}{1 + e^{\beta^\top \mathbf{X}_i}}\right)^{1-Y_i} \\ &= \prod_{i=1}^n \frac{e^{Y_i \beta^\top \mathbf{X}_i}}{1 + e^{\beta^\top \mathbf{X}_i}} \end{aligned}$$

From which we deduce the log-likelihood:

$$\ell_n(\beta) = \sum_{i=1}^{n} \left\{ Y_i \beta^\top \mathbf{X}_i - \ln\left(1 + e^{\beta^\top \mathbf{X}_i}\right) \right\}$$

and then the score equation:

$$\frac{\partial \ell_n(\beta)}{\partial \beta} = \sum_{i=1}^{n} \mathbf{X}_i \left(Y_i - \frac{e^{\beta^\top \mathbf{X}_i}}{1 + e^{\beta^\top \mathbf{X}_i}} \right) = 0$$

which, of course, coincides with [2.17] (here with $k_i = 1$ for each i). Recall that the MLE does not admit an explicit expression and should therefore be obtained numerically.

Now let us calculate the matrix of second derivatives:

$$\begin{aligned} \frac{\partial^2 \ell_n(\beta)}{\partial \beta \partial \beta^\top} &= -\sum_{i=1}^{n} \mathbf{X}_i \mathbf{X}_i^\top \frac{e^{\beta^\top \mathbf{X}_i}}{(1 + e^{\beta^\top \mathbf{X}_i})^2} \\ &= -\sum_{i=1}^{n} \mathbf{X}_i \mathbf{X}_i^\top \pi_i(\beta)(1 - \pi_i(\beta)) \end{aligned}$$

If $\mathbb{X}$ is of full rank, then this matrix is negative definite. Indeed, let $\mathbf{u}$ be a non-zero vector in $\mathbb{R}^p$. For every β, we have:

$$\begin{aligned} \mathbf{u}^\top \frac{\partial^2 \ell_n(\beta)}{\partial \beta \partial \beta^\top} \mathbf{u} &= -\sum_{i=1}^{n} (\mathbf{X}_i^\top \mathbf{u})^2 \, \pi_i(\beta)(1 - \pi_i(\beta)) \\ &\leq 0 \end{aligned}$$

Suppose that $\mathbf{u}^\top \frac{\partial^2 \ell_n(\beta)}{\partial \beta \partial \beta^\top} \mathbf{u} = 0$. Then $\mathbf{X}_i^\top \mathbf{u} = 0$ for each $i = 1, \ldots, n$ (since $0 < \pi_i(\beta) < 1$) and thus $\mathbb{X}\mathbf{u} = 0$. If $\mathbb{X}$ is of full rank, then we have $\mathbf{u} = 0$, which is a contradiction. Therefore, $\mathbf{u}^\top \frac{\partial^2 \ell_n(\beta)}{\partial \beta \partial \beta^\top} \mathbf{u} < 0$ and hence $\frac{\partial^2 \ell_n(\beta)}{\partial \beta \partial \beta^\top}$ is negative definite for every β.

The log-likelihood is therefore a strictly concave function of β. This has an important consequence numerically: the MLE is a global maximum of the likelihood, which ensures that the Newton–Raphson algorithm converges.

Let us set $\mathcal{I}_n(\beta) = -\partial^2 \ell_n(\beta)/\partial \beta \partial \beta^\top$. From theorem 2.4, the sequence $(\hat{\beta}_n)$ of maximum likelihood estimators is consistent:

$$\hat{\beta}_n \xrightarrow[n \to \infty]{\mathbb{P}} \beta$$

and asymptotically Gaussian:

$$\left(\frac{\mathcal{I}_n(\hat{\beta}_n)}{n}\right)^{\frac{1}{2}} \sqrt{n}(\hat{\beta}_n - \beta) \xrightarrow[n\to\infty]{\mathcal{L}} \mathcal{N}(0, I_p)$$

Statistical inference in the logistic regression model then proceeds as described in section 2.3.2.

2.4.2. *Poisson regression model*

Consider the Poisson regression model:

$$Y_i \sim \mathcal{P}(\mu_i), \text{ with } \mu_i = e^{\beta^\top \mathbf{X}_i} \qquad [2.23]$$

The coefficients of the model are interpreted in the following way. If the explanatory variable X_{ij} increases by one unit, with all other things being equal, then the mean of Y_i is multiplied by a factor of e^{β_j}. Depending on the sign of β_j, this will either increase (if $\beta_j > 0$) or decrease (if $\beta_j < 0$) the mean of Y_i. In the case when $\beta_j = 0$, then the mean of Y_i remains unchanged as X_{ij} varies (X_{ij} has no effect on the response).The model is identifiable when $\mathbb{X}$ is of full rank. The likelihood of β can be written as:

$$\begin{aligned} L_n(\beta) &= \prod_{i=1}^{n} e^{-\mu_i} \frac{\mu_i^{Y_i}}{Y_i!} \\ &= \prod_{i=1}^{n} \frac{\exp(Y_i \beta^\top \mathbf{X}_i - e^{\beta^\top \mathbf{X}_i})}{Y_i!} \end{aligned}$$

from which we get the log-likelihood:

$$\ell_n(\beta) = \sum_{i=1}^{n} \left\{ Y_i \beta^\top \mathbf{X}_i - e^{\beta^\top \mathbf{X}_i} - \ln(Y_i!) \right\}$$

and then the score equation:

$$\frac{\partial \ell_n(\beta)}{\partial \beta} = \sum_{i=1}^{n} \mathbf{X}_i \left(Y_i - e^{\beta^\top \mathbf{X}_i} \right) = 0$$

which, of course, coincides with [2.18] (the score equation obtained from the general formulation of a generalized linear model). Calculating the matrix of second derivatives:

$$\frac{\partial^2 \ell_n(\beta)}{\partial \beta \partial \beta^\top} = -\sum_{i=1}^{n} \mathbf{X}_i \mathbf{X}_i^\top e^{\beta^\top \mathbf{X}_i}$$

let us ensure that, if $\mathbb{X}$ is of full rank, the log-likelihood is strictly concave and admits a unique maximum. Finally, the asymptotic results of theorem 2.4 can be applied here. In particular, for n sufficiently large, $\hat{\beta}_n \approx \mathcal{N}(\beta, \mathcal{I}_n(\hat{\beta}_n)^{-1})$ where $\mathcal{I}_n(\beta) = -\partial^2 \ell_n(\beta)/\partial\beta\partial\beta^\top$.

2.4.3. *Gamma regression model*

The gamma regression model is used to model a quantitative and positive response variable. It has found applications in medicine (tumor size modeling, duration of hospitalization), meteorology (amount of precipitation) as well as insurance (claim amounts). Its density is of the form:

$$f(y|\mathbf{X}_i) = y^{\nu-1} \exp\left(-\frac{y\nu}{\mu_i}\right)\left(\frac{\nu}{\mu_i}\right)^{\nu} \frac{1}{\Gamma(\nu)}, \quad y \in \mathbb{R}_+ \qquad [2.24]$$

(where $\Gamma(x) = \int_0^\infty e^{-t} t^{x-1}\, dt$). Here, we continue to use the parameterization adopted in section 1.3, where $\mathbb{E}(Y|\mathbf{X}_i) = \mu_i$, var$(Y|\mathbf{X}_i) = \mu_i^2/\nu$, and the dispersion parameter ϕ is such that $\phi = 1/\nu$.

As mentioned in section 2.2, the canonical link function of the gamma distribution, which is given by $g(\mu_i) = -\frac{1}{\mu_i} = \beta^\top \mathbf{X}_i$, imposes the condition $\beta^\top \mathbf{X}_i < 0$ since $\mu_i > 0$. To avoid this type of constraint, we prefer to use the log-link function and hence we set:

$$\ln \mu_i = \beta^\top \mathbf{X}_i$$

so that: $\mu_i = e^{\beta^\top \mathbf{X}_i}$. The interpretation of β here is the same as that in the Poisson regression model.

Suppose that we have a sample of independent observations $\{(Y_i, \mathbf{X}_i), i = 1, \ldots, n\}$ of the model [2.24]. The likelihood is calculated as follows:

$$L_n(\beta, \nu) = \prod_{i=1}^n \left\{ Y_i^{\nu-1} \exp\left(-\frac{Y_i\nu}{\mu_i}\right)\left(\frac{\nu}{\mu_i}\right)^{\nu} \frac{1}{\Gamma(\nu)} \right\}$$

from which we obtain the log-likelihood:

$$\ell_n(\beta, \nu) = \sum_{i=1}^n \left\{ (\nu - 1)\ln Y_i - \nu Y_i e^{-\beta^\top \mathbf{X}_i} - \nu\beta^\top \mathbf{X}_i + \nu \ln \nu - \ln \Gamma(\nu) \right\}$$

and then the score equation:

$$\sum_{i=1}^n \mathbf{X}_i \left\{ Y_i e^{-\beta^\top \mathbf{X}_i} - 1 \right\} = 0 \qquad [2.25]$$

(note that this equation does not depend on ν). In practice, the MLE will be approximated by the means of a Newton–Raphson type algorithm. As for the parameter ν, it can be estimated using either the maximum likelihood or the inverse $\hat{\phi}^{-1}$ of the moment estimator [2.20] (recall the fact that $\phi = \nu^{-1}$). The variance function of the gamma distribution is $v(\mu) = \mu^2$; hence $\hat{\phi}$ is given by:

$$\hat{\phi} = \frac{1}{n-p}\sum_{i=1}^{n}\left(\frac{Y_i - \hat{\mu}_i}{\hat{\mu}_i}\right)^2$$

The interested reader can find further developments on the gamma regression model in McCullagh and Nelder (1989).

2.5. Generalized linear models in R: Poisson regression example

In this section, we briefly describe the implementation and outputs of the `glm` function in R (R Core Team 2020). R is a free software dedicated to statistics, as well as the analysis and visualization of data. It is used largely in academic and research environments, but also in industry.

The `glm` function is dedicated to generalized linear models (estimation and hypothesis testing). The linear Gaussian model can be implemented using `glm`, but the `lm` function is generally used as it is specifically dedicated to it (of course, the results obtained from either function will coincide).

As an illustration, we will cover how the Poisson model can be adjusted to an actual data set. Our aim here is not to undertake a complete analysis of these data (in particular, we will not consider any question regarding variable selection, model adequacy or residual analysis), but instead simply to describe, explain and interpret the outputs of the `glm` function, with emphasis placed upon inferential aspects. The reader interested in understanding more can consult one of the many books dedicated to generalized linear models in R such as Faraway (2016) or Dunn and Smyth (2018).

The `docvisits` data set used for this illustration is supplied by the R package `zic` (Jochmann 2017). It comes from the "German Socio-Economic Panel" (SOEP), which is a longitudinal study that began in 1984 and covers approximately 11,000 households in Germany. Each year, participants in this study provide information on subjects as varied as their professional experience, training, income and health. A full description of the data set is provided in Riphahn et al. (2003).

The `docvisits` data set is a sample of the SOEP study, involving 1,812 men aged between 25 and 65. For each participant, we have the number of times he consulted a doctor (in office) during the last three months of 1994 (the `docvisits` response variable), as well as a specific amount of information that will serve as the explanatory variables:

– age: age (in years);

– health: measures the level of health satisfaction of the individual (from 0: minimum level to 10: maximum level);

– handicap: 1 if the individual has a disability, 0 otherwise;

– hdegree: degree of disability (percentage);

– married: 1 if the individual is married, 0 otherwise;

– schooling: number of schooling years;

– hhincome: monthly household net income (Deutsch mark/1,000);

– children: 1 if the household has one or more children below the age of 16 years, 0 otherwise;

– self: 1 if the individual is self-employed, 0 otherwise;

– civil: 1 if the individual is a civil servant, 0 otherwise;

– bluec: 1 if the individual is a blue-collar worker, 0 otherwise;

– employed: 1 if the individual is employed, 0 otherwise;

– public: 1 if the individual is insured in public health insurance, 0 otherwise;

– addon: 1 if the individual is insured in add-on insurance, 0 otherwise.

The script below loads the zic package and docvisits data set, before plotting a histogram of the docvisits response variable (Figure 2.4):

```
library(zic)
data(docvisits)
barplot(with(docvisits, table(docvisits)),
    xlab="Number of consultations",
    ylab="Frequency",col="lightblue")
```

In this histogram, note that the "peak at zero" corresponds to a significantly large proportion of individuals that did not consult a doctor over these last three months (about 41%). This peak is accompanied by a significant difference between the empirical mean and variance of the response variable:

```
mean(docvisits[,1])
[1] 2.958057
var(docvisits[,1])
[1] 27.28924
```

We will return to these observations in Chapter 4. For the moment, let us fit a Poisson regression model to the docvisits data set. The response variable is renamed nbvisits. Each available explanatory variable is used in the linear predictor. The model is therefore the following:

$$Y_i \sim \mathcal{P}(\mu_i), \quad i = 1, \ldots, n$$

where:

$$\begin{aligned}\mu_i = &\exp(\beta_1 + \beta_2\texttt{age}_i + \beta_3\texttt{health}_i + \beta_4\texttt{handicap}_i + \beta_5\texttt{hdegree}_i + \beta_6\texttt{married}_i \\ &+ \beta_7\texttt{schooling}_i + \beta_8\texttt{hhincome}_i + \beta_9\texttt{children}_i + \beta_{10}\texttt{self}_i + \beta_{11}\texttt{civil}_i \\ &+ \beta_{12}\texttt{bluec}_i + \beta_{13}\texttt{employed}_i + \beta_{14}\texttt{public}_i + \beta_{15}\texttt{addon}_i)\end{aligned} \quad [2.26]$$

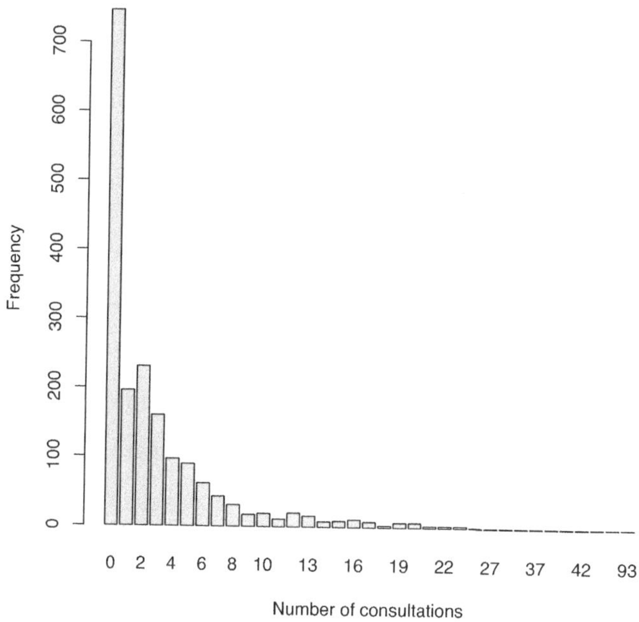

Figure 2.4. *Histogram of the number of consultations* (docvisits *data set)*

It suffices to indicate which variables to use in the glm function, as well as which family the model should belong to for the fitting (thanks to the family command which supports the binomial(link="logit"), gaussian(link="identity"), Gamma (link="inverse") and poisson(link="log") families, among others). The functions indicated inside of the parentheses are the default link functions used by glm. It is not actually necessary to enter them in (unless you wish to use another link function).

The script:

```
attach(docvisits)
datadoc=data.frame(age,health,handicap,hdegree,
    married,schooling,hhincome,children,self,
    civil,bluec,employed,public,addon)

nbvisits=docvisits[,1]
mod_pois=glm(nbvisits~.,data=datadoc,family=
    poisson(link="log"))
printCoefmat(coef(summary(mod_pois)))
```

produces the following output:

```
Estimate Std. Error  z value  Pr(>|z|)
(Intercept)  2.0731874  0.1345255  15.4111 < 2.2e
    -16 ***
age          0.0123011  0.0015040   8.1787 2.870e
    -16 ***
health      -0.2434786  0.0056891 -42.7971 < 2.2e
    -16 ***
handicap     0.4060363  0.0727500   5.5813 2.388e
    -08 ***
hdegree     -0.0048258  0.0012464  -3.8717
    0.0001081 ***
married     -0.0611258  0.0385844  -1.5842
    0.1131459
schooling   -0.0034508  0.0069532  -0.4963
    0.6196875
hhincome     0.0105722  0.0075109   1.4076
    0.1592526
children    -0.0389413  0.0357513  -1.0892
    0.2760537
self        -0.2650078  0.0664960  -3.9853 6.739e
    -05 ***
civil       -0.1613567  0.0726127  -2.2222
    0.0262728 *
bluec        0.0733666  0.0379492   1.9333
    0.0532013 .
employed    -0.1680440  0.0429818  -3.9097 9.243e
    -05 ***
public       0.1301053  0.0636595   2.0438
    0.0409763 *
addon        0.2697033  0.0928141   2.9058
    0.0036626 **
---
Signif. codes:  0 '***' 0.001 '**' 0.01 '*' 0.05
    '.' 0.1 ' ' 1
```

The `Estimate` column returns the estimated values of each β_j. The corresponding standard errors are presented in the `Std. Error` column. The `z` `value` column returns the Wald test statistic for $\mathcal{H}_0 : \beta_j = 0$ against $\mathcal{H}_1 : \beta_j \neq 0$ (calculated for each j as the ratio `Estimate/Std. Error`). For each test statistic, the column `Pr(>|z|)` returns the corresponding p-value, namely, the value $\mathbb{P}(\mathcal{N}(0,1) > |z|)$. The asterisks allow for the significance level of each test to be easily visualized.

The results obtained here indicate that the age, health satisfaction level, presence of a disability and the disability degree are very significantly related to the number of consultations. On average, the number of care requests increases with age and for individuals presenting a disability. As we would expect, the average number of consultations decreases as the health satisfaction level increases. It furthermore decreases as the disability degree increases, which could be related to mobility difficulties experienced by the patients, or to specific care requests that require a consultation in a specialized health structure rather than an office.

Furthermore, on average, observe that beneficiaries of public health insurance have more frequent consultations than those without (and this phenomenon is all the more present and statistically significant for those with add-on health insurance).

Being self-employed is associated to lower health care consumption. This could be due to health insurance coverage being less favorable toward the self-employed (in Germany, self-employed workers can opt out of having public health insurance; add-on health insurance is also less widespread there).

2.5.1. *Confidence intervals and hypothesis tests*

The command:

```
confint.default(mod_pois)
```

returns the confidence intervals $[\hat{\beta}_{n,j} - u_{1-\frac{\alpha}{2}} \times \text{se}(\hat{\beta}_{n,j}), \hat{\beta}_{n,j} + u_{1-\frac{\alpha}{2}} \times \text{se}(\hat{\beta}_{n,j})]$ for each of the β_j:

```
2.5 %         97.5 %
(Intercept)    1.809522238   2.336852643
age            0.009353193   0.015248929
health        -0.254629139  -0.232328104
handicap       0.263448855   0.548623749
hdegree       -0.007268787  -0.002382877
married       -0.136749746   0.014498221
schooling     -0.017078933   0.010177245
hhincome      -0.004148822   0.025293321
children      -0.109012615   0.031129993
self          -0.395337494  -0.134678038
```

```
civil        -0.303674933 -0.019038476
bluec        -0.001012494  0.147745637
employed     -0.252286812 -0.083801227
public        0.005335002  0.254875600
addon         0.087791059  0.451615533
```

By default, $\alpha = 0.05$ and the intervals are at the (asymptotic) confidence level 0.95. We can modify this level using the `level` option. For example:

```
confint.default(mod_pois,level=0.99)
```

returns intervals at the confidence level 0.99. Finally, we can produce confidence intervals for just a selection of the β_j. For example:

```
confint.default(mod_pois,c("age","health"))
```

returns the intervals for β_2 and β_3:

```
2.5 %          97.5 %
age        0.009353193   0.01524893
health  -0.254629139  -0.23232810
```

We can easily perform tests between nested models too, either by calculating the likelihood ratio statistic "by hand", or by using the `lrtest` function from the `lmtest` package (Zeileis and Hothorn 2002).

Suppose that we want to test the hypothesis that holding an insurance (public or private) does not influence the average number of consultations. This amounts to testing:

$$\mathcal{H}_0 : \beta_{14} = \beta_{15} = 0 \text{ against } \mathcal{H}_1 : \beta_{14} \neq 0 \text{ or } \beta_{15} \neq 0$$

The model defined by $\mathcal{H}_0$ is nested within that defined by $\mathcal{H}_1$ (it is obtained by dropping the `public` and `addon` variables of the model under $\mathcal{H}_1$).

The log-likelihood of the model under $\mathcal{H}_1$ is the same as that for the model [2.26]. It can be obtained by the means of the `logLik` function:

```
logLik(mod_pois)
'log Lik.' -5375.863 (df=15)
```

The following script adjusts the model under $\mathcal{H}_0$ and returns its log-likelihood:

```
mod_pois_H0=update(mod_pois,formula=.~.-public-
    addon)
logLik(mod_pois_H0)
'log Lik.' -5382.266 (df=13)
```

Under $\mathcal{H}_0$, the likelihood ratio statistic R_n asymptotically follows a χ^2-distribution with two degrees of freedom. A decision rule at the level 0.05 will therefore consist of rejecting $\mathcal{H}_0$ when R_n is greater than $c_{0.95}(2) \approx 5.991$. Here, $R_n = 2 \times (-5,375.863 - (-5,382.266)) = 12.806$, and the $\mathcal{H}_0$ hypothesis is therefore rejected. The p-value of the test is the probability $\mathbb{P}(\chi^2_2 > 12.806)$, which can be easily obtained using R:

```
1-pchisq(12.806,2)
[1] 0.00165658
```

These results can also be obtained directly using the `lrtest` function from the `lmtest` package. The syntax is the following:

```
lrtest(mod_pois, c("public","addon"))
```

It suffices to indicate to `lrtest` which variables are to be dropped under $\mathcal{H}_0$. We obtain the following output:

```
Likelihood ratio test

Model 1: nbvisits ~ age + health + handicap +
    hdegree + married + schooling + hhincome +
    children + self + civil + bluec + employed +
    public + addon
Model 2: nbvisits ~ age + health + handicap +
    hdegree + married + schooling + hhincome +
    children + self + civil + bluec + employed
#Df  LogLik Df  Chisq Pr(>Chisq)
1  15 -5375.9
2  13 -5382.3 -2 12.806   0.001657 **
```

When the models that we wish to compare are not nested, then the likelihood ratio test is no longer valid. Instead, penalized likelihood criteria can be used, such as the AIC (*Akaike's information criterion*) and the BIC (*Bayesian information criterion*).

2.5.2. *AIC and BIC, variable selection*

If we view likelihood as a measure of how well a model fits the data, then it is natural to choose the model with the greatest likelihood. However, this would lead to the most complex model being chosen, that being the one with the most explanatory variables. Intuitively, the more explanatory variables that are included in a model, the more "flexible" it will be and therefore appropriate to fit to the data. The adjustment will be maximal when every available explanatory variable is included.

However, the more variables that are included, the more the variance of the estimators increases, and hence also the variance of the predictions. A model that fits the data very well could therefore turn out to perform poorly when it comes to making predictions.

It is necessary therefore to control the number of explanatory variables included when constructing a model. To achieve a compromise between adjustment and complexity, one solution consists of maximizing a likelihood *penalized* by the complexity of the model, which is to say, by the number of parameters to be estimated. This leads to the definition of Akaike's criterion:

$$AIC = -2\ell_n(\hat{\beta}_n, \hat{\phi}) + 2(p+1)$$

where p represents the dimension of β, and $p+1$ is the number of parameters to be estimated, which includes ϕ, should it be unknown. When ϕ is known, this criterion becomes:

$$AIC = -2\ell_n(\hat{\beta}_n, \phi) + 2p$$

On the other hand, the BIC adopts an alternative penalty. When ϕ is unknown, it is written as:

$$BIC = -2\ell_n(\hat{\beta}_n, \hat{\phi}) + (p+1)\ln n$$

and, when ϕ is known:

$$BIC = -2\ell_n(\hat{\beta}_n, \phi) + p\ln n$$

We keep the model that minimizes the AIC or the BIC. Generally speaking, the models retained on the BIC basis are more parsimonious (they contain fewer explanatory variables). Indeed, as soon as $n \geq 8$, the penalty of the BIC is greater than that of the AIC. Therefore, using the BIC can be interesting when we wish to favor the interpretation of the model.

The `AIC` and `BIC` functions in `R` return the values of these two criteria:

```
AIC(mod_pois)
[1] 10781.73
BIC(mod_pois)
[1] 10864.26
```

In particular, the AIC and BIC are used in automatic variable selection procedures. Even for a moderate value of p, it is not possible to compare the AIC or the BIC for every model that can be formed from p explanatory variables: the algorithmic cost would be too high.

Automatic selection consists of going step-by-step through the set of all possible models, sequentially removing or adding explanatory variables, on the basis of a given criterion (e.g. minimization of the AIC or BIC, or consideration of the p-value from the Wald test).

Multiple procedures exist: forward selection (start with the model in which the linear predictor is reduced to the constant β_1 and then, at each step, for example, add the variable which minimizes the AIC), backward selection (same principle as in the forward procedure, but now the algorithm starts with the model containing each available explanatory variable, before removing them one by one) or mixed (or *stepwise*, also the same principle as before, but either adds or removes a variable at each step). The principles, advantages and disadvantages of each method are described in more detail in Dunn and Smyth (2018) (see also Hastie et al. (2009)). In `R`, they are implemented using the `step` function.

2.5.3. *Prediction, confidence intervals for a prediction*

Suppose that we want to make some predictions using an adjusted model. We have the explanatory variables $\mathbf{X}_{n+1}$ from individual $n+1$ (which is not included in the sample used to adjust the model), and we want to estimate $\mu_{n+1} = \mathbb{E}(Y_{n+1}|\mathbf{X}_{n+1})$. In the Poisson model, for example, we have $\mu_{n+1} = e^{\beta^\top \mathbf{X}_{n+1}}$. It is therefore natural to estimate μ_{n+1} by:

$$\hat{\mu}_{n+1} = e^{\hat{\beta}_n^\top \mathbf{X}_{n+1}}$$

where $\hat{\beta}_n$ denotes the maximum likelihood estimator of β, obtained from the sample made up of the previous n individuals.

To construct a confidence interval for μ_{n+1}, first let us note, if n is sufficiently large, that:

$$\hat{\beta}_n^\top \mathbf{X}_{n+1} \approx \mathcal{N}(\beta^\top \mathbf{X}_{n+1}, \mathbf{X}_{n+1}^\top \text{var}(\hat{\beta}_n) \mathbf{X}_{n+1})$$

where $\text{var}(\hat{\beta}_n) = \mathcal{I}_n(\hat{\beta}_n)^{-1}$. From this, we obtain a confidence interval at the confidence level $1-\alpha$ of $\beta^\top \mathbf{X}_{n+1}$:

$$[L_n, U_n] := \left[\hat{\beta}_n^\top \mathbf{X}_{n+1} - u_{1-\frac{\alpha}{2}} \times \text{se}(\hat{\beta}_n^\top \mathbf{X}_{n+1}), \hat{\beta}_n^\top \mathbf{X}_{n+1} + u_{1-\frac{\alpha}{2}} \times \text{se}(\hat{\beta}_n^\top \mathbf{X}_{n+1})\right]$$

where $\text{se}(\hat{\beta}_n^\top \mathbf{X}_{n+1}) = \sqrt{\mathbf{X}_{n+1}^\top \text{var}(\hat{\beta}_n) \mathbf{X}_{n+1}}$. The confidence interval for the prediction μ_{n+1} is therefore obtained as $[e^{L_n}, e^{U_n}]$.

The `predict` function in R does not directly return the interval $[e^{L_n}, e^{U_n}]$, but allows for it to be easily constructed. For example, consider the Poisson model $Y_i \sim \mathcal{P}(\mu_i)$, where:

$$\mu_i = \exp(\beta_1 + \beta_2 \texttt{age}_i + \beta_3 \texttt{health}_i + \beta_4 \texttt{handicap}_i)$$

(so that the code can be easily read afterwards, we will only include three explanatory variables). Suppose that we want to obtain a confidence interval at the confidence level 0.95 for the average number of consultations of a 50-year-old man, who does not present a disability, and whose health satisfaction level is 7. Then we would search for an interval of $\mu_{n+1} = \mathbb{E}(Y_{n+1}|\mathbf{X}_{n+1})$, where $\mathbf{X}_{n+1} = (1, \texttt{age}_{n+1}, \texttt{health}_{n+1}, \texttt{handicap}_{n+1}) = (1, 50, 7, 0)$ (here, the 1 corresponds to the constant term of the linear predictor).

We begin by adjusting the model, before then recovering the values of $\hat{\beta}_n^\top \mathbf{X}_{n+1}$ and $\text{se}(\hat{\beta}_n^\top \mathbf{X}_{n+1})$ using the `predict` function:

```
mod_pois_2=glm(nbvisits~age+health+handicap,data=
    datadoc,family=poisson(link="log"))
out=predict(mod_pois_2,newdata=data.frame(age=50,
    health=7,handicap=0),se.fit=TRUE)
```

The `out$fit` and `out$se.fit` commands return $\hat{\beta}_n^\top \mathbf{X}_{n+1}$ and $\text{se}(\hat{\beta}_n^\top \mathbf{X}_{n+1})$, respectively. The confidence interval for μ_{n+1} can be calculated from these easily enough:

```
ci.lo=exp(out$fit-qnorm(0.975)*out$se.fit)
ci.hi=exp(out$fit+qnorm(0.975)*out$se.fit)

c(lower=ci.lo,estimate=exp(out$fit),upper=ci.hi)
lower.1  estimate.1    upper.1
2.352269    2.445076   2.541544
```

To obtain $\hat{\mu}_{n+1}$, we have calculated `exp(out$fit)`. It is possible to directly recover the prediction by including the option `type="response"` within the argument of the `predict` function:

```
out=predict(mod_pois_2,newdata=data.frame(age=50,
    health=7,handicap=0),se.fit=TRUE,type="
    response")
```

The out$fit command now returns $\hat{\mu}_{n+1} = 2.445076$.

We can adapt this code to calculate confidence intervals for the average number of consultations for men aged between 30 and 50 years (with a step of, for example, four years), who do not present a disability, and whose health satisfaction level is 7:

```
newage=seq(30,50, by=4)
out_2=predict(mod_pois_2,newdata=data.frame(age=
    newage,health=7,handicap=0),se.fit=TRUE)
ci.lo=exp(out_2$fit-qnorm(0.975)*out_2$se.fit)
ci.hi=exp(out_2$fit+qnorm(0.975)*out_2$se.fit)
cbind(newage,ci.lo,prediction=exp(out_2$fit),ci.
    hi)
```

```
newage     ci.lo prediction    ci.hi
1       30 1.826504    1.910666 1.998705
2       34 1.930007    2.007272 2.087630
3       38 2.035701    2.108763 2.184447
4       42 2.141930    2.215385 2.291360
5       46 2.247457    2.327399 2.410184
6       50 2.352269    2.445076 2.541544
```

2.6. Technical appendix

2.6.1. *Some probability distributions*

Let us briefly recall some probability distributions that are constructed from the normal distribution. These distributions arise naturally in the setting of the linear Gaussian model. These are the χ^2-, Student's t-, and Fisher's distributions.

Let $X_1, \dots, X_n$ denote a set of i.i.d. random variables that follow the standard normal distribution $\mathcal{N}(0, 1)$. The χ^2-distribution with n degrees of freedom, which we denote by χ^2_n, is then the distribution of the sum $X_1^2 + X_2^2 + \ldots + X_n^2$.

The χ^2-distribution is in turn involved in the definition of Student's t-distribution. If X is a random variable following the $\mathcal{N}(0, 1)$ distribution, and if Y is a random variable, independent of X, that follows the χ^2_n-distribution, then the distribution that the variable:

$$Z = \frac{X}{\sqrt{Y/n}} \qquad [2.27]$$

follows is called Student's t-distribution with n degrees of freedom; we denote it by $\mathcal{T}_n$. Student's t-distribution is symmetrical and centered.

REMARK.– If n is sufficiently large ($n > 30$ is generally accepted as being sufficient), then the $\mathcal{T}_n$-distribution can be approximated by the normal distribution $\mathcal{N}(0, 1)$.

To see this, note that the denominator in [2.27], with distribution $\sqrt{\chi^2_n/n}$, converges in probability to 1 when n tends toward infinity. Indeed, $\mathbb{E}(\chi^2_n/n) = 1$ and $\text{var}(\chi^2_n/n) = 2/n$, which tends toward 0 when n goes to infinity. Hence, the denominator converges in quadratic mean, and consequently, in probability, to 1. Finally, Z converges in distribution to the distribution of X, namely, the $\mathcal{N}(0, 1)$ distribution. ■

Lastly, if U_1 is a random variable of the $\chi^2_{n_1}$-distribution, and if U_2 is a random variable, independent of U_1, of the $\chi^2_{n_2}$-distribution, then the distribution that the variable:

$$U = \frac{U_1/n_1}{U_2/n_2}$$

follows is called Fisher's distribution with (n_1, n_2) degrees of freedom. We denote it by F_{n_1,n_2}.

2.6.2. *Cochran's theorem*

Let $\mathbf{Y}$ be a Gaussian random vector of the $\mathcal{N}(\mu, \sigma^2 I_n)$ distribution, where I_n denotes the identity matrix of order n. Also, let $\mathcal{M}$ be a p-dimensional subspace of $\mathbb{R}^n$, and let P denote the orthogonal projection matrix from $\mathbb{R}^n$ onto $\mathcal{M}$.

Then, the following properties hold:

1) $P\mathbf{Y} \sim \mathcal{N}(P\mu, \sigma^2 P)$.

2) The vectors $P\mathbf{Y}$ and $\mathbf{Y} - P\mathbf{Y}$ are independent.

3) $\|P\mathbf{Y} - P\mu\|^2/\sigma^2 \sim \chi^2_p$.

2.7. Exercises

Exercise 1 – Maximum likelihood in the GLM

Let $\{(Y_i, \mathbf{X}_i), i = 1, \ldots, n\}$ be a sample of independent observations of the model [2.13], where $\mu_i = \mathbb{E}(Y_i|\mathbf{X}_i)$ and $g(\mu_i) = \beta^\top \mathbf{X}_i$ (g denotes the link function and $\beta = (\beta_1, \ldots, \beta_p)^\top$ is an unknown parameter). Further, we denote $\eta_i = \beta^\top \mathbf{X}_i$.

To simplify the notation, in the following we will adopt Leibniz's notation when differentiating a composition of functions: if $z = f(y)$ and $y = g(x)$, then the derivative $\partial f(g(x))/\partial x = \dot{f}(g(x))\dot{g}(x)$ will be denoted by $\frac{\partial z}{\partial x} = \frac{\partial z}{\partial y}\frac{\partial y}{\partial x}$.

The aim of this exercise is to determinate the estimating equation for β when g can be any link function (in section 2.3.1, we restricted ourselves to the case where g is the canonical link function of the model).

1) Show that the log-likelihood of (β, ϕ) can be written as $\ell_n(\beta, \phi) = \sum_{i=1}^n \ell_{n,i}(\beta, \phi)$, where $\ell_{n,i}(\beta, \phi)$ is a function to be determined.

2) Starting from the decomposition:

$$\frac{\partial \ell_{n,i}}{\partial \beta_j} = \frac{\partial \ell_{n,i}}{\partial \theta_i}\frac{\partial \theta_i}{\partial \mu_i}\frac{\partial \mu_i}{\partial \eta_i}\frac{\partial \eta_i}{\partial \beta_j}$$

show that the estimating equation of β can be written as:

$$\sum_{i=1}^n \mathbf{X}_i \frac{(Y_i - \mu_i)}{v(\mu_i)}\frac{\partial \mu_i}{\partial \eta_i} = 0 \qquad [2.28]$$

where $v(\mu_i)$ is the variance function.

APPLICATION.– Consider the gamma regression model:

$$f(y|\mathbf{X}_i) = y^{\nu-1}\exp\left(-\frac{y\nu}{\mu_i}\right)\left(\frac{\nu}{\mu_i}\right)^{\nu}\frac{1}{\Gamma(\nu)}, \quad y \in \mathbb{R}_+$$

and take the logarithm function to be the link function: $\ln \mu_i = \beta^\top \mathbf{X}_i$. Show that [2.28] reduces to the equation [2.25].

3) If g is the canonical link function, show that [2.28] reduces to equation [2.15].

Exercise 2 – Iteratively reweighted least squares

The MLE of β in the GLM is obtained by solving the equation $\frac{\partial \ell_n(\beta,\phi)}{\partial \beta} = 0$ (equation [2.14], section 2.3.1). Except in the special case of the linear Gaussian model, the MLE does not admit an explicit expression. Therefore, it must be approximated numerically using an iterative algorithm (e.g. the Newton–Raphson algorithm).

NEWTON-RAPHSON ALGORITHM.– At each iteration, the algorithm approximates the function $\beta \mapsto \partial \ell_n(\beta, \phi)/\partial \beta$ using its first-order Taylor expansion. At the $(k+1)$-th iteration, we have:

$$\frac{\partial \ell_n(\beta^{(k+1)},\phi)}{\partial \beta} \approx \frac{\partial \ell_n(\beta^{(k)},\phi)}{\partial \beta} + \frac{\partial^2 \ell_n(\beta^{(k)},\phi)}{\partial \beta \partial \beta^\top}(\beta^{(k+1)} - \beta^{(k)})$$

and we search for the value of $\beta^{(k+1)}$ that causes this approximation to vanish, which is to say that we solve:

$$\frac{\partial \ell_n(\beta^{(k)},\phi)}{\partial \beta} + \frac{\partial^2 \ell_n(\beta^{(k)},\phi)}{\partial \beta \partial \beta^\top}(\beta^{(k+1)} - \beta^{(k)}) = 0$$

Doing so, we obtain:

$$\beta^{(k+1)} = \beta^{(k)} - \left(\frac{\partial^2 \ell_n(\beta^{(k)},\phi)}{\partial \beta \partial \beta^\top}\right)^{-1} \frac{\partial \ell_n(\beta^{(k)},\phi)}{\partial \beta} \qquad [2.29]$$

Starting with an initial value $\beta^{(0)}$, we reiterate this process to obtain a sequence $\beta^{(1)}, \beta^{(2)}, \ldots$ until some convergence criterion has been satisfied. Then the MLE is approximated using the last iterated value that was obtained for $\beta^{(k)}$.

In the following, we will use the same notation as that used in section 2.3.1.

1) In the model [2.13] (to simplify the calculation, we will consider the canonical link function), show that:

$$\frac{\partial \ell_n(\beta,\phi)}{\partial \beta} = \frac{1}{\phi}\mathbb{X}^\top(\mathbf{Y} - \mu(\beta))$$

where $\mathbb{X}$ is the design matrix [2.2] and $\mu(\beta)$ denotes the vector[3] $(\mu_1(\beta), \ldots, \mu_n(\beta))^\top$.

2) Calculate $\frac{\partial^2 \ell_n(\beta,\phi)}{\partial \beta_j \partial \beta_k}$, and deduce from this that $\frac{\partial^2 \ell_n(\beta,\phi)}{\partial \beta \partial \beta^\top}$ can be written as:

$$\frac{\partial^2 \ell_n(\beta,\phi)}{\partial \beta \partial \beta^\top} = -\frac{1}{\phi}\mathbb{X}^\top \mathbb{W}(\beta)\mathbb{X}$$

where $\mathbb{W}(\beta)$ is the diagonal $(n \times n)$-matrix whose ith diagonal term is $v(\mu_i(\beta))$.

3) Show that [2.29] can be written as:

$$\beta^{(k+1)} = (\mathbb{X}^\top \mathbb{W}(\beta^{(k)})\mathbb{X})^{-1}\mathbb{X}^\top \mathbb{W}(\beta^{(k)})\mathbf{U}(\beta^{(k)})$$

where $\mathbf{U}(\beta) = \mathbb{X}\beta + \mathbb{W}(\beta)^{-1}(\mathbf{Y} - \mu(\beta))$.

REMARK.– At each iteration, $\beta^{(k+1)}$ takes on the form $(\mathbb{X}^\top \mathbb{W}\mathbb{X})^{-1}\mathbb{X}^\top \mathbb{W}\mathbf{U}$ of a weighted LSE (by the matrix $\mathbb{W}$), hence the name "iteratively reweighted least

3 We will include β in the notation when it will be helpful to understand the calculations.

squares" attributed to the algorithm. This is the algorithm implemented by the `glm` function in R. There, the vector $\mathbf{U}$ plays the role of the response variable. It depends on β and is updated after each iteration, just like $\mathbb{W}$ is. ■

4) In the case of the linear Gaussian model, show that $\beta^{(k+1)}$ becomes $(\mathbb{X}^\top\mathbb{X})^{-1}\mathbb{X}^\top\mathbf{Y}$. Comment on this result.

Exercise 3 – Fisher scoring algorithm

The Fisher scoring algorithm is a modified version of the Newton–Raphson, one in which the matrix $-\partial^2\ell_n(\beta^{(k)}, \phi)/\partial\beta\partial\beta^\top$ is replaced by its expectation, improving the stability of the algorithm[4]. When the canonical link function is used, the two matrices – and hence the two algorithms – coincide.

1) Let $Y_1, \ldots, Y_n$ be an i.i.d. sample of the distribution $\mathcal{P}(\mu)$. We want to estimate μ. Denote $\bar{Y}_n = n^{-1}\sum_{i=1}^n Y_i$. For the Newton–Raphson algorithm, show that the update equation of $\mu^{(k+1)}$ can be written as:

$$\mu^{(k+1)} = 2\mu^{(k)} - \frac{(\mu^{(k)})^2}{\bar{Y}_n} \qquad [2.30]$$

What does this equation become if $\mu^{(k)} = \bar{Y}_n$?

HINT.– Start with equation [2.29].

2) Let us rewrite [2.30] in the form:

$$\mu^{(k+1)} = \mu^{(k)}\left(2 - \frac{\mu^{(k)}}{\bar{Y}_n}\right)$$

How does the algorithm adjust the value of $\mu^{(k+1)}$ when $\mu^{(k)} < \bar{Y}_n$?

3) For the Fisher scoring algorithm, show that the update equation of $\mu^{(k+1)}$ can be written as:

$$\mu^{(k+1)} = \bar{Y}_n$$

4) Let $Y_1, \ldots, Y_n$ be a sample of independent observations of the model:

$$Y_i \sim \mathcal{P}(e^{\beta^\top \mathbf{X}_i})$$

where $\mathbf{X}_i$ is a vector of fixed explanatory variables (which is to say, non-random). Denote the log-likelihood of β in this model by $\ell_n(\beta)$.

4 $-\partial^2\ell_n(\beta, \phi)/\partial\beta\partial\beta^\top$ is often called the *observed information*; its expectation is called the *expected information*.

a) Write $\ell_n(\beta)$, then determine $\partial \ell_n(\beta)/\partial\beta$ and $\partial^2 \ell_n(\beta)/\partial\beta\partial\beta^\top$. Explain why the Newton–Raphson and Fisher scoring algorithms coincide.

b) Consider the case when $\mathbf{X}_i$ is reduced to the constant 1 (and thus $\beta^\top \mathbf{X}_i = \beta$). Show that the updated equation for $\beta^{(k+1)}$ can be written as:

$$\beta^{(k+1)} = \beta^{(k)} + \frac{\bar{Y}_n}{e^{\beta^{(k)}}} - 1$$

How does the algorithm adjust the value of $\beta^{(k+1)}$ when $e^{\beta^{(k)}} < \bar{Y}_n$?

Exercise 4 – A binomial regression model

Let $Y_1, \ldots, Y_n$ be a sample of independent observations such that:

$$Y_i \sim \mathcal{B}(n_i, \pi_i(\beta)), \quad i = 1, \ldots, n$$

where $\pi_i(\beta) = F(x_i\beta)$, F is a cumulative distribution function, $f(x) = \partial F(x)/\partial x$ is its derivative, x_i is a scalar explanatory variable and $\beta \in \mathbb{R}$ is a parameter to be estimated.

1) Calculate the likelihood of β, and then show that the scoring equation can be written as:

$$\sum_{i=1}^{n} x_i(Y_i - n_i F(x_i\beta)) \frac{f(x_i\beta)}{F(x_i\beta)(1 - F(x_i\beta))} = 0$$

2) In the following, F will denote the cdf of the logistic distribution. Show that $f/\{F(1-F)\} = 1$. From this, deduce a simplified expression of the scoring equation.

3) Show that:

$$\frac{\partial^2 \ell_n(\beta)}{\partial\beta^2} = -\sum_{i=1}^{n} x_i^2 n_i \frac{e^{x_i\beta}}{(1 + e^{x_i\beta})^2}$$

where $\ell_n(\beta)$ denotes the log-likelihood of β. Show that the updated formula [2.29] of $\beta^{(k+1)}$ in the Newton–Raphson algorithm can be written as:

$$\beta^{(k+1)} = \beta^{(k)} + \frac{\sum_{i=1}^{n} x_i(Y_i - n_i\pi_i(\beta^{(k)}))}{\sum_{j=1}^{n} x_j^2 n_j \pi_j(\beta^{(k)})(1 - \pi_j(\beta^{(k)}))}$$

Exercise 5 – A Poisson regression model

Suppose that $Y_i|X_i \sim \mathcal{P}(e^{\beta_0+\beta_1 X_i})$, where:

$$X_i = \begin{cases} 1 & \text{for } i = 1, \ldots, n_A, \\ 0 & \text{for } i = n_A + 1, \ldots, n_A + n_B \end{cases}$$

Here, the Y_i are assumed to be independent. Let $\beta = (\beta_0, \beta_1)^\top$, $\mathbf{X}_i = (1, X_i)^\top$, $\mu_0 := \mathbb{E}(Y_i|X_i = 0) = e^{\beta_0}$ and $\mu_1 := \mathbb{E}(Y_i|X_i = 1) = e^{\beta_0+\beta_1}$. The MLE of β is obtained by solving equation [2.18] (see section 2.3.1):

$$\sum_{i=1}^{n} \mathbf{X}_i \left(Y_i - e^{\beta^\top \mathbf{X}_i} \right) = 0$$

Starting with this equation, show that we obtain the following estimators for μ_0 and μ_1:

$$\hat{\mu}_0 = \frac{1}{n_B} \sum_{i=n_A+1}^{n_A+n_B} Y_i \quad \text{and} \quad \hat{\mu}_1 = \frac{1}{n_A} \sum_{i=1}^{n_A} Y_i$$

Exercise 6 – Deviance

The deviance of a model measures how well it adjusts to the data. It is calculated by taking the difference between the log-likelihood of the *saturated* model and that of the model under consideration. The saturated model is the model which associates a parameter $\mu_i = \mathbb{E}(Y_i)$ to each individual i. Thus, it has n parameters $\mu_1, \ldots, \mu_n$ (we will write $\mu = (\mu_1, \ldots, \mu_n)^\top$). This model does not have any practical interest, but it serves as a reference to judge the fit of the other models.

Consider a GLM defined by $g(\mu_i) = \beta^\top \mathbf{X}_i$. Denote the log-likelihood of this model by $\ell_n(\beta)$, and by $\hat{\beta}_n$ the MLE of β. Further, denote the log-likelihood of the saturated model by $\ell_n(\mu)$, and the MLE of μ by $\hat{\mu} = (\hat{\mu}_1, \ldots, \hat{\mu}_n)^\top$. Then the normalized deviance is defined to be the quantity:

$$D^* = 2(\ell_n(\hat{\mu}) - \ell_n(\hat{\beta}_n))$$

The quantity $D = D^*\phi$ (where ϕ denotes the dispersion parameter of the GLM under consideration) is called the deviance. If $\phi = 1$, then the deviance and the normalized deviance coincide (e.g. in the binomial and Poisson distributions).We can compare two models by comparing their deviances (see Dobson 1990).

1) Suppose we have n independent observations $Y_i \sim \mathcal{B}(m_i, \pi_i)$, $i = 1, \ldots, n$. Show that the MLE of μ_i in the saturated model is given by:

$$\hat{\mu}_i = Y_i$$

and, from this, deduce $\ell_n(\hat{\mu})$.

Now consider the model where π_i is of the form $\pi_i = \pi_i(\beta) = h(\beta^\top \mathbf{X}_i)$, $\beta \in \mathbb{R}^p$ is an unknown parameter and h is a given function (e.g. the logistic or probit functions). Denote $\mu_i(\hat{\beta}_n) = m_i \pi_i(\hat{\beta}_n)$. Show that the deviance of this model is given by:

$$D = 2 \sum_{i=1}^{n} \left\{ Y_i \ln \left(\frac{Y_i}{\mu_i(\hat{\beta}_n)} \right) + (m_i - Y_i) \ln \left(\frac{m_i - Y_i}{m_i - \mu_i(\hat{\beta}_n)} \right) \right\}$$

2) Consider an independent sample $Y_i \sim \mathcal{P}(\mu_i)$, where $\mu_i = \mu_i(\beta) = \exp(\beta^\top \mathbf{X}_i)$, $i = 1, \ldots, n$. By reasoning as in the first question of this exercise, show that the deviance of the model is given by:

$$D = 2 \sum_{i=1}^{n} \left\{ Y_i \ln \left(\frac{Y_i}{\mu_i(\hat{\beta}_n)} \right) - (Y_i - \mu_i(\hat{\beta}_n)) \right\}$$

If $\mathbf{X}_i$ contains the constant term 1, show that D becomes:

$$D = 2 \sum_{i=1}^{n} Y_i \ln \left(\frac{Y_i}{\mu_i(\hat{\beta}_n)} \right)$$

3) Consider an independent sample $Y_i \sim \mathcal{N}(\mu_i, \sigma^2)$, $i = 1, \ldots, n$. For the model with $\mu_i = \mu_i(\beta)$, show that the deviance is given by:

$$D = \sum_{i=1}^{n} (Y_i - \mu_i(\hat{\beta}_n))^2$$

4) Consider an independent sample $Y_i \sim G(\mu_i, \nu)$, $i = 1, \ldots, n$. In the model $\mu_i = \mu_i(\beta)$, show that the deviance is given by:

$$D = 2 \sum_{i=1}^{n} \left\{ \frac{Y_i - \mu_i(\hat{\beta}_n)}{\mu_i(\hat{\beta}_n)} + \ln \left(\frac{\mu_i(\hat{\beta}_n)}{Y_i} \right) \right\}$$

Exercise 7 – A logistic random-effect model

Introducing a random effect into a regression model allows for correlations between the observations of the response variable to be modeled. This correlation can be a correlation between individuals due to a group effect (patients treated in the same hospital, inhabitants of the same region, members of the same family, etc.), or a correlation between repeated measurements of the same individual.

In this exercise, the model is the following: for each individual $i = 1, \dots, n$, we observe a pair (Y_{i1}, Y_{i2}) of binary variables, and assume that:

$$\operatorname{logit}(\mathbb{P}(Y_{ij} = 1|u_i)) = \beta_0 + \beta_1 X_{ij} + u_i, \quad j = 1, 2$$

where X_{i1} and X_{i2} are fixed explanatory variables and u_i is a random effect (which is to say, an *unobserved* random variable, whose presence allows for a correlation between Y_{i1} and Y_{i2}).

Suppose that $u_i \sim \mathcal{N}(0, \sigma_u^2)$, and that Y_{i1} and Y_{i2} are independent given u_i. Further suppose that the individuals are independent.

REMARK.– In this model, β_1 is considered to be the parameter of interest. ■

1) Show that $\operatorname{cov}(Y_{i1}, Y_{i2}) \geq 0$. Comment on this result.

HINT.– Use the equality:

$$\operatorname{cov}(Y_{i1}, Y_{i2}) = \mathbb{E}(\operatorname{cov}(Y_{i1}, Y_{i2}|u_i)) + \operatorname{cov}(\mathbb{E}(Y_{i1}|u_i), \mathbb{E}(Y_{i2}|u_i))$$

Also recall that, if X is a random variable and $f, g : \mathbb{R} \to \mathbb{R}$ are two increasing functions, then $\operatorname{cov}(f(X), g(X)) \geq 0$.

2) Determine the marginal probabilities $\mathbb{P}(Y_{ij} = 1)$ and $\mathbb{P}(Y_{i1} = y_{i1}, Y_{i2} = y_{i2})$. Write down the marginal likelihood of β_0, β_1, and σ_u^2. Comment on this result.

3) Show that:

$$\mathbb{P}(Y_{i1} = 1|Y_{i1} + Y_{i2} = 1, u_i) = \frac{\exp(\beta_1(X_{i1} - X_{i2}))}{1 + \exp(\beta_1(X_{i1} - X_{i2}))}$$

What are the values of $\mathbb{P}(Y_{i1} = 1|Y_{i1} + Y_{i2} = 2, u_i)$ and $\mathbb{P}(Y_{i1} = 1|Y_{i1} + Y_{i2} = 0, u_i)$? From these results, deduce a method that allows for β_1 to be easily estimated.

Exercise 8 – A Poisson random-effect model

Consider a population that can be structured into groups (e.g. patients treated in the same hospital and salaries in the same business). For individual i from jth group, we observe a count Y_{ij} as well as a fixed explanatory variable X_{ij}. Denote by u_j a random group effect. Suppose that $u_j \sim \mathcal{N}(0, \sigma_u^2)$ and $Y_{ij}|u_j \sim \mathcal{P}(\mu_{ij})$, where:

$$\mu_{ij} = e^{\beta_0+\beta_1 X_{ij}+u_j}$$

If $i \neq \ell$, suppose that Y_{ij} and $Y_{\ell j}$ are conditionally independent of u_j.

1) Show that:

$$\mathbb{E}(Y_{ij}) = e^{\beta_0+\beta_1 X_{ij}+\sigma_u^2/2}$$

and:

$$\text{var}(Y_{ij}) = \mathbb{E}(Y_{ij}) + [\mathbb{E}(Y_{ij})]^2 \left(e^{\sigma_u^2} - 1\right)$$

Compare $\mathbb{E}(Y_{ij})$ and $\text{var}(Y_{ij})$.

2) Calculate $\text{cov}(Y_{ij}, Y_{\ell j})$ for $i \neq \ell$. What can we say about the observations of the same group?

HINT.– If $u_j \sim \mathcal{N}(0, \sigma_u^2)$, its moment generating function is given by $\mathbb{E}(e^{tu_j}) = \exp\left(\sigma_u^2 t^2/2\right)$. Recall the equality $\text{var}(Y_{ij}) = \mathbb{E}(\text{var}(Y_{ij}|u_j)) + \text{var}(\mathbb{E}(Y_{ij}|u_j))$. Also use the hints given for Exercise 7.

Exercise 9 – Median lethal dose

Consider the logistic regression model:

$$\text{logit}\left(\mathbb{P}(Y_i = 1|X_i)\right) = \beta_0 + \beta_1 X_i$$

where X_i is a continuous explanatory variable. In this model, the MLE $\hat{\beta} = (\hat{\beta}_0, \hat{\beta}_1)^\top$ of $\beta = (\beta_0, \beta_1)^\top$ satisfies $\sqrt{n}(\hat{\beta} - \beta) \xrightarrow[n\to\infty]{\mathcal{L}} \mathcal{N}(0, \Sigma^{-1})$ (see theorem 2.4, section 2.3.2). In this exercise, denote:

$$\Sigma^{-1} = \begin{pmatrix} \sigma_0^2 & \sigma_{01} \\ \sigma_{01} & \sigma_1^2 \end{pmatrix}$$

Let x_0 be the value of X_i such that $\mathbb{P}(Y_i = 1|X_i = x_0) = \frac{1}{2}$.

REMARK.– In toxicology, x_0 is called the *median lethal dose* and is denoted by DL_{50}, referring to how much of a toxic substance is required to cause 50% from a group of test animals to die – often mice or rats. ■

1) Show that $x_0 = -\beta_0/\beta_1$.

2) A natural estimator of x_0 is $\hat{x}_0 = -\hat{\beta}_0/\hat{\beta}_1$. Show that:

$$\sqrt{n}(\hat{x}_0 - x_0) \xrightarrow[n\to\infty]{\mathcal{L}} \mathcal{N}(0, \sigma_{x_0}^2)$$

where:

$$\sigma_{x_0}^2 = x_0^2 \left(\frac{\sigma_0^2}{\beta_0^2} + \frac{\sigma_1^2}{\beta_1^2} - \frac{2\sigma_{01}}{\beta_0\beta_1} \right)$$

HINT.– Use the delta method. In the one-dimensional case, this method is described in section 1.5. Here, a slightly more general version is required. Let (T_n) be a sequence of random vectors in $\mathbb{R}^k$, and let φ be a mapping from $\mathbb{R}^k$ into $\mathbb{R}^m$. If:

$$\sqrt{n}\,(T_n - \theta) \xrightarrow[n\to\infty]{\mathcal{L}} \mathcal{N}(0, V)$$

and if φ is differentiable[5] at θ, then:

$$\sqrt{n}\,(\varphi(T_n) - \varphi(\theta)) \xrightarrow[n\to\infty]{\mathcal{L}} \mathcal{N}(0, D\varphi(\theta) V D\varphi(\theta)^\top)$$

3) From this, deduce a confidence interval at the confidence level 0.95 for x_0.

Exercise 10 – AIC for the linear Gaussian model

In this exercise, the notation is the same as that used in section 2.1.5.

Consider the linear Gaussian model $\mathcal{M}_1$, defined by:

$$Y_i = \beta^\top \mathbf{X}_i + \varepsilon_i, \quad i = 1, \dots, n$$

where $\varepsilon_i \sim \mathcal{N}(0, \sigma^2)$ and $\beta \in \mathbb{R}^p$. We denote the MLE of β by $\hat{\beta}_n$. The MLE of σ^2 is given by $\hat{\sigma}_{\mathcal{M}_1}^2 = \frac{1}{n} RSS(\mathcal{M}_1)$, where $RSS(\mathcal{M}_1) = \sum_{i=1}^n (Y_i - \hat{\beta}_n^\top \mathbf{X}_i)^2$ denotes the RSS for the model.

5 Recall that a mapping $\varphi : \mathbb{R}^k \to \mathbb{R}^m$ is said to be differentiable at $\theta \in \mathbb{R}^k$ if there exists a linear mapping $D\varphi(\theta) : \mathbb{R}^k \to \mathbb{R}^m$ such that $\varphi(\theta + h) - \varphi(\theta) = D\varphi(\theta)(h) + o(\|h\|)$, $h \to 0$.

1) Show that the AIC of $\mathcal{M}_1$ is given by:

$$AIC(\mathcal{M}_1) = n\left[\ln(2\pi\hat{\sigma}^2_{\mathcal{M}_1}) + 1\right] + 2(p+1)$$

2) Consider the model $\mathcal{M}_2$, obtained by adding q explanatory variables onto the model $\mathcal{M}_1$. Show that $AIC(\mathcal{M}_2) < AIC(\mathcal{M}_1)$ if, and only if:

$$\frac{RSS(\mathcal{M}_2)}{RSS(\mathcal{M}_1)} < e^{-\frac{2q}{n}}$$

Comment on this result.

3

Censored and Missing Data in GLMs

In the previous chapter, the variables Y and $\mathbf{X}$ were fully observed for each individual. In practice, it is often the case that they are only partially observed (censored and missing data problems). The aim of this chapter is to describe – only in the GLM setting – some of these problems, as well as some solutions formulated to solve them.

3.1. Censored data

3.1.1. *Introduction*

Censoring, in the statistical sense of the term, refers to the case when we do not know the exact data value, but we have access to information of the type: "the data are greater than such a value". This type of censoring carries the name of *right censoring*. On the other hand, when we have the information "the data are less than such a value", we call this type *left censoring*. Sometimes, we know that the data are located between two thresholds, in which case, we call this *interval* censoring. In each of these three cases, the information available is clearly less precise than the data itself.

REMARK.– It is necessary to distinguish between censored and missing data. Data are said to be missing when we do not know its value. We could represent it as a "hole" in a data table: an unmeasured variable for an individual, a lost value, etc. A contrario, censored data still provide information regarding the value of an observation. However, this information is only partially available or incomplete. ■

Censoring occurs in particular when we observe time durations (survival times of cancer patients, periods of unemployment, machine operating times, etc.).

For a color version of the code in this chapter, see www.iste.co.uk/dupuy/linearmodels.zip.

EXAMPLE 3.1.– Consider the example of a clinical trial whose objective is to evaluate the efficacy of a new treatment against a specific illness. Patients are recruited, receive the treatment and then are followed until the end of the trial (let τ denote its duration, for example, $\tau = 12$ months). For each patient, the data to be observed is the duration T that elapses between the start of the treatment and the patient's recovery.

Consider a patient who leaves the trial before its end. This patient, for example, may move after six months to a different region, and can no longer visit the hospital leading the trial. Suppose that the patient has not yet recovered at the time of their departure.

The information available for this patient is of the form $\{T \geq \text{ six months}\}$: we do not know precisely the time required for their recovery, only that it is longer than six months. We say that these data are *right* censored. It would be a bad idea to drop them from the sample since they provide some information regarding T, even if it is only partial.

In this example, the censoring is said to be *random*, since it takes place at a time which was not known in advance.

EXAMPLE 3.2.– Now consider a patient who reaches the end of the trial without having recovered. Here again, the time required to recover is not know precisely: we only know that it is greater than τ. The information available for this patient is of the form $\{T \geq \tau\}$. In this example, the censoring is said to be *fixed*, because it occurs at a non-random time (the end of the trial). We also call this administrative censoring.

If we know T precisely (e.g. $T = 3$), we say that the data are *complete*. Time durations are not the only data susceptible to censoring (however, note that the statistical methods for censored data have essentially been developed in the context of lifespan analysis, since the pioneering work of Kaplan and Meier (1958)). Counts can also be censored, as the following example illustrates.

EXAMPLE 3.3.– Suppose we are interested in the consumption of healthcare for a given population. Each person is asked the number of times (denoted by Y) when they have consulted a doctor over the course of the previous three months. If this person does not remember precisely, and answers "at least five times", then this is a censored observation of a counting variable (the information available is of the form $\{Y \geq 5\}$). This is random right censoring.

Fixed right censoring can also play a role in this context, if the respondents have to tick one of the following responses: "no consultation", "1 consultation", "2 consultations", "3 consultations" and "4 consultations or more". The censoring here is due to the observation having an upper threshold given by a predefined value.

Fixed right censoring typically plays a role when taking measurements (physical, biological, etc.) and when the value to be observed lies beyond a maximum measurement threshold (think of the height of a river which passes above the maximum level of a flood measurement gauge). Fixed *left* censoring occurs, for example, when measuring a viral load[1] C, but the measuring instrument cannot register a value below a certain threshold τ (known as the detection threshold). The information available is consequently of the form $\{C < \tau\}$.

There are many other examples of situations that produce censored data. Furthermore, there exist many other forms of censoring other than the left, right and interval censorings described above, and the interested reader can consult the book of Klein and Moeschberger (2013), for example, to learn more.

The aim of this chapter is not to draw up an exhaustive panorama of the techniques used to handle censored data, but rather to describe some estimation problems involving GLMs in the presence of censoring, as well as some of the solutions that can be implemented. This remains an area of active research, and most of the results have thus far essentially been exclusively disseminated via research articles. The literature dedicated to censoring in durations models (in particular, in duration regression models) is much richer and the reader will have no difficulties in finding books on the subject (we cite Fleming and Harrington (1991) and Andersen et al. (1993), among many other references).

In general, discarding censored observations risks introducing bias into the statistical analysis and degrading the precision of the estimators, as they are then calculated using a smaller number of observations. On the other hand, keeping censored data, yet still treating them as if they were complete observations, leads to these observations being underestimated, which also gives rise to a bias.

These remarks therefore ask for censoring to be considered appropriately, prior to obtaining a valid statistical inference. Below, we will explain how the maximum likelihood method can be adapted to the censored setting. We limit ourselves to the case of right censoring. The case of left and interval censoring can be treated analogously by adapting the arguments used for right censoring. To illustrate the principle of the method, we will first consider the case of a randomly right-censored response in the Poisson regression model.

3.1.2. *Poisson regression with a right-censored response*

Consider the Poisson regression model described in section 2.4.2, defined by:

$$Y_i \sim \mathcal{P}(\mu_i) \quad \text{and} \quad \mu_i = e^{\beta^\top \mathbf{x}_i}, \quad i = 1, \ldots, n$$

1 A viral load is the number of copies of a virus in a given volume of fluid.

Suppose that Y_i can be randomly right-censored. To model this censoring, a positive random variable C_i, called the censoring variable, is introduced. The observation available for individual i is then defined to be the minimum of Y_i and C_i, namely:

$$Y_i^* = \min(Y_i, C_i)$$

In the case of administrative censoring, C_i is a constant, equal to the threshold τ beyond which Y_i is no longer observed. We then have $Y_i^* = \min(Y_i, \tau)$.

Therefore, for each individual i, we assume that there exist two variables, Y_i and C_i, and that observing one prevents us from observing the other. If C_i is less than Y_i, then C_i is observed and Y_i is censored. If the converse holds, then Y_i is observed instead.

The roles of these two variables are not interchangeable. Indeed, Y_i is the variable of interest, that is to say, the variable that we wish to model. As for C_i, it perturbs the observation of Y_i. Therefore, we will not consider C_i to be censored by Y_i when Y_i is less than C_i. If Y_i is available to us, then the value of C_i serves no further purpose.

After having defined Y_i^*, we construct a variable δ_i (called the censoring indicator), which will inform us on the nature of the observed data. Recall that $1\{A\}$ is the indicator function of the event A, which is to say $1\{A\}$ equals 1 if A is realized and 0 otherwise. Then we set:

$$\delta_i = 1\{Y_i < C_i\}$$

Hence, by convention, we have $\delta_i = 1$ if the observed data are complete, namely, if $Y_i < C_i$. In this case, $Y_i^* = Y_i$. If the observed data are censored (i.e. if $C_i \leq Y_i$), then we have $\delta_i = 0$ and $Y_i^* = C_i$.

With this convention, when $C_i = Y_i$, then we assume that the data are censored. It is of course possible to adopt the opposite convention by adapting the upcoming calculations appropriately.

3.1.2.1. *Estimation*

The data available to us are made up of a sample of observations $\{(Y_i^*, \delta_i, \mathbf{X}_i), i = 1, \ldots, n\}$. If $\delta_i = 1$, then the observation is the pair $(Y_i, \mathbf{X}_i)$. If $\delta_i = 0$, the observation is the pair $(C_i, \mathbf{X}_i)$. The likelihood contribution of an uncensored observation can be written as:

$$\mathbb{P}(Y_i = y_i^*, C_i > y_i^* | \mathbf{X}_i)$$

This contribution clearly reflects the information available for an uncensored individual: Y_i takes on the value y_i^* and C_i is strictly greater than y_i^* (if this were not the case, then the observation would be censored).

The likelihood contribution of a censored observation can be written as:

$$\mathbb{P}(Y_i \geq y_i^*, C_i = y_i^* | \mathbf{X}_i)$$

Here again, the contribution clearly reflects the information available for a censored individual: C_i equals y_i^* and Y_i is greater than or equal to y_i^*. We can then form the likelihood as:

$$\prod_{i=1}^{n} \mathbb{P}(Y_i = y_i^*, C_i > y_i^* | \mathbf{X}_i)^{\delta_i} \times \prod_{i=1}^{n} \mathbb{P}(Y_i \geq y_i^*, C_i = y_i^* | \mathbf{X}_i)^{1-\delta_i} \qquad [3.1]$$

The first product contains the contributions from the complete observations, whereas the second contains those from the censored observations.

Two assumptions are commonly made when analyzing censored data, which we will make here. First, we assume that the variable of interest Y_i and the censoring variable C_i are independent given the explanatory variables $\mathbf{X}_i$ (this is the so-called *independent* censoring hypothesis). Intuitively, the value of C_i is not influenced by that of Y_i, and vice versa. This is true, in particular, in the case of administrative censoring, where the value of C_i is a constant.

Under this hypothesis, the likelihood [3.1] can be rewritten as:

$$\prod_{i=1}^{n} \{\mathbb{P}(Y_i = y_i^* | \mathbf{X}_i)\mathbb{P}(C_i > y_i^* | \mathbf{X}_i)\}^{\delta_i} \times \prod_{i=1}^{n} \{\mathbb{P}(Y_i \geq y_i^* | \mathbf{X}_i)\mathbb{P}(C_i = y_i^* | \mathbf{X}_i)\}^{1-\delta_i}$$

If the independent censoring hypothesis is not satisfied, then it would be appropriate to jointly model the distributions of Y_i and C_i.

The second hypothesis is that of *non-informative* censoring. It assumes that the probability distribution of C_i does not depend on the parameters of the distribution of Y_i (here, the regression parameter β). Under this hypothesis, the $\mathbb{P}(C_i > y_i^* | \mathbf{X}_i)$ and $\mathbb{P}(C_i = y_i^* | \mathbf{X}_i)$ terms can be ignored when maximizing the likelihood (with respect to β). Therefore, the "useful" part of the likelihood [3.1] reduces to:

$$\prod_{i=1}^{n} \mathbb{P}(Y_i = y_i^* | \mathbf{X}_i)^{\delta_i} \mathbb{P}(Y_i \geq y_i^* | \mathbf{X}_i)^{1-\delta_i}$$

This is the classic expression of the likelihood for a sample of right censored observations, under the independent censoring and non-informative censoring hypothesis. A complete observation contributes via its probability, namely, $\mathbb{P}(Y_i = y_i^*|\mathbf{X}_i)$. A censored observation contributes via the $\mathbb{P}(Y_i \geq y_i^*|\mathbf{X}_i)$ term, which reflects the fact that Y_i is at least equal to y_i^*.

As in the uncensored case, the MLE of β is obtained by maximizing the log-likelihood, which is written here as:

$$\sum_{i=1}^{n} \{\delta_i \ln \mathbb{P}(Y_i = y_i^*|\mathbf{X}_i) + (1 - \delta_i) \ln \mathbb{P}(Y_i \geq y_i^*|\mathbf{X}_i)\}$$

For a discrete distribution (on $\mathbb{N}$):

$$\mathbb{P}(Y_i \geq y_i^*|\mathbf{X}_i) = 1 - \sum_{k=0}^{y_i^*-1} \mathbb{P}(Y_i = k|\mathbf{X}_i), \quad y_i^* \geq 1$$

and $\mathbb{P}(Y_i \geq 0|\mathbf{X}_i) = 1$. For the Poisson model, the log-likelihood therefore becomes:

$$\begin{aligned} \ell_n(\beta) = \sum_{i=1}^{n} \Big\{ & \delta_i \left(Y_i^* \beta^\top \mathbf{X}_i - e^{\beta^\top \mathbf{X}_i} - \ln(Y_i^*!) \right) \\ & + (1 - \delta_i) \ln \left(1 - \sum_{k=0}^{Y_i^*-1} \frac{e^{-\exp(\beta^\top \mathbf{X}_i) + k\beta^\top \mathbf{X}_i}}{k!} \right) \Big\} \end{aligned} \qquad [3.2]$$

The MLE of β can be obtained by solving the equation $\partial \ell_n(\beta)/\partial \beta = 0$. We denote[2] it by $\hat{\beta}_n$.

REMARK.– If $\delta_i = 1$ for each $i = 1, \ldots, n$ (that is to say, if no data are censored), then $Y_i^* = Y_i$ and [3.2] reduces to:

$$\sum_{i=1}^{n} \left\{ Y_i \beta^\top \mathbf{X}_i - e^{\beta^\top \mathbf{X}_i} - \ln(Y_i!) \right\}$$

which is the log-likelihood of the Poisson model obtained in section 2.4.2. ■

3.1.2.2. *Some notation*

If Y follows a Poisson distribution with parameter μ, then, for each integer u:

$$\mathbb{P}(Y \leq u) = \sum_{k=0}^{u} e^{-\mu} \frac{\mu^k}{k!} = \frac{\Gamma(u+1, \mu)}{u!}$$

2 We use the same notation as in the uncensored case in order to avoid overburdening the notation. Afterward, the context will be sufficiently clear so that the reader will know whether $\hat{\beta}_n$ denotes the MLE in the censored or uncensored case.

where:

$$\Gamma(u,\mu) = \int_{\mu}^{\infty} t^{u-1} e^{-t} dt$$

denotes the incomplete gamma function. The derivative of $\Gamma(u,\mu)$ with respect to μ is:

$$\frac{\partial \Gamma(u,\mu)}{\partial \mu} = -\mu^{u-1} e^{-\mu}$$

With this notation, the log-likelihood [3.2] becomes:

$$\ell_n(\beta) = \sum_{i=1}^{n} \left\{ \delta_i \left(Y_i^* \beta^\top \mathbf{X}_i - e^{\beta^\top \mathbf{X}_i} - \ln(Y_i^*!) \right) \right.$$
$$\left. +(1-\delta_i) \ln\left(1 - \frac{\Gamma(Y_i^*, e^{\beta^\top \mathbf{X}_i})}{(Y_i^* - 1)!}\right) \right\}$$

This expression lends itself well when calculating derivatives with respect to β. Indeed, let us denote:

$$h_\beta(y,x) = \frac{e^{-e^{\beta^\top x} + \beta^\top x y}}{(y-1)! - \Gamma(y, e^{\beta^\top x})}, \text{ for every } \beta \in \mathbb{R}^p, x \in \mathbb{R}^p, y \in \mathbb{N}\backslash\{0\}$$

Also, denote $\Sigma_1(\beta) = -\mathbb{E}\left[\frac{\partial^2 \ell_1(\beta)}{\partial\beta\partial\beta^\top}\right]$.

Then it can be shown that:

$$\Sigma_1(\beta) = \mathbb{E}\left[\mathbf{X}_1\mathbf{X}_1^\top \left(\delta_1 e^{\beta^\top \mathbf{X}_1} + (\delta_1 - 1)\left\{Y_1^* - e^{\beta^\top \mathbf{X}_1}\right.\right.\right.$$
$$\left.\left.\left. - h_\beta(Y_1^*, \mathbf{X}_1)\right\} h_\beta(Y_1^*, \mathbf{X}_1)\right)\right]$$

3.1.2.3. *Asymptotic properties of the MLE*

The following theorem states the consistency and asymptotic normality of $\hat{\beta}_n$ (see Bousselmi et al. (2021) for the proof).

THEOREM 3.1.– *Suppose that the explanatory variables $X_{ij}, j = 1,\dots,p$ are bounded, the true value of β belongs to the interior of a compact subset of $\mathbb{R}^p$ and the following conditions are satisfied: $\mathbb{P}(Y^* \geq 1|\delta = 0) = 1$ and $\mathbb{P}(\delta = 1) > 0$. Then $\hat{\beta}_n \xrightarrow[n\to\infty]{\mathbb{P}} \beta$ and:*

$$\sqrt{n}(\hat{\beta}_n - \beta) \xrightarrow[n\to\infty]{\mathcal{L}} \mathcal{N}(0, \Sigma_1^{-1}(\beta))$$

The hypothesis $\mathbb{P}(Y^* \geq 1|\delta = 0) = 1$ implies that the observation 0 cannot be a censored data. A censored 0 would not provide any information, since an observation from the Poisson distribution is always greater than or equal to 0. The hypothesis $\mathbb{P}(\delta = 1) > 0$ implies that some complete data have been observed.

To calculate confidence intervals and realize hypothesis tests on β_j, it is necessary to have a consistent estimator for the asymptotic variance $\Sigma_1^{-1}(\beta)$. Let us denote:

$$\Sigma_{1,n}(\beta) = \frac{1}{n}\sum_{i=1}^{n} \mathbf{X}_i\mathbf{X}_i^\top \Big(\delta_i e^{\beta^\top \mathbf{X}_i} \\ + (\delta_i - 1)\left\{Y_i^* - e^{\beta^\top \mathbf{X}_i} - h_\beta(Y_i^*, \mathbf{X}_i)\right\} h_\beta(Y_i^*, \mathbf{X}_i)\Big)$$

This is an empirical version of $\Sigma_1(\beta)$, obtained by replacing the mean in Σ_1 by its empirical version. A consistent estimator of the asymptotic variance $\Sigma_1^{-1}(\beta)$ is therefore given by $\Sigma_{1,n}^{-1}(\hat{\beta}_n)$ (Bousselmi et al. 2021). When n is sufficiently large, $\hat{\beta}_n \approx \mathcal{N}(\beta, \Sigma_{1,n}^{-1}(\hat{\beta}_n)/n)$.

REMARK.– In the absence of censoring, $\Sigma_1(\beta)$ becomes:

$$\Sigma_1(\beta) = \mathbb{E}\left[\mathbf{X}_1\mathbf{X}_1^\top e^{\beta^\top \mathbf{X}_1}\right]$$

which is the asymptotic variance of the MLE in the uncensored Poisson model, and $\Sigma_{1,n}(\beta)$ reduces to $\frac{1}{n}\sum_{i=1}^{n} \mathbf{X}_i\mathbf{X}_i^\top e^{\beta^\top \mathbf{X}_i}$. We therefore recover the asymptotic results from section 2.4.2. ■

3.1.2.4. *A small simulation study*

The R package VGAM (Yee 2010, 2015) provides a very large number of regression models, including GLMs. In particular, its `vglm` function allows for the censored Poisson model (right, left or interval censoring) to be estimated. Here, we will use it in the setting of a small simulation study intended to evaluate the effect that censoring has on the precision of the MLE.

Let us simulate $N = 1,000$ samples of size n from the Poisson model:

$$Y_i \sim \mathcal{P}(\exp(0.2X_{i1} - 0.1X_{i2} + 0.4X_{i3} + 0.3X_{i4} + 0.5X_{i5}))$$

where $X_{i2} \sim \mathcal{N}(0, 1)$, $X_{i3} \sim \mathcal{B}(0.3)$, $X_{i4} \sim \mathcal{N}(1, 2.25)$ and $X_{i5} \sim \mathcal{U}[2, 5]$ are independent variables, and $X_{i1} = 1$. Then, for each individual, we simulate a censoring variable C_i by using a truncated Poisson distribution at 0 (so that $C_i \geq 1$ and $\mathbb{P}(Y_i^* \geq 1|\delta_i = 0) = 1$). For each sample, we construct a data set of the form

$\{(Y_i^*, \delta_i, \mathbf{X}_i), i = 1, \ldots, n\}$, with $Y_i^* = \min(Y_i, C_i)$ and $\delta_i = 1\{Y_i < C_i\}$. Finally, we adjust a right censored Poisson model to each sample using each explanatory variable that is available. The R syntax is the following:

```
fit=vglm(SurvS4(yi,delta)~X2+X3+X4+X5,cens.poisson)
```

By default, the vglm function includes the constant term in the linear predictor. The printCoefmat(coef(summary(fit))) command returns the following output, similar to that of glm:

```
            Estimate Std. Error z value  Pr(>|z|)
(Intercept)  0.251073   0.094378  2.6603  0.007807 **
X2          -0.110795   0.018714 -5.9205 3.209e-09 ***
X3           0.348834   0.043429  8.0324 9.562e-16 ***
X4           0.309125   0.016201 19.0803 < 2.2e-16 ***
X5           0.485207   0.024662 19.6745 < 2.2e-16 ***
---
Signif. codes:  0 '***' 0.001 '**' 0.01 '*' 0.05 '.' 0.1 ' ' 1
```

We can obtain confidence intervals and carry out hypothesis testing by using the functions previously introduced.

The mean squared error (MSE) of an estimator is a measure of its precision. The MSE of $\hat{\beta}_{n,j}$ is defined as $\mathbb{E}[(\hat{\beta}_{n,j} - \beta_j)^2]$. It cannot be calculated, but it can be approximated by:

$$\text{MSE}(\hat{\beta}_{n,j}) = \frac{1}{N}\sum_{k=1}^{N}(\hat{\beta}_{n,j}^{(k)} - \beta_j)^2$$

where $\hat{\beta}_{n,j}^{(k)}$ denotes the MLE of β_j calculated from the kth sample. In order to evaluate the effect that censoring has on the estimations of the β_j, let us calculate $\text{MSE}(\hat{\beta}_{n,j})$ for different proportions of censored data in the simulated samples. We are going to adjust the proportion (let us denote it by p) by adjusting the parameter of the distribution of C_i. Table 3.1 displays the results for $p = 0, 0.1, 0.2, 0.4$ (the $p = 0$ case corresponds to the uncensored case) when $n = 150$, $n = 500$ (we actually report the roots of the MSEs, as they are easier to read than the MSEs themselves as they possess multiple 0s after the decimal point).

Conforming to our intuition, for a fixed sample size, the precision of the $\hat{\beta}_{n,j}$ degrades when the proportion of censored data increases. For a fixed p, the precision of each MLE increases with the sample size.

n	p	$\hat{\beta}_{n,1}$	$\hat{\beta}_{n,2}$	$\hat{\beta}_{n,3}$	$\hat{\beta}_{n,4}$	$\hat{\beta}_{n,5}$
150	0	0.1112	0.0234	0.0473	0.0158	0.0270
	0.1	0.1247	0.0254	0.0548	0.0202	0.0304
	0.2	0.1407	0.0284	0.0616	0.0213	0.0344
	0.4	0.1661	0.0346	0.0747	0.0273	0.0425
500	0	0.0624	0.0122	0.0248	0.0085	0.0152
	0.1	0.0705	0.0141	0.0292	0.0099	0.0170
	0.2	0.0752	0.0147	0.0317	0.0118	0.0184
	0.4	0.0891	0.0181	0.0410	0.0142	0.0228

Table 3.1. *Square roots of the MSE's for the* $\hat{\beta}_{n,j}$

For each estimator $\hat{\beta}_{n,j}$, Figure 3.1 presents the histogram of its N values obtained from the N simulated samples. More precisely, we plot the histograms of the normalized MLEs:

$$\frac{\hat{\beta}^{(k)}_{n,j} - \beta_j}{\text{se}(\hat{\beta}^{(k)}_{n,j})}, \quad k = 1, \dots, N \tag{3.3}$$

where $\text{se}(\hat{\beta}^{(k)}_{n,j})$ denotes the standard error of $\hat{\beta}_{n,j}$ in the kth simulated sample (namely, the square root of the jth diagonal term of $\Sigma^{-1}_{1,n}(\hat{\beta}_n)/n$). For n sufficiently large:

$$\frac{\hat{\beta}_{n,j} - \beta_j}{\text{se}(\hat{\beta}_{n,j})} \approx \mathcal{N}(0, 1)$$

from theorem 3.1. The histogram of values [3.3] should hence approximately reflect the density of the standard normal distribution. We represent these histograms with $n = 150$ and a censoring proportion equal to 0.4. The density of the $\mathcal{N}(0, 1)$ distribution is superposed onto them.

These histograms illustrate the approximate normality of the distribution of the MLE.

REMARK.– The maximum likelihood method in the censored Poisson model was first described in Terza (1985) and Caudill and Mixon (1995), without any theoretical results. Since then, it has been applied to other censored count data models: mixtures of Poisson regressions (Karlis et al. 2016), generalized Poisson regression (Famoye and Wang 2004), zero-truncated Poisson (Yeh et al. 2012) and zero-inflated Poisson (Nguyen and Dupuy 2021) models (we will revisit the last model in Chapter 4). ■

In the following section, a second example of a censored GLM will be described, this time for a continuous response variable.

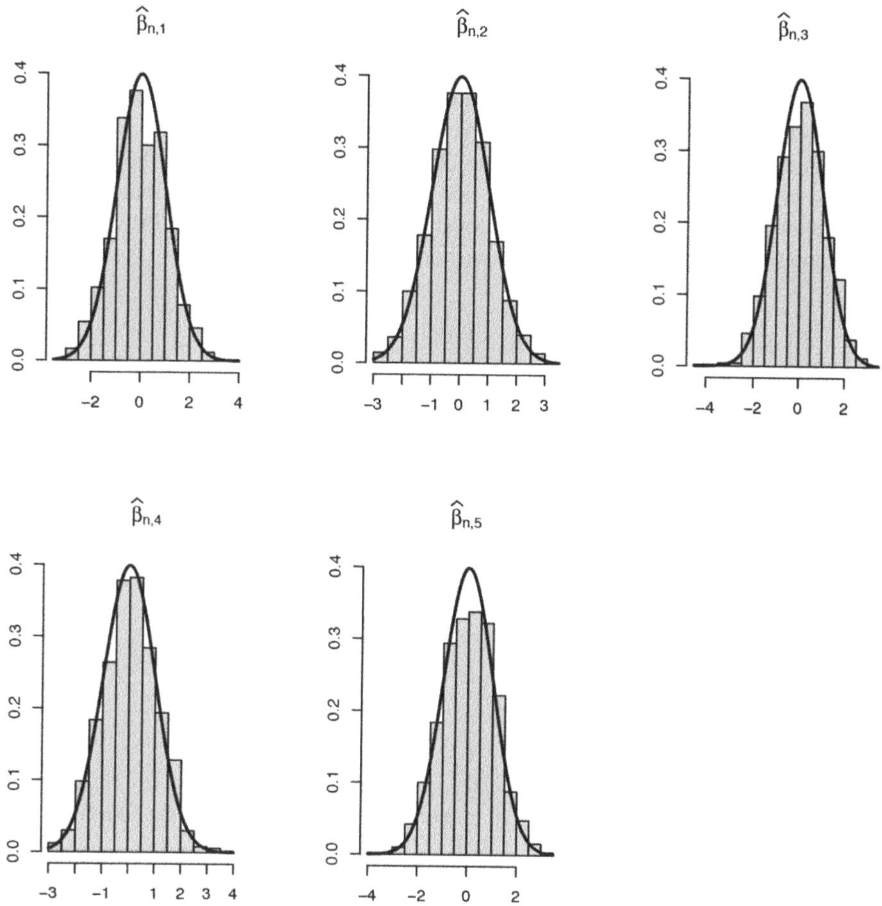

Figure 3.1. *Histograms of the* $(\hat{\beta}_{n,j}^{(k)} - \beta_j)/\text{se}(\hat{\beta}_{n,j}^{(k)}), k = 1, \ldots, N$ *(*$n = 150, p = 0.4$*)*

3.1.3. *Gamma regression with a right-censored response*

In the gamma regression model, recall that the conditional density of Y_i is written as:

$$f(y|\mathbf{X}_i) = y^{\nu-1} \exp\left(-\frac{y\nu}{\mu_i}\right)\left(\frac{\nu}{\mu_i}\right)^{\nu} \frac{1}{\Gamma(\nu)}, \quad y \in \mathbb{R}_+$$

where $\Gamma(u) = \int_0^\infty e^{-t} t^{u-1}\, dt$. With this parameterization, $\mathbb{E}(Y|\mathbf{X}_i) = \mu_i$ and $\text{var}(Y|\mathbf{X}_i) = \mu_i^2/\nu$. The most commonly used link function is the logarithm function:

$$\ln \mu_i = \beta^\top \mathbf{X}_i$$

(recall that it is not the canonical link function, see section 2.4.3). The parameters of the model are β and ν. Suppose that we have a sample $\{(Y_i^*, \delta_i, \mathbf{X}_i), i = 1, \dots, n\}$ of independent and right censored observations from this model. Under the hypothesis that the censoring is non-informative, and independent of Y_i conditionally on $\mathbf{X}_i$, the likelihood can be calculated analogously as in the previous case. Provided some adjustments of the notations, it can be written as:

$$\prod_{i=1}^{n} f(Y_i^*|\mathbf{X}_i)^{\delta_i}(1 - F(Y_i^*|\mathbf{X}_i))^{1-\delta_i} \qquad [3.4]$$

where $1 - F(y|\mathbf{X})$, the (conditional) *survival function* of Y_i, is given by:

$$\begin{aligned} 1 - F(y|\mathbf{X}_i) &= \int_y^\infty f(t|\mathbf{X}_i)\,dt \\ &= \frac{1}{\Gamma(\nu)} \int_{\frac{\nu y}{\mu(\mathbf{X}_i)}}^\infty t^{\nu-1} e^{-t}\,dt \\ &= \frac{\Gamma\left(\nu, \frac{\nu y}{\mu(\mathbf{X}_i)}\right)}{\Gamma(\nu)} \end{aligned}$$

(recall that $\Gamma(\nu, y) = \int_y^\infty t^{\nu-1} e^{-t}\,dt$ denotes the incomplete gamma function). By inserting the expressions of $f(y|\mathbf{X}_i)$ and $1 - F(y|\mathbf{X}_i)$ into [3.4] and then taking the logarithm, we obtain the log-likelihood:

$$\begin{aligned} \ell_n(\nu, \beta) = \sum_{i=1}^{n} \Big\{ &\delta_i \left((\nu - 1)\ln Y_i^* + \nu \ln \nu - \nu\beta^\top \mathbf{X}_i - Y_i^* \nu e^{-\beta^\top \mathbf{X}_i} - \ln \Gamma(\nu) \right) \\ &+ (1 - \delta_i) \ln \left(\frac{\Gamma(\nu, \nu Y_i^* e^{-\beta^\top \mathbf{X}_i})}{\Gamma(\nu)} \right) \Big\} \end{aligned} \qquad [3.5]$$

The MLE $(\hat{\nu}_n, \hat{\beta}_n)$ is the solution of the system $\partial \ell_n(\nu, \beta)/\partial(\nu, \beta^\top)^\top = 0$. It does not admit an explicit expression, so it is numerically approximated using a Newton–Raphson type algorithm. In the uncensored case, ν is typically estimated using $\hat{\phi}^{-1}$, where:

$$\hat{\phi} = \frac{1}{n - p} \sum_{i=1}^{n} \left(\frac{Y_i - \hat{\mu}_i}{\hat{\mu}_i} \right)^2$$

is the Pearson estimator of $\phi = \nu^{-1}$ (see section 2.4.3). When Y_i is censored, this estimator can no longer be used.

REMARK.– In the absence of censoring (i.e. if $\delta_i = 1$ for each $i = 1, \ldots, n$), then the log-likelihood [3.5] simplifies to:

$$\ell_n(\beta, \nu) = \sum_{i=1}^{n} \left\{ (\nu - 1) \ln Y_i - \nu Y_i e^{-\beta^\top \mathbf{X}_i} - \nu \beta^\top \mathbf{X}_i + \nu \ln \nu - \ln \Gamma(\nu) \right\}$$

which, of course, coincides with the log-likelihood for the complete case. ■

3.1.3.1. *Some notation*

Let us introduce some notation that will be useful when stating the asymptotic properties of the MLE. For every $\beta \in \mathbb{R}^p, \nu > 0, y > 0$, and $x \in \mathbb{R}^p$, denote:

$$g_{\nu,\beta}(y, x) = \frac{(\nu y e^{-\beta^\top x})^\nu \exp(-\nu y e^{-\beta^\top x})}{\Gamma\left(\nu, \nu y e^{-\beta^\top x}\right)}$$

and:

$$h_{\nu,\beta}(y, x) = \frac{\partial \Gamma(\nu)/\partial \nu - \int_0^{\nu y e^{-\beta^\top x}} t^{\nu-1} e^{-t} (\ln t)\, dt}{\Gamma\left(\nu, \nu y e^{-\beta^\top x}\right)} - \frac{g_{\nu,\beta}(y, x)}{\nu}$$

The derivatives of $g_{\nu,\beta}$ and $h_{\nu,\beta}$ with respect to ν are given by:

$$\frac{\partial}{\partial \nu} g_{\nu,\beta}(y, x) = g_{\nu,\beta}(y, x) \left(-h_{\nu,\beta}(y, x) + \ln(\nu y e^{-\beta^\top x}) + 1 - y e^{-\beta^\top x} \right)$$

and:

$$\frac{\partial}{\partial \nu} h_{\nu,\beta}(y, x) = -h^2_{\nu,\beta}(y, x) + \frac{\frac{\partial^2}{\partial \nu^2} \Gamma(\nu)}{\Gamma\left(\nu, \nu y e^{-\beta^\top x}\right)}$$
$$- \frac{\int_0^{\nu y e^{-\beta^\top x}} t^{\nu-1} e^{-t} (\ln t)^2\, dt}{\Gamma\left(\nu, \nu y e^{-\beta^\top x}\right)}$$
$$- \frac{1}{\nu} g_{\nu,\beta}(y, x) \left(2 \ln(\nu y e^{-\beta^\top x}) + 1 - \frac{1}{\nu} - y e^{-\beta^\top x} \right)$$

Then let us define:

$$\Omega_1^{\nu,\nu}(\nu,\beta) = \mathbb{E}\left[-\frac{\delta}{\nu} + (\delta-1)\frac{\partial}{\partial\nu}h_{\nu,\beta}(Y^*,\mathbf{X}) + \frac{\partial^2}{\partial\nu^2}\ln\Gamma(\nu)\right]$$

$$\Omega_1^{\beta,\beta}(\nu,\beta) = \mathbb{E}\Big[\mathbf{X}\mathbf{X}^\top \Big\{\delta Y^*\nu e^{-\beta^\top\mathbf{X}} + (\delta-1)g_{\nu,\beta}(Y^*,\mathbf{X})$$
$$\times \Big(\nu Y^* e^{-\beta^\top\mathbf{X}} - \nu - g_{\nu,\beta}(Y^*,\mathbf{X})\Big)\Big\}\Big]$$

and:

$$\Omega_1^{\nu,\beta}(\nu,\beta) = \mathbb{E}\left[\mathbf{X}^\top\left(\delta(1-Y^*e^{-\beta^\top\mathbf{X}}) + (\delta-1)\frac{\partial}{\partial\nu}g_{\nu,\beta}(Y^*,\mathbf{X})\right)\right]$$

Note that $\Omega_1^{\nu,\nu}$ is a scalar quantity, $\Omega_1^{\beta,\beta}$ is a $(p\times p)$-matrix and that $\Omega_1^{\nu,\beta}$ is a p-dimensional row-vector. Finally, define the matrix $\Omega_1(\nu,\beta)$, of size $(p+1)\times(p+1)$, as:

$$\Omega_1(\nu,\beta) = \begin{pmatrix} \Omega_1^{\nu,\nu}(\nu,\beta) & \Omega_1^{\nu,\beta}(\nu,\beta) \\ (\Omega_1^{\nu,\beta}(\nu,\beta))^\top & \Omega_1^{\beta,\beta}(\nu,\beta) \end{pmatrix}$$

3.1.3.2. *Asymptotic properties of the MLE*

The following theorem states the consistency and asymptotic normality of the MLE in the right censored gamma regression model (see Dupuy (2020) for the proof).

THEOREM 3.2.– *Suppose that the explanatory variables $X_{ij}, j = 1,\ldots,p$ are bounded and that the true values of ν and β belong to the interiors of compact subsets of $\mathbb{R}_+^*$ and $\mathbb{R}^p$, respectively. Then $(\hat\nu_n,\hat\beta_n) \xrightarrow[n\to\infty]{\mathbb{P}} (\nu,\beta)$ and:*

$$\sqrt{n}\begin{pmatrix}\hat\nu_n - \nu \\ \hat\beta_n - \beta\end{pmatrix} \xrightarrow[n\to\infty]{\mathcal{L}} \mathcal{N}\left(0, \Omega_1^{-1}(\nu,\beta)\right)$$

As was done in the previous section, a consistent estimator of the asymptotic variance of the MLE can be constructed by replacing the expectations with their empirical versions and the parameters ν and β with their MLEs in the matrix $\Omega_1(\nu,\beta)$. The result is the estimator:

$$\widehat{\Omega}_{1,n} = \begin{pmatrix} \widehat{\Omega}_{1,n}^{\nu,\nu}(\hat\nu_n,\hat\beta_n) & \widehat{\Omega}_{1,n}^{\nu,\beta}(\hat\nu_n,\hat\beta_n) \\ (\widehat{\Omega}_{1,n}^{\nu,\beta}(\hat\nu_n,\hat\beta_n))^\top & \widehat{\Omega}_{1,n}^{\beta,\beta}(\hat\nu_n,\hat\beta_n) \end{pmatrix}$$

where:

$$\widehat{\Omega}_{1,n}^{\nu,\nu}(\hat{\nu}_n,\hat{\beta}_n) = \frac{1}{n}\sum_{i=1}^{n}\left\{-\frac{\delta_i}{\hat{\nu}_n} + (\delta_i - 1)\frac{\partial}{\partial\nu}h_{\hat{\nu}_n,\hat{\beta}_n}(Y_i^*,\mathbf{X}_i) + \frac{\partial^2}{\partial\nu^2}\ln\Gamma(\hat{\nu}_n)\right\}$$

$$\widehat{\Omega}_{1,n}^{\beta,\beta}(\hat{\nu}_n,\hat{\beta}_n) = \frac{1}{n}\sum_{i=1}^{n}\mathbf{X}_i\mathbf{X}_i^\top\left\{\delta_i Y_i^*\hat{\nu}_n e^{-\hat{\beta}_n^\top\mathbf{X}_i} + (\delta_i - 1)g_{\hat{\nu}_n,\hat{\beta}_n}(Y_i^*,\mathbf{X}_i)\right.$$

$$\left.\times\left(\hat{\nu}_n Y_i^* e^{-\hat{\beta}_n^\top\mathbf{X}_i} - \hat{\nu}_n - g_{\hat{\nu}_n,\hat{\beta}_n}(Y_i^*,\mathbf{X}_i)\right)\right\}$$

$$\widehat{\Omega}_{1,n}^{\nu,\beta}(\hat{\nu}_n,\hat{\beta}_n,) = \frac{1}{n}\sum_{i=1}^{n}\mathbf{X}_i^\top\left(\delta_i(1 - Y_i^* e^{-\hat{\beta}_n^\top\mathbf{X}_i}) + (\delta_i - 1)\frac{\partial}{\partial\nu}g_{\hat{\nu}_n,\hat{\beta}_n}(Y_i^*,\mathbf{X}_i)\right)$$

For n sufficiently large:

$$\begin{pmatrix}\hat{\nu}_n\\ \hat{\beta}_n\end{pmatrix} \approx \mathcal{N}\left(\begin{pmatrix}\nu\\ \beta\end{pmatrix}, \frac{1}{n}\widehat{\Omega}_{1,n}^{-1}\right)$$

3.1.3.3. *A small simulation study*

Let us simulate $N = 1,000$ samples of size n of the gamma regression model with $\nu = 1.5$, and:

$$\mu_i = \exp(0.2X_{i1} - 0.1X_{i2} + 0.4X_{i3} + 0.3X_{i4} + 0.5X_{i5})$$

where $X_{i2} \sim \mathcal{N}(0,1)$, $X_{i3} \sim \mathcal{B}(0.3)$, $X_{i4} \sim \mathcal{N}(1, 2.25)$ and $X_{i5} \sim \mathcal{U}[2,5]$ are independent, and $X_{i1} = 1$. Censoring is simulated from an exponential distribution, whose parameter is chosen so that a proportion p of each sample is censored (we successively consider $p = 0.1, 0.2, 0.4$ and $n = 150, 500$). For each sample, we subsequently construct a data set of the form $\{(Y_i^*, \delta_i, \mathbf{X}_i), i = 1,\ldots,n\}$, where $Y_i^* = \min(Y_i, C_i)$ and $\delta_i = 1\{Y_i < C_i\}$.

We also consider the uncensored case ($p = 0$). In this case, the `glm` function allows for ν and β to be estimated. The syntax is the following (for one sample):

```
fit=glm(Y~X2+X3+X4+X5,family=Gamma(link="log"))
```

The constant term of the linear predictor is included by default by `glm`. It is therefore not necessary to mention X_{i1}. We obtain the output:

```
Coefficients:
             Estimate Std. Error t value Pr(>|t|)
(Intercept)  0.09498    0.16502   0.576  0.56518
X2          -0.10452    0.04003  -2.611  0.00931 **
X3           0.39646    0.08436   4.700 3.38e-06 ***
X4           0.26883    0.02653  10.133  < 2e-16 ***
X5           0.52340    0.04436  11.799  < 2e-16 ***
---
Signif. codes:  0 '***' 0.001 '**' 0.01 '*' 0.05 '.' 0.1 ' ' 1

(Dispersion parameter for Gamma family taken to be 0.7544596)
```

REMARK.– By default, glm returns the Pearson estimator of $\phi = 1/\nu$ (here, $\hat{\phi} = 0.7544596$ and hence $\hat{\nu} = 1/0.7544596 = 1.325452$). The gamma.dispersion function from the MASS package (Venables and Ripley 2002) returns the MLE of ϕ:

```
gamma.dispersion(fit)
[1] 0.7118316
```

from which we obtain the MLE of ν: $\hat{\nu}_n = 1/0.7118316 = 1.404827$. ■

To our knowledge, there is no R function (or at least, no function in any widely available package) that calculates the MLE for the censored gamma regression model. Nevertheless, it is easy enough to code this calculation by using one of the many R packages dedicated to numerical optimization. It suffices to code the log-likelihood, before applying an optimization function to it. Here, we will use the maxLik package (Henningsen and Toomet 2011).

The code below forms a loglik.gamma.cens function that calculates the log-likelihood [3.5]. Yc denotes the vector of the Y_i^*, $i = 1, \ldots, n$ and X is the design matrix. The pgamma function returns the cumulative distribution function of the gamma distribution. Then we use the maxLik function (maxLik package), which approximates the MLEs with the help of the Newton–Raphson algorithm. It suffices to use loglik.gamma.cens as the argument of maxLik.

```
loglik.gamma.cens=function(param){
nu=param[1]
b=param[-1]
sum(delta*((nu-1)*log(Yc)+nu*log(nu)-nu*t(b)%*%X-Yc*nu*exp(-t(b)%
     *%X)-log(gamma(nu)))+(1-delta)*log(1-pgamma(Yc,shape=nu,scale
     =exp(t(b)%*%X)/nu)))
}

fit=maxLik(logLik=loglik.gamma.cens,start=val.init)
```

The `start=...` command provides the initial values for the Newton–Raphson algorithm. Some reasonable values can be obtained by adjusting a gamma regression model to the data $\{(Y_i^*, \mathbf{X}_i), i = 1, \ldots, n\}$ (i.e. we ignore any censoring and we treat the Y_i^* as uncensored data). The code is the following:

```
fit.init=glm(Yc~X2+X3+X4+X5,family=Gamma(link="log"))
val.init=c(1/gamma.dispersion(fit.init),fit.init$coeff)
```

The `coef(fit)` command displays the estimates produced by the `maxLik` function (for one sample):

```
           (Intercept)         X2          X3           X4          X5
1.5227927   0.3730795 -0.1475665   0.5692299   0.2831021   0.4419077
```

The value 1.5227927 corresponds to the MLE of ν since, in the `loglik.gamma.cens` function, the parameters have been entered in the order of ν, β.

This code is applied to each one of the 1,000 samples simulated (an additional script calculates $\widehat{\Omega}_{1,n}^{-1}$). The bias and standard error of each estimator are displayed in Table 3.2 (the results are averaged over the 1,000 samples). Also displayed are the coverage probability and the average length (over the N samples) of the confidence intervals at the confidence level 0.95 for each parameter (Table 3.3).

n	p	$\hat{\nu}_n$	$\hat{\beta}_{n,1}$	$\hat{\beta}_{n,2}$	$\hat{\beta}_{n,3}$	$\hat{\beta}_{n,4}$	$\hat{\beta}_{n,5}$
150	0	0.0607	−0.0155	0.0000	−0.0004	−0.0004	0.0012
		(0.1646)	(0.2863)	(0.0679)	(0.1466)	(0.0450)	(0.0777)
	0.1	0.0685	−0.0147	−0.0013	−0.0039	0.0023	0.0003
		(0.1713)	(0.3002)	(0.0709)	(0.1548)	(0.0476)	(0.0819)
	0.2	0.0544	−0.0021	0.0017	−0.0026	0.0021	−0.0037
		(0.1760)	(0.3162)	(0.0756)	(0.1654)	(0.0508)	(0.0869)
	0.4	0.0617	−0.0121	−0.0002	0.0003	0.0030	0.0008
		(0.1951)	(0.3568)	(0.0858)	(0.1919)	(0.0585)	(0.1006)
500	0	0.0191	0.0013	−0.0011	−0.0012	−0.0013	−0.0011
		(0.0876)	(0.1560)	(0.0366)	(0.0799)	(0.0244)	(0.0422)
	0.1	0.0179	−0.0059	0.0002	0.0011	0.0003	0.0006
		(0.0905)	(0.1635)	(0.0386)	(0.0846)	(0.0259)	(0.0446)
	0.2	0.0193	−0.0004	−0.0006	−0.0046	0.0000	−0.0004
		(0.0940)	(0.1716)	(0.0405)	(0.0898)	(0.0275)	(0.0472)
	0.4	0.0234	−0.0034	−0.0017	0.0034	0.0003	−0.0006
		(0.1036)	(0.1935)	(0.0461)	(0.1040)	(0.0317)	(0.0544)

Table 3.2. *Bias (s.e.) of the MLE*

n	p	$\hat{\nu}_n$	$\hat{\beta}_{n,1}$	$\hat{\beta}_{n,2}$	$\hat{\beta}_{n,3}$	$\hat{\beta}_{n,4}$	$\hat{\beta}_{n,5}$
150	0	0.951	0.943	0.957	0.953	0.942	0.945
		(0.6451)	(1.1222)	(0.2662)	(0.5746)	(0.1766)	(0.3045)
	0.1	0.951	0.946	0.949	0.949	0.939	0.945
		(0.6715)	(1.1768)	(0.2778)	(0.6069)	(0.1866)	(0.3209)
	0.2	0.965	0.934	0.942	0.941	0.949	0.939
		(0.6900)	(1.2394)	(0.2962)	(0.6486)	(0.1990)	(0.3407)
	0.4	0.943	0.935	0.944	0.943	0.955	0.946
		(0.7647)	(1.3987)	(0.3363)	(0.7522)	(0.2295)	(0.3943)
500	0	0.956	0.943	0.941	0.957	0.942	0.945
		(0.3432)	(0.6115)	(0.1436)	(0.3131)	(0.0957)	(0.1655)
	0.1	0.953	0.951	0.951	0.946	0.943	0.957
		(0.3547)	(0.6409)	(0.1515)	(0.3317)	(0.1015)	(0.1750)
	0.2	0.951	0.961	0.956	0.954	0.948	0.956
		(0.3683)	(0.6726)	(0.1588)	(0.3521)	(0.1076)	(0.1852)
	0.4	0.954	0.956	0.951	0.967	0.948	0.950
		(0.4062)	(0.7586)	(0.1808)	(0.4076)	(0.1244)	(0.2133)

Table 3.3. *Coverage probabilities (average lengths of the confidence intervals)*

When the proportion of censored data increases, the biases are observed to remain relatively stable, whereas the standard errors increase, reflecting how the precision of the MLE deteriorates. The estimate of the asymptotic standard deviation is nonetheless of good quality, ensuring that the coverage probabilities are close to the nominal confidence level of 0.95.

Of course, the average length of the confidence interval increases with the amount of censoring, due to an increase in the standard errors.

We also represent the histograms of the normalized MLEs $(\hat{\nu}_n^{(k)} - \nu)/\text{se}(\hat{\nu}_n^{(k)})$ and $(\hat{\beta}_{n,j}^{(k)} - \beta_j)/\text{se}(\hat{\beta}_{n,j}^{(k)})$, $k = 1, \ldots, N$ for $n = 150$ and $p = 0.4$ (Figure 3.2).

The Gaussian approximation of the distribution of the MLEs, stated in theorem 3.2, is here again reasonably satisfied (the bias in $\hat{\nu}_n$ becomes more apparent. In the uncensored case, this bias is known and often leads to the Pearson estimator being preferred over the MLE to estimate ν).

REMARK.– Several authors have considered estimation in GLMs when the covariates are censored (either randomly or due to some detection limit). In May et al. (2011); Tsimikas et al. (2012); Bernhardt et al. (2015); Lee et al. (2018), the interested reader will find several adapted estimation methods, as well as many more references. ■

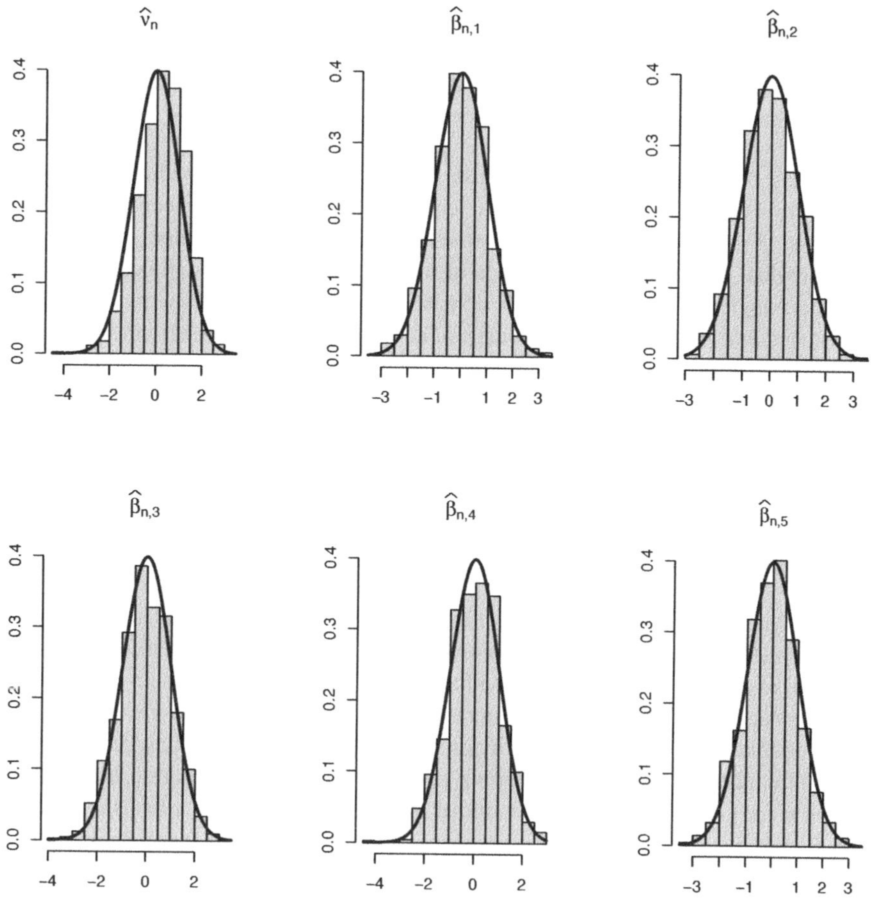

Figure 3.2. *Histograms of the* $(\hat{\nu}_n^{(k)} - \nu)/\mathrm{se}(\hat{\nu}_n^{(k)})$ *and* $(\hat{\beta}_{n,j}^{(k)} - \beta_j)/\mathrm{se}(\hat{\beta}_{n,j}^{(k)}), k = 1, \ldots, N$ *(for* $n = 150$, $p = 0.4$*)*

3.2. Missing data problems

3.2.1. *Introduction*

The question of missing data is central in statistics because, despite all the care which can be taken when collecting data, it is rare to obtain a complete data set. The term “missing data” refers to the situation in which the values of one or more variables are not observed for several individuals in the sample.

The causes of missing data are many in number: broken measuring devices, data being accidentally lost or destroyed, incorrect entry, non-responses from some individuals, etc. Contrary to censored data, which at least provide partial information, missing data offer no information whatsoever.

Missing data are problematic because most of the statistical methods cannot be applied directly using incomplete data sets. Many methods have been proposed to take missing data into account: *complete-case* analysis, which consists of removing any individual having at least one piece of missing data from the sample; *imputation* methods (single or multiple), which consist of "filling the gaps" with "plausible" values; *weighting* methods, which consist of adding additional weight to individuals in a complete-case analysis in order to eliminate any bias introduced when withdrawing part of the individuals, etc. Each of these methods have given rise to many variants. In Imbert and Vialaneix (2018), the reader will find a very complete state of the art along with a comprehensive bibliography. Furthermore, among the many books dedicated to the subject, we cite Rubin (1987); Little and Rubin (2002); Tsiatis (2006). Our bibliography is not exhaustive, but the reader should have no difficulty in finding references appropriate to their needs.

Complete-case analysis, which is often used by default in statistical softwares, can generate bias and a large loss of precision in the estimators. We can easily see that this method is less than optimal: if an individual has a value missing, then they are dropped from the sample. Doing so deprives ourselves of all the information provided by the other variables observed for this individual. A great deal of work has been devoted (and still continues to be) to developing and improving more elaborate methods, in particular for GLMs. It is obviously out of the question to give an exhaustive review here. Rather, we will approach this vast subject from the point of view of a particular problem – the problem of missing censoring indicators in regression models with a right censored response variable – for which we will describe many estimation methods. This will allow the reader to know the principles, specifics, advantages and disadvantages of these methods. Before doing so, let us describe the different mechanisms that can give rise to missing data.

3.2.2. *Missing data typology*

Missing data can be classified into three categories, depending on the mechanism that generates them. In the following, the probability that some data are missing (respectively, observed) will be called the "missingness probability" (respectively, the "selection probability"). Of course, the sum of these two probabilities must equal 1.

3.2.2.1. *Data missing completely at random*

Data are said to be *missing completely at random (MCAR)* if the missingness probability is the same for each observation. In particular, this means that the missingness probability does not depend on either the observed nor the missing variables that play a role in the problem.

The breakdown of a measuring instrument during an experiment, the loss of a biological sample, etc., are some potential causes of data missing completely at random. Ignoring missing data when it is MCAR does not cause the results to be biased, but it does cause a loss of precision in the estimators. In practice, MCAR data are rare.

3.2.2.2. *Data missing at random*

When the missingness probability depends on the values of one or more completely observed variables, then the data are said to be *missing at random* (MAR). The missingness probability is therefore not the same for each data, but depends only on the information observed.

Consider a case–control study in which participants are questioned on their past exposure ("yes" or "no") to a given risk factor. We can expect the proportion of missing responses to be lower for cases when compared to controls, as the cases will have thought about the possible causes of their illness and questioned their past more acutely than the control patients. The missingness probability is not the same for each individual (the missing data are therefore not MCAR), but only depends on the information observed (case or control status).

3.2.2.3. *Data missing not at random*

Data are said to be *missing not at random* (MNAR) if the missingness probability depends on the missing data itself. MNAR data typically occur in studies that address sensitive subjects: addiction, sexuality, etc.

In a survey on the risk factors for cirrhosis, if people with significant alcohol consumption refuse to indicate their level, the missing data – here the level of alcohol consumption – will be MNAR.

When the data are MNAR, the reason as to why the data are missing depends on the data itself. To construct a valid inference in this case, it would be necessary to have the distribution of complete observations among the individuals whose data are missing. Unfortunately, this is rarely the case, and any hypothesis that could be made about this distribution is therefore unverifiable.

3.2.3. *Methods for treating missing data*

In the presence of missing data, one approach consists of performing the statistical analysis using only the available data. This is the complete-case analysis. Let us examine the properties of this method under the MCAR, MAR and MNAR hypotheses, with the simple example of estimating the mean of an i.i.d. sample. The context is the following.

A clinical study is established to evaluate a new drug which lowers the cholesterol level. We wish to estimate the average decrease of this level after six months of treatment. Let X_i $(i = 1, \ldots, n)$ denote the decrease in the cholesterol level of patient i at the end of treatment. It is natural to estimate $\mu = \mathbb{E}(X)$ by:

$$\hat{\mu} = \frac{1}{n} \sum_{i=1}^{n} X_i$$

The law of large numbers ensures that $\hat{\mu} \xrightarrow[n\to\infty]{\mathbb{P}} \mathbb{E}(X)$. Now suppose that X_i is missing for some of the patients. We define the missing data indicator ξ as follows:

$$\xi_i = \begin{cases} 1 & \text{if } X_i \text{ is observed} \\ 0 & \text{if } X_i \text{ is missing} \end{cases}$$

The *complete-case estimator* of μ is defined by:

$$\hat{\mu}_{cc} = \frac{\sum_{i=1}^{n} X_i \xi_i}{\sum_{i=1}^{n} \xi_i}$$

It is simply the empirical mean of the observed data. The law of large numbers ensures that:

$$\hat{\mu}_{cc} = \frac{\sum_{i=1}^{n} X_i \xi_i}{\sum_{i=1}^{n} \xi_i} = \frac{\frac{1}{n}\sum_{i=1}^{n} X_i \xi_i}{\frac{1}{n}\sum_{i=1}^{n} \xi_i} \xrightarrow[n\to\infty]{\mathbb{P}} \frac{\mathbb{E}(X\xi)}{\mathbb{E}(\xi)}$$

3.2.3.1. *The different cases*

3.2.3.1.1. MCAR case

If the missing data is MCAR, then the selection probability is the same for each patient, which is to say that there exists a constant α such that $\mathbb{P}(\xi_i = 1|X_i) = \alpha$ for each i. The ξ_i and X_i variables are therefore independent. In this case:

$$\frac{\mathbb{E}(X\xi)}{\mathbb{E}(\xi)} = \frac{\mathbb{E}(X)\mathbb{E}(\xi)}{\mathbb{E}(\xi)} = \mathbb{E}(X) = \mu$$

and the complete-case estimator is consistent. This agrees with our intuition: if the data is MCAR, then the observations form a random subsample of the original sample. Thus, there is no reason to introduce a bias when estimating μ with complete cases. The estimator $\hat{\mu}_{cc}$ will be less precise than $\hat{\mu}$, however, since it has been calculated from fewer observations.

We can equally show that:

$$\sqrt{n}(\hat{\mu}_{cc} - \mu) \xrightarrow[n\to\infty]{\mathcal{L}} \mathcal{N}\left(0, \frac{\text{var}(X)}{\mathbb{E}(\xi)}\right)$$

while $\sqrt{n}(\hat{\mu}-\mu) \xrightarrow[n\to\infty]{\mathcal{L}} \mathcal{N}(0, \text{var}(X))$ from the central limit theorem. The asymptotic variance of $\hat{\mu}_{cc}$ is therefore greater than that of $\hat{\mu}$ (it is all the greater as the selection probability is small, which also agrees with our intuition).

3.2.3.1.2. MNAR case

If the missing data are MNAR, the selection probability $\mathbb{P}(\xi_i = 1|X_i)$ depends on X_i. Let us write $\mathbb{P}(\xi_i = 1|X_i) = \alpha(X_i)$, where α denotes a particular function. We have:

$$\hat{\mu}_{cc} \xrightarrow[n\to\infty]{\mathbb{P}} \frac{\mathbb{E}(X\xi)}{\mathbb{E}(\xi)} = \frac{\mathbb{E}\left[\mathbb{E}(X\xi|X)\right]}{\mathbb{E}\left[\mathbb{E}(\xi|X)\right]} = \frac{\mathbb{E}\left[X\alpha(X)\right]}{\mathbb{E}\left[\alpha(X)\right]}$$

However, $\mathbb{E}\left[X\alpha(X)\right]/\mathbb{E}\left[\alpha(X)\right]$ has no reason to equal $\mathbb{E}(X)$. For example, if α is an increasing function, the probability of observing X_i will be even greater as X_i is large. Patients with large values of X will therefore be overrepresented among the complete data, and we can expect $\hat{\mu}_{cc}$ to overestimate μ. This can be easily shown.

Let X_i and X_j be two independent copies of X. If α is increasing, then:

$$(X_i - X_j)(\alpha(X_i) - \alpha(X_j)) \geq 0$$

and therefore:

$$\begin{aligned} 0 &\leq \mathbb{E}[(X_i - X_j)(\alpha(X_i) - \alpha(X_j))] \\ &\leq 2\mathbb{E}[X_i\alpha(X_i)] - 2\mathbb{E}(X_i)\mathbb{E}(\alpha(X_i)) \end{aligned}$$

from which $\mathbb{E}[X_i\alpha(X_i)] \geq \mathbb{E}(X_i)\mathbb{E}(\alpha(X_i))$, and finally:

$$\frac{\mathbb{E}\left[X_i\alpha(X_i)\right]}{\mathbb{E}\left[\alpha(X_i)\right]} \geq \mathbb{E}(X_i) = \mu$$

So, $\hat{\mu}_{cc}$ overestimates μ, agreeing with our intuition.

3.2.3.1.3. MAR case

For each patient i, suppose that one or more supplementary variables W_i without missing data (variables relating to diet, smoking, physical activity, etc.) are observed. These variables are sometimes called *auxiliary* variables, because they are not of direct interest. The available data are therefore either (X_i, W_i) if $\xi_i = 1$, or W_i if $\xi_i = 0$.

Under the MAR hypothesis, the selection probability does not depend on X_i, but it can depend on W_i:

$$\mathbb{P}(\xi_i = 1|X_i, W_i) = \mathbb{P}(\xi_i = 1|W_i)$$

In other words, ξ_i and X_i are conditionally independent given W_i.

REMARK.– The conditional independence of ξ_i and X_i given W_i does not imply the independence of ξ_i and X_i. Suppose that W_i denotes the decrease in the cholesterol level of patient i after three months, and that this data is available for each patient. Suppose also that the patients who think that their levels have not sufficiently decreased are more inclined to stop the treatment. Then, ξ_i and W_i are linked. On the other hand, it is reasonable to think that, given W_i, the decision to stop treatment does not depend on X_i (namely, on the cholesterol level after six months, of which the patient is not yet aware of after three months). Therefore, we have $\mathbb{P}(\xi_i = 1|X_i, W_i) = \mathbb{P}(\xi_i = 1|W_i)$, and the mechanism of the missing data is MAR.

However, the variables ξ_i and X_i are certainly linked, since each one is linked to W_i (it is reasonable to think that the cholesterol level after six months is linked to the level after three months). If we do not condition on W_i, then we have $\mathbb{P}(\xi_i = 1|X_i) = \alpha(X_i)$ and are back in the MNAR case again. ■

The problem posed by MNAR data is that it is impossible to estimate the selection probabilities $\mathbb{P}(\xi_i = 1|X_i) = \alpha(X_i)$, since the X_i are not observed when $\xi_i = 0$. On the other hand, when the data are MAR and auxiliary variables W_i are available, it becomes possible to estimate $\mathbb{P}(\xi_i = 1|W_i)$, allowing for consistent estimators (of μ in our example) to be constructed using weighted complete-case or imputation methods. This is what we will now describe (using the example of estimating μ; we will then consider a more complicated problem involving missing data in a GLM).

3.2.3.2. *Weighted complete-case methods*

Suppose that the data are MAR, which is to say that ξ_i and X_i are independent given W_i:

$$\mathbb{P}(\xi_i = 1|X_i, W_i) = \mathbb{P}(\xi_i = 1|W_i) = \alpha(W_i)$$

which can be rewritten as:

$$\mathbb{E}(\xi_i|X_i, W_i) = \mathbb{E}(\xi_i|W_i) = \alpha(W_i)$$

since ξ_i is binary. The MAR hypothesis does not imply the independence of ξ_i and X_i, and the complete-case estimator may be biased. The weighted complete-case estimation method (IPW[3]) uses only complete cases, but overweighs them to

3 *Inverse probability weighting* or weighting by the inverse of the (selection) probability.

compensate for this bias (the reader can consult Seaman and White (2013) for a review of this method).

The intuition is the following. Suppose that patient i is a complete case and that their selection probability equals 1/3, that is:

$$\mathbb{P}(\xi_i = 1|W_i) = \frac{1}{3} \qquad [3.6]$$

We can interpret [3.6] in saying that for a patient observed with the auxiliary variable W_i, there exist two other patients sharing the same value W_i, who are unobserved. The IPW method then consists of weighting the complete cases by $1/\mathbb{P}(\xi_i = 1|W_i)$ in the complete-case estimator. If $\mathbb{P}(\xi_i = 1|W_i) = 1/3$, the contribution from patient i is weighted by $1/(1/3) = 3$, and this patient is "counted three times" in the estimate. Hence, we get the estimator:

$$\hat{\mu}_{IPW} = \frac{1}{n}\sum_{i=1}^{n}\frac{X_i\xi_i}{\alpha(W_i)}$$

The law of large numbers ensures that:

$$\hat{\mu}_{IPW} \xrightarrow[n\to\infty]{\mathbb{P}} \mathbb{E}\left(\frac{X\xi}{\alpha(W)}\right)$$

However:

$$\begin{aligned}
\mathbb{E}\left(\frac{X\xi}{\alpha(W)}\right) &= \mathbb{E}\left(\mathbb{E}\left[\frac{X\xi}{\alpha(W)}\middle| X, W\right]\right) \\
&= \mathbb{E}\left(\frac{X}{\alpha(W)}\mathbb{E}\left[\xi|X, W\right]\right) \\
&= \mathbb{E}\left(\frac{X}{\alpha(W)}\mathbb{E}\left[\xi|W\right]\right) \qquad \text{(since the data are MAR)} \\
&= \mathbb{E}\left(\frac{X}{\alpha(W)}\alpha(W)\right) \\
&= \mathbb{E}(X) \\
&= \mu
\end{aligned}$$

Therefore, $\hat{\mu}_{IPW}$ is a consistent estimator of μ.

In practice, the selection probabilities are more often not known. We can estimate them parametrically by assuming that they are of the form:

$$\mathbb{P}(\xi_i = 1|W_i) = \alpha(W_i, \theta)$$

where α is a known function (e.g. logistic and probit), and θ is an unknown parameter (that we estimate using the maximum likelihood method, for example, using the observations $(\xi_i, W_i), i = 1, \ldots, n$). We denote the MLE of θ by $\hat{\theta}$, obtained by maximizing the likelihood:

$$\prod_{i=1}^{n} \{\alpha(W_i, \theta)\}^{\xi_i} \{1 - \alpha(W_i, \theta)\}^{1-\xi_i}$$

The IPW estimator of μ is calculated thus as follows:

$$\hat{\mu}_{IPW} = \frac{1}{n} \sum_{i=1}^{n} \frac{X_i \xi_i}{\alpha(W_i, \hat{\theta})}$$

The selection probabilities can also be estimated using local, non-parametric, semi-parametric regressions, etc.

3.2.3.3. *Imputation methods*

Imputation methods are based on a different principle. They are undoubtedly the most widely used approach when it comes to handling missing data (with the exception of complete-case analysis, which is the default method implemented in softwares).

Imputation involves replacing the missing data with "plausible" values, before then performing the statistical inference on the completed sample as if it were the "true" one. There are many ways of constructing these plausible values (see Imbert and Vialaneix (2018), for example). We restrict ourselves here to the methods that will be used in sections 3.2.4 and 3.2.5.

Imputation by prediction, or by regression (called *regression calibration*), proceeds in two steps: (i) estimate a regression model for X using the observed variables, and then (ii) replace the missing X_i with their predictions provided by the model. We denote by

$$\mathbb{E}(X_i | W_i) = \mu(W_i, \gamma)$$

the regression of X_i on the auxiliary variables W_i. Here, μ denotes a known function and γ an unknown parameter (although the method is illustrated here using a parametric model, local, non-parametric and semi-parametric regressions, etc., can also be used).

The parameter γ can be estimated using, for example, complete cases by maximum likelihood (for complete cases, recall that we observe both X_i and W_i). Denote by

$f_{X|W}(x|w;\gamma)$ the conditional density of X given W. The MLE $\hat{\gamma}$ of γ is obtained by maximizing the likelihood:

$$\prod_{\{i:\xi_i=1\}} f_{X|W}(X_i|W_i;\gamma)$$

We can then estimate $\mathbb{E}(X_i|W_i)$ by $\mu(W_i,\hat{\gamma})$ and use $\mu(W_i,\hat{\gamma})$ in the place of X_i to estimate μ. We obtain the estimator:

$$\hat{\mu}_{imp} = \frac{1}{n}\sum_{i=1}^{n}\{X_i\xi_i + \mu(W_i,\hat{\gamma})(1-\xi_i)\}$$

If the model $\mathbb{E}(X_i|W_i) = \mu(W_i,\gamma)$ is correct, then $\hat{\gamma}$ is a consistent estimator of γ and $\hat{\mu}_{imp}$ is asymptotically equivalent to:

$$\frac{1}{n}\sum_{i=1}^{n}[X_i\xi_i + \mu(W_i,\gamma)(1-\xi_i)]$$

The law of large numbers then ensures that:

$$\hat{\mu}_{imp} \xrightarrow[n\to\infty]{\mathbb{P}} \mathbb{E}\left[X\xi + \mu(W,\gamma)(1-\xi)\right]$$

However:

$$\begin{aligned}\mathbb{E}\left[X\xi + \mu(W,\gamma)(1-\xi)\right] &= \mathbb{E}\left[\mathbb{E}\left(X\xi + \mu(W,\gamma)(1-\xi)|\xi,W\right)\right]\\ &= \mathbb{E}\left[\xi\mathbb{E}\left(X|\xi,W\right) + \mu(W,\gamma)(1-\xi)\right]\\ &= \mathbb{E}\left[\xi\mu(W,\gamma) + \mu(W,\gamma)(1-\xi)\right]\end{aligned}$$

since, if the data are MAR, $\mathbb{E}\left(X|\xi,W\right) = \mathbb{E}\left(X|W\right) = \mu(W,\gamma)$. We have therefore:

$$\begin{aligned}\mathbb{E}\left[X\xi + \mu(W,\gamma)(1-\xi)\right] &= \mathbb{E}\left[\mu(W,\gamma)\right]\\ &= \mathbb{E}\left[\mathbb{E}\left(X|W\right)\right]\\ &= \mathbb{E}(X)\\ &= \mu\end{aligned}$$

and $\hat{\mu}_{imp}$ is a consistent estimator of μ.

REMARK.– In the absence of auxiliary variables, regression calibration involves replacing X_i with the mean of the observed X_j (and if W_i is a categorical variable, with the mean of the X_j for which $W_j = W_i$). We speak of *mean imputation*. This is a special case of imputation, in which missing values are replaced by a value that is identical for each individual (see Imbert and Vialaneix (2018)). ■

An alternative to regression calibration consists of randomly simulating a value according to the estimated density $f_{X|W}(X_i|W_i;\hat{\gamma})$ and using it to replace the missing X_i. This method, along with regression calibration, are *single imputation* methods: a unique value is used to replace the missing data. *Multiple imputation* consists of simulating multiple values from $f_{X|W}(X_i|W_i;\hat{\gamma})$ to construct multiple completed samples. Statistical analysis is performed on each sample in turn; then the results are combined to produce a single final result. For example, we can calculate the average of the estimates obtained from each completed sample.

The IPW method requires a model for the distribution of ξ_i given W_i. Imputation methods require a model for X_i given W_i. In the two cases, a misspecification of the model risks biasing the statistical analyses. This leads to the introduction of the AIPW method (for *augmented inverse probability weighted*), which is doubly robust (Scharfstein et al. 1999) (also see Tsiatis (2006) for a complete – albeit rather theoretical – treatment of the method as well as multiple references).

3.2.3.4. *AIPW estimator*

Let us reconsider the example of estimating $\mu = \mathbb{E}(X)$ under the MAR hypothesis. To construct the AIPW estimator of μ, a model for the distribution of X_i given W_i as well as a model for the distribution of ξ_i given W_i are both required (this may seem strange, in light of what we wrote above about the risk of bias if these models are misspecified). Let us denote these models by:

$$\mathbb{E}(X_i|W_i) = \mu(W_i, \gamma)$$

and:

$$\mathbb{E}(\xi_i|W_i) = \alpha(W_i, \theta)$$

and by $\hat{\gamma}, \hat{\theta}$ the MLEs of γ and θ, obtained in the same way as in the previous sections.

REMARK.– If the model for X_i given W_i is specified correctly, $\hat{\gamma}$ converges to the true value of γ and $\mu(W_i, \hat{\gamma})$ converges to $\mu(W_i, \gamma)$. If the model is incorrect, $\hat{\gamma}$ will be biased and will converge to a value γ^* that differs from the true value γ (this is the consequence of the results of White (1982) regarding the properties of the MLE in misspecified models). In this case, $\mu(W_i, \hat{\gamma})$ converges to $\mu(W_i, \gamma^*) \neq \mathbb{E}(X_i|W_i)$.

In the same way, if the model for ξ_i given W_i is correct, then $\hat{\theta}$ is a consistent estimator of the true θ and $\alpha(W_i, \hat{\theta})$ converges to $\alpha(W_i, \theta)$. If the model is incorrect, then $\hat{\theta}$ will converge to a value θ^* that differs from the true θ and $\alpha(W_i, \hat{\theta})$ will converge to $\alpha(W_i, \theta^*) \neq \mathbb{E}(\xi_i | W_i)$. ■

The AIPW estimator of μ is therefore defined as:

$$\hat{\mu}_{AIPW} = \frac{1}{n} \sum_{i=1}^{n} \left\{ \frac{X_i \xi_i}{\alpha(W_i, \hat{\theta})} + \frac{(\alpha(W_i, \hat{\theta}) - \xi_i)}{\alpha(W_i, \hat{\theta})} \mu(W_i, \hat{\gamma}) \right\}$$

The first term in the brackets can be recognized as being the IPW estimator of μ, which only uses complete cases. This term is further "augmented" by the term $\frac{(\alpha(W_i, \hat{\theta}) - \xi_i)}{\alpha(W_i, \hat{\theta})} \mu(W_i, \hat{\gamma})$, which involves each individual, regardless of whether they are complete cases ($\xi_i = 1$) or not ($\xi_i = 0$).

We can rewrite $\hat{\mu}_{AIPW}$ as follows:

$$\hat{\mu}_{AIPW} = \frac{1}{n} \sum_{i=1}^{n} \left\{ \mu(W_i, \hat{\gamma}) + \xi_i \frac{(X_i - \mu(W_i, \hat{\gamma}))}{\alpha(W_i, \hat{\theta})} \right\}$$

The AIPW estimator can therefore be understood as the sum of two terms: the average, over all individuals, of the predictions $\mu(W_i, \hat{\gamma})$ of the X_i, and the average, over complete cases, of the $X_i - \mu(W_i, \hat{\gamma})$. These latter terms can be interpreted as the residuals from regressing X_i on W_i. These residuals are weighted by the inverse of their observation probabilities to take into account the fact that not all of them are observed.

This estimator is consistent for μ when at least one of the two models, $\mu(W_i, \gamma)$ or $\alpha(W_i, \theta)$, is correctly specified, justifying the *doubly robust* name attributed to the estimator. This is easily checked informally (these arguments will be dealt with more rigorously in the following sections).

3.2.3.4.1. Case 1: correctly specified $\mu(W_i, \gamma)$

In this case, $\hat{\mu}_{AIPW}$ is asymptotically equivalent to:

$$\hat{\mu}_{AIPW} = \frac{1}{n} \sum_{i=1}^{n} \left\{ \frac{X_i \xi_i}{\alpha(W_i, \theta^*)} - \frac{(\xi_i - \alpha(W_i, \theta^*))}{\alpha(W_i, \theta^*)} \mu(W_i, \gamma) \right\}$$

which, by the law of large numbers, converges in probability to:

$$\mathbb{E}\left[\frac{X\xi}{\alpha(W, \theta^*)} - \frac{(\xi - \alpha(W, \theta^*))}{\alpha(W, \theta^*)} \mu(W, \gamma) \right]$$

$$= \mathbb{E}\left[\mathbb{E}\left\{ \frac{X\xi}{\alpha(W, \theta^*)} - \frac{(\xi - \alpha(W, \theta^*))}{\alpha(W, \theta^*)} \mu(W, \gamma) \middle| \xi, W \right\} \right]$$

$$= \mathbb{E}\left[\frac{\mathbb{E}\left(X|\xi, W\right)\xi}{\alpha(W,\theta^*)} - \frac{(\xi - \alpha(W,\theta^*))}{\alpha(W,\theta^*)}\mu(W,\gamma)\right]$$

$$= \mathbb{E}\left[\frac{\mathbb{E}\left(X|W\right)\xi}{\alpha(W,\theta^*)} - \frac{(\xi - \alpha(W,\theta^*))}{\alpha(W,\theta^*)}\mu(W,\gamma)\right]$$

because, if the data are MAR, then X and ξ are independent given W and hence $\mathbb{E}\left(X|\xi, W\right) = \mathbb{E}\left(X|W\right) = \mu(W,\gamma)$. Thus, $\hat{\mu}_{AIPW}$ converges to:

$$\begin{aligned}
\mathbb{E}\left[\frac{\mu(W,\gamma)\xi}{\alpha(W,\theta^*)} - \frac{(\xi - \alpha(W,\theta^*))}{\alpha(W,\theta^*)}\mu(W,\gamma)\right] &= \mathbb{E}\left[\mu(W,\gamma)\right] \\
&= \mathbb{E}\left[\mathbb{E}\left(X|W\right)\right] \\
&= \mathbb{E}(X) \\
&= \mu
\end{aligned}$$

and is indeed consistent.

3.2.3.4.2. Case 2: correctly specified $\alpha(W_i, \theta)$

In this case, $\hat{\mu}_{AIPW}$ is asymptotically equivalent to:

$$\hat{\mu}_{AIPW} = \frac{1}{n}\sum_{i=1}^{n}\left\{\frac{X_i\xi_i}{\alpha(W_i,\theta)} - \frac{(\xi_i - \alpha(W_i,\theta))}{\alpha(W_i,\theta)}\mu(W_i,\gamma^*)\right\}$$

and converges in probability to:

$$\begin{aligned}
&\mathbb{E}\left[\frac{X\xi}{\alpha(W,\theta)} - \frac{(\xi - \alpha(W,\theta))}{\alpha(W,\theta)}\mu(W,\gamma^*)\right] \\
&\quad = \mathbb{E}\left[\mathbb{E}\left\{\frac{X\xi}{\alpha(W,\theta)} - \frac{(\xi - \alpha(W,\theta))}{\alpha(W,\theta)}\mu(W,\gamma^*)\middle| X, W\right\}\right] \\
&\quad = \mathbb{E}\left[\frac{X\mathbb{E}\left(\xi|X,W\right)}{\alpha(W,\theta)} - \frac{(\mathbb{E}\left(\xi|X,W\right) - \alpha(W,\theta))}{\alpha(W,\theta)}\mu(W,\gamma^*)\right] \\
&\quad = \mathbb{E}\left[\frac{X\mathbb{E}\left(\xi|W\right)}{\alpha(W,\theta)} - \frac{(\mathbb{E}\left(\xi|W\right) - \alpha(W,\theta))}{\alpha(W,\theta)}\mu(W,\gamma^*)\right]
\end{aligned}$$

because, under the MAR hypothesis, $\mathbb{E}\left(\xi|X,W\right) = \mathbb{E}\left(\xi|W\right) = \alpha(W,\theta)$. Thus, $\hat{\mu}_{AIPW}$ converges to:

$$\mathbb{E}\left[\frac{X\alpha(W,\theta)}{\alpha(W,\theta)} - \frac{(\alpha(W,\theta) - \alpha(W,\theta))}{\alpha(W,\theta)}\mu(W,\gamma^*)\right] = \mathbb{E}(X) = \mu$$

and is also consistent in this case.

Therefore, the AIPW estimator is consistent for μ if at least one of the two models for X_i given W_i or ξ_i given W_i is correctly specified (the so-called doubly robust property). If the two models are correct, it is also more efficient than the IPW estimator, as we will illustrate in the next two sections. If the probabilities $\alpha(W_i, \hat{\theta})$ are very small, the IPW estimator may be numerically unstable when n is small. Tsiatis (2006) indicates that the AIPW estimator is less sensitive to this effect.

We have just described the general principle of three estimation methods, which produce consistent estimators when the missing data are MAR. Now let us apply them to a missing data problem in two GLMs.

3.2.4. *A missing data problem in the Poisson model*

The context is that of the right-censored Poisson regression model. We adopt the notations from section 3.1.2.

Suppose we have available a sample of independent observations:

$$\{(Y_i^*, \delta_i, \mathbf{X}_i), i = 1, \ldots, n\}$$

where:

1) $Y_i^* = \min(Y_i, C_i)$ is the observation, eventually censored, of a count variable $Y_i \sim \mathcal{P}(e^{\beta^\top \mathbf{X}_i})$;

2) C_i is a censoring variable and $\delta_i = 1\{Y_i < C_i\}$ is the censoring indicator;

3) $\mathbf{X}_i$ is a vector of p explanatory variables.

The censoring is assumed to be independent and non-informative. Recall the expression for the log-likelihood of β in this context:

$$\ell_n(\beta) = \sum_{i=1}^{n} \left\{ \delta_i \left(Y_i^* \beta^\top \mathbf{X}_i - e^{\beta^\top \mathbf{X}_i} - \ln(Y_i^*!) \right) \right.$$
$$\left. +(1 - \delta_i) \ln \left(1 - \frac{\Gamma(Y_i^*, e^{\beta^\top \mathbf{X}_i})}{(Y_i^* - 1)!} \right) \right\}$$

with:

$$\Gamma(u, \mu) = \int_{\mu}^{\infty} t^{u-1} e^{-t} dt$$

Now, for certain individuals of the sample, assume that the censoring indicator δ_i is not observed (we assume that it is missing at random, MAR). Define the indicator:

$$\xi_i = \begin{cases} 1 & \text{if } \delta_i \text{ is observed} \\ 0 & \text{otherwise} \end{cases}$$

The data available for individual i is therefore of the form:

$$\mathcal{O}_i = (Y_i^*, \mathbf{X}_i, \delta_i, \xi_i = 1) \quad \text{or} \quad \mathcal{O}_i = (Y_i^*, \mathbf{X}_i, \xi_i = 0)$$

In what follows, we will show how the regression calibration, multiple imputation and AIPW methods can be adapted to estimate β, and we will state the asymptotic properties of the resulting estimators. Section 3.2.4 is based on Bousselmi et al. (2021).

3.2.4.1. *Regression calibration*

Regression calibration consists of replacing δ_i by its prediction obtained from a regression model of δ_i on the observed variables. We denote by $\mathbf{W}_i$ the set of completely observed variables: $\mathbf{W}_i = (Y_i^*, \mathbf{X}_i^\top)^\top$. If some auxiliary variables $\mathbf{V}_i$ are available, we denote $\mathbf{W}_i = (Y_i^*, \mathbf{X}_i^\top, \mathbf{V}_i^\top)^\top$. In the following, we will denote the dimension of $\mathbf{W}_i$ by q.

Suppose that the distribution of δ_i given $\mathbf{W}_i$ can be described by a parametric model:

$$\mathbb{P}(\delta_i = 1 | \mathbf{W}_i) = m(\mathbf{W}_i, \theta_0)$$

where $\theta_0 \in \mathbb{R}^q$ is an unknown parameter[4] and m is a known function with values between 0 and 1. For example, $m(\mathbf{W}_i, \theta) = e^{\theta^\top \mathbf{W}_i}/(1 + e^{\theta^\top \mathbf{W}_i})$ corresponds to the logistic regression model. Regression calibration consists of replacing the missing δ_i by $\mathbb{E}(\delta_i | \mathbf{W}_i) = m(\mathbf{W}_i, \theta_0)$. In general, θ_0 is unknown. We can estimate it using the maximum likelihood method applied to the complete cases. The likelihood is calculated as follows:

$$L_n(\theta) = \prod_{i=1}^{n} m(\mathbf{W}_i, \theta)^{\xi_i \delta_i} (1 - m(\mathbf{W}_i, \theta))^{\xi_i (1 - \delta_i)}$$

We calculate the MLE:

$$\hat{\theta}_n = \arg\max_{\theta} L_n(\theta) \qquad [3.7]$$

4 In the following, it will be useful to distinguish the true value of a parameter by using 0 as a subscript.

which allows for the prediction $m(\mathbf{W}_i, \hat{\theta}_n)$ to be calculated. Then, we estimate β by maximizing an approximated version of $\ell_n(\beta)$, in which the missing δ_i are replaced by their predictions. We denote by:

$$\hat{\delta}_i(\hat{\theta}_n) = \xi_i\delta_i + (1-\xi_i)m(\mathbf{W}_i, \hat{\theta}_n)$$

the variable which equals δ_i if δ_i is observed, or equals its prediction if δ_i is missing. The approximate log-likelihood is written as:

$$\widetilde{\ell_n}(\beta, \hat{\theta}_n) = \sum_{i=1}^{n} \Big\{ \hat{\delta}_i(\hat{\theta}_n) \left(Y_i^* \beta^\top \mathbf{X}_i - e^{\beta^\top \mathbf{X}_i} - \ln(Y_i^*!) \right) \\ +(1-\hat{\delta}_i(\hat{\theta}_n)) \ln \left(1 - \frac{\Gamma\left(Y_i^*, e^{\beta^\top \mathbf{X}_i}\right)}{(Y_i^*-1)!} \right) \Big\} \qquad [3.8]$$

The estimator of β will be denoted by:

$$\widetilde{\beta}_n = \arg\max_{\beta} \widetilde{\ell_n}(\beta, \hat{\theta}_n)$$

REMARK.– Let us denote:

$$\dot{m}(\mathbf{W}_i, \theta) = \frac{\partial m(\mathbf{W}_i, \theta)}{\partial \theta} \quad \text{and} \quad \widetilde{m_i}(\theta) = \frac{\dot{m}(\mathbf{W}_i, \theta)}{m(\mathbf{W}_i, \theta)(1 - m(\mathbf{W}_i, \theta))}$$

If u is a column vector, denote by $u^{\otimes}2$ the product $uu^\top$. Define the $(q \times q)$-matrix:

$$\Theta(\theta) = \mathbb{E}\left[\frac{\dot{m}^{\otimes 2}(\mathbf{W}, \theta)}{m(\mathbf{W}, \theta)(1 - m(\mathbf{W}, \theta))} \xi \right]$$

By expanding the score function $\partial \ln L_n(\theta)/\partial\theta$ as a Taylor series, it can be shown that $\hat{\theta}_n$ satisfies the equation:

$$\sqrt{n}(\hat{\theta}_n - \theta_0) = \frac{1}{\sqrt{n}} \sum_{i=1}^{n} \Theta^{-1}(\theta_0)\widetilde{m_i}(\theta_0)\xi_i(\delta_i - m(\mathbf{W}_i, \theta_0)) + o_{\mathbb{P}}(1) \qquad [3.9]$$

where $o_{\mathbb{P}}(1)$ denotes a sequence of random variables that tends toward 0 in probability (see, for example, section 3.2 of Tsiatis (2006)). We say that $\hat{\theta}_n$ is *asymptotically linear*. The function $\mathcal{O}_i \mapsto \varphi(\mathcal{O}_i) = \Theta^{-1}(\theta_0)\widetilde{m_i}(\theta_0)\xi_i(\delta_i - m(\mathbf{W}_i, \theta_0))$ is called the *influence function* of $\hat{\theta}_n$.

The expression [3.9] implies that $\hat{\theta}_n \xrightarrow[n\to\infty]{\mathbb{P}} \theta_0$. Indeed, we can rewrite [3.9] as follows:

$$\begin{aligned}\hat{\theta}_n - \theta_0 &= \frac{1}{n}\sum_{i=1}^{n} \Theta^{-1}(\theta_0)\widetilde{m_i}(\theta_0)\xi_i(\delta_i - m(\mathbf{W}_i, \theta_0)) + o_{\mathbb{P}}(1/\sqrt{n}) \\ &= \frac{1}{n}\sum_{i=1}^{n} \varphi(\mathcal{O}_i) + o_{\mathbb{P}}(1/\sqrt{n})\end{aligned}$$

From the law of large numbers, $\frac{1}{n}\sum_{i=1}^{n} \varphi(\mathcal{O}_i)$ converges in probability to:

$$\Theta^{-1}(\theta_0)\mathbb{E}\left[\widetilde{m_i}(\theta_0)\xi_i(\delta_i - m(\mathbf{W}_i, \theta_0))\right]$$

However:

$$\begin{aligned}\mathbb{E}\left[\widetilde{m_i}(\theta_0)\xi_i(\delta_i - m(\mathbf{W}_i, \theta_0))\right] &= \mathbb{E}\left[\widetilde{m_i}(\theta_0)\mathbb{E}\left\{\xi_i\delta_i - \xi_i m(\mathbf{W}_i, \theta_0)|\mathbf{W}_i\right\}\right] \\ &= \mathbb{E}\left[\widetilde{m_i}(\theta_0)\left\{\mathbb{E}(\xi_i\delta_i|\mathbf{W}_i) - \mathbb{E}(\xi_i|\mathbf{W}_i)m(\mathbf{W}_i, \theta_0)\right\}\right]\end{aligned}$$

Under the MAR hypothesis:

$$\begin{aligned}\mathbb{E}(\xi_i\delta_i|\mathbf{W}_i) &= \mathbb{E}(\xi_i|\mathbf{W}_i)\mathbb{E}(\delta_i|\mathbf{W}_i) \\ &= \mathbb{E}(\xi_i|\mathbf{W}_i)m(\mathbf{W}_i, \theta_0)\end{aligned}$$

from which:

$$\mathbb{E}\left[\widetilde{m_i}(\theta_0)\xi_i(\delta_i - m(\mathbf{W}_i, \theta_0))\right] = 0$$

Therefore, $\frac{1}{n}\sum_{i=1}^{n} \varphi(\mathcal{O}_i) \xrightarrow[n\to\infty]{\mathbb{P}} 0$, and consequently $\hat{\theta}_n \xrightarrow[n\to\infty]{\mathbb{P}} \theta_0$.

The expression [3.9] implies equally that $\hat{\theta}_n$ is asymptotically Gaussian. From the central limit theorem:

$$\frac{1}{\sqrt{n}}\sum_{i=1}^{n} \Theta^{-1}(\theta_0)\widetilde{m_i}(\theta_0)\xi_i(\delta_i - m(\mathbf{W}_i, \theta_0)) \xrightarrow[n\to\infty]{\mathcal{L}} \mathcal{N}(0, \Lambda)$$

where:

$$\begin{aligned}
\Lambda &= \text{var}(\varphi(\mathcal{O}_i)) \\
&= \Theta^{-1}(\theta_0)\text{var}(\widetilde{m_i}(\theta_0)\xi_i(\delta_i - m(\mathbf{W}_i, \theta_0)))\Theta^{-1}(\theta_0) \\
&= \Theta^{-1}(\theta_0)\mathbb{E}\left(\widetilde{m_i}^{\otimes 2}(\theta_0)\xi_i(\delta_i - m(\mathbf{W}_i, \theta_0))^2\right)\Theta^{-1}(\theta_0) \\
&= \Theta^{-1}(\theta_0)\mathbb{E}\left(\widetilde{m_i}^{\otimes 2}(\theta_0)\mathbb{E}(\xi_i|\mathbf{W}_i)\mathbb{E}\{(\delta_i - m(\mathbf{W}_i, \theta_0))^2|\mathbf{W}_i\}\right)\Theta^{-1}(\theta_0)
\end{aligned}$$

However:

$$\begin{aligned}
\mathbb{E}\{(\delta_i - m(\mathbf{W}_i, \theta_0))^2|\mathbf{W}_i\} &= \text{var}(\delta_i|\mathbf{W}_i) \\
&= m(\mathbf{W}_i, \theta_0)(1 - m(\mathbf{W}_i, \theta_0))
\end{aligned}$$

and so:

$$\begin{aligned}
\Lambda &= \Theta^{-1}(\theta_0)\mathbb{E}\left(\widetilde{m_i}^{\otimes 2}(\theta_0)\mathbb{E}(\xi_i|\mathbf{W}_i)m(\mathbf{W}_i, \theta_0)(1 - m(\mathbf{W}_i, \theta_0))\right)\Theta^{-1}(\theta_0) \\
&= \Theta^{-1}(\theta_0)\mathbb{E}\left(\frac{\dot{m}^{\otimes 2}(\mathbf{W}_i, \theta_0)}{m(\mathbf{W}_i, \theta_0)(1 - m(\mathbf{W}_i, \theta_0))}\xi_i\right)\Theta^{-1}(\theta_0) \\
&= \Theta^{-1}(\theta_0)\Theta(\theta_0)\Theta^{-1}(\theta_0) \\
&= \Theta^{-1}(\theta_0)
\end{aligned}$$

Finally, Slutsky's theorem implies that:

$$\sqrt{n}(\hat{\theta}_n - \theta_0) \xrightarrow[n\to\infty]{\mathcal{L}} \mathcal{N}(0, \Theta^{-1}(\theta_0))$$

■

3.2.4.1.1. Asymptotic properties

To state the asymptotic properties of $\tilde{\beta}_n$, some regularity conditions are necessary:

– *C1*: the explanatory variables $\mathbf{X}_i$ (and the auxiliary variables $\mathbf{V}_i$ if there are any) are bounded.

– *C2*: the true values β_0 and θ_0 belong to the interiors of compact subsets $\mathcal{B} \subseteq \mathbb{R}^p$ and $\Theta \subseteq \mathbb{R}^q$, respectively.

– *C3*: $\mathbb{P}(Y^* \geq 1|\xi\delta = 0) = 1$ and $\mathbb{P}(\delta = 1) > 0$.

– *C4*: the function $m(\mathbf{w}, \theta)$ is differentiable with respect to θ for every $\mathbf{w}$, and there exists a bounded function h such that for every θ and $\tilde{\theta} \in \Theta$, $|m(\mathbf{w}, \theta) - m(\mathbf{w}, \tilde{\theta})| \leq h(\mathbf{w})\|\theta - \tilde{\theta}\|$ (we will denote $\mathbb{E}[h(\mathbf{W})] = v$).

Condition C3 is interpreted in the same way as that in theorem 3.1: a 0 cannot be a censored data, and shall not be a data for whom we ignore if it is censored or not.

Some additional notation is also required. First, denote $\pi(\mathbf{W}) = \mathbb{P}(\xi = 1|\mathbf{W})$. In section 3.1.2.2, we had defined the function:

$$h_\beta(y, x) = \frac{e^{-e^{\beta^\top x} + \beta^\top xy}}{(y-1)! - \Gamma(y, e^{\beta^\top x})}$$

for every $\beta \in \mathbb{R}^p, x \in \mathbb{R}^p$ and $y \in \mathbb{N}\backslash\{0\}$.

Now define the matrices:

$$\Sigma_1(\beta) = \mathbb{E}\left[\mathbf{X}\mathbf{X}^\top \left(\delta e^{\beta^\top \mathbf{X}} + (\delta - 1)\left\{Y^* - e^{\beta^\top \mathbf{X}} - h_\beta(Y^*, \mathbf{X})\right\} h_\beta(Y^*, \mathbf{X})\right)\right]$$

$$\Sigma_2(\beta, \theta) = \mathbb{E}\left[\mathbf{X}\dot{m}^\top(\mathbf{W}, \theta)\left(Y^* - e^{\beta^\top \mathbf{X}} - h_\beta(Y^*, \mathbf{X})\right)(1 - \pi(\mathbf{W}))\right]$$

$$\Sigma_3(\beta, \theta) = \mathbb{E}\left[\mathbf{X}\dot{m}^\top(\mathbf{W}, \theta)\left(Y^* - e^{\beta^\top \mathbf{X}} - h_\beta(Y^*, \mathbf{X})\right)\right]$$

of sizes $(p \times p)$, $(p \times q)$, and $(p \times q)$, respectively.

The following theorem states the consistency and asymptotic normality of $\tilde{\beta}_n$. Its proof is provided in section 3.3.2.

THEOREM 3.3.– *Suppose that conditions C1 to C4 are satisfied. Then* $\tilde{\beta}_n \xrightarrow[n\to\infty]{\mathbb{P}} \beta$ *and:*

$$\sqrt{n}(\tilde{\beta}_n - \beta_0) \xrightarrow[n\to\infty]{\mathcal{L}} \mathcal{N}(0, \Sigma)$$

where:

$$\Sigma = \Sigma_1^{-1}(\beta_0)\left\{\Sigma_1(\beta_0) + (2\Sigma_3(\beta_0, \theta_0) - \Sigma_2(\beta_0, \theta_0))\,\Theta^{-1}(\theta_0)\Sigma_2^\top(\beta_0, \theta_0)\right\}\Sigma_1^{-1}(\beta_0)$$

REMARK.– If $\pi(\mathbf{W}) = 1$, Σ reduces to $\Sigma_1^{-1}(\beta_0)$, the asymptotic variance matrix of the MLE of β in the censored Poisson regression model but without missing data (see theorem 3.1). ■

A consistent estimator of Σ is given by:

$$\Sigma_{1,n}^{-1}(\tilde{\beta}_n, \hat{\theta}_n)\left\{\Sigma_{1,n}(\tilde{\beta}_n, \hat{\theta}_n) + \left(2\Sigma_{3,n}(\tilde{\beta}_n, \hat{\theta}_n) - \Sigma_{2,n}(\tilde{\beta}_n, \hat{\theta}_n)\right)\Theta_n^{-1}(\hat{\theta}_n)\Sigma_{2,n}^\top(\tilde{\beta}_n, \hat{\theta}_n)\right\}\Sigma_{1,n}^{-1}(\tilde{\beta}_n, \hat{\theta}_n)$$

which is an empirical version of Σ, where:

$$\Sigma_{1,n}(\beta,\theta) = \frac{1}{n}\sum_{i=1}^{n} \mathbf{X}_i\mathbf{X}_i^\top \Big(\hat{\delta}_i(\theta)e^{\beta^\top \mathbf{X}_i}$$

$$+ (\hat{\delta}_i(\theta)-1)\left\{Y_i^* - e^{\beta^\top \mathbf{X}_i} - h_\beta(Y_i^*,\mathbf{X}_i)\right\} h_\beta(Y_i^*,\mathbf{X}_i)\Big)$$

$$\Sigma_{2,n}(\beta,\theta) = \frac{1}{n}\sum_{i=1}^{n} \mathbf{X}_i\dot{m}^\top(\mathbf{W}_i,\theta)\left(Y_i^* - e^{\beta^\top \mathbf{X}_i} - h_\beta(Y_i^*,\mathbf{X}_i)\right)(1-\xi_i)$$

$$\Sigma_{3,n}(\beta,\theta) = \frac{1}{n}\sum_{i=1}^{n} \mathbf{X}_i\dot{m}^\top(\mathbf{W}_i,\theta)\left(Y_i^* - e^{\beta^\top \mathbf{X}_i} - h_\beta(Y_i^*,\mathbf{X}_i)\right)$$

$$\Theta_n(\theta) = \frac{1}{n}\sum_{i=1}^{n} \frac{\dot{m}^{\otimes 2}(\mathbf{W}_i,\theta)}{m(\mathbf{W}_i,\theta)(1-m(\mathbf{W}_i,\theta))}\xi_i$$

3.2.4.2. *Multiple imputation*

Single imputation consists of completing a sample by replacing each missing δ_i with a value randomly drawn from the distribution of δ_i given $\mathbf{W}_i$. We estimate β on the resulting sample (called the completed, or imputed, sample). Multiple imputation consists of repeating this procedure M times, so that M imputed samples are obtained, and estimating β on each one of them, before averaging the results to obtain a unique estimate (see, for example, Schafer (1999) and Kenward and Carpenter (2007)).

Imputation by random simulation, whether be it single or multiple, allows us to realize the statistical inference as if a complete sample was available (i.e. by directly using the available functions and packages to estimate β). This is not always the case for regression calibration.

As in the previous section, assume that the distribution of δ_i given $\mathbf{W}_i$ is described by a parametric model $\mathbb{P}(\delta_i = 1|\mathbf{W}_i) = m(\mathbf{W}_i,\theta_0)$. θ_0 is estimated by the maximum likelihood method applied to the complete cases (see [3.7]). The imputed values are obtained by simulating from the estimated distribution of δ_i, here the Bernoulli distribution $\mathcal{B}(m(\mathbf{W}_i,\hat{\theta}_n))$.

We denote by $D_{i,j}(\hat{\theta}_n)$ (for $j = 1,\dots,M$) the jth value imputed from the $\mathcal{B}(m(\mathbf{W}_i,\hat{\theta}_n))$ distribution, and:

$$\delta_{i,j}^*(\hat{\theta}_n) = \xi_i\delta_i + (1-\xi_i)D_{i,j}(\hat{\theta}_n)$$

the variable which equals δ_i if δ_i is observed, and equals the imputed value $D_{i,j}(\hat{\theta}_n)$ if δ_i is missing. We estimate β in the jth imputed sample by maximizing the log-likelihood:

$$\ell^*_{n,j}(\beta, \hat{\theta}_n) = \sum_{i=1}^{n} \left\{ \delta^*_{i,j}(\hat{\theta}_n) \left(Y_i^* \beta^\top \mathbf{X}_i - e^{\beta^\top \mathbf{X}_i} - \ln(Y_i^*!) \right) \right.$$
$$\left. +(1 - \delta^*_{i,j}(\hat{\theta}_n)) \ln \left(1 - \frac{\Gamma\left(Y_i^*, e^{\beta^\top \mathbf{X}_i}\right)}{(Y_i^* - 1)!} \right) \right\}$$

Let us denote by:

$$\hat{\beta}^*_{n,j} = \arg\max_{\beta} \ell^*_{n,j}(\beta, \hat{\theta}_n)$$

the estimator of β obtained from the jth completed sample. We average the M estimators $\hat{\beta}^*_{n,1}, \ldots, \hat{\beta}^*_{n,M}$ to obtain the final estimator:

$$\hat{\beta}^*_n = \frac{1}{M} \sum_{j=1}^{M} \hat{\beta}^*_{n,j}$$

REMARK.– The `vglm` function from the `VGAM` package (Yee 2010, 2015) can be used to obtain the $\hat{\beta}^*_{n,j}$. Indeed, $\ell^*_{n,j}(\beta, \hat{\theta}_n)$ is none other than the log-likelihood [3.2] of the censored Poisson model in which the missing δ_i are replaced by the $D_{i,j}(\hat{\theta}_n)$, which equal either 0 or 1.

On the other hand, `vglm` cannot be used in the regression calibration. Indeed, $\hat{\delta}_i(\hat{\theta}_n)$ is a number that lies between 0 and 1 (since $m(\mathbf{W}_i, \theta) \in (0, 1)$), which is not supported by `vglm`. ■

3.2.4.2.1. Asymptotic properties

The following theorem states the asymptotic properties of $\hat{\beta}^*_n$. Its proof is given in section 3.3.3.

THEOREM 3.4.– *Suppose that conditions C1 to C4 are satisfied. For each* $j = 1, \ldots, M$, *we denote:*

$$f_{\beta,\theta,j}(\mathcal{O}_i) = \mathbf{X}_i\{\delta^*_{i,j}(\theta)[Y_i^* - e^{\beta^\top \mathbf{X}_i} - h_\beta(Y_i^*, \mathbf{X}_i)] + h_\beta(Y_i^*, \mathbf{X}_i)\}$$

Also, denote:

$$\Sigma_1^*(\beta,\theta) = var\left(\frac{1}{M}\sum_{j=1}^{M} f_{\beta,\theta,j}(\mathcal{O}_1)\right)$$

Then $\hat{\beta}_n^* \xrightarrow[n\to\infty]{\mathbb{P}} \beta_0$, *and:*

$$\sqrt{n}(\hat{\beta}_n^* - \beta_0) \xrightarrow[n\to\infty]{\mathcal{L}} \mathcal{N}(0,\Sigma^*)$$

where:

$$\Sigma^* = \Sigma_1^{-1}(\beta_0)\left\{\Sigma_1^*(\beta_0,\theta_0) + (2\Sigma_3(\beta_0,\theta_0) - \Sigma_2(\beta_0,\theta_0))\,\Theta^{-1}(\theta_0)\Sigma_2^\top(\beta_0,\theta_0)\right\}\Sigma_1^{-1}(\beta_0)$$

A consistent estimator of Σ^* is given by:

$$\Sigma_n^* = \bar{\Sigma}_{1,n}^{-1}(\hat{\beta}_n^*,\hat{\theta}_n)\left\{\Sigma_{1,n}^*(\hat{\beta}_n^*,\hat{\theta}_n) + \left(2\Sigma_{3,n}(\hat{\beta}_n^*,\hat{\theta}_n) - \Sigma_{2,n}(\hat{\beta}_n^*,\hat{\theta}_n)\right)\Theta_n^{-1}(\hat{\theta}_n)\Sigma_{2,n}^\top(\hat{\beta}_n^*,\hat{\theta}_n)\right\}\bar{\Sigma}_{1,n}^{-1}(\hat{\beta}_n^*,\hat{\theta}_n)$$

where $\Sigma_{1,n}^*(\beta,\theta)$ denotes the empirical variance of the $\frac{1}{M}\sum_{j=1}^{M} f_{\beta,\theta,j}(\mathcal{O}_i)$, $i=1,\ldots,n$, and $\bar{\Sigma}_{1,n}(\beta,\theta) = \frac{1}{M}\sum_{j=1}^{M}\Sigma_{1,n,j}(\beta,\theta)$, where:

$$\Sigma_{1,n,j}(\beta,\theta) = \frac{1}{n}\sum_{i=1}^{n}\mathbf{X}_i\mathbf{X}_i^\top\left(\delta_{i,j}^*(\theta)e^{\beta^\top\mathbf{X}_i} + (\delta_{i,j}^*(\theta)-1)\left\{Y_i^* - e^{\beta^\top\mathbf{X}_i} - h_\beta(Y_i^*,\mathbf{X}_i)\right\}h_\beta(Y_i^*,\mathbf{X}_i)\right)$$

The matrices $\Sigma_{2,n}$, $\Sigma_{3,n}$ and Θ_n are the same as those in section 3.2.4.1.1.

Theorem 3.4 provides us with an analytical expression for the asymptotic variance of $\hat{\beta}_n^*$. However, it is not always easy to determine the asymptotic variance of a multiple imputation estimator.

Also, an estimator of this variance is necessary to construct confidence intervals and hypothesis tests. A simple estimator has been proposed by Rubin (1987). Its principle is the following.

We denote by $\hat{\beta}_1, \ldots, \hat{\beta}_M$ the estimators of a real parameter β, obtained from M imputed samples (the following formulas can be easily generalized to the vectorial case). These estimators can be combined to produce a single value:

$$\hat{\beta}^* = \frac{1}{M} \sum_{j=1}^{M} \hat{\beta}_j$$

Suppose that we have an estimator of $\text{var}(\hat{\beta}_j)$ available. For example, if $\hat{\beta}_j$ is an MLE, its asymptotic variance is estimated using the inverse of the empirical Fisher information. Denote by $\widehat{\text{var}}(\hat{\beta}_j)$ the variance estimator calculated on the j-th imputed sample, as if it were a complete sample.

The estimator of the variance of $\hat{\beta}^*$ proposed by Rubin (1987) is calculated as the sum of two terms. The first, called the *within-imputation variance*, is the average of the $\widehat{\text{var}}(\hat{\beta}_j)$. It is often denoted by W:

$$W = \frac{1}{M} \sum_{j=1}^{M} \widehat{\text{var}}(\hat{\beta}_j)$$

The second term, called the *between-imputation variance*, is the empirical variance of the $\hat{\beta}_j$. It is often denoted by B:

$$B = \frac{1}{M-1} \sum_{j=1}^{M} (\hat{\beta}_j - \hat{\beta}^*)^2$$

The estimator of the variance of $\hat{\beta}^*$ proposed by Rubin (1987) is:

$$\widehat{\text{var}}(\hat{\beta}^*) = W + \left(1 + \frac{1}{M}\right) B$$

The correction factor $(1 + 1/M)$ has been proposed to improve the precision of the estimator.

In the case of the Poisson regression model with missing censoring indicators, Σ_n^* and Rubin's estimator produce very similar results.

3.2.4.3. *AIPW estimator*

To construct the AIPW estimator of β, we need the selection probability $\mathbb{P}(\xi_i = 1|\mathbf{W}_i)$ and conditional mean $\mathbb{E}(\delta_i|\mathbf{W}_i)$. Suppose that they can be specified using the parametric models:

$$\mathbb{P}(\xi_i = 1|\mathbf{W}_i) = \pi(\mathbf{W}_i, \gamma_0)$$

and:

$$\mathbb{P}(\delta_i = 1|\mathbf{W}_i) = m(\mathbf{W}_i, \theta_0)$$

If the parameters $\gamma_0, \theta_0 \in \mathbb{R}^q$ are unknown, which is most often the case in practice, then they are estimated using the maximum likelihood method. As before, the MLE of θ_0 is obtained on complete cases:

$$\hat{\theta}_n = \arg\max_{\theta} \prod_{i=1}^{n} m(\mathbf{W}_i, \theta)^{\xi_i \delta_i}(1 - m(\mathbf{W}_i, \theta))^{\xi_i(1-\delta_i)}$$

The MLE of γ_0 is obtained from the observations $(\xi_i, \mathbf{W}_i), i = 1, \ldots, n$:

$$\hat{\gamma}_n = \arg\max_{\gamma} \prod_{i=1}^{n} \pi(\mathbf{W}_i, \gamma)^{\xi_i}(1 - \pi(\mathbf{W}_i, \gamma))^{1-\xi_i}$$

Just like $\hat{\theta}_n$, $\hat{\gamma}_n$ is asymptotically linear. It satisfies the equation:

$$\sqrt{n}(\hat{\gamma}_n - \gamma_0) = \frac{1}{\sqrt{n}} \sum_{i=1}^{n} \Sigma_4^{-1}(\gamma_0)\widetilde{\pi}_i(\gamma_0)(\xi_i - \pi(\mathbf{W}_i, \gamma_0)) + o_{\mathbb{P}}(1) \qquad [3.10]$$

with:

$$\dot{\pi}(\mathbf{W}_i, \gamma) = \frac{\partial \pi(\mathbf{W}_i, \gamma)}{\partial \gamma}, \quad \widetilde{\pi}_i(\gamma) = \frac{\dot{\pi}(\mathbf{W}_i, \gamma)}{\pi(\mathbf{W}_i, \gamma)(1 - \pi(\mathbf{W}_i, \gamma))}$$

and:

$$\Sigma_4(\gamma) = \mathbb{E}\left[\frac{\dot{\pi}^{\otimes 2}(\mathbf{W}, \gamma)}{\pi(\mathbf{W}, \gamma)(1 - \pi(\mathbf{W}, \gamma))}\right]$$

REMARK.– If the models $\pi(\mathbf{W}_i, \gamma_0)$ and $m(\mathbf{W}_i, \theta_0)$ are misspecified (which is to say, if the models used do not correspond to the "true" ones underlying the data), $\hat{\gamma}_n$ and $\hat{\theta}_n$ converge, respectively, to the values $\gamma^* \neq \gamma_0$ and $\theta^* \neq \theta_0$, which follows from the results of White (1982) on the MLE in misspecified models. In the opposite case, $\hat{\gamma}_n$ and $\hat{\theta}_n$ converge to γ_0 and θ_0. ■

Let us adapt the principle of the AIPW method described in section 3.2.3.4. First, define the quantity:

$$\breve{\delta}_i(\hat{\theta}_n, \hat{\gamma}_n) = m(\mathbf{W}_i, \hat{\theta}_n) + \xi_i\left(\frac{\delta_i - m(\mathbf{W}_i, \hat{\theta}_n)}{\pi(\mathbf{W}_i, \hat{\gamma}_n)}\right) \qquad [3.11]$$

which, as before, should be interpreted as the prediction $m(\mathbf{W}_i, \hat{\theta}_n)$ of δ_i to which the weighted residual $(\delta_i - m(\mathbf{W}_i, \hat{\theta}_n))/\pi(\mathbf{W}_i, \hat{\gamma}_n)$ – if the individual i is a complete case – is added. Then [3.11] can be rewritten as:

$$\breve{\delta}_i(\hat{\theta}_n, \hat{\gamma}_n) = \frac{\xi_i \delta_i}{\pi(\mathbf{W}_i, \hat{\gamma}_n)} + \left(1 - \frac{\xi_i}{\pi(\mathbf{W}_i, \hat{\gamma}_n)}\right) m(\mathbf{W}_i, \hat{\theta}_n)$$

where we recognize the weighted contribution $\frac{\xi_i \delta_i}{\pi(\mathbf{W}_i, \hat{\gamma}_n)}$ of a complete case, with the additional $(1 - \frac{\xi_i}{\pi(\mathbf{W}_i, \hat{\gamma}_n)}) m(\mathbf{W}_i, \hat{\theta}_n)$ term.

To obtain the AIPW estimator of β, replace δ_i by $\breve{\delta}_i(\hat{\theta}_n, \hat{\gamma}_n)$ in the log-likelihood [3.2] of the censored Poisson model and maximize with respect to β. This is equivalent to solving the estimating equation $\breve{\ell}_n(\beta, \hat{\theta}_n, \hat{\gamma}_n) = 0$, where:

$$\breve{\ell}_n(\beta, \hat{\theta}_n, \hat{\gamma}_n) = \sum_{i=1}^{n} \mathbf{X}_i \left[\breve{\delta}_i(\hat{\theta}_n, \hat{\gamma}_n)\left(Y_i^* - e^{\beta^\top \mathbf{X}_i} - h_\beta(Y_i^*, \mathbf{X}_i)\right) + h_\beta(Y_i^*, \mathbf{X}_i)\right] \tag{3.12}$$

Denote by $\breve{\beta}_n$ the resulting estimator.

3.2.4.3.1. Asymptotic properties

First, define the matrices:

$$\Sigma_5(\beta, \theta, \gamma) = \mathbb{E}\left[\mathbf{X}\left(Y^* - e^{\beta^\top \mathbf{X}} - h_\beta(Y^*, \mathbf{X})\right)\left(1 - \frac{\xi}{\pi(\mathbf{W}, \gamma)}\right) \dot{m}^\top(\mathbf{W}, \theta)\right]$$

$$\Sigma_6(\beta, \theta, \gamma) = \mathbb{E}\left[\mathbf{X}\left(Y^* - e^{\beta^\top \mathbf{X}} - h_\beta(Y^*, \mathbf{X})\right) \xi \frac{\dot{\pi}^\top(\mathbf{W}, \gamma)}{\pi^2(\mathbf{W}, \gamma)} (m(\mathbf{W}, \theta) - \delta)\right]$$

$$\Sigma_7(\beta, \theta, \gamma) = \Sigma_1(\beta) + (2\Sigma_3(\beta, \theta) - \Sigma_5(\beta, \theta, \gamma))\, \Theta^{-1}(\theta) \Sigma_5^\top(\beta, \theta, \gamma)$$

and:

$$\Sigma_8(\beta, \theta, \gamma) = \Sigma_1(\beta) - \Sigma_6(\beta, \theta, \gamma)\Sigma_4^{-1}(\gamma)\Sigma_6^\top(\beta, \theta, \gamma)$$

of sizes $(p \times q)$, $(p \times q)$, $(p \times p)$, and $(p \times p)$, respectively. The following regularity hypotheses will be required:

– *C5*: the space of the parameters γ is a bounded subset $\mathcal{G} \subseteq \mathbb{R}^q$ and γ_0 belongs to the interior of $\mathcal{G}$.

– *C6*: the function $\pi(\cdot, \cdot)$ satisfies $\pi(\mathbf{w}, \gamma) > 0$ for every $\mathbf{w}$ in the support of $\mathbf{W}$ and $\gamma \in \mathcal{G}$.

– *C7*: the function $\pi(\mathbf{w}, \gamma)$ is differentiable with respect to γ for every $\mathbf{w}$, and there exists a bounded function g such that for every $\gamma, \tilde{\gamma} \in \mathcal{G}$, $|\pi(\mathbf{w}, \gamma) - \pi(\mathbf{w}, \tilde{\gamma})| \leq g(\mathbf{w})\|\gamma - \tilde{\gamma}\|$ (we will denote $\mathbb{E}[g(\mathbf{W})] = u$).

We can now state the asymptotic properties of $\breve{\beta}_n$ (the proofs are given in sections 3.3.4 and 3.3.5).

THEOREM 3.5.– *Suppose that C1 to C7 are satisfied. If at least one of the two models $m(\mathbf{W}_i, \theta)$ and $\pi(\mathbf{W}_i, \gamma)$ is well-specified, then $\breve{\beta}_n \xrightarrow[n\to\infty]{\mathbb{P}} \beta_0$.*

We recover the double robustness property of the AIPW estimator, which is consistent even if one of the two models $m(\mathbf{W}_i, \theta)$ or $\pi(\mathbf{W}_i, \gamma)$ is incorrect. The AIPW estimator is also asymptotically Gaussian even if one of the two models is misspecified. The asymptotic variance depends on the situation.

THEOREM 3.6.– *Under the conditions C1 to C7, $\sqrt{n}(\breve{\beta}_n - \beta_0) \xrightarrow[n\to\infty]{\mathcal{L}} \mathcal{N}(0, \mathbf{J})$, where:*

$$\mathbf{J} = \begin{cases} \Sigma_1^{-1}(\beta_0)\Sigma_7(\beta_0, \theta_0, \gamma^*)\Sigma_1^{-1}(\beta_0) \text{ if } m(\mathbf{W}_i, \theta) \text{ is well-specified} \\ \Sigma_1^{-1}(\beta_0)\Sigma_8(\beta_0, \theta^*, \gamma_0)\Sigma_1^{-1}(\beta_0) \text{ if } \pi(\mathbf{W}_i, \gamma) \text{ is well-specified} \\ \Sigma_1^{-1}(\beta_0) \text{ if } m(\mathbf{W}_i, \theta) \text{ and } \pi(\mathbf{W}_i, \gamma) \text{ are both well-specified} \end{cases}$$

REMARK.– When $m(\mathbf{W}_i, \theta)$ and $\pi(\mathbf{W}_i, \gamma)$ are both correct, the asymptotic variance of $\breve{\beta}_n$ coincides with that of the MLE in the censored Poisson regression model without missing data. ■

To construct a consistent estimator of $\mathbf{J}$, we form the following matrices, which are empirical versions of the ones that feature in the expression for $\mathbf{J}$:

$$\breve{\Sigma}_{1,n}(\beta, \theta, \gamma) = \frac{1}{n}\sum_{i=1}^{n} \mathbf{X}_i\mathbf{X}_i^\top \Big(\breve{\delta}_i(\theta, \gamma)e^{\beta^\top \mathbf{X}_i}$$

$$+(\breve{\delta}_i(\theta, \gamma) - 1)\left\{Y_i^* - e^{\beta^\top \mathbf{X}_i} - h_\beta(Y_i^*, \mathbf{X}_i)\right\} h_\beta(Y_i^*, \mathbf{X}_i)\Big)$$

$$\Sigma_{4,n}(\gamma) = \frac{1}{n}\sum_{i=1}^{n} \frac{\dot{\pi}^{\otimes 2}(\mathbf{W}_i, \gamma)}{\pi(\mathbf{W}_i, \gamma)(1 - \pi(\mathbf{W}_i, \gamma))}$$

$$\Sigma_{5,n}(\beta,\theta,\gamma) = \frac{1}{n}\sum_{i=1}^{n} \mathbf{X}_i \left(Y_i^* - e^{\beta^\top \mathbf{X}_i} - h_\beta(Y_i^*, \mathbf{X}_i)\right)$$
$$\times \left(1 - \frac{\xi_i}{\pi(\mathbf{W}_i,\gamma)}\right) \dot{m}^\top(\mathbf{W}_i,\theta)$$
$$\Sigma_{6,n}(\beta,\theta,\gamma) = \frac{1}{n}\sum_{i=1}^{n} \mathbf{X}_i \left(Y_i^* - e^{\beta^\top \mathbf{X}_i} - h_\beta(Y_i^*, \mathbf{X}_i)\right)\xi_i$$
$$\times \frac{\dot{\pi}^\top(\mathbf{W}_i,\gamma)}{\pi^2(\mathbf{W}_i,\gamma)} \left(m(\mathbf{W}_i,\theta) - \delta_i\right)$$
$$\Sigma_{7,n}(\beta,\theta,\gamma) = \breve{\Sigma}_{1,n}(\beta,\theta,\gamma) + (2\Sigma_{3,n}(\beta,\theta)$$
$$-\Sigma_{5,n}(\beta,\theta,\gamma))\,\Theta_n^{-1}(\theta)\Sigma_{5,n}^\top(\beta,\theta,\gamma)$$

and:

$$\Sigma_{8,n}(\beta,\theta,\gamma) = \breve{\Sigma}_{1,n}(\beta,\theta,\gamma) - \Sigma_{6,n}(\beta,\theta,\gamma)\Sigma_{4,n}^{-1}(\gamma)\Sigma_{6,n}^\top(\beta,\theta,\gamma)$$

The matrices $\Sigma_{3,n}$ and Θ_n are the ones given in section 3.2.4.1.1. A consistent estimator of $\mathbf{J}$ is therefore:

$$\mathbf{J}_n = \begin{cases} \breve{\Sigma}_{1,n}^{-1}(\breve{\beta}_n,\hat{\theta}_n,\hat{\gamma}_n)\Sigma_{7,n}(\breve{\beta}_n,\hat{\theta}_n,\hat{\gamma}_n)\breve{\Sigma}_{1,n}^{-1}(\breve{\beta}_n,\hat{\theta}_n,\hat{\gamma}_n) \text{ if } m(\mathbf{W}_i,\theta) \\ \text{is well-specified} \\ \breve{\Sigma}_{1,n}^{-1}(\breve{\beta}_n,\hat{\theta}_n,\hat{\gamma}_n)\Sigma_{8,n}(\breve{\beta}_n,\hat{\theta}_n,\hat{\gamma}_n)\breve{\Sigma}_{1,n}^{-1}(\breve{\beta}_n,\hat{\theta}_n,\hat{\gamma}_n) \text{ if } \pi(\mathbf{W}_i,\gamma) \\ \text{is well-specified} \\ \breve{\Sigma}_{1,n}^{-1}(\breve{\beta}_n,\hat{\theta}_n,\hat{\gamma}_n) \text{ if } m(\mathbf{W}_i,\theta) \text{ and } \pi(\mathbf{W}_i,\gamma) \text{ are both} \\ \text{well-specified} \end{cases}$$

In Bousselmi et al. (2021), the authors report the results of a simulation study that compares the complete-case and AIPW estimators, along with those obtained from regression calibration and multiple imputation. Doing so, several observations can be made:

– If the selection probabilities of the complete cases ($\pi(\mathbf{W}_i,\gamma)$ model) are misspecified and $m(\mathbf{W}_i,\theta)$ is well-specified, the estimators obtained by regression calibration, multiple imputation and the AIPW estimator perform equivalently (in terms of bias, standard error, mean squared error and coverage probabilities). This illustrates the robustness of the AIPW estimator, which is the only one susceptible of being sensitive to this misspecification, since the imputation methods do not use the $\pi(\mathbf{W}_i,\gamma)$ model.

– If the model for δ_i given $\mathbf{W}_i$ ($m(\mathbf{W}_i,\theta)$ model) is misspecified and $\pi(\mathbf{W}_i,\gamma)$ is well-specified, the imputation estimators are affected by a bias which degrades their performances, notably the coverage probabilities. On the other hand, the performances of the AIPW estimator are maintained at a correct level when the proportion of the censored data remains moderate (around 0.2 in the simulations reported in Bousselmi et al. (2021), but this proportion can depend on the number of explanatory variables or the size of the sample). When the proportion of censored data is greater (0.4 in the simulations), the AIPW estimator has a more important bias, suggesting that although it is doubly robust, it is more sensitive to a misspecification of $m(\mathbf{W}_i,\theta)$ than of $\pi(\mathbf{W}_i,\gamma)$. This can be explained by the expression for $\breve{\delta}_i(\theta,\gamma)$:

$$\begin{aligned}\breve{\delta}_i(\theta,\gamma) &= m(\mathbf{W}_i,\theta)+\xi_i\left(\frac{\delta_i-m(\mathbf{W}_i,\theta)}{\pi(\mathbf{W}_i,\gamma)}\right)\\ &= \begin{cases} m(\mathbf{W}_i,\theta) & \text{if } \xi_i=0\\ m(\mathbf{W}_i,\theta)+\left(\frac{\delta_i-m(\mathbf{W}_i,\theta)}{\pi(\mathbf{W}_i,\gamma)}\right) & \text{if } \xi_i=1\end{cases}\end{aligned}$$

When $m(\mathbf{W}_i,\theta)$ is incorrect, each individual contributes to the likelihood with a misspecified term, whether ξ_i is equal to either 0 or to 1. On the other hand, when $\pi(\mathbf{W}_i,\gamma)$ is incorrect, only the complete cases contribute to the likelihood with a misspecified term. Thus, a misspecification of $\pi(\mathbf{W}_i,\gamma)$ affects the estimator less than a misspecification of $m(\mathbf{W}_i,\theta)$ does.

– When the two models are specified correctly, the different estimators perform similarly.

– The complete-case estimator is outperformed by its three competitors in each scenario.

To summarize, the imputation and AIPW estimators have comparable performances when either $m(\mathbf{W}_i,\theta)$ or both of the two models $m(\mathbf{W}_i,\theta)$ and $\pi(\mathbf{W}_i,\gamma)$ are well-specified. The AIPW estimator is better than the imputation ones when $m(\mathbf{W}_i,\theta)$ is misspecified.

3.2.5. *A missing data problem in the gamma regression model*

The context here is that of the gamma regression model with a right-censored response, as described in section 3.1.3. Again, we adopt the notation of section 3.2.4.

Suppose we have available a sample of independent observations $\{\mathcal{O}_i, i=1,\dots,n\}$, where $\mathcal{O}_i=(Y_i^*,\mathbf{X}_i,\delta_i)$ if $\xi_i=1$ and $\mathcal{O}_i=(Y_i^*,\mathbf{X}_i)$ if $\xi_i=0$, $Y_i^*=\min(Y_i,C_i)$, and Y_i given $\mathbf{X}_i$ follows a gamma distribution of density:

$$f(y|\mathbf{X}_i)=y^{\nu-1}\exp\left(-\frac{y\nu}{\mu_i}\right)\left(\frac{\nu}{\mu_i}\right)^{\nu}\frac{1}{\Gamma(\nu)},\quad y\in\mathbb{R}_+$$

where $\mu_i = \exp(\beta^\top \mathbf{X}_i)$ and C_i is an independent and non-informative censoring variable.

As in section 3.2.4, we assume that the distributions of δ_i and ξ_i given $\mathbf{W}_i$ can be described by the parametric models $\mathbb{P}(\delta_i = 1|\mathbf{W}_i) = m(\mathbf{W}_i, \theta_0)$ and $\mathbb{P}(\xi_i = 1|\mathbf{W}_i) = \pi(\mathbf{W}_i, \gamma_0)$. The parameters $\theta_0, \gamma_0 \in \mathbb{R}^q$ are estimated by maximum likelihood.

In the absence of missing data, recall that the log-likelihood of (ν, β) is written as:

$$\ell_n(\nu, \beta) = \sum_{i=1}^{n} \Big\{ \delta_i \Big((\nu - 1) \ln Y_i^* + \nu \ln \nu - \nu \beta^\top \mathbf{X}_i - Y_i^* \nu e^{-\beta^\top \mathbf{X}_i} - \ln \Gamma(\nu) \Big)$$

$$+ (1 - \delta_i) \ln \left(\frac{\Gamma(\nu, \nu Y_i^* e^{-\beta^\top \mathbf{X}_i})}{\Gamma(\nu)} \right) \Big\} \qquad [3.13]$$

3.2.5.1. *Imputation estimators*

An estimator of (ν, β) based upon regression calibration is obtained by replacing δ_i with:

$$\delta_i^{(1)}(\hat{\theta}_n) = \xi_i \delta_i + (1 - \xi_i) m(\mathbf{W}_i, \hat{\theta}_n)$$

in [3.13], and then by maximizing with respect to (ν, β). We will denote this estimator by $(\hat{\nu}_n^{(1)}, \hat{\beta}_n^{(1)})$.

To construct an estimator using multiple imputation, we begin by forming J completed samples. A completed sample is obtained by replacing each missing δ_i by a value simulated from the Bernoulli distribution $\mathcal{B}(m(\mathbf{W}_i, \hat{\theta}_n))$. Denote by $D_{i,j}(\hat{\theta}_n) \sim \mathcal{B}(m(\mathbf{W}_i, \hat{\theta}_n))$ the imputed value for individual i in the j-th sample. Also denote by:

$$\delta_{i,j}^{(2)}(\theta) = \xi_i \delta_i + (1 - \xi_i) D_{i,j}(\theta)$$

the variable which equals δ_i if δ_i is observed and equals $D_{i,j}(\theta)$ otherwise.

We estimate (ν, β) in the jth completed sample by maximizing the log-likelihood [3.13], in which each δ_i is replaced by $\delta_{i,j}^{(2)}(\hat{\theta}_n)$. We denote the resulting estimator by $(\hat{\nu}_{n,j}^{(2)}, \hat{\beta}_{n,j}^{(2)})$. The final estimator of (ν, β) is produced by averaging over the $(\hat{\nu}_{n,j}^{(2)}, \hat{\beta}_{n,j}^{(2)})$:

$$\hat{\nu}_n^{(2)} = \frac{1}{J} \sum_{j=1}^{J} \hat{\nu}_{n,j}^{(2)} \quad \text{and} \quad \hat{\beta}_n^{(2)} = \frac{1}{J} \sum_{j=1}^{J} \hat{\beta}_{n,j}^{(2)}$$

3.2.5.1.1. Some notation and regularity hypotheses

Here, we will resume – and furthermore complete – the notation first introduced in sections 3.1.3 and 3.2.4. In particular, recall that we defined the matrices $\Omega_1(\nu, \beta)$ and $\Theta(\theta)$. Now let us define the following ones:

$$\Omega_2(\nu, \beta, \theta) = \begin{pmatrix} \mathbb{E}\left(\dot{m}^\top(\mathbf{W}, \theta)\left(\ln Y^* + \ln \nu + 1 - \beta^\top \mathbf{X} - Y^* e^{-\beta^\top \mathbf{X}} - h_{\nu,\beta}(Y^*, \mathbf{X})\right) \\ (1 - \pi(\mathbf{W}))\right) \\ \mathbb{E}\left(\mathbf{X}\dot{m}^\top(\mathbf{W}, \theta)\left(Y^* \nu e^{-\beta^\top \mathbf{X}} - \nu - g_{\nu,\beta}(Y^*, \mathbf{X})\right)(1 - \pi(\mathbf{W}))\right) \end{pmatrix}$$

and:

$$\Omega_3(\nu, \beta, \theta) = \begin{pmatrix} \mathbb{E}\left(\dot{m}^\top(\mathbf{W}, \theta)\left(\ln Y^* + \ln \nu + 1 - \beta^\top \mathbf{X} - Y^* e^{-\beta^\top \mathbf{X}} - h_{\nu,\beta}(Y^*, \mathbf{X})\right) \\ (\pi(\mathbf{W}) + 1)\right) \\ \mathbb{E}\left(\mathbf{X}\dot{m}^\top(\mathbf{W}, \theta)\left(Y^* \nu e^{-\beta^\top \mathbf{X}} - \nu - g_{\nu,\beta}(Y^*, \mathbf{X})\right)(\pi(\mathbf{W}) + 1)\right) \end{pmatrix}$$

where $\pi(\mathbf{W}) = \mathbb{P}(\xi = 1|\mathbf{W})$. For each individual $i = 1, \ldots, n$ and each completed sample $j = 1, \ldots, J$, we also denote:

$$L^{(j)}_{1,\nu,\beta,\theta}(\mathcal{O}_i) = \delta^{(2)}_{i,j}(\theta)\left(\ln Y_i^* + \ln \nu + 1 - \beta^\top \mathbf{X}_i - Y_i^* e^{-\beta^\top \mathbf{X}_i} - h_{\nu,\beta}(Y_i^*, \mathbf{X}_i)\right)$$
$$+ h_{\nu,\beta}(Y_i^*, \mathbf{X}_i) - \psi(\nu)$$

where $\psi(\nu) := \partial \log \Gamma(\nu)/\partial \nu$, and:

$$L^{(j)}_{2,\nu,\beta,\theta}(\mathcal{O}_i) = \mathbf{X}_i\left(\delta^{(2)}_{i,j}(\theta)\left[Y_i^* \nu e^{-\beta^\top \mathbf{X}_i} - \nu - g_{\nu,\beta}(Y_i^*, \mathbf{X}_i)\right] + g_{\nu,\beta}(Y_i^*, \mathbf{X}_i)\right)$$

Finally, denote by $L^{(j)}_{\nu,\beta,\theta}(\mathcal{O}_i)$ the column vector $L^{(j)}_{\nu,\beta,\theta}(\mathcal{O}_i) := (L^{(j)}_{1,\nu,\beta,\theta}(\mathcal{O}_i), L^{(j)}_{2,\nu,\beta,\theta}(\mathcal{O}_i)^\top)^\top$, and:

$$\Omega_4(\nu, \beta, \theta) = \text{var}\left(\frac{1}{J}\sum_{j=1}^{J} L^{(j)}_{\nu,\beta,\theta}(\mathcal{O}_1)\right)$$

Some regularity hypotheses will be necessary in what follows:

– *H1*: the true values ν_0, β_0, and θ_0 of the parameters belong to the interiors of compact subsets of $\mathbb{R}_+^*$, $\mathbb{R}^p$, and $\mathbb{R}^q$, respectively.

– *H2*: the variables $\mathbf{X}_i$ are bounded.

– *H3*: the function $m(\mathbf{w}, \theta)$ is differentiable with respect to θ for every $\mathbf{w}$, and there exists a bounded function h such that for every θ and $\tilde{\theta} \in \Theta$, $|m(\mathbf{w}, \theta) - m(\mathbf{w}, \tilde{\theta})| \leq h(\mathbf{w})\|\theta - \tilde{\theta}\|$.

3.2.5.1.2. Asymptotic results

The two theorems below state some asymptotic properties of imputation estimators. To simplify the notation, denote $\Omega_{1,0} = \Omega_1(\nu_0, \beta_0)$ and $\Omega_{j,0} = \Omega_j(\nu_0, \beta_0, \theta_0)$, $j = 2, 3, 4$.

THEOREM 3.7.– *Suppose that conditions H1, H2 and H3 are satisfied. Then* $(\hat{\nu}_n^{(1)}, \hat{\beta}_n^{(1)}) \xrightarrow[n\to\infty]{\mathbb{P}} (\nu_0, \beta_0)$ *and:*

$$\sqrt{n}\begin{pmatrix} \hat{\nu}_n^{(1)} - \nu_0 \\ \hat{\beta}_n^{(1)} - \beta_0 \end{pmatrix} \xrightarrow[n\to\infty]{\mathcal{L}} \mathcal{N}(0, \Omega^{(1)})$$

where $\Omega^{(1)} = \Omega_{1,0}^{-1}(\Omega_{1,0} + \Omega_{3,0}\Theta_{\theta_0}^{-1}\Omega_{2,0}^\top)\Omega_{1,0}^{-1}$.

A consistent estimator of $\Omega^{(1)}$ is obtained by replacing the expectations with empirical means, and the parameters with their estimators, in $\Omega_{1,0}, \Omega_{2,0}, \Omega_{3,0}$ and Θ_{θ_0}.

So let us form the matrices:

$$\widehat{\Omega}_{1,n} = \begin{pmatrix} \widehat{\Omega}_{1,n}^{\nu,\nu}(\hat{\nu}_n^{(1)}, \hat{\beta}_n^{(1)}, \hat{\theta}_n) & \widehat{\Omega}_{1,n}^{\nu,\beta}(\hat{\nu}_n^{(1)}, \hat{\beta}_n^{(1)}, \hat{\theta}_n) \\ (\widehat{\Omega}_{1,n}^{\nu,\beta}(\hat{\nu}_n^{(1)}, \hat{\beta}_n^{(1)}, \hat{\theta}_n))^\top & \widehat{\Omega}_{1,n}^{\beta,\beta}(\hat{\nu}_n^{(1)}, \hat{\beta}_n^{(1)}, \hat{\theta}_n) \end{pmatrix}$$

where:

$$\widehat{\Omega}_{1,n}^{\nu,\nu}(\hat{\nu}_n^{(1)}, \hat{\beta}_n^{(1)}, \hat{\theta}_n) =$$

$$\frac{1}{n}\sum_{i=1}^n \left\{ -\frac{\delta_i^{(1)}(\hat{\theta}_n)}{\hat{\nu}_n^{(1)}} + (\delta_i^{(1)}(\hat{\theta}_n) - 1)\frac{\partial}{\partial \nu} h_{\hat{\nu}_n^{(1)}, \hat{\beta}_n^{(1)}}(Y_i^*, \mathbf{X}_i) + \frac{\partial^2}{\partial \nu^2} \ln\Gamma(\hat{\nu}_n^{(1)}) \right\}$$

$$\widehat{\Omega}_{1,n}^{\beta,\beta}(\hat{\nu}_n^{(1)}, \hat{\beta}_n^{(1)}, \hat{\theta}_n) = \frac{1}{n}\sum_{i=1}^n \left\{ \mathbf{X}_i\mathbf{X}_i^\top \left(\delta_i^{(1)}(\hat{\theta}_n) Y_i^* \hat{\nu}_n^{(1)} e^{-\hat{\beta}_n^{(1)\top}\mathbf{X}_i} \right.\right.$$

$$\left.\left. + (\delta_i^{(1)}(\hat{\theta}_n) - 1) g_{\hat{\nu}_n^{(1)}, \hat{\beta}_n^{(1)}}(Y_i^*, \mathbf{X}_i) \left(\hat{\nu}_n^{(1)} Y_i^* e^{-\hat{\beta}_n^{(1)\top}\mathbf{X}_i} - \hat{\nu}_n^{(1)} - g_{\hat{\nu}_n^{(1)}, \hat{\beta}_n^{(1)}}(Y_i^*, \mathbf{X}_i) \right) \right) \right\}$$

$$\widehat{\Omega}_{1,n}^{\nu,\beta}(\hat{\nu}_n^{(1)}, \hat{\beta}_n^{(1)}, \hat{\theta}_n) =$$

$$\frac{1}{n}\sum_{i=1}^{n}\left\{\mathbf{X}_i^\top\left(\delta_i^{(1)}(\hat{\theta}_n)(1 - Y_i^* e^{-\hat{\beta}_n^{(1)\top}\mathbf{X}_i}) + (\delta_i^{(1)}(\hat{\theta}_n) - 1)\frac{\partial}{\partial \nu} g_{\hat{\nu}_n^{(1)}, \hat{\beta}_n^{(1)}}(Y_i^*, \mathbf{X}_i)\right)\right\}$$

and:

$$\widehat{\Omega}_{2,n} =$$

$$\begin{pmatrix} \frac{1}{n}\sum_{i=1}^n \dot{m}^\top(\mathbf{W}_i, \hat{\theta}_n) \\ \quad \times\left(\ln Y_i^* + \ln \hat{\nu}_n^{(1)} + 1 - \hat{\beta}_n^{(1)\top}\mathbf{X}_i - Y_i^* e^{-\hat{\beta}_n^{(1)\top}\mathbf{X}_i} - h_{\hat{\nu}_n^{(1)}, \hat{\beta}_n^{(1)}}(Y_i^*, \mathbf{X}_i)\right)(1 - \xi_i) \\ \frac{1}{n}\sum_{i=1}^n \mathbf{X}_i \dot{m}^\top(\mathbf{W}_i, \hat{\theta}_n)\left(Y_i^* \hat{\nu}_n^{(1)} e^{-\hat{\beta}_n^{(1)\top}\mathbf{X}_i} - \hat{\nu}_n^{(1)} - g_{\hat{\nu}_n^{(1)}, \hat{\beta}_n^{(1)}}(Y_i^*, \mathbf{X}_i)\right)(1 - \xi_i) \end{pmatrix}$$

$$\widehat{\Omega}_{3,n} =$$

$$\begin{pmatrix} \frac{1}{n}\sum_{i=1}^n \dot{m}^\top(\mathbf{W}_i, \hat{\theta}_n) \\ \quad \times\left(\ln Y_i^* + \ln \hat{\nu}_n^{(1)} + 1 - \hat{\beta}_n^{(1)\top}\mathbf{X}_i - Y_i^* e^{-\hat{\beta}_n^{(1)\top}\mathbf{X}_i} - h_{\hat{\nu}_n^{(1)}, \hat{\beta}_n^{(1)}}(Y_i^*, \mathbf{X}_i)\right)(1 + \xi_i) \\ \frac{1}{n}\sum_{i=1}^n \mathbf{X}_i \dot{m}^\top(\mathbf{W}_i, \hat{\theta}_n)\left(Y_i^* \hat{\nu}_n^{(1)} e^{-\hat{\beta}_n^{(1)\top}\mathbf{X}_i} - \hat{\nu}_n^{(1)} - g_{\hat{\nu}_n^{(1)}, \hat{\beta}_n^{(1)}}(Y_i^*, \mathbf{X}_i)\right)(1 + \xi_i) \end{pmatrix}$$

Also recall the expression:

$$\Theta_n(\theta) = \frac{1}{n}\sum_{i=1}^{n}\frac{\dot{m}^{\otimes 2}(\mathbf{W}_i, \theta)}{m(\mathbf{W}_i, \theta)(1 - m(\mathbf{W}_i, \theta))}\xi_i$$

A consistent estimator of $\Omega^{(1)}$ is:

$$\widehat{\Omega}_{1,n}^{-1}(\widehat{\Omega}_{1,n} + \widehat{\Omega}_{3,n}\Theta_n^{-1}(\hat{\theta}_n)\widehat{\Omega}_{2,n}^\top)\widehat{\Omega}_{1,n}^{-1}$$

THEOREM 3.8.– *Suppose that conditions H1, H2 and H3 are satisfied. Then* $(\hat{\nu}_n^{(2)}, \hat{\beta}_n^{(2)}) \xrightarrow[n\to\infty]{\mathbb{P}} (\nu_0, \beta_0)$ *and:*

$$\sqrt{n}\begin{pmatrix} \hat{\nu}_n^{(2)} - \nu_0 \\ \hat{\beta}_n^{(2)} - \beta_0 \end{pmatrix} \xrightarrow[n\to\infty]{\mathcal{L}} \mathcal{N}(0, \Omega^{(2)})$$

where $\Omega^{(2)} = \Omega_{1,0}^{-1}(\Omega_{4,0} + \Omega_{3,0}\Theta_{\theta_0}^{-1}\Omega_{2,0}^\top)\Omega_{1,0}^{-1}$.

We denote by $\widehat{\Omega}_{1,n,j}$ the matrix calculated in the same way that $\widehat{\Omega}_{1,n}$ was, albeit now with $(\hat{\nu}_n^{(1)}, \hat{\beta}_n^{(1)})$ replaced by $(\hat{\nu}_n^{(2)}, \hat{\beta}_n^{(2)})$ and $\delta_i^{(1)}(\hat{\theta}_n)$ by $\delta_{i,j}^{(2)}(\hat{\theta}_n)$.

Set:

$$\overline{\Omega}_{1,n} = \frac{1}{J}\sum_{j=1}^{J}\widehat{\Omega}_{1,n,j}$$

and let $\widehat{\Omega}_{4,n}$ denote the empirical variance of:

$$\frac{1}{J}\sum_{j=1}^{J} L^{(j)}_{\hat{\nu}_n^{(2)},\hat{\beta}_n^{(2)},\hat{\theta}_n}(\mathcal{O}_1),\ldots,\frac{1}{J}\sum_{j=1}^{J} L^{(j)}_{\hat{\nu}_n^{(2)},\hat{\beta}_n^{(2)},\hat{\theta}_n}(\mathcal{O}_n)$$

Finally, calculate $\widehat{\Omega}_{2,n}$ and $\widehat{\Omega}_{3,n}$ by replacing $(\hat{\nu}_n^{(1)},\hat{\beta}_n^{(1)})$ by $(\hat{\nu}_n^{(2)},\hat{\beta}_n^{(2)})$. A consistent estimator of $\Omega^{(2)}$ is:

$$\overline{\Omega}_{1,n}^{-1}(\widehat{\Omega}_{4,n} + \widehat{\Omega}_{3,n}\Theta_n^{-1}(\hat{\theta}_n)\widehat{\Omega}_{2,n}^{\top})\overline{\Omega}_{1,n}^{-1}$$

3.2.5.2. *AIPW estimator*

The AIPW estimator of (ν,β) is obtained by replacing δ_i in [3.13] by:

$$\delta_i^{(3)}(\hat{\theta}_n,\hat{\gamma}_n) = m(\mathbf{W}_i,\hat{\theta}_n) + \xi_i\left(\frac{\delta_i - m(\mathbf{W}_i,\hat{\theta}_n)}{\pi(\mathbf{W}_i,\hat{\gamma}_n)}\right)$$

We denote it by $(\hat{\nu}_n^{(3)},\hat{\beta}_n^{(3)})$.

Recall that, if the models $\pi(\mathbf{W}_i,\gamma_0)$ and $m(\mathbf{W}_i,\theta_0)$ are misspecified, then $\hat{\gamma}_n$ and $\hat{\theta}_n$ converge to the values $\gamma^* \neq \gamma_0$ and $\theta^* \neq \theta_0$, as shown in White (1982). Otherwise, $\hat{\gamma}_n$ and $\hat{\theta}_n$ converge to γ_0 and θ_0. Also recall the notation:

$$\Sigma_4(\gamma) = \mathbb{E}\left[\frac{\dot{\pi}^{\otimes 2}(\mathbf{W},\gamma)}{\pi(\mathbf{W},\gamma)(1-\pi(\mathbf{W},\gamma))}\right]$$

and define the matrices:

$$\Omega_5(\nu,\beta,\theta,\gamma) =$$
$$\begin{pmatrix} \mathbb{E}\left(\left\{1-\frac{\xi}{\pi(\mathbf{W},\gamma)}\right\}\dot{m}^{\top}(\mathbf{W}_i,\theta)\right. \\ \quad\left.\times\left(\ln Y^* + \ln\nu + 1 - \beta^{\top}\mathbf{X} - Y^*e^{-\beta^{\top}\mathbf{X}} - h_{\nu,\beta}(Y^*,\mathbf{X})\right)\right) \\ \mathbb{E}\left(\mathbf{X}\left\{1-\frac{\xi}{\pi(\mathbf{W},\gamma)}\right\}\dot{m}^{\top}(\mathbf{W}_i,\theta)\left(Y^*\nu e^{-\beta^{\top}\mathbf{X}} - \nu - g_{\nu,\beta}(Y^*,\mathbf{X})\right)\right) \end{pmatrix}$$

and:

$$\Omega_6(\nu,\beta,\theta,\gamma) =$$
$$\begin{pmatrix} \mathbb{E}\left((m(\mathbf{W},\theta)-\delta)\xi\frac{\dot{\pi}^\top(\mathbf{W},\gamma)}{\pi^2(\mathbf{W},\gamma)} \right. \\ \left. \times\left(\ln Y^* + \ln\nu + 1 - \beta^\top\mathbf{X} - Y^* e^{-\beta^\top\mathbf{X}} - h_{\nu,\beta}(Y^*,\mathbf{X})\right)\right) \\ \mathbb{E}\left(\mathbf{X}(m(\mathbf{W},\theta)-\delta)\xi\frac{\dot{\pi}^\top(\mathbf{W},\gamma)}{\pi^2(\mathbf{W},\gamma)}\left(Y^*\nu e^{-\beta^\top\mathbf{X}} - \nu - g_{\nu,\beta}(Y^*,\mathbf{X})\right)\right) \end{pmatrix}$$

Some additional regularity hypotheses are required:

– *H4*: the true value γ_0 of γ belongs to the interior of a compact subset $\mathcal{G}$ of $\mathbb{R}^q$.

– *H5*: the function $\pi(\cdot,\cdot)$ is such that $\pi(\mathbf{w},\gamma) > 0$ for every $\mathbf{w}$ in the support of $\mathbf{W}$ and every γ. Furthermore, $\pi(\mathbf{w},\gamma)$ is differentiable with respect to γ for every $\mathbf{w}$, and there exists a bounded function g such that for every $\gamma,\tilde{\gamma}\in\mathcal{G}$, $|\pi(\mathbf{w},\gamma)-\pi(\mathbf{w},\tilde{\gamma})| \leq g(\mathbf{w})\|\gamma-\tilde{\gamma}\|$.

We can now state the asymptotic properties of the AIPW estimator:

THEOREM 3.9.– *Suppose that conditions H1 to H5 are satisfied. If at least one of the two models $m(\mathbf{W}_i,\theta)$ and $\pi(\mathbf{W}_i,\gamma)$ is well-specified, then:*

$$(\hat{\nu}_n^{(3)},\hat{\beta}_n^{(3)}) \xrightarrow[n\to\infty]{\mathbb{P}} (\nu_0,\beta_0)$$

Furthermore:

$$\sqrt{n}\begin{pmatrix}\hat{\nu}_n^{(3)}-\nu_0\\ \hat{\beta}_n^{(3)}-\beta_0\end{pmatrix} \xrightarrow{d} N\left(0,\mathbf{J}(\nu_0,\beta_0,\theta_*,\gamma_*)\right)$$

where:

$$\mathbf{J}(\nu_0,\beta_0,\theta_*,\gamma_*) = \begin{cases} \Omega_{1,0}^{-1}(\Omega_{1,0}+\{\Omega_{2,0}+\Omega_{3,0}-\Omega_5(\nu_0,\beta_0,\theta_0,\gamma_*)\} \\ \quad\times\Theta^{-1}(\theta_0)\Omega_5^\top(\nu_0,\beta_0,\theta_0,\gamma_*))\Omega_{1,0}^{-1} \\ \text{if } m(\mathbf{W}_i,\theta) \text{ is well-specified} \\ \\ \Omega_{1,0}^{-1}(\Omega_{1,0}-\Omega_6(\nu_0,\beta_0,\theta_*,\gamma_0)\Sigma_4^{-1}(\gamma_0)\Omega_6^\top(\nu_0,\beta_0,\theta_*,\gamma_0))\Omega_{1,0}^{-1} \\ \text{if } \pi(\mathbf{W}_i,\gamma) \text{ is well-specified} \\ \\ \Omega_{1,0}^{-1} \text{ if } m(\mathbf{W}_i,\theta) \text{ and } \pi(\mathbf{W}_i,\gamma) \text{ are both well-specified} \end{cases}$$

Here again, the AIPW estimator is doubly robust (i.e. it is consistent even when one of the two models $m(\mathbf{W}_i,\theta)$ or $\pi(\mathbf{W}_i,\gamma)$ is incorrect). It is also asymptotically

Gaussian even when $m(\mathbf{W}_i, \theta)$ or $\pi(\mathbf{W}_i, \gamma)$ is misspecified. When $m(\mathbf{W}_i, \theta)$ and $\pi(\mathbf{W}_i, \gamma)$ are both correct, its asymptotic variance coincides with that of the MLE in the censored gamma regression model but without missing data (theorem 3.2).

To estimate $\mathbf{J}$, consider the matrices $\widehat{\Omega}_{1,n}, \widehat{\Omega}_{2,n}$ and $\widehat{\Omega}_{3,n}$ again, which were introduced in section 3.2.5.1.2 (they are now calculated using $\hat{\nu}_n^{(3)}, \hat{\beta}_n^{(3)}$ and $\delta_i^{(3)}(\hat{\theta}_n, \hat{\gamma}_n)$), along with the matrix $\Sigma_{4,n}(\gamma)$ (section 3.2.4.3.1). Introduce the empirical versions of Ω_5 and Ω_6:

$$\widehat{\Omega}_{5,n} =$$

$$\begin{pmatrix} \frac{1}{n}\sum_{i=1}^{n}\left\{1 - \frac{\xi_i}{\pi(\mathbf{W}_i, \hat{\gamma}_n)}\right\} \dot{m}^{\top}(\mathbf{W}_i, \hat{\theta}_n)\left(\ln Y_i^* + \ln \hat{\nu}_n^{(3)} + 1 - \hat{\beta}_n^{(3)\top}\mathbf{X}_i \right. \\ \left. -Y_i^* e^{-\hat{\beta}_n^{(3)\top}\mathbf{X}_i} - h_{\hat{\nu}_n^{(3)}, \hat{\beta}_n^{(3)}}(Y_i^*, \mathbf{X}_i)\right) \\ \frac{1}{n}\sum_{i=1}^{n}\mathbf{X}_i\left\{1 - \frac{\xi_i}{\pi(\mathbf{W}_i, \hat{\gamma}_n)}\right\} \dot{m}^{\top}(\mathbf{W}_i, \hat{\theta}_n) \\ \times\left(Y_i^* \hat{\nu}_n^{(3)} e^{-\hat{\beta}_n^{(3)\top}\mathbf{X}_i} - \hat{\nu}_n^{(3)} - g_{\hat{\nu}_n^{(3)}, \hat{\beta}_n^{(3)}}(Y_i^*, \mathbf{X}_i)\right) \end{pmatrix}$$

and:

$$\widehat{\Omega}_{6,n} =$$

$$\begin{pmatrix} \frac{1}{n}\sum_{i=1}^{n}(m(\mathbf{W}_i, \hat{\theta}_n) - \delta_i^3(\hat{\theta}_n, \hat{\gamma}_n))\xi_i \frac{\dot{\pi}^{\top}(\mathbf{W}_i, \hat{\gamma}_n)}{\pi^2(\mathbf{W}_i, \hat{\gamma}_n)}\left(\ln Y_i^* + \ln \hat{\nu}_n^{(3)} + 1 \right. \\ \left. -\hat{\beta}_n^{(3)\top}\mathbf{X}_i - Y_i^* e^{-\hat{\beta}_n^{(3)\top}\mathbf{X}_i} - h_{\hat{\nu}_n^{(3)}, \hat{\beta}_n^{(3)}}(Y_i^*, \mathbf{X}_i)\right) \\ \frac{1}{n}\sum_{i=1}^{n}\mathbf{X}_i(m(\mathbf{W}_i, \hat{\theta}_n) - \delta_i^3(\hat{\theta}_n, \hat{\gamma}_n))\xi_i \frac{\dot{\pi}^{\top}(\mathbf{W}_i, \hat{\gamma}_n)}{\pi^2(\mathbf{W}_i, \hat{\gamma}_n)} \\ \times\left(Y_i^* \hat{\nu}_n^{(3)} e^{-\hat{\beta}_n^{(3)\top}\mathbf{X}_i} - \hat{\nu}_n^{(3)} - g_{\hat{\nu}_n^{(3)}, \hat{\beta}_n^{(3)}}(Y_i^*, \mathbf{X}_i)\right) \end{pmatrix}$$

A consistent estimator of $\mathbf{J}$ is:

$$\mathbf{J}_n = \begin{cases} \widehat{\Omega}_{1,n}^{-1}(\widehat{\Omega}_{1,n} + \{\widehat{\Omega}_{2,n} + \widehat{\Omega}_{3,n} - \widehat{\Omega}_{5,n}\}\Theta_n^{-1}(\hat{\theta}_n)\widehat{\Omega}_{5,n}^{\top})\widehat{\Omega}_{1,n}^{-1} \text{ if } m(\mathbf{W}_i, \theta) \\ \text{is well-specified} \\ \widehat{\Omega}_{1,n}^{-1}(\widehat{\Omega}_{1,n} - \widehat{\Omega}_{6,n}\Sigma_{4,n}^{-1}(\hat{\gamma}_n)\widehat{\Omega}_{6,n}^{\top})\widehat{\Omega}_{1,n}^{-1} \text{ if } \pi(\mathbf{W}_i, \gamma) \text{ is well-specified} \\ \widehat{\Omega}_{1,n}^{-1} \text{ if } m(\mathbf{W}_i, \theta) \text{ and } \pi(\mathbf{W}_i, \gamma) \text{ are both well-specified} \end{cases}$$

Missing data problems in GLMs have given rise to a great number of works. Among them, we mention some previous studies (Ibrahim 1990; Horton and Laird 1999; Ibrahim et al. 1999, 2005; Sinha 2008; Zhao and Shao 2015), which themselves provide a great number of references. Some authors have also considered GLMs with missing data in the covariates and/or the response variable. They have proposed imputation and AIPW estimators adapted to these settings. Obviously, the methods for missing data described in this chapter are not limited to just GLMs, and the reader should have no difficulty in finding applications to other regression models, such as duration models.

3.3. Technical appendix

In this section, we state the main lines of the proofs of theorems 3.3–3.6. They provide an idea of the techniques which can be used to establish the asymptotic results in regression models with missing data. The proofs of the other theorems stated in this chapter utilize similar arguments and are not discussed in detail.

Two technical lemmas that are useful for the proofs are the subject of section 3.3.1. Section 3.3.6 collects together some definitions and results related to empirical processes (these results are useful when proving lemma 3.1).

3.3.1. *Two lemmas*

First, let us introduce some notation:

$$\begin{aligned}\dot{\ell}^*_{n,j}(\beta,\theta) &= \frac{\partial \ell^*_{n,j}(\beta,\theta)}{\partial\beta}, \quad j=1,\ldots,M\\ &= \sum_{i=1}^n \mathbf{X}_i\left\{\delta^*_{i,j}(\theta)\left[Y_i^* - e^{\beta^\top \mathbf{X}_i} - h_\beta(Y_i^*,\mathbf{X}_i)\right] + h_\beta(Y_i^*,\mathbf{X}_i)\right\}\\ &= \sum_{i=1}^n f_{\beta,\theta,j}(\mathcal{O}_i)\end{aligned}$$

We have the following two lemmas:

LEMMA 3.1.– *Under the conditions C1, C2 and C4:*

$$\begin{aligned}&\frac{1}{\sqrt{n}}\left[\dot{\ell}^*_{n,j}(\beta_0,\hat{\theta}_n) - n\mathbb{E}[\dot{\ell}^*_{1,j}(\beta_0,\hat{\theta}_n)]\right.\\ &\left.\quad - \left(\dot{\ell}^*_{n,j}(\beta_0,\theta_0) - n\mathbb{E}[\dot{\ell}^*_{1,j}(\beta_0,\theta_0)]\right)\right] \xrightarrow[n\to\infty]{\mathbb{P}} 0\end{aligned} \qquad [3.14]$$

LEMMA 3.2.– *For each $j=1,\ldots,M$, we have:*

$$\frac{\partial \mathbb{E}[\dot{\ell}^*_{1,j}(\beta,\theta)]}{\partial\theta^\top} = \Sigma_2(\beta,\theta) \quad \textit{and} \quad \frac{1}{n}\frac{\partial \dot{\ell}^*_{n,j}(\beta_0,\hat{\theta}_n)}{\partial\beta^\top} \xrightarrow[n\to\infty]{\mathbb{P}} -\Sigma_1(\beta_0)$$

PROOF OF LEMMA 3.1.– To simplify the notation, we will write f_θ in the place of $f_{\beta_0,\theta,j}$. First of all, note that:

$$\frac{1}{\sqrt{n}}\left[\dot{\ell}^*_{n,j}(\beta_0,\theta) - n\mathbb{E}[\dot{\ell}^*_{1,j}(\beta_0,\theta)]\right] = \frac{1}{\sqrt{n}}\left[\sum_{i=1}^{n} f_\theta(\mathcal{O}_i) - n\mathbb{E}[f_\theta(\mathcal{O}_1)]\right]$$
$$= \mathbb{G}_n f_\theta$$

where $\mathbb{G}_n f_\theta$ denotes the empirical process at f_θ (we refer the reader to section 3.3.6 for the definition of an empirical process and related notions: Glivenko–Cantelli and Donsker classes, etc.). To prove this lemma, first let us show that the class $\{f_\theta : \theta \in \Theta\}$ of functions is Donsker. For this, decompose f_θ as:

$$f_\theta(\mathcal{O}_i) = \mathbf{X}_i(f_{1,\theta}(\mathcal{O}_i) + f_{2,\theta}(\mathcal{O}_i) + f_{3,\theta}(\mathcal{O}_i))$$

where $f_{1,\theta}(\mathcal{O}_i) = -\delta^*_{i,j}(\theta)e^{\beta_0^\top \mathbf{X}_i} + h_{\beta_0}(Y_i^*, \mathbf{X}_i)$, $f_{2,\theta}(\mathcal{O}_i) = \delta^*_{i,j}(\theta)Y_i^*$ and $f_{3,\theta}(\mathcal{O}_i) = -\delta^*_{i,j}(\theta)h_{\beta_0}(Y_i^*, \mathbf{X}_i)$, and show that the classes $\mathcal{F}_1 := \{f_{1,\theta} : \theta \in \Theta\}$, $\mathcal{F}_2 := \{f_{2,\theta} : \theta \in \Theta\}$ and $\mathcal{F}_3 := \{f_{3,\theta} : \theta \in \Theta\}$ are Donsker. By way of an illustration, let us show that $\mathcal{F}_1$ is Donsker.

In the following, it will be useful to view $D_{i,j}(\theta) \sim \mathcal{B}(m(\mathbf{W}_i, \theta))$ as the random variable $1_{\{U_i \leq m(\mathbf{W}_i,\theta)\}}$, where U_i is a uniform variable on $[0,1]$ that is independent of $\mathcal{O}_i$.

Let $d = \text{diam}(\Theta)$ denote the diameter of $\Theta \subseteq \mathbb{R}^q$. We can cover Θ with no more than $(d/\kappa)^q$ cubes with side length κ. The radius $\kappa^* := \alpha\kappa$ of the circumscribed balls of these cubes is a multiple of κ ($\alpha > 0$), and these balls also cover Θ. Now, for a fixed $\theta \in \Theta$, consider the set:

$$\{f_{1,\tilde{\theta}} : \tilde{\theta} \in \Theta \cap \mathcal{B}(\theta, \kappa^*)\}$$

where $\mathcal{B}(\theta,\kappa^*) = \{\tilde{\theta} \in \mathbb{R}^q : \|\theta - \tilde{\theta}\| \leq \kappa^*\}$ denotes the ball of radius κ^* and center θ. If $\tilde{\theta} \in \mathcal{B}(\theta,\kappa^*)$, condition C4 implies that:

$$|m(\mathbf{w},\theta) - m(\mathbf{w},\tilde{\theta})| \leq h(\mathbf{w})\kappa^*$$

implying that $m(\mathbf{w},\theta) - h(\mathbf{w})\kappa^* \leq m(\mathbf{w},\tilde{\theta}) \leq m(\mathbf{w},\theta) + h(\mathbf{w})\kappa^*$, and hence:

$$1_{\{U_i \leq m(\mathbf{w},\theta) - h(\mathbf{w})\kappa^*\}} \leq 1_{\{U_i \leq m(\mathbf{w},\tilde{\theta})\}} \leq 1_{\{U_i \leq m(\mathbf{w},\theta) + h(\mathbf{w})\kappa^*\}}$$

From this, we deduce that:

$$f_\theta^L(\mathcal{O}_i) \leq f_{1,\tilde{\theta}}(\mathcal{O}_i) \leq f_\theta^U(\mathcal{O}_i)$$

where:

$$f_\theta^L(\mathcal{O}_i) = h_{\beta_0}(Y_i^*, \mathbf{X}_i) - (\xi_i\delta_i + (1-\xi_i)1_{\{U_i \leq m(\mathbf{W}_i,\theta)+h(\mathbf{W}_i)\kappa^*\}})e^{\beta_0^\top \mathbf{X}_i}$$

and:

$$f_\theta^U(\mathcal{O}_i) = h_{\beta_0}(Y_i^*, \mathbf{X}_i) - (\xi_i\delta_i + (1-\xi_i)1_{\{U_i \leq m(\mathbf{W}_i,\theta)-h(\mathbf{W}_i)\kappa^*\}})e^{\beta_0^\top \mathbf{X}_i}$$

Furthermore, under conditions C1, C2 and C4, there exists a positive constant c_1 such that:

$$\mathbb{E}\left[\left(f_\theta^U(\mathcal{O}_i) - f_\theta^L(\mathcal{O}_i)\right)^2\right] \leq 2c_1\kappa^* v$$

$[f_\theta^L, f_\theta^U]$ is therefore an ε-bracket for $\{f_{1,\tilde{\theta}} : \tilde{\theta} \in \Theta \cap \mathcal{B}(\theta, \kappa^*)\}$, where $\varepsilon^2 = 2c_1\kappa^* v$. We can cover Θ with no more than $(d/\kappa)^q$ balls of radius κ^*, and hence we can cover $\mathcal{F}_1 = \{f_{1,\tilde{\theta}} : \tilde{\theta} \in \Theta\}$ with at most $(d/\kappa)^q$ ε-brackets $[f_\theta^L, f_\theta^U]$, where $\varepsilon = \sqrt{2c_1\kappa^* v}$. The number of such ε-brackets is therefore bounded by $(\alpha d/\kappa^*)^q = (2\alpha c_1 dv/\varepsilon^2)^q$, which is of the order ε^{-2q}. The bracketing integral is therefore of the order $\int_0^1 \sqrt{-2q \ln \varepsilon}\, d\varepsilon$, which is finite. The $\mathcal{F}_1$ class of functions is therefore Donsker from theorem 3.13 (section 3.3.6).

We can show that $\mathcal{F}_2$ and $\mathcal{F}_3$ are Donsker too by using similar arguments (omitted). A sum of Donsker classes is also Donsker, hence the class $\{f_{1,\theta} + f_{2,\theta} + f_{3,\theta} : \theta \in \Theta\}$ of functions is Donsker too. Finally, as $\mathbf{X}$ is bounded (condition C1), the class $\{f_\theta : \theta \in \Theta\}$ of functions is Donsker.

The sequence $\{\mathbb{G}_n f_\theta : \theta \in \Theta\}$ of processes therefore converges weakly to a tight limit and is equicontinuous. Lemma 14.3 from Tsiatis (2006) and the consistency of $\hat{\theta}_n$ imply that $\mathbb{G}_n f_{\hat{\theta}_n} - \mathbb{G}_n f_{\theta_0} \xrightarrow[n\to\infty]{\mathbb{P}} 0$, which coincides with [3.14]. ■

PROOF OF LEMMA 3.2.–

– *First statement*. First, note that:

$$\begin{aligned}\mathbb{E}[\delta_{1,j}^*(\theta)|\mathbf{W}_1] &= \mathbb{E}[\xi_1\delta_1 + (1-\xi_1)D_{1,j}(\theta)|\mathbf{W}_1] \\ &= \pi(\mathbf{W}_1)m(\mathbf{W}_1, \theta_0) + (1-\pi(\mathbf{W}_1))m(\mathbf{W}_1, \theta)\end{aligned} \quad [3.15]$$

From this, we deduce that:

$$\begin{aligned}\mathbb{E}[\dot{\ell}_{1,j}^*(\beta,\theta)] &= \mathbb{E}\left[\mathbf{X}_1\left(\delta_{1,j}^*(\theta)\left[Y_1^* - e^{\beta^\top \mathbf{X}_1} - h_\beta(Y_1^*, \mathbf{X}_1)\right] + h_\beta(Y_1^*, \mathbf{X}_1)\right)\right] \\ &= \mathbb{E}\left[\mathbf{X}_1\left((\pi(\mathbf{W}_1)m(\mathbf{W}_1,\theta_0) + (1-\pi(\mathbf{W}_1))m(\mathbf{W}_1,\theta)\right)\right. \\ &\quad \times \left.\left.\left[Y_1^* - e^{\beta^\top \mathbf{X}_1} - h_\beta(Y_1^*, \mathbf{X}_1)\right] + h_\beta(Y_1^*, \mathbf{X}_1)\right)\right]\end{aligned}$$

(the second equality is obtained by taking the conditional expectation given $\mathbf{W}_1$). Finally, we easily calculate:

$$\frac{\partial \mathbb{E}[\dot{\ell}^*_{1,j}(\beta,\theta)]}{\partial \theta^\top} = \mathbb{E}\left[\mathbf{X}_1(1-\pi(\mathbf{W}_1))\dot{m}^\top(\mathbf{W}_1,\theta)\left(Y_1^* - e^{\beta^\top \mathbf{X}_1} - h_\beta(Y_1^*,\mathbf{X}_1)\right)\right]$$

which coincides with $\Sigma_2(\beta,\theta)$.

– *Second statement.* It is straightforward to calculate:

$$\begin{aligned}\frac{\partial \dot{\ell}^*_{n,j}(\beta_0,\hat{\theta}_n)}{\partial \beta^\top} &= \sum_{i=1}^n \mathbf{X}_i\mathbf{X}_i^\top \left[-\delta^*_{i,j}(\hat{\theta}_n)e^{\beta_0^\top \mathbf{X}_i}\right.\\ &\left.+(1-\delta^*_{i,j}(\hat{\theta}_n))h_{\beta_0}(Y_i^*,\mathbf{X}_i)\left(Y_i^* - e^{\beta_0^\top \mathbf{X}_i} - h_{\beta_0}(Y_i^*,\mathbf{X}_i)\right)\right]\end{aligned}$$

Then decompose $n^{-1}\partial \dot{\ell}^*_{n,j}(\beta_0,\hat{\theta}_n)/\partial \beta^\top$:

$$\begin{aligned}\frac{1}{n}\frac{\partial \dot{\ell}^*_{n,j}(\beta_0,\hat{\theta}_n)}{\partial \beta^\top} &= \left(\frac{1}{n}\frac{\partial \dot{\ell}^*_{n,j}(\beta_0,\hat{\theta}_n)}{\partial \beta^\top} - \frac{1}{n}\frac{\partial \dot{\ell}^*_{n,j}(\beta_0,\theta_0)}{\partial \beta^\top}\right) + \frac{1}{n}\frac{\partial \dot{\ell}^*_{n,j}(\beta_0,\theta_0)}{\partial \beta^\top}\\ &= \frac{1}{n}\sum_{i=1}^n \mathbf{X}_i\mathbf{X}_i^\top \left[-e^{\beta_0^\top \mathbf{X}_i}(1-\xi_i)(D_{i,j}(\hat{\theta}_n) - D_{i,j}(\theta_0))\right.\\ &+ h_{\beta_0}(Y_i^*,\mathbf{X}_i)\left(Y_i^* - e^{\beta_0^\top \mathbf{X}_i} - h_{\beta_0}(Y_i^*,\mathbf{X}_i)\right)\\ &\times \left.(1-\xi_i)(D_{i,j}(\theta_0) - D_{i,j}(\hat{\theta}_n))\right] + \frac{1}{n}\frac{\partial \dot{\ell}^*_{n,j}(\beta_0,\theta_0)}{\partial \beta^\top}\\ &= \frac{1}{n}\sum_{i=1}^n \mathbf{X}_i\mathbf{X}_i^\top(1-\xi_i)\left[e^{\beta_0^\top \mathbf{X}_i} + h_{\beta_0}(Y_i^*,\mathbf{X}_i)\right.\\ &\times \left.\left(Y_i^* - e^{\beta_0^\top \mathbf{X}_i} - h_{\beta_0}(Y_i^*,\mathbf{X}_i)\right)\right]\\ &\times (D_{i,j}(\theta_0) - D_{i,j}(\hat{\theta}_n)) + \frac{1}{n}\frac{\partial \dot{\ell}^*_{n,j}(\beta_0,\theta_0)}{\partial \beta^\top}\\ &= \frac{1}{n}\sum_{i=1}^n \mathcal{Z}_i(1_{\{U_{i,j}\le m(\mathbf{W}_i,\theta_0)\}} - 1_{\{U_{i,j}\le m(\mathbf{W}_i,\hat{\theta}_n)\}})\\ &+ \frac{1}{n}\frac{\partial \dot{\ell}^*_{n,j}(\beta_0,\theta_0)}{\partial \beta^\top}\end{aligned} \qquad [3.16]$$

where $\mathcal{Z}_i := \mathbf{X}_i\mathbf{X}_i^\top(1-\xi_i)[e^{\beta_0^\top \mathbf{X}_i} + h_{\beta_0}(Y_i^*, \mathbf{X}_i)(Y_i^* - e^{\beta_0^\top \mathbf{X}_i} - h_{\beta_0}(Y_i^*, \mathbf{X}_i))]$ (in the following, we will denote by $\mathcal{Z}_{i,(\ell,k)}$ the element (ℓ,k) of $\mathcal{Z}_i$) and $U_{i,j}$ is a uniform random variable on $[0,1]$, independent of each other variable in the problem.

First of all, consider the first term to the right of the $=$ sign in [3.16]. The variable $|1_{\{U_{i,j}\leq m(\mathbf{W}_i,\theta_0)\}} - 1_{\{U_{i,j}\leq m(\mathbf{W}_i,\hat{\theta}_n)\}}|$ equals either 0 or 1, and takes on the value 1 with probability $|m(\mathbf{W}_i,\theta_0) - m(\mathbf{W}_i,\hat{\theta}_n)|$. Let $\varepsilon > 0$. Then, for each $\ell, k \in \{1,\ldots,p\}$, from the Markov inequality, we can write:

$$\mathbb{P}\left(\left|\frac{1}{n}\sum_{i=1}^{n}\mathcal{Z}_{i,(\ell,k)}(1_{\{U_{i,j}\leq m(\mathbf{W}_i,\theta_0)\}} - 1_{\{U_{i,j}\leq m(\mathbf{W}_i,\hat{\theta}_n)\}})\right| > \varepsilon\right)$$
$$\leq \frac{1}{\varepsilon}\mathbb{E}\left[\left|\frac{1}{n}\sum_{i=1}^{n}\mathcal{Z}_{i,(\ell,k)}(1_{\{U_{i,j}\leq m(\mathbf{W}_i,\theta_0)\}} - 1_{\{U_{i,j}\leq m(\mathbf{W}_i,\hat{\theta}_n)\}})\right|\right]$$

Under the conditions C1 and C2, there exists a finite positive constant c_2 such that $|\mathcal{Z}_{i,(\ell,k)}| \leq c_2$. We have therefore:

$$\mathbb{P}\left(\left|\frac{1}{n}\sum_{i=1}^{n}\mathcal{Z}_{i,(\ell,k)}(1_{\{U_{i,j}\leq m(\mathbf{W}_i,\theta_0)\}} - 1_{\{U_{i,j}\leq m(\mathbf{W}_i,\hat{\theta}_n)\}})\right| > \varepsilon\right)$$
$$\leq \frac{c_2}{\varepsilon n}\sum_{i=1}^{n}|m(\mathbf{W}_i,\theta_0) - m(\mathbf{W}_i,\hat{\theta}_n)|$$
$$\leq \frac{c_2}{\varepsilon n}\sum_{i=1}^{n}h(\mathbf{W}_i)\|\theta_0 - \hat{\theta}_n\|$$
$$\leq \frac{c_2}{\varepsilon}\|\theta_0 - \hat{\theta}_n\|(v + o_{\mathbb{P}}(1))$$

(the last two lines are a consequence of condition C4). Finally, the consistency of $\hat{\theta}_n$ implies that $\frac{1}{n}\sum_{i=1}^{n}\mathcal{Z}_{i,(\ell,k)}(1_{\{U_{i,j}\leq m(\mathbf{W}_i,\theta_0)\}} - 1_{\{U_{i,j}\leq m(\mathbf{W}_i,\hat{\theta}_n)\}})$ converges in probability to 0, and thus also the first term to the right of the $=$ sign in [3.16].

Now consider the second term to the right of the $=$ sign in [3.16]. From the law of large numbers, $n^{-1}\partial\dot{\ell}_{n,j}^*(\beta_0,\theta_0)/\partial\beta^\top$ converges in probability to:

$$\mathbb{E}\left[\mathbf{X}_1\mathbf{X}_1^\top\left[-\delta_{1,j}^*(\theta_0)e^{\beta_0^\top\mathbf{X}_1} + (1-\delta_{1,j}^*(\theta_0))h_{\beta_0}(Y_1^*,\mathbf{X}_1)\right.\right.$$
$$\left.\left.\times\left(Y_1^* - e^{\beta_0^\top\mathbf{X}_1} - h_{\beta_0}(Y_1^*,\mathbf{X}_1)\right)\right]\right] \quad [3.17]$$

From [3.15], $\mathbb{E}[\delta^*_{1,j}(\theta_0)|\mathbf{W}_1] = m(\mathbf{W}_1, \theta_0)$. Hence, by taking the conditional expectation given $\mathbf{W}_1$ in [3.17], we can verify that [3.17] is equal to $-\Sigma_1(\beta_0)$.

Finally, we have shown that $n^{-1}\partial\dot{\ell}^*_{n,j}(\beta_0, \hat{\theta}_n)/\partial\beta^\top$ converges in probability to $-\Sigma_1(\beta_0)$, which concludes the proof. ■

3.3.2. *Proof of theorem 3.3*

3.3.2.1. *Consistency*

The consistency of $\widetilde{\beta}_n$ can be proven by verifying that the conditions of the inverse function theorem stated in Foutz (1977) are satisfied.

Denote $\dot{\widetilde{\ell}}_n(\beta, \theta) = \partial\widetilde{\ell}_n(\beta, \theta)/\partial\beta$, where $\widetilde{\ell}_n(\beta, \theta)$ is given by [3.8]. We can show that:

$$\dot{\widetilde{\ell}}_n(\beta, \theta) = \sum_{i=1}^n \mathbf{X}_i \left[\hat{\delta}_i(\theta)(Y^*_i - e^{\beta^\top \mathbf{X}_i}) + (1 - \hat{\delta}_i(\theta))h_\beta(Y^*_i, \mathbf{X}_i)\right]$$

The first condition to check is the continuity of the function $\beta \mapsto \partial\dot{\widetilde{\ell}}_n(\beta, \hat{\theta}_n)/\partial\beta^\top$ in a neighborhood of β_0. We can easily check that $\beta \mapsto \dot{\widetilde{\ell}}_n(\beta, \hat{\theta}_n)$ is differentiable with respect to β, and that its derivative equals:

$$\begin{aligned}\frac{\partial\dot{\widetilde{\ell}}_n(\beta, \hat{\theta}_n)}{\partial\beta^\top} &= \sum_{i=1}^n \mathbf{X}_i\mathbf{X}_i^\top \Big(-\hat{\delta}_i(\hat{\theta}_n)e^{\beta^\top \mathbf{X}_i} \\ &+(1 - \hat{\delta}_i(\hat{\theta}_n))\left\{Y^*_i - e^{\beta^\top \mathbf{X}_i} - h_\beta(Y^*_i, \mathbf{X}_i)\right\} h_\beta(Y^*_i, \mathbf{X}_i)\Big)\end{aligned}$$

which is continuous with respect to β.

The second condition to check is the following: $n^{-1}\dot{\widetilde{\ell}}_n(\beta_0, \hat{\theta}_n) = o_{\mathbb{P}}(1)$. Decompose $n^{-1}\dot{\widetilde{\ell}}_n(\beta_0, \hat{\theta}_n)$ as follows:

$$\frac{1}{n}\dot{\widetilde{\ell}}_n(\beta_0, \hat{\theta}_n) = \frac{1}{n}(\dot{\widetilde{\ell}}_n(\beta_0, \hat{\theta}_n) - \dot{\widetilde{\ell}}_n(\beta_0, \theta_0)) + \frac{1}{n}\dot{\widetilde{\ell}}_n(\beta_0, \theta_0)$$

The law of large numbers ensures that $n^{-1}\dot{\widetilde{\ell}}_n(\beta_0, \theta_0)$ converges in probability to:

$$\begin{aligned}&\mathbb{E}\left[\mathbf{X}\left(\hat{\delta}(\theta_0)(Y^* - e^{\beta_0^\top \mathbf{X}}) + (1 - \hat{\delta}(\theta_0))h_{\beta_0}(Y^*, \mathbf{X})\right)\right] \qquad [3.18]\\ &= \mathbb{E}\left[\mathbf{X}\left(\mathbb{E}(\hat{\delta}(\theta_0)|\mathbf{W})(Y^* - e^{\beta_0^\top \mathbf{X}}) + (1 - \mathbb{E}(\hat{\delta}(\theta_0)|\mathbf{W}))h_{\beta_0}(Y^*, \mathbf{X})\right)\right]\end{aligned}$$

(the equality is obtained by taking the conditional expectation given $\mathbf{W}$). Under the MAR hypothesis:

$$\begin{aligned}\mathbb{E}(\hat{\delta}(\theta_0)|\mathbf{W}) &= \mathbb{E}(\xi\delta + (1-\xi)\mathbb{E}(\delta|\mathbf{W})|\mathbf{W}) \\ &= \mathbb{E}(\xi|\mathbf{W})\mathbb{E}(\delta|\mathbf{W}) + (1-\mathbb{E}(\xi|\mathbf{W}))\mathbb{E}(\delta|\mathbf{W}) \\ &= \mathbb{E}(\delta|\mathbf{W})\end{aligned}$$

(the MAR hypothesis comes into play via the equality $\mathbb{E}(\xi\delta|\mathbf{W}) = \mathbb{E}(\xi|\mathbf{W})\mathbb{E}(\delta|\mathbf{W})$). Therefore, [3.18] can be rewritten as:

$$\begin{aligned}&\mathbb{E}\left[\mathbf{X}\left(\mathbb{E}(\delta|\mathbf{W})(Y^* - e^{\beta_0^\top \mathbf{X}}) + (1-\mathbb{E}(\delta|\mathbf{W}))h_{\beta_0}(Y^*, \mathbf{X})\right)\right] \\ &\quad = \mathbb{E}\left[\mathbf{X}\left(\delta(Y^* - e^{\beta_0^\top \mathbf{X}}) + (1-\delta)h_{\beta_0}(Y^*, \mathbf{X})\right)\right]\end{aligned}$$

which is equal to 0 (take the conditional expectation given $\{\delta = 1\}$ and $\mathbf{X}$). The convergence in probability of $n^{-1}(\dot{\tilde{\ell}}_n(\beta_0, \hat{\theta}_n) - \dot{\tilde{\ell}}_n(\beta_0, \theta_0))$ to 0 is a consequence of the consistency of $\hat{\theta}_n$ and of the conditions C1, C2 and C4. This completes the proof of the second condition.

The third condition in Foutz (1977) is the following: the sequence $(n^{-1}\partial\dot{\tilde{\ell}}_n(\beta, \hat{\theta}_n)/\partial\beta^\top)_n$ converges in probability, uniformly in a neighborhood of β_0. We have:

$$\begin{aligned}\frac{1}{n}\frac{\partial\dot{\tilde{\ell}}_n(\beta,\theta)}{\partial\beta^\top} &= \frac{1}{n}\sum_{i=1}^{n}\mathbf{X}_i\mathbf{X}_i^\top\left(-\hat{\delta}_i(\theta)e^{\beta^\top\mathbf{X}_i}\right. \\ &\quad \left. +(1-\hat{\delta}_i(\theta))\left\{Y_i^* - e^{\beta^\top\mathbf{X}_i} - h_\beta(Y_i^*, \mathbf{X}_i)\right\}h_\beta(Y_i^*, \mathbf{X}_i)\right)\end{aligned}$$

Following the same principle as above, decompose $n^{-1}\partial\dot{\tilde{\ell}}_n(\beta, \hat{\theta}_n)/\partial\beta^\top$ as:

$$\frac{1}{n}\frac{\partial\dot{\tilde{\ell}}_n(\beta,\hat{\theta}_n)}{\partial\beta^\top} = \frac{1}{n}\left(\frac{\partial\dot{\tilde{\ell}}_n(\beta,\hat{\theta}_n)}{\partial\beta^\top} - \frac{\partial\dot{\tilde{\ell}}_n(\beta,\theta_0)}{\partial\beta^\top}\right) + \frac{1}{n}\frac{\partial\dot{\tilde{\ell}}_n(\beta,\theta_0)}{\partial\beta^\top}$$

The first term converges in probability to 0 (a consequence of the consistency of $\hat{\theta}_n$ and the conditions C1, C2 and C4) and, by the law of large numbers, $n^{-1}\partial\dot{\tilde{\ell}}_n(\beta, \theta_0)/$

$\partial\beta^\top$ converges in probability to $-\Sigma_1(\beta)$. Hence, $n^{-1}\partial\dot{\tilde{\ell}}_n(\beta,\hat{\theta}_n)/\partial\beta^\top$ converges in probability to $-\Sigma_1(\beta)$.

Under the conditions C1 and C2, the derivative of $n^{-1}\partial\dot{\tilde{\ell}}_n(\beta,\hat{\theta}_n)/\partial\beta^\top$ with respect to β is bounded for each n. The sequence $(n^{-1}\partial\dot{\tilde{\ell}}_n(\beta,\hat{\theta}_n)/\partial\beta^\top)_n$ is therefore equicontinuous and hence $n^{-1}\partial\dot{\tilde{\ell}}_n(\beta,\hat{\theta}_n)/\partial\beta^\top$ converges uniformly to $-\Sigma_1(\beta)$ in a neighborhood of β_0.

The conditions of the inverse function theorem stated in Foutz (1977) are thus satisfied, ensuring the consistency of $\tilde{\beta}_n$.

3.3.2.2. *Asymptotic normality*

By expanding $\dot{\tilde{\ell}}_n(\tilde{\beta}_n,\hat{\theta}_n)$ as a Taylor series about the point (β_0,θ_0), we have:

$$\sqrt{n}(\tilde{\beta}_n-\beta_0)=\left(-\frac{1}{n}\frac{\partial\dot{\tilde{\ell}}_n(\beta_0,\theta_0)}{\partial\beta^\top}\right)^{-1}$$
$$\times\left(\frac{1}{\sqrt{n}}\dot{\tilde{\ell}}_n(\beta_0,\theta_0)+\frac{1}{n}\frac{\partial\dot{\tilde{\ell}}_n(\beta_0,\theta_0)}{\partial\theta^\top}\sqrt{n}(\hat{\theta}_n-\theta_0)\right)+o_{\mathbb{P}}(1)$$

We also have:

$$\begin{aligned}\frac{1}{n}\frac{\partial\dot{\tilde{\ell}}_n(\beta,\theta)}{\partial\theta^\top}&=\frac{1}{n}\sum_{i=1}^{n}\mathbf{X}_i\left(Y_i^*-e^{\beta^\top\mathbf{X}_i}-h_\beta(Y_i^*,\mathbf{X}_i)\right)(1-\xi_i)\dot{m}^\top(\mathbf{W}_i,\theta)\\&=\Sigma_2(\beta,\theta)+o_{\mathbb{P}}(1)\end{aligned}\qquad[3.19]$$

By combining [3.9] and [3.19], we can therefore rewrite $\sqrt{n}(\tilde{\beta}_n-\beta_0)$ in the form:

$$\sqrt{n}(\tilde{\beta}_n-\beta_0)=\left(-\frac{1}{n}\frac{\partial\dot{\tilde{\ell}}_n(\beta_0,\theta_0)}{\partial\beta^\top}\right)^{-1}\frac{1}{\sqrt{n}}\sum_{i=1}^{n}\mathcal{U}_i+o_{\mathbb{P}}(1)$$

with:

$$\begin{aligned}\mathcal{U}_i&=\mathbf{X}_i\left\{\hat{\delta}_i(\theta_0)(Y_i^*-e^{\beta_0^\top\mathbf{X}_i})+(1-\hat{\delta}_i(\theta_0))h_{\beta_0}(Y_i^*,\mathbf{X}_i)\right\}\\&\quad+\Sigma_2(\beta_0,\theta_0)\Theta^{-1}(\theta_0)\widetilde{m_i}(\theta_0)\xi_i(\delta_i-m(\mathbf{W}_i,\theta_0))\\&=\mathcal{U}_{i,1}+\mathcal{U}_{i,2}\end{aligned}$$

The variance of $\mathcal{U}_i$ is obtained by calculating:

$$\begin{aligned}\text{var}(\mathcal{U}_i) &= \text{var}(\mathcal{U}_{i,1}) + \text{var}(\mathcal{U}_{i,2}) + 2\,\text{cov}(\mathcal{U}_{i,1}, \mathcal{U}_{i,2}) \\ &= \Sigma_1(\beta_0) + (2\Sigma_3(\beta_0, \theta_0) - \Sigma_2(\beta_0, \theta_0))\,\Theta^{-1}(\theta_0)\Sigma_2^\top(\beta_0, \theta_0)\end{aligned}$$

Convergence of $\sqrt{n}(\tilde{\beta}_n - \beta_0)$ follows from the central limit theorem, the convergence of $\frac{1}{n}\frac{\partial \tilde{\dot{\ell}}_n(\beta_0,\theta_0)}{\partial \beta^\top}$ to $-\Sigma_1(\beta_0)$ and Slutsky's theorem.

3.3.3. *Proof of theorem 3.4*

As the proof of consistency is essentially the same as that for theorem 3.3, we will not reproduce it here.

To prove asymptotic normality, we begin by expanding $\dot{\ell}^*_{n,j}(\hat{\beta}^*_{n,j}, \hat{\theta}_n)$ as a Taylor series about the point β_0:

$$\begin{aligned}0 &= \frac{1}{\sqrt{n}}\dot{\ell}^*_{n,j}(\hat{\beta}^*_{n,j}, \hat{\theta}_n) \\ &= \frac{1}{\sqrt{n}}\dot{\ell}^*_{n,j}(\beta_0, \hat{\theta}_n) + \frac{1}{n}\frac{\partial \dot{\ell}^*_{n,j}(\beta_0, \hat{\theta}_n)}{\partial \beta^\top}\sqrt{n}(\hat{\beta}^*_{n,j} - \beta_0) + o_{\mathbb{P}}(1)\end{aligned}$$

By using lemma 3.1 and then a Taylor series expansion of $\mathbb{E}[\dot{\ell}^*_{1,j}(\beta_0, \hat{\theta}_n)]$ about the point θ_0, we can write:

$$\begin{aligned}0 &= \frac{1}{\sqrt{n}}\dot{\ell}^*_{n,j}(\beta_0, \theta_0) - \sqrt{n}\mathbb{E}[\dot{\ell}^*_{1,j}(\beta_0, \theta_0)] + \sqrt{n}\mathbb{E}[\dot{\ell}^*_{1,j}(\beta_0, \hat{\theta}_n)] \\ &+ \frac{1}{n}\frac{\partial \dot{\ell}^*_{n,j}(\beta_0, \hat{\theta}_n)}{\partial \beta^\top}\sqrt{n}(\hat{\beta}^*_{n,j} - \beta_0) + o_{\mathbb{P}}(1) \\ &= \frac{1}{\sqrt{n}}\dot{\ell}^*_{n,j}(\beta_0, \theta_0) + \sqrt{n}\left(\frac{\partial \mathbb{E}[\dot{\ell}^*_{1,j}(\beta_0, \theta_0)]}{\partial \theta^\top}(\hat{\theta}_n - \theta_0) + o_{\mathbb{P}}(\|\hat{\theta}_n - \theta_0\|)\right) \\ &+ \frac{1}{n}\frac{\partial \dot{\ell}^*_{n,j}(\beta_0, \hat{\theta}_n)}{\partial \beta^\top}\sqrt{n}(\hat{\beta}^*_{n,j} - \beta_0) + o_{\mathbb{P}}(1)\end{aligned} \quad [3.20]$$

Then, by combining [3.20] and lemma 3.2, we obtain the following approximation of $\hat{\beta}^*_{n,j}$:

$$\begin{aligned}
&\sqrt{n}(\hat{\beta}^*_{n,j} - \beta_0) \\
&= \Sigma_1^{-1}(\beta_0)\frac{1}{\sqrt{n}}\sum_{i=1}^{n}\Big[\mathbf{X}_i\left\{\delta^*_{i,j}(\theta_0)[Y_i^* - e^{\beta_0^\top \mathbf{X}_i} - h_{\beta_0}(Y_i^*, \mathbf{X}_i)] + h_{\beta_0}(Y_i^*, \mathbf{X}_i)\right\} \\
&+ \Sigma_2(\beta_0, \theta_0)\Theta^{-1}(\theta_0)\widetilde{m_i}(\theta_0)\xi_i(\delta_i - m(\mathbf{W}_i, \theta_0))\Big] + o_{\mathbb{P}}(1)
\end{aligned}$$

from which we deduce:

$$\begin{aligned}
&\sqrt{n}(\hat{\beta}^*_n - \beta_0) \\
&= \frac{1}{M}\sum_{j=1}^{M}\left(\sqrt{n}(\hat{\beta}^*_{n,j} - \beta_0)\right) \\
&= \Sigma_1^{-1}(\beta_0)\frac{1}{\sqrt{n}}\sum_{i=1}^{n}\left[\frac{1}{M}\sum_{j=1}^{M}\mathbf{X}_i\left\{\delta^*_{i,j}(\theta_0)[Y_i^* - e^{\beta_0^\top \mathbf{X}_i} - h_{\beta_0}(Y_i^*, \mathbf{X}_i)]\right.\right. \\
&+ h_{\beta_0}(Y_i^*, \mathbf{X}_i)\} + \Sigma_2(\beta_0, \theta_0)\Theta^{-1}(\theta_0)\widetilde{m_i}(\theta_0)\xi_i(\delta_i - m(\mathbf{W}_i, \theta_0))\Big] + o_{\mathbb{P}}(1) \\
&:= \Sigma_1^{-1}(\beta_0)\frac{1}{\sqrt{n}}\sum_{i=1}^{n}\left[\frac{1}{M}\sum_{j=1}^{M} f_{\beta_0,\theta_0,j}(\mathcal{O}_i) + \mathcal{V}_i\right] + o_{\mathbb{P}}(1) \qquad [3.21]
\end{aligned}$$

where $\mathcal{V}_i := \Sigma_2(\beta_0, \theta_0)\Theta^{-1}(\theta_0)\widetilde{m_i}(\theta_0)\xi_i(\delta_i - m(\mathbf{W}_i, \theta_0))$. Calculating the variance of $\frac{1}{M}\sum_{j=1}^{M} f_{\beta_0,\theta_0,j}(\mathcal{O}_i) + \mathcal{V}_i$ does not present any difficulty (we refer to Bousselmi et al. (2021) for the details):

$$\begin{aligned}
&\mathrm{var}\left(\frac{1}{M}\sum_{j=1}^{M} f_{\beta_0,\theta_0,j}(\mathcal{O}_i) + \mathcal{V}_i\right) \\
&= \mathrm{var}\left(\frac{1}{M}\sum_{j=1}^{M} f_{\beta_0,\theta_0,j}(\mathcal{O}_i)\right) + \mathrm{var}(\mathcal{V}_i) + \frac{2}{M}\sum_{j=1}^{M}\mathrm{cov}(f_{\beta_0,\theta_0,j}(\mathcal{O}_i), \mathcal{V}_i) \\
&= \Sigma_1^*(\beta_0, \theta_0) + \Sigma_2(\beta_0, \theta_0)\Theta^{-1}(\theta_0)\Sigma_2^\top(\beta_0, \theta_0) \\
&+2\left(\Sigma_3(\beta_0, \theta_0) - \Sigma_2(\beta_0, \theta_0)\right)\Theta^{-1}(\theta_0)\Sigma_2^\top(\beta_0, \theta_0) \\
&= \Sigma_1^*(\beta_0, \theta_0) + \left(2\Sigma_3(\beta_0, \theta_0) - \Sigma_2(\beta_0, \theta_0)\right)\Theta^{-1}(\theta_0)\Sigma_2^\top(\beta_0, \theta_0) \qquad [3.22]
\end{aligned}$$

Finally, applying the central limit theorem to [3.21] implies the convergence in distribution of $\sqrt{n}(\hat{\beta}_n^* - \beta_0)$ to a centered Gaussian vector, whose variance can be obtained from [3.22]:

$$\Sigma_1^{-1}(\beta_0)\left\{\Sigma_1^*(\beta_0,\theta_0) + (2\Sigma_3(\beta_0,\theta_0) - \Sigma_2(\beta_0,\theta_0))\,\Theta^{-1}(\theta_0)\Sigma_2^\top(\beta_0,\theta_0)\right\}\Sigma_1^{-1}(\beta_0)$$

3.3.4. *Proof of theorem 3.5*

Suppose that the model $m(\mathbf{W}_i,\theta)$ is correctly specified. The consistency of $\breve{\beta}_n$ can be proven by checking that the conditions of the inverse function theorem from Foutz (1977) are satisfied.

First, it is easy to check that the function $\beta \mapsto \partial\breve{\ell}_n(\beta,\hat{\theta}_n,\hat{\gamma}_n)/\partial\beta^\top$ is continuous in a neighborhood of β_0, where $\breve{\ell}_n(\beta,\hat{\theta}_n,\hat{\gamma}_n)$ is given by [3.12] (condition i).

The second condition to check is: $n^{-1}\breve{\ell}_n(\beta_0,\hat{\theta}_n,\hat{\gamma}_n) = o_{\mathbb{P}}(1)$ (condition ii). Decompose $n^{-1}\breve{\ell}_n(\beta_0,\hat{\theta}_n,\hat{\gamma}_n)$ as:

$$\begin{aligned}
\frac{1}{n}\breve{\ell}_n(\beta_0,\hat{\theta}_n,\hat{\gamma}_n) &= \frac{1}{n}\sum_{i=1}^n \mathbf{X}_i\frac{\xi_i}{\pi(\mathbf{W}_i,\hat{\gamma}_n)}\left(\delta_i - m(\mathbf{W}_i,\hat{\theta}_n)\right)\\
&\times\left(Y_i^* - e^{\beta_0^\top\mathbf{X}_i} - h_{\beta_0}(Y_i^*,\mathbf{X}_i)\right)\\
&+\frac{1}{n}\sum_{i=1}^n \mathbf{X}_i\left\{m(\mathbf{W}_i,\hat{\theta}_n)\left(Y_i^* - e^{\beta_0^\top\mathbf{X}_i}\right)\right.\\
&+\left.\left(1 - m(\mathbf{W}_i,\hat{\theta}_n)\right)h_{\beta_0}(Y_i^*,\mathbf{X}_i)\right\}\\
&= Q_n^{(1)}(\hat{\theta}_n,\hat{\gamma}_n) + Q_n^{(2)}(\hat{\theta}_n)
\end{aligned}$$

First, consider the term $Q_n^{(1)}(\hat{\theta}_n,\hat{\gamma}_n)$. Set $\mathcal{Q}_i := \mathbf{X}_i\xi_i(Y_i^* - e^{\beta_0^\top\mathbf{X}_i} - h_{\beta_0}(Y_i^*,\mathbf{X}_i))$. Then we can write:

$$\begin{aligned}
Q_n^{(1)}(\hat{\theta}_n,\hat{\gamma}_n) &= \frac{1}{n}\sum_{i=1}^n \frac{1}{\pi(\mathbf{W}_i,\hat{\gamma}_n)}(\delta_i - m(\mathbf{W}_i,\hat{\theta}_n))\mathcal{Q}_i\\
&= \frac{1}{n}\sum_{i=1}^n\left(\frac{1}{\pi(\mathbf{W}_i,\hat{\gamma}_n)} - \frac{1}{\pi(\mathbf{W}_i,\gamma^*)} + \frac{1}{\pi(\mathbf{W}_i,\gamma^*)}\right)\\
&\times\ (\delta_i - m(\mathbf{W}_i,\hat{\theta}_n))\mathcal{Q}_i
\end{aligned}$$

$$
\begin{aligned}
&= \frac{1}{n}\sum_{i=1}^{n}\left(\frac{1}{\pi(\mathbf{W}_i,\hat{\gamma}_n)} - \frac{1}{\pi(\mathbf{W}_i,\gamma^*)}\right)(\delta_i - m(\mathbf{W}_i,\hat{\theta}_n))\mathcal{Q}_i \\
&+ \frac{1}{n}\sum_{i=1}^{n}\frac{1}{\pi(\mathbf{W}_i,\gamma^*)}(\delta_i - m(\mathbf{W}_i,\theta_0))\mathcal{Q}_i \\
&+ \frac{1}{n}\sum_{i=1}^{n}\frac{1}{\pi(\mathbf{W}_i,\gamma^*)}(m(\mathbf{W}_i,\theta_0) - m(\mathbf{W}_i,\hat{\theta}_n))\mathcal{Q}_i \\
&:= Q_{n,1}^{(1)} + Q_{n,2}^{(1)} + Q_{n,3}^{(1)}
\end{aligned}
$$

Denote by $Q_{n,1,\ell}^{(1)}$ and $\mathcal{Q}_{i,\ell}$ (for $\ell = 1,\ldots,p$) the components of the vectors $Q_{n,1}^{(1)}$ and $\mathcal{Q}_i$, respectively. We have:

$$
|Q_{n,1,\ell}^{(1)}| \leq \frac{1}{n}\sum_{i=1}^{n}\left|\frac{\pi(\mathbf{W}_i,\gamma^*) - \pi(\mathbf{W}_i,\hat{\gamma}_n)}{\pi(\mathbf{W}_i,\hat{\gamma}_n)\pi(\mathbf{W}_i,\gamma^*)}\right| |\delta_i - m(\mathbf{W}_i,\hat{\theta}_n)||\mathcal{Q}_{i,\ell}|
$$

Conditions C1 and C6 imply that there exists a finite positive constant c_3 such that:

$$
|Q_{n,1,\ell}^{(1)}| \leq \frac{c_3}{n}\sum_{i=1}^{n}|\pi(\mathbf{W}_i,\gamma^*) - \pi(\mathbf{W}_i,\hat{\gamma}_n)|
$$

and condition C7 implies that:

$$
\begin{aligned}
|Q_{n,1,\ell}^{(1)}| &\leq \frac{c_3}{n}\sum_{i=1}^{n} g(\mathbf{W}_i)\|\gamma^* - \hat{\gamma}_n\| \\
&\leq c_3(u + o_{\mathbb{P}}(1))\|\gamma^* - \hat{\gamma}_n\|
\end{aligned}
$$

Finally, convergence of $\hat{\gamma}_n$ to γ^* implies that $Q_{n,1,\ell}^{(1)}$ ($\ell = 1,\ldots,p$) converges to 0, and hence $Q_{n,1}^{(1)}$ does too. In the same way, under conditions C1 and C6, there exists a finite positive constant c_4 such that:

$$
|Q_{n,3,\ell}^{(1)}| \leq \frac{c_4}{n}\sum_{i=1}^{n}|m(\mathbf{W}_i,\theta_0) - m(\mathbf{W}_i,\hat{\theta}_n)|, \quad \ell = 1,\ldots,p
$$

Condition C4 then implies that:

$$
|Q_{n,3,\ell}^{(1)}| \leq c_4(v + o_{\mathbb{P}}(1))\|\theta_0 - \hat{\theta}_n\|
$$

If the model $m(\mathbf{W}_i, \theta)$ is correctly specified (and thus, if $\hat{\theta}_n$ is consistent for θ_0), then $Q^{(1)}_{n,3,\ell}$ ($\ell = 1, \ldots, p$) converges to 0, and hence $Q^{(1)}_{n,3}$ does too. Finally, from the law of large numbers, $Q^{(1)}_{n,2}$ converges in probability to:

$$\mathbb{E}\left[\frac{1}{\pi(\mathbf{W}_i, \gamma^*)}(\delta_i - m(\mathbf{W}_i, \theta_0))\mathcal{Q}_i\right]$$

$$= \mathbb{E}\left[\frac{\mathbf{X}_i(Y_i^* - e^{\beta_0^\top \mathbf{X}_i} - h_{\beta_0}(Y_i^*, \mathbf{X}_i))}{\pi(\mathbf{W}_i, \gamma^*)}\mathbb{E}(\xi_i|\mathbf{W}_i)(\mathbb{E}(\delta_i|\mathbf{W}_i) - m(\mathbf{W}_i, \theta_0))\right]$$

which equals 0 if $m(\mathbf{W}_i, \theta)$ is well-specified (because then $m(\mathbf{W}_i, \theta_0) = \mathbb{E}(\delta_i|\mathbf{W}_i)$). We have therefore $Q^{(1)}_n(\hat{\theta}_n, \hat{\gamma}_n) = o_{\mathbb{P}}(1)$, and:

$$\frac{1}{n}\breve{\ell}_n(\beta_0, \hat{\theta}_n, \hat{\gamma}_n) = Q^{(2)}_n(\hat{\theta}_n) + o_{\mathbb{P}}(1)$$

Now decompose $Q^{(2)}_n(\hat{\theta}_n)$ in the following way: $Q^{(2)}_n(\hat{\theta}_n) = Q^{(2)}_n(\hat{\theta}_n) - Q^{(2)}_n(\theta_0) + Q^{(2)}_n(\theta_0)$. From the law of large numbers, $Q^{(2)}_n(\theta_0)$ converges in probability to $\mathbb{E}[\mathbf{X}\{m(\mathbf{W}, \theta_0)(Y^* - e^{\beta_0^\top \mathbf{X}}) + (1 - m(\mathbf{W}, \theta_0))h_{\beta_0}(Y^*, \mathbf{X})\}]$ which equals 0 (we have shown this in the proof of theorem 3.3). Furthermore:

$$Q^{(2)}_n(\hat{\theta}_n) - Q^{(2)}_n(\theta_0)$$
$$= \frac{1}{n}\sum_{i=1}^{n}\mathbf{X}_i(m(\mathbf{W}_i, \hat{\theta}_n) - m(\mathbf{W}_i, \theta_0))(Y_i^* - e^{\beta_0^\top \mathbf{X}_i} - h_{\beta_0}(Y_i^*, \mathbf{X}_i))$$

and, by using the same arguments as those for $Q^{(1)}_{n,3}$, it can be shown that this quantity converges to 0 if the model $m(\mathbf{W}_i, \theta)$ is correct. Therefore, $Q^{(2)}_n(\hat{\theta}_n) = o_{\mathbb{P}}(1)$, which finishes the proof of condition *ii*.

The third condition (condition *iii*) to check is the following: the sequence $(n^{-1}\partial\breve{\ell}_n(\beta, \hat{\theta}_n, \hat{\gamma}_n)/\partial\beta^\top)_n$ converges in probability (to $-\Sigma_1(\beta)$) uniformly in a neighborhood of β_0. Denote $\mathcal{Q}_{i,\beta} = (Y_i^* - e^{\beta^\top \mathbf{X}_i} - h_\beta(Y_i^*, \mathbf{X}_i))h_\beta(Y_i^*, \mathbf{X}_i)$. After a few straightforward calculations, we get:

$$\frac{1}{n}\frac{\partial\breve{\ell}_n(\beta, \theta, \gamma)}{\partial\beta^\top} = \frac{1}{n}\sum_{i=1}^{n}\mathbf{X}_i\mathbf{X}_i^\top\left[-\breve{\delta}_i(\theta, \gamma)(e^{\beta^\top \mathbf{X}_i} + \mathcal{Q}_{i,\beta}) + \mathcal{Q}_{i,\beta}\right]$$

$$= -\frac{1}{n}\sum_{i=1}^{n}\mathbf{X}_i\mathbf{X}_i^\top(e^{\beta^\top\mathbf{X}_i} + \mathcal{Q}_{i,\beta})m(\mathbf{W}_i,\theta) + \frac{1}{n}\sum_{i=1}^{n}\mathbf{X}_i\mathbf{X}_i^\top\mathcal{Q}_{i,\beta}$$

$$+ \frac{1}{n}\sum_{i=1}^{n}\mathbf{X}_i\mathbf{X}_i^\top\frac{\xi_i}{\pi(\mathbf{W}_i,\gamma)}(m(\mathbf{W}_i,\theta) - \delta_i)(e^{\beta^\top\mathbf{X}_i} + \mathcal{Q}_{i,\beta})$$

Now decompose $n^{-1}\partial\breve{\ell}_n(\beta,\hat{\theta}_n,\hat{\gamma}_n)/\partial\beta^\top$ as:

$$\begin{aligned}
\frac{1}{n}\frac{\partial\breve{\ell}_n(\beta,\hat{\theta}_n,\hat{\gamma}_n)}{\partial\beta^\top} &= \frac{1}{n}\frac{\partial\breve{\ell}_n(\beta,\hat{\theta}_n,\hat{\gamma}_n)}{\partial\beta^\top} - \frac{1}{n}\frac{\partial\breve{\ell}_n(\beta,\theta_0,\gamma^*)}{\partial\beta^\top} + \frac{1}{n}\frac{\partial\breve{\ell}_n(\beta,\theta_0,\gamma^*)}{\partial\beta^\top} \\
&= \frac{1}{n}\sum_{i=1}^{n}\mathbf{X}_i\mathbf{X}_i^\top(e^{\beta^\top\mathbf{X}_i} + \mathcal{Q}_{i,\beta})(m(\mathbf{W}_i,\theta_0) - m(\mathbf{W}_i,\hat{\theta}_n)) \\
&+ \frac{1}{n}\sum_{i=1}^{n}\mathbf{X}_i\mathbf{X}_i^\top\xi_i(e^{\beta^\top\mathbf{X}_i} + \mathcal{Q}_{i,\beta})\frac{m(\mathbf{W}_i,\hat{\theta}_n) - \delta_i}{\pi(\mathbf{W}_i,\hat{\gamma}_n)} \\
&- \frac{1}{n}\sum_{i=1}^{n}\mathbf{X}_i\mathbf{X}_i^\top\xi_i(e^{\beta^\top\mathbf{X}_i} + \mathcal{Q}_{i,\beta})\frac{m(\mathbf{W}_i,\theta_0) - \delta_i}{\pi(\mathbf{W}_i,\gamma^*)} \\
&+ \frac{1}{n}\frac{\partial\breve{\ell}_n(\beta,\theta_0,\gamma^*)}{\partial\beta^\top} \\
&:= T_n^{(1)} + T_n^{(2)} + T_n^{(3)} + \frac{1}{n}\frac{\partial\breve{\ell}_n(\beta,\theta_0,\gamma^*)}{\partial\beta^\top}
\end{aligned}$$

By using the same arguments as those for $Q_{n,3}^{(1)}$ (respectively, $Q_n^{(1)}$ and $Q_{n,2}^{(1)}$), it can be shown that $T_n^{(1)}$ (respectively, $T_n^{(2)}$ and $T_n^{(3)}$) converges to 0 (we omit the details). From the law of large numbers, the term $n^{-1}\partial\breve{\ell}_n(\beta,\theta_0,\gamma^*)/\partial\beta^\top$ converges in probability to $\mathbb{E}[\mathbf{X}_i\mathbf{X}_i^\top\{-\breve{\delta}_i(\theta_0,\gamma^*)(e^{\beta^\top\mathbf{X}_i} + \mathcal{Q}_{i,\beta}) + \mathcal{Q}_{i,\beta}\}]$.

If the model $m(\mathbf{W}_i,\theta)$ is well-specified, we get:

$$\begin{aligned}
\mathbb{E}[\breve{\delta}_i(\theta_0,\gamma^*)|\mathbf{W}_i] &= \frac{\mathbb{E}[\xi_i|\mathbf{W}_i]\mathbb{E}[\delta_i|\mathbf{W}_i]}{\pi(\mathbf{W}_i,\gamma^*)} + \left(1 - \frac{\mathbb{E}[\xi_i|\mathbf{W}_i]}{\pi(\mathbf{W}_i,\gamma^*)}\right)m(\mathbf{W}_i,\theta_0) \\
&= \mathbb{E}[\delta_i|\mathbf{W}_i]
\end{aligned}$$

and therefore:

$$\begin{aligned}
&\mathbb{E}\left[\mathbf{X}_i\mathbf{X}_i^\top\left(-\breve{\delta}_i(\theta_0,\gamma^*)(e^{\beta^\top\mathbf{X}_i}+\mathcal{Q}_{i,\beta})+\mathcal{Q}_{i,\beta}\right)\right]\\
&=\mathbb{E}\left[\mathbf{X}_i\mathbf{X}_i^\top\left(-\mathbb{E}[\delta_i|\mathbf{W}_i](e^{\beta^\top\mathbf{X}_i}+\mathcal{Q}_{i,\beta})+\mathcal{Q}_{i,\beta}\right)\right]\\
&=-\mathbb{E}\left[\mathbf{X}_i\mathbf{X}_i^\top\left(\delta_i e^{\beta^\top\mathbf{X}_i}+(\delta_i-1)\mathcal{Q}_{i,\beta}\right)\right]\\
&=-\Sigma_1(\beta)
\end{aligned}$$

Hence, $n^{-1}\partial\breve{\ell}_n(\beta,\hat{\theta}_n,\hat{\gamma}_n)/\partial\beta^\top$ converges in probability to $-\Sigma_1(\beta)$ (uniform convergence is obtained from the same arguments as those used in the proof of theorem 3.3).

Conditions i–iii of the inverse function theorem from Foutz (1977) are therefore satisfied, which ensures the consistency of $\breve{\beta}_n$ provided that $m(\mathbf{W}_i,\theta)$ is well-specified. In an analogous way, the consistency of $\breve{\beta}_n$ can be shown provided that the model $\pi(\mathbf{W}_i,\gamma)$ is well-specified.

3.3.5. *Proof of theorem 3.6*

First of all, note that:

$$\frac{\partial\breve{\delta}_i(\theta,\gamma)}{\partial\theta^\top}=\left(1-\frac{\xi_i}{\pi(\mathbf{W}_i,\gamma)}\right)\dot{m}^\top(\mathbf{W}_i,\theta)$$

and:

$$\frac{\partial\breve{\delta}_i(\theta,\gamma)}{\partial\gamma^\top}=(m(\mathbf{W}_i,\theta)-\delta_i)\xi_i\frac{\dot{\pi}^\top(\mathbf{W}_i,\gamma)}{\pi^2(\mathbf{W}_i,\gamma)}$$

It is easy to check that:

$$\frac{1}{n}\frac{\partial\breve{\ell}_n(\beta_0,\theta^*,\gamma^*)}{\partial\theta^\top}\xrightarrow[n\to\infty]{\mathbb{P}}\Sigma_5(\beta_0,\theta^*,\gamma^*)\qquad[3.23]$$

and:

$$\frac{1}{n}\frac{\partial\breve{\ell}_n(\beta_0,\theta^*,\gamma^*)}{\partial\gamma^\top}\xrightarrow[n\to\infty]{\mathbb{P}}\Sigma_6(\beta_0,\theta^*,\gamma^*)\qquad[3.24]$$

Furthermore, if $m(\mathbf{W}_i,\theta)$ is well-specified (and hence $\theta^*=\theta_0$), then $\Sigma_6(\beta_0,\theta_0,\gamma^*)=0$. In the same way, if the model $\pi(\mathbf{W}_i,\gamma)$ is well-specified (and hence $\gamma^* = \gamma_0$), then $\Sigma_5(\beta_0, \theta_0, \gamma^*) = 0$. By expanding $\breve{\ell}_n(\breve{\beta}_n, \hat{\theta}_n, \hat{\gamma}_n)$ as a Taylor series about the point $(\beta_0, \theta^*, \gamma^*)$, we obtain:

$$\begin{aligned}
&\sqrt{n}(\breve{\beta}_n - \beta_0) \\
&= \left(-\frac{1}{n}\frac{\partial \breve{\ell}_n(\beta_0, \theta^*, \gamma^*)}{\partial \beta^\top}\right)^{-1} \left(\frac{1}{\sqrt{n}}\breve{\ell}_n(\beta_0, \theta^*, \gamma^*) + \frac{1}{n}\frac{\partial \breve{\ell}_n(\beta_0, \theta^*, \gamma^*)}{\partial \theta^\top}\right. \\
&\left.\times \sqrt{n}(\hat{\theta}_n - \theta^*) + \frac{1}{n}\frac{\partial \breve{\ell}_n(\beta_0, \theta^*, \gamma^*)}{\partial \gamma^\top}\sqrt{n}(\hat{\gamma}_n - \gamma^*)\right) + o_{\mathbb{P}}(1)
\end{aligned} \quad [3.25]$$

Finally, by applying the central limit theorem to [3.25] and using [3.9], [3.10], [3.23] and [3.24], we can show that $\sqrt{n}(\breve{\beta}_n - \beta_0)$ converges in distribution to a Gaussian vector, whose variance depends on whether the models $m(\mathbf{W}_i, \theta)$ and $\pi(\mathbf{W}_i, \gamma)$ are well-specified or not (the calculations are omitted). If $m(\mathbf{W}_i, \theta)$ and $\pi(\mathbf{W}_i, \gamma)$ are well-specified, then $\Sigma_7(\beta_0, \theta_0, \gamma_0) = \Sigma_8(\beta_0, \theta_0, \gamma_0) = \Sigma_1(\beta_0)$ and the variance reduces to $\Sigma_1^{-1}(\beta_0)$.

3.3.6. *Elements of empirical processes*

In this section, we summarize the concepts of empirical processes that are helpful in understanding the proof of lemma 3.1 (it is not necessary to read this section to have a general understanding of the book). The presentation that follows here is strongly inspired by Chapter 19 of van der Vaart (1998). Readers who are interested in more detailed information are strongly invited to refer to it.

3.3.6.1. *Empirical measure, distribution function and processes*

Let $X_1, X_2, \ldots$ be a sequence of i.i.d. random variables with distribution function F. To the sample $X_1, \ldots, X_n$, let us associate the quantity $\mathbb{P}_n$ defined by:

$$\mathbb{P}_n = \frac{1}{n}\sum_{i=1}^{n} \delta_{X_i}$$

We call it the *empirical distribution* (δ_x denotes the Dirac measure at x). This is the discrete uniform measure on the observations $\{X_1, \ldots, X_n\}$. We have: $\mathbb{P}_n(A) = \frac{1}{n}\sum_{i=1}^{n} \delta_{X_i}(A) = \text{card}\{1 \le i \le n : X_i \in A\}/n$.

Also, define the *empirical distribution function* $\mathbb{F}_n : \mathbb{R} \to [0, 1]$ as:

$$\begin{aligned}
\mathbb{F}_n(t) &= \mathbb{P}_n((-\infty, t]) \\
&= \frac{1}{n}\sum_{i=1}^{n} 1\{X_i \le t\}
\end{aligned}$$

REMARK.– The quantities $\mathbb{P}_n$ and $\mathbb{F}_n$ are random variables (to simplify the notation, we have omitted the random ω in the definitions): $\mathbb{P}_n$ is a random variable with values in the set of probability distributions on $\mathbb{R}$, and $\mathbb{F}_n$ is a random variable with values in the set of distribution functions on $\mathbb{R}$. ■

Finally, the family of random variables $\{\alpha_n(t) = \sqrt{n}\,(\mathbb{F}_n(t) - F(t)), t \in \mathbb{R}\}$ is called the *empirical process* (indexed by t). One realization of α_n is a function $t \mapsto \alpha_n(t)$, which is called the sample path.

For every $t \in \mathbb{R}$, the $1\{X_i \leq t\}$ are independent Bernoulli variables $\mathcal{B}(F(t))$. For every $t \in \mathbb{R}$, the strong law of large numbers ensures that:

$$\mathbb{F}_n(t) \xrightarrow[n\to\infty]{a.s.} F(t)$$

and from the central limit theorem:

$$\forall t \in \mathbb{R},\ \alpha_n(t) \xrightarrow[n\to\infty]{\mathcal{L}} \mathcal{N}(0, F(t)(1 - F(t)))$$

The multivariate central limit theorem states a slightly stronger result: for every $(t_1, \ldots, t_k) \in \mathbb{R}^k$, the vector $(\alpha_n(t_1), \ldots, \alpha_n(t_k))$ converges in distribution to a centered Gaussian vector with variance–covariance matrix $\mathbf{V} = (V_{i,j})$, where:

$$\begin{aligned} V_{i,j} &= \text{cov}(1\{X \leq t_i\}, 1\{X \leq t_j\}) \\ &= F(t_i \wedge t_j) - F(t_i)F(t_j) \end{aligned}$$

where $s \wedge t := \min(s, t)$.

The Glivenko–Cantelli and Donsker theorems provide uniform versions of these results.

3.3.6.2. *Glivenko–Cantelli and Donsker theorems*

The (random) quantity $\sup_{t\in\mathbb{R}} |\mathbb{F}_n(t) - F(t)| = \|\mathbb{F}_n - F\|_\infty$ is known as the *Kolmogorov–Smirnov statistic*. The Glivenko–Cantelli and Donsker theorems set out its convergence properties (we provide them without proof; see van der Vaart (1998)).

THEOREM 3.10 (GLIVENKO–CANTELLI THEOREM).– *Let $X_1, X_2, \ldots$ be a sequence of i.i.d. random variables with distribution function F. Then:*

$$\|\mathbb{F}_n - F\|_\infty \xrightarrow[n\to\infty]{a.s.} 0$$

We denote by $D[-\infty, \infty]$ the space of càdlàg functions (continues à droite, avec limite à gauche, in French) endowed with the supremum norm. Donsker's theorem states a "uniform" version of the central limit theorem.

THEOREM 3.11 (DONSKER'S THEOREM).– *Let $X_1, X_2, \dots$ be a sequence of i.i.d. random variables with distribution function F. Then the sequence of empirical processes $(\alpha_n)_n$ converges in distribution in $D[-\infty, \infty]$ to a centered Gaussian process G_F with covariance function:*

$$cov(G_F(s), G_F(t)) = \mathbb{E}(G_F(s)G_F(t)) = F(s \wedge t) - F(s)F(t), \quad \forall s, t \in \mathbb{R}$$

The Glivenko–Cantelli and Donsker theorems for real empirical processes can be thought of as special cases of more general results that apply to empirical processes indexed by classes of functions.

3.3.6.3. *Empirical processes indexed by functions*

Consider a sequence $X, X_1, X_2, \dots$ of i.i.d. random variables from a distribution P on the space $(\mathcal{X}, \mathcal{A})$. Let $\mathcal{F}$ be a class of measurable functions from $\mathcal{X}$ into $\mathbb{R}$. For every $f \in \mathcal{F}$, set:

$$Pf = \mathbb{E}[f(X)] = \int f\, dP \text{ and } \mathbb{P}_n f = \frac{1}{n}\sum_{i=1}^{n} f(X_i) = \int f\, d\mathbb{P}_n$$

The stochastic process $\{\mathbb{G}_n f, f \in \mathcal{F}\}$ defined by:

$$\mathbb{G}_n f = \sqrt{n}(\mathbb{P}_n f - Pf) = \frac{1}{\sqrt{n}}\sum_{i=1}^{n}(f(X_i) - Pf)$$

is called the empirical process indexed by $\mathcal{F}$. It is a random function from $\mathcal{F}$ into $\mathbb{R}$.

REMARK.– If $\mathcal{X} = \mathbb{R}$, the process $\{\alpha_n(t), t \in \mathbb{R}\}$ can be rewritten in the form $\{\mathbb{G}_n f, f \in \mathcal{F}\}$, where $\mathcal{F} = \{1\{\cdot \le t\}, t \in \mathbb{R}\}$ is the set of indicators of the half-line $(-\infty, t]$. So we can think of a real empirical process as being indexed by either $t \in \mathbb{R}$ or by $f \in \mathcal{F}$. ■

For $f \in \mathcal{F}$, the strong law of large numbers ensures that $\mathbb{P}_n f \xrightarrow[n\to\infty]{a.s.} Pf$. A class $\mathcal{F}$ of functions for which this convergence is satisfied uniformly is called a Glivenko–Cantelli class.

DEFINITION 3.1 (GLIVENKO–CANTELLI CLASS).– *A class $\mathcal{F}$ of functions $f : \mathcal{X} \to \mathbb{R}$ is said to be P-Glivenko–Cantelli (or simply Glivenko–Cantelli) if:*

$$\|\mathbb{P}_n - P\|_{\mathcal{F}} = \sup_{f\in\mathcal{F}} |\mathbb{P}_n f - Pf| \xrightarrow[n\to\infty]{a.s.} 0$$

A Glivenko–Cantelli class provides a uniform law of large numbers, because the property:

$$\lim_{n\to\infty} \sup_{f\in\mathcal{F}} \left| \frac{1}{n}\sum_{i=1}^{n} f(X_i) - \mathbb{E}[f(X)] \right| = 0 \; a.s.$$

controls an infinite number of laws of large numbers simultaneously. We also say that $\mathcal{F}$ is a Glivenko–Cantelli class when the convergence holds in probability.

If $f \in \mathcal{F}$ and $Pf^2 < \infty$, the central limit theorem ensures that:

$$\mathbb{G}_n f \xrightarrow[n\to\infty]{\mathcal{L}} \mathcal{N}(0, P(f - Pf)^2)$$

and from the multivariate central limit theorem, for any finite set $(f_1, \dots, f_k)$ of functions in $\mathcal{F}$ such that $Pf_i^2 < \infty$, $(\mathbb{G}_n f_1, \dots, \mathbb{G}_n f_k)$ converges in distribution to a Gaussian vector $(Gf_1, \dots, Gf_k)$ with mean zero and covariances $P(f_i f_j) - Pf_i Pf_j$. A class of functions for which there exists a "uniform" version of this convergence is called a Donsker class.

In what follows, denote by $\ell^\infty(\mathcal{F})$ the space of bounded functions $z : \mathcal{F} \to \mathbb{R}$, endowed with the norm $\|z\|_\mathcal{F} = \sup_{f\in\mathcal{F}} |z(f)|$. Recall that a sequence of processes $\{Z_n(f), f \in \mathcal{F}\}$ converges in distribution in $\ell^\infty(\mathcal{F})$ to the process $\{Z(f), f \in \mathcal{F}\}$ if, for every continuous and bounded function h from $\ell^\infty(\mathcal{F})$ into $\mathbb{R}$, we have: $\mathbb{E}[h(Z_n)] \longrightarrow \mathbb{E}[h(Z)]$ (see van der Vaart (1998)).

DEFINITION 3.2 (DONSKER CLASS).– *A class $\mathcal{F}$ of functions $f : \mathcal{X} \to \mathbb{R}$ is said to be P-Donsker if the sequence of processes $\{\mathbb{G}_n f, f \in \mathcal{F}\}$ converges in distribution in the space $\ell^\infty(\mathcal{F})$ to a process $\{Gf, f \in \mathcal{F}\}$. The limit process G, called a P-Brownian bridge, is a centered Gaussian process with covariance function cov$(Gf_1, Gf_2) = P(f_1 f_2) - Pf_1 Pf_2$.*

A Donsker class provides a uniform central limit theorem because the property:

$$\sqrt{n}\left(\frac{1}{n}\sum_{i=1}^{n} f(X_i) - Pf\right) \xrightarrow[n\to\infty]{\mathcal{L}} \mathcal{N}(0, \text{var}(f(X)))$$

is satisfied for every $f \in \mathcal{F}$ simultaneously.

REMARK.– If $\mathcal{F}$ is Donsker, by continuity of the norm, we have: $\|\mathbb{G}_n\|_\mathcal{F} \xrightarrow[n\to\infty]{\mathcal{L}} \|G\|_\mathcal{F}$. Similarly, we have: $n^{-1/2}\|\mathbb{G}_n\|_\mathcal{F} \xrightarrow[n\to\infty]{\mathcal{L}} 0$, and hence also: $n^{-1/2}\|\mathbb{G}_n\|_\mathcal{F} \xrightarrow[n\to\infty]{\mathbb{P}} 0$. From this, we deduce that $\|\mathbb{P}_n - P\|_\mathcal{F} \xrightarrow[n\to\infty]{\mathbb{P}} 0$ and thus every Donsker class is also a Glivenko–Cantelli class. ■

Whether a given class $\mathcal{F}$ is a Glivenko–Cantelli or Donsker class depends on its size, which can be measured in terms of bracketing entropy.

3.3.6.4. *Sufficient conditions for $\mathcal{F}$ to be Glivenko–Cantelli or Donsker*

First, let us introduce some notation. If $1 \leq r < \infty$, we will use $L_r(P)$ to denote the set of functions $g : \mathcal{X} \to \mathbb{R}$ such that $\|g\|_{P,r} = (P|c|^r)^{1/r} < \infty$.

If l and u are two functions, the *bracket* $[l, u]$ is the set of functions f such that $l \leq f \leq u$.

An ε*-bracket* in $L_r(P)$ is a bracket $[l, u]$ that satisfies $\|u - l\|_{P,r} \leq \varepsilon$. Also denote by $N_{[]}(\varepsilon, \mathcal{F}, L_r(P))$ the minimum number of ε-brackets required to cover $\mathcal{F}$ (the number $\ln(N_{[]}(\varepsilon, \mathcal{F}, L_r(P)))$ is called the *entropy with bracketing*). Finally, the quantity:

$$J_{[]}(1, \mathcal{F}, L_2(P)) = \int_0^1 \sqrt{\ln N_{[]}(\varepsilon, \mathcal{F}, L_2(P))}\, d\varepsilon$$

is called the *bracketing integral.*

The two following theorems state some conditions under which a class of functions is a Glivenko–Cantelli or Donsker class (the interested reader can refer to van der Vaart (1998) for the proofs).

THEOREM 3.12.– *If $N_{[]}(\varepsilon, \mathcal{F}, L_1(P)) < \infty$ for every $\varepsilon > 0$, then $\mathcal{F}$ is Glivenko–Cantelli.*

THEOREM 3.13.– *If $\mathcal{F}$ is such that $J_{[]}(1, \mathcal{F}, L_2(P)) < \infty$, then $\mathcal{F}$ is P-Donsker.*

3.4. Exercises

Recall that a random variable Y follows an exponential distribution with parameter λ (where $\lambda > 0$) if its density is: $f(y) = \lambda e^{-\lambda y}$, $y \in \mathbb{R}_+$. Denote $Y \sim \mathcal{E}(\lambda)$, and recall that $\mathbb{E}(Y) = 1/\lambda$.

Exercise 1 – On censoring

If not properly taken into account, censoring can induce a bias into the estimate. This exercise seeks to illustrate this by the means of a few examples.

Let Y be a positive random variable. Denote by f_Y its density, F_Y its distribution function and $S_Y = 1 - F_Y$ its survival function. Suppose that Y can be right-censored by a variable C. Then, we observe the pair (Y^*, δ), where $Y^* = \min(Y, C)$ and $\delta = 1\{Y \leq C\}$. We wish to estimate $S_Y(t) = \mathbb{P}(Y > t)$ based on the i.i.d. sample (Y_i^*, δ_i), $i = 1, \ldots, n$.

1) The first estimator that we will consider is the empirical survival function of the Y_i^*:

$$\hat{S}_1(t) = \frac{1}{n} \sum_{i=1}^{n} 1\{Y_i^* > t\}$$

From the law of large numbers, $\hat{S}_1(t)$ converges in probability to $\mathbb{P}(Y^* > t)$ when $n \to \infty$. Show that $\mathbb{P}(Y^* > t) \leq S_Y(t)$. Explain why we might expect $\hat{S}_1(t)$ to underestimate $S_Y(t)$.

a) Suppose that Y and C are independent. Give a sufficient condition on the distribution of C for which $\mathbb{P}(Y^* > t) < S_Y(t)$.

2) We can construct a second estimator (also non-parametric) of $S_Y(t)$ by removing the censored data of the sample and then by calculating the empirical survival function using the remaining data:

$$\hat{S}_2(t) = \frac{\sum_{i=1}^{n} 1\{Y_i^* > t, \delta_i = 1\}}{\sum_{i=1}^{n} \delta_i}$$

a) Suppose that the censoring is fixed and occurs at $C = c$. Show that $\hat{S}_2(t)$ converges in probability to a limit $s(t)$ such that $s(t) \leq S_Y(t)$.

b) Suppose that C is random and independent of Y. Denote by S_C its survival function. Show that:

$$\hat{S}_2(t) \xrightarrow[n \to \infty]{\mathbb{P}} h(t) = \frac{\int_t^{\infty} f_Y(y) S_C(y)\, dy}{\int_0^{\infty} f_Y(y) S_C(y)\, dy}$$

Suppose that $Y \sim \mathcal{E}(\lambda_Y)$ and $C \sim \mathcal{E}(\lambda_C)$. Show that:

$$h(t) = e^{-(\lambda_Y + \lambda_C)t}$$

Compare $h(t)$ and $S_Y(t)$. How does the asymptotic bias of $\hat{S}_2(t)$ vary as a function of λ_C?

REMARK.– The usual non-parametric estimator of the survival function in the presence of random right-censoring is the *Kaplan–Meier estimator* (Kaplan and Meier 1958). It takes into account the censoring while being consistent and asymptotically Gaussian (the interested reader can find more detailed information in Andersen et al. (1993)). ■

Exercise 2 – Censored likelihood

Let Y be a continuous and positive random variable (e.g. this could represent a hospitalization duration, or a period of unemployment). Suppose that Y is right-censored by a continuous and positive random variable C. Let $Y^* = \min(Y, C)$ denote the duration observed and $\delta = 1\{Y \leq C\}$ the censoring indicator.

Denote by f_Y the density of Y and $S_Y(y) = \mathbb{P}(Y > y)$ its survival function (also denote by f_C and S_C the density and survival function of C, respectively). Suppose that Y and C are independent.

1) Let $t \geq 0$. Show that $\mathbb{P}(Y^* \leq t, \delta = 1) = \int_0^t f_Y(u) S_C(u)\, du$ and $\mathbb{P}(Y^* \leq t, \delta = 0) = \int_0^t S_Y(u) f_C(u)\, du$. Deduce from this, the density of the pair (Y^*, δ).

2) Suppose that the distribution of Y is known up to some parameter $\theta \in \mathbb{R}^p$. Denote $f_\theta = f_Y$ and $S_\theta = S_Y$. Suppose we have available an i.i.d. sample (Y_i^*, δ_i), $i = 1, \ldots, n$ of (Y^*, δ).

a) Write down the likelihood of θ in the form:

$$L_n(\theta) = \prod_{i=1}^{n} A_i^{\delta_i} B_i^{1-\delta_i}$$

where A_i and B_i are two terms to be determined.

b) Suppose that the distribution of C does not depend on θ (the non-informative censoring hypothesis). Explain why the part of L_n that is useful when estimating θ reduces down to:

$$\prod_{i=1}^{n} \{f_\theta(Y_i^*)\}^{\delta_i} \{S_\theta(Y_i^*)\}^{1-\delta_i} \qquad [3.26]$$

c) Suppose that $Y \sim \mathcal{E}(\theta)$. By using [3.26], show that the MLE of θ is given by:

$$\hat{\theta}_n = \frac{\sum_{i=1}^{n} \delta_i}{\sum_{i=1}^{n} Y_i^*}$$

REMARK.– If no observation is censored (so that $\delta_i = 1$ for each i), then $\hat{\theta}_n$ reduces to $1/\bar{Y}_n$ and, from the law of large numbers, $\hat{\theta}_n \xrightarrow[n\to\infty]{\mathbb{P}} 1/\mathbb{E}(Y) = \theta$.

■

d) Suppose that $Y \sim \mathcal{E}(\theta)$ and $C \sim \mathcal{E}(\lambda)$. Show that $Y^* \sim \mathcal{E}(\theta + \lambda)$ and also that:

$$\mathbb{E}(\delta) = \frac{\theta}{\theta + \lambda}$$

From this, deduce that $\hat{\theta}_n \xrightarrow[n\to\infty]{\mathbb{P}} \theta$.

Exercise 3 – Exponential regression model

Consider a random duration Y that follows an exponential distribution with parameter $\lambda e^{\beta^\top \mathbf{X}}$, where $\mathbf{X}$ is a vector of p explanatory variables (with no constant term), β is a regression parameter (the parameter of interest of the model) and $\lambda > 0$. This model is called the *exponential regression model*, and it is used in lifetime data analysis (see, for example, Klein and Moeschberger (2013)). In R, this model can be estimated using the `survreg` function from the `survival` package (Therneau and Grambsch 2013).

Let C be a right-censoring time, assumed to be independent of Y and non-informative. Set $Y^* = \min(Y, C)$ and $\delta = 1\{Y \leq C\}$. Suppose that we have available an i.i.d. sample $(Y_i^*, \delta_i, \mathbf{X}_i)$, $i = 1, \ldots, n$.

1) Show that the likelihood of (λ, β) can be written as:

$$L_n(\lambda, \beta) = \lambda^{\sum_{i=1}^n \delta_i} \exp\left(\beta \sum_{i=1}^n \delta_i \mathbf{X}_i - \lambda \sum_{i=1}^n Y_i^* e^{\beta^\top \mathbf{X}_i}\right)$$

HINT.– Use [3.26].

2) In this question, let $\{\delta_i, i = 1, \ldots, n\}$ be the observations and suppose that, for each i, δ_i follows the $\mathcal{P}(Y_i^* \lambda e^{\beta^\top \mathbf{X}_i})$ distribution. Calculate the likelihood of (λ, β) under this model and show that it is proportional to $L_n(\lambda, \beta)$.

REMARK.– This observation allows us to estimate the parameters λ and β of an exponential regression model using the `glm` function: it suffices to adjust the model $\mathcal{P}(\mu_i)$ to the $\delta_i, i = 1, \ldots, n$, using:

$$\mu_i = \exp(\ln \lambda + \beta^\top \mathbf{X}_i + \ln Y_i^*)$$

The linear predictor can be rewritten in the form $\tilde{\beta}^\top \tilde{\mathbf{X}}_i + \ln Y_i^*$, where $\tilde{\beta} = (\ln \lambda, \beta^\top)^\top$ and $\tilde{\mathbf{X}}_i = (1, \mathbf{X}_i^\top)^\top$. The $\ln Y_i^*$ term is treated like an explanatory variable, but whose coefficient is known and fixed to be equal to 1 (which is indicated in `glm` by `offset(log(Ycens))`, where `Ycens` denotes the variable Y_i^*). ■

Exercise 4 – Complete-case estimator

Reusing the notation from section 3.2.3, show that:

$$\sqrt{n}(\hat{\mu}_{cc} - \mu) \xrightarrow[n\to\infty]{\mathcal{L}} \mathcal{N}\left(0, \frac{\text{var}(X)}{\mathbb{E}(\xi)}\right)$$

HINT.– Determine the limit distribution of:

$$\sqrt{n}\begin{pmatrix} n^{-1}\sum_{i=1}^{n} X_i\xi_i - \mathbb{E}(X\xi) \\ n^{-1}\sum_{i=1}^{n} \xi_i - \mathbb{E}(\xi) \end{pmatrix}$$

and then use the multivariate version of the delta method, which was described in exercise 9 of Chapter 2.

4

Zero-Inflated Models

4.1. Introduction

In Chapter 2, we applied the Poisson regression model to the `docvisits` data set (provided by the R package `zic` (Jochmann 2017)). This data set comes from a longitudinal study of approximately 11,000 German households. Each year, participants provide information regarding their income, health, professional career, etc. A summarized description of the data is provided in section 2.5 of this book. Let us just remember that the statistical individuals are the survey participants, and that the response variable is the number of times that a participant consulted a doctor (at a practice) during the last three months of 1994 (the `docvisits` variable).

4.1.1. *Overdispersion*

In section 2.5, we presented a histogram of the response variable, which is reproduced below. Two points were observed: (i) the presence in the histogram of a "peak at zero", corresponding to a very large proportion of participants who did not consult a doctor during the last three months (about 41%); and (ii) a large difference between the empirical mean and variance of the response variable:

```
mean(docvisits[,1])
[1] 2.958057
var(docvisits[,1])
[1] 27.28924
```

For a color version of the code in this chapter, see www.iste.co.uk/dupuy/linearmodels.zip.

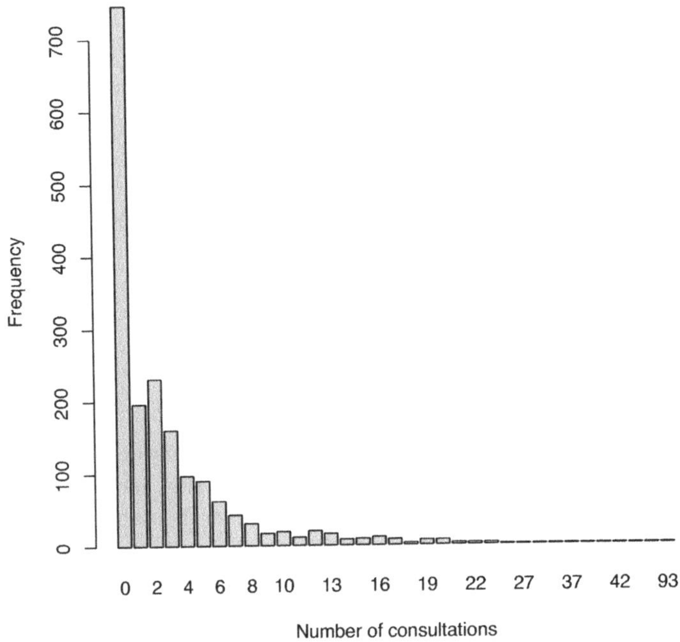

Figure 4.1. *Histogram of the number of consultations (*`docvisits` *data set)*

The ratio (empirical variance)/(empirical mean) equals:

```
var(docvisits[,1])/mean(docvisits[,1])
[1] 9.225392
```

This value does not align with the equidispersion property (that the mean and variance are equal) of the Poisson distribution. The variance of the observations is greater than their mean, in which case we say that the data are *overdispersed*. Of course, comparing the empirical mean and variance is not completely relevant here.

Indeed, it is not reasonable to assume that the observations of the `docvisits` variable all follow a single Poisson distribution. On the contrary, it is likely that some of their variability can be attributed to the explanatory variables described in section 2.5, which characterize individual participants.

A refined analysis of the data dispersion can be obtained by calculating the ratio:

$$\phi = \frac{\mathrm{var}(Y|\mathbf{X})}{\mathbb{E}(Y|\mathbf{X})}$$

Equidispersion corresponds to the case when $\phi = 1$, and overdispersion to the case when $\phi > 1$. If $\phi < 1$, we speak of underdispersion. ϕ is unknown, but it can be estimated once a Poisson regression has been adjusted to the data. Consider the model[1] from section 2.5:

$$Y_i \sim \mathcal{P}(\mu_i), i = 1, \ldots, n$$

where:

$$\begin{aligned}\mu_i = \exp(&\beta_1 + \beta_2\mathtt{age}_i + \beta_3\mathtt{health}_i + \beta_4\mathtt{handicap}_i + \beta_5\mathtt{hdegree}_i + \beta_6\mathtt{married}_i \\ &+\beta_7\mathtt{schooling}_i + \beta_8\mathtt{hhincome}_i + \beta_9\mathtt{children}_i + \beta_{10}\mathtt{self}_i + \beta_{11}\mathtt{civil}_i \\ &+\beta_{12}\mathtt{bluec}_i + \beta_{13}\mathtt{employed}_i + \beta_{14}\mathtt{public}_i + \beta_{15}\mathtt{addon}_i)\end{aligned} \quad [4.1]$$

It is natural to estimate:

$$\phi = \frac{\mathrm{var}(Y|\mathbf{X})}{\mathbb{E}(Y|\mathbf{X})} = \mathbb{E}\left[\frac{(Y_i - \mu_i)^2}{\mu_i}\middle|\mathbf{X}_i\right]$$

by:

$$\widehat{\phi} = \frac{1}{n-p}\sum_{i=1}^{n}\frac{(Y_i - \hat{\mu}_i)^2}{\hat{\mu}_i}$$

where $\hat{\mu}_i$ is obtained by replacing the β_j by their MLEs in [4.1]. The $(Y_i - \hat{\mu}_i)/\sqrt{\hat{\mu}_i}$, $i = 1, \ldots, n$ are the Pearson residuals. In R, they are given by the `residuals` function, which allows for $\widehat{\phi}$ to be easily calculated:

```
datadoc=data.frame(age,health,handicap,hdegree,married,schooling,
    hhincome,children,self,civil,bluec,employed,public,addon)
mod_pois=glm(nbvisits~.,data=datadoc,family=poisson(link="log"))
p.res=residuals(mod_pois,"pearson")
phi=sum(p.res^2)/df.residual(mod_pois)
phi
[1] 5.316671
```

1 The notation is the same as that from section 2.5. It is not recalled here.

The inclusion of the explanatory variables has reduced the overdispersion, but its level still remains significant ($\widehat{\phi} \approx 5.3$). Why is this overdispersion a problem? Intuitively, adjusting the Poisson model to overdispersed data induces the variance of the MLE to be underestimated. Therefore, the standard errors obtained will be "too small". However, these standard errors are used to calculate the Wald tests and confidence intervals. The first consequence of this is that the nonsignificant explanatory variables are at risk of appearing significant (in fact, underestimating a standard error causes the corresponding Wald statistic to increase). The confidence intervals obtained will also have a lower confidence level compared to the nominal one.

REMARK.– There are many causes that can give rise to overdispersion: unobserved heterogeneity, the omission of important explanatory variables (meaning that the heterogeneity of the data will not be taken into account correctly), an excess of zeros, the presence of outliers, etc. Many of these causes may also occur simultaneously. ■

The following example illustrates what is meant by "unobserved heterogeneity". Consider a population composed of smokers and nonsmokers. We denote by Y the number of illnesses reported by an individual over the course of a given time period. Suppose that $Y \sim \mathcal{P}(\mu_0)$ for the nonsmoking individuals, and $Y \sim \mathcal{P}(\mu_1)$ for the smoking individuals (where $\mu_0 \neq \mu_1$). Furthermore, we denote by X the variable which equals 1 if an individual smokes and 0 if not, and suppose that $X \sim \mathcal{B}(p)$, where $0 < p < 1$.

Smoking status is a factor of population heterogeneity, relative to the number of illnesses reported. Indeed, the distribution of Y differs according to the value of X, but it is equidistributed within each of the two subpopulations of smoking and nonsmoking individuals.

Suppose now that X is not observed (or is ignored by the modeler). We can easily calculate the marginal mean and marginal variance of Y as:

$$\begin{aligned}\mathbb{E}(Y) &= \mathbb{E}(\mathbb{E}(Y|X)) \\ &= \mathbb{E}(\mu_0(1-X) + \mu_1 X) \\ &= \mu_0(1-p) + \mu_1 p\end{aligned}$$

and:

$$\begin{aligned}\text{var}(Y) &= \mathbb{E}(\text{var}(Y|X)) + \text{var}(\mathbb{E}(Y|X)) \\ &= \mathbb{E}(Y) + \text{var}(\mu_0(1-X) + \mu_1 X) \\ &= \mathbb{E}(Y) + (\mu_1 - \mu_0)^2 p(1-p)\end{aligned}$$

We see that var$(Y) > \mathbb{E}(Y)$. The marginal distribution of Y is therefore overdispersed. Intuitively, if the heterogeneity induced by X in the distribution of Y is not explicitly taken into account, then it manifests itself in the form of overdispersion in the marginal distribution of Y. This overdispersion corresponds to the part of the variability in Y explained by X.

Having seen this example, we can easily understand why overdispersion occurs frequently in count data. Despite the care taken when collecting data, it is rare to observe or to be able to measure every explanatory variable that can influence a given response variable.

For the rest of this book, we will focus on excess zeros, also called "zero inflation", which calls for specific modeling techniques, as described in the remainder of this chapter. Other methods are available to take overdispersion arising from unobserved heterogeneity into account: the quasi-Poisson model, generalized Poisson model, negative-binomial model, etc. For more on these subjects, the reader can consult Cameron and Trivedi (1998); Hilbe (2011); Dupuy (2018); Hardin and Hilbe (2018) and the literature review by Coly et al. (2016), for example.

4.1.2. *Excess of zeros*

An excess of zeros is said to occur when the proportion of observed zeros in the sample is greater than the amount expected with the adjusted model. It is not difficult to modify a discrete distribution so that it can handle an excess of zeros. Starting with a discrete distribution (let us say, the probability distribution of a random variable Y^* taking on the values $0, 1, 2\ldots$ with probabilities $p_0, p_1, p_2\ldots$), we can define a *zero-inflated* probability distribution by setting:

$$\mathbb{P}(Y = y) = \begin{cases} \pi + (1-\pi)p_0 & \text{if } y = 0 \\ (1-\pi)p_y & \text{if } y = 1, 2, \ldots \end{cases} \qquad [4.2]$$

where π represents the proportion of additional zeros (which we will call the "zero-inflation probability"). Note that:

$$\mathbb{P}(Y = 0) = p_0 + \pi(1 - p_0) > p_0$$

if $\pi > 0$. The probability p_0 of observing zero in the original model has therefore been increased ("inflated") by the quantity $\pi(1 - p_0)$.

The mean and variance of Y are calculated based upon those of Y^*:

$$\begin{aligned}\mathbb{E}(Y) &= \sum_{y=0}^{+\infty} y\,\mathbb{P}(Y=y) \\ &= (1-\pi)\sum_{y=0}^{+\infty} y\,p_y \\ &= (1-\pi)\mathbb{E}(Y^*)\end{aligned} \qquad [4.3]$$

and:

$$\begin{aligned}\text{var}(Y) &= \sum_{y=0}^{+\infty} y^2\,\mathbb{P}(Y=y) - (\mathbb{E}Y)^2 \\ &= (1-\pi)\sum_{y=0}^{+\infty} y^2\,p_y - (\mathbb{E}Y)^2 \\ &= (1-\pi)\left\{\text{var}(Y^*) + (\mathbb{E}Y^*)^2\right\} - (1-\pi)^2(\mathbb{E}Y^*)^2 \\ &= (1-\pi)\text{var}(Y^*) + \pi(1-\pi)(\mathbb{E}Y^*)^2\end{aligned} \qquad [4.4]$$

We can therefore calculate the coefficient of dispersion $\phi = \text{var}(Y)/\mathbb{E}(Y)$ of Y as a function of the coefficient of dispersion $\phi^* = \text{var}(Y^*)/\mathbb{E}(Y^*)$ of Y^*:

$$\phi = \phi^* + \pi\mathbb{E}(Y^*)$$

We see that $\phi > \phi^*$: introducing an excess of zeros into the distribution of Y^* has therefore increased the dispersion of the variable. We also see that the overdispersion increases with π, which makes sense.

The construction [4.2] defines a mixture model: the mixture of the distribution $p_y, y = 0, 1, 2, \ldots$ along with the Dirac measure at 0. It is based on the assumption that the observed individuals can be partitioned into two subpopulations: one subpopulation for which the response variable definitely equals 0 (this subpopulation represents the proportion π of the population being studied), and the other subpopulation of individuals for whom the response is randomly drawn from the distribution $p_0, p_1, p_2 \ldots$ This second subpopulation represents the proportion $1-\pi$ of the population being studied. Numerous examples of how this kind of modeling can be applied are provided in the literature. Here, we present three examples.

EXAMPLE 4.1 (FOREGOING HEALTHCARE).– In studies on medical healthcare consumption (measured by the number of visits to a doctor over a given time period), it is common to observe a significant proportion of zeros (e.g. see Yen et al. (2001);

Sarma and Simpson (2006); Sari (2009); Pizer and Prentice (2011); Staub and Winkelmann (2013); Diallo et al. (2017, 2018); Chen et al. (2019).

This usually corresponds to two situations: (i) individuals who have not needed to consult a doctor over the time period in question, or (ii) individuals who have given up on consulting a doctor, regardless of their health status (usually for economical reasons).

In the first case, we speak of "random" zeros (Staub and Winkelmann 2013) to indicate that an observed zero is the realization of a random variable, which otherwise would have been able to provide a nonzero observation, if the individual's state of health permitted. The corresponding subpopulation is sometimes known as the *population at risk* (in the sense of "at risk of experiencing the event of interest", which here would be a medical consultation). In case (ii), we speak of "structural zeros" (Staub and Winkelmann 2013), and the corresponding subpopulation is sometimes known as *population not at risk*.

EXAMPLE 4.2 (AUTOMOBILE INSURANCE).– An excess of zeros can also manifest itself in the domain of automobile insurance. The distribution of insurance claims for material damage (accidents, glass damage cover, etc.) often presents a peak at zero. This peak corresponds to the coexistence of two insured subpopulations: a subpopulation with no claims over the time period in question, and a subpopulation that refrains from making a claim to avoid affecting their no-claims bonus (see, for example, Yip and Yau (2005); Boucher and Denuit (2008); Boucher et al. (2009); Zhang et al. (2022)).

EXAMPLE 4.3 (HIGH-RISK BEHAVIORS).– Studying the determinants of risky behavior (e.g. in matters of sexuality or drug consumption) often leads to observing count data with an excess of zeros. The peak at zero corresponds to the presence of two subpopulations: (i) one subpopulation of individuals who have not engaged in any risky behavior over the time period in question (but who are nonetheless likely to report such behavior), and produce random zeros; and (ii) the other subpopulation of individuals who have eliminated this type of behavior from their habits and produce structural zeros (see, for example, Hu et al. (2011); Long et al. (2015); Tross et al. (2015)).

REMARK.– Let S denote a variable, which equals 0 if an individual systematically produces a zero, and equals 1 if not. We have $\mathbb{P}(Y = 0|S = 0) = 1$, $\mathbb{P}(Y = y|S = 1) = p_y$, and $S \sim \mathcal{B}(1 - \pi)$. In practice, S is not observed.

We can redefine the model [4.2] in light of its interpretation as a mixture model, where the variable S indicates which subpopulation an individual belongs to (either at risk or not at risk). The distribution of Y is thus defined by:

$$Y|S = 0 \sim \delta_0 \quad \text{and} \quad Y|S = 1 \sim \{p_y, y = 0, 1, 2, \ldots\}$$

where δ_0 denotes the Dirac measure at 0. We recover the model [4.2]:

$$\begin{aligned}\mathbb{P}(Y=0) &= \mathbb{P}(Y=0|S=0)\pi + \mathbb{P}(Y=0|S=1)(1-\pi) \\ &= \pi + (1-\pi)p_0\end{aligned}$$

and for $y = 1, 2, \ldots$:

$$\begin{aligned}\mathbb{P}(Y=y) &= \mathbb{P}(Y=y|S=0)\pi + \mathbb{P}(Y=y|S=1)(1-\pi) \\ &= 0 \times \pi + (1-\pi)p_y \\ &= (1-\pi)p_y\end{aligned}$$

This interpretation has led multiple authors (e.g. Lambert (1992); Hall (2000)) to use the EM algorithm to estimate zero-inflated models. The EM algorithm (which stands for *expectation-maximization* (Dempster et al. 1977)) is an estimation algorithm that is often used in missing-data problems and mixture models. In zero-inflated models, the variable S is treated like the missing data. ■

4.2. Zero-inflated Poisson models and extensions

4.2.1. *The zero-inflated Poisson model*

When the probabilities p_y of the model [4.2] are given by a Poisson distribution, we obtain the zero-inflated Poisson model, often abbreviated as the ZIP model. It is one of the most commonly used zero-inflated models and can be written as:

$$\mathbb{P}(Y=y) = \begin{cases} \pi + (1-\pi)e^{-\mu} & \text{if } y = 0 \\ (1-\pi)\frac{e^{-\mu}\mu^y}{y!} & \text{if } y = 1, 2, \ldots \end{cases} \qquad [4.5]$$

We denote $Y \sim \text{ZIP}(\pi, \mu)$. We also note:

$$Y \sim \pi\delta_0 + (1-\pi)\mathcal{P}(\mu)$$

which can be interpreted as:

$$Y \sim \begin{cases} 0 & \text{with probability } \pi \\ \mathcal{P}(\mu) & \text{with probability } 1-\pi \end{cases}$$

Figure 4.2 represents the frequency distributions for the ZIP$(0.2, 5)$ and $\mathcal{P}(5)$ distributions. It can be obtained using the `dzipois` function from the `R` package

VGAM (Yee 2010, 2015), which produces the probabilities $\mathbb{P}(\text{ZIP}(0.2, 5) = y)$. These probabilities and the $\mathbb{P}(\mathcal{P}(5) = y)$ ones are also presented in the following table. The code is:

```
barplot(rbind(dzipois(0:12,5,0.2),dpois(0:12,5)),beside=TRUE,col=
    c("blue","white"),names.arg=as.character(0:12))
cbind("Poisson"=dpois(0:12,5),"ZIP(0.2,5)"=dzipois(0:12,5,0.2))
```

```
          Poisson   ZIP(0.2,5)
 [1,] 0.006737947 0.205390358
 [2,] 0.033689735 0.026951788
 [3,] 0.084224337 0.067379470
 [4,] 0.140373896 0.112299117
 [5,] 0.175467370 0.140373896
 [6,] 0.175467370 0.140373896
 [7,] 0.146222808 0.116978247
 [8,] 0.104444863 0.083555890
 [9,] 0.065278039 0.052222431
[10,] 0.036265577 0.029012462
[11,] 0.018132789 0.014506231
[12,] 0.008242177 0.006593741
[13,] 0.003434240 0.002747392
```

The expectation and variance of the $\text{ZIP}(\pi, \mu)$ distribution are derived from the formulas [4.3] and [4.4] with $Y^* \sim \mathcal{P}(\mu)$:

$$\mathbb{E}(Y) = (1 - \pi)\mu$$

and:

$$\begin{aligned}\text{var}(Y) &= (1 - \pi)\text{var}(Y^*) + \pi(1 - \pi)(\mathbb{E}Y^*)^2 \\ &= (1 - \pi)\mu + \pi(1 - \pi)\mu^2 \\ &= (1 + \pi\mu)(1 - \pi)\mu \\ &= (1 + \pi\mu)\mathbb{E}(Y)\end{aligned}$$

The coefficient of dispersion equals:

$$\phi = 1 + \pi\mu$$

The excess of zeros has caused some overdispersion.

REMARK.– A large proportion of zeros is not, a priori, incompatible with a Poisson distribution. Indeed, the probability $\mathbb{P}(\mathcal{P}(\mu) = 0) = e^{-\mu}$ tends toward 1 when μ tends toward 0. But this constrains the mean and variance of the observations, both equal to μ, as very small. For example, for the $\mathcal{P}(0.3)$ distribution, the probability of observing 0 is high: $\mathbb{P}(\mathcal{P}(0.3) = 0) = e^{-0.3} \approx 0.741$, yet the mean and variance are both equal to 0.3.

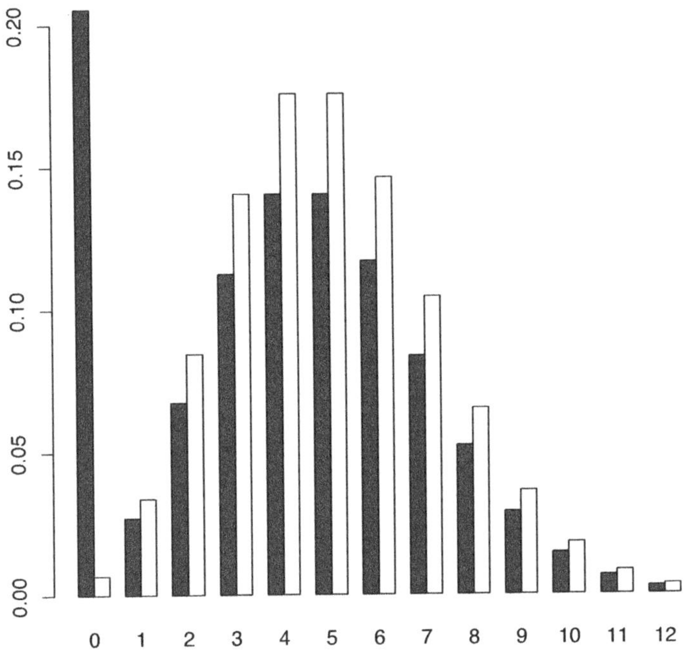

Figure 4.2. *Frequency distributions of the ZIP(0.2, 5) (blue) and $\mathcal{P}(5)$ (white) distributions. For a color version of this figure, see www.iste.co.uk/dupuy/linearmodels.zip*

A small numerical experiment also illustrates this observation. Let us simulate 1,000 realizations of the $\mathcal{P}(0.3)$ distribution using the `x=rpois(1 000, 0.3)` command. The proportion of zeros in the obtained sample is given by `mean(x==0)`. It equals 0.733, which is close to the theoretical probability of 0.741. The empirical mean and variance, given by `mean(x)` and `var(x)`, equal 0.299 and 0.276, respectively. They are both similarly close to the mean of 0.3. But note that the only values appearing in the sample are 0, 1, 2 and 3. The number of occurrences of each is provided by the `table` command:

```
table(x)
x
  0   1   2   3
733 236  30   1
```

The small value of μ strongly restricts the observable values. A sample containing the same proportion of zeros, but with a larger range (and therefore a greater mean and variance) could not therefore be correctly modeled by a Poisson distribution. The ZIP distribution thus offers an interesting alternative. ■

The model [4.5] can be extended to the case when π and/or μ depend on explanatory variables. The first work in this area dates back to Mullahy (1986) and Lambert (1992). For each individual i, suppose that we have some explanatory variables available and that we think a priori – or that we wish to test the hypothesis – that these variables influence the zero-inflation probability and/or the mean of Y. We define a ZIP regression model by allowing π and μ to depend on these variables. The model can be written as:

$$\mathbb{P}(Y_i = y) = \begin{cases} \pi(\mathbf{Z}_i) + (1 - \pi(\mathbf{Z}_i))e^{-\mu(\mathbf{X}_i)} & \text{if } y = 0 \\ (1 - \pi(\mathbf{Z}_i))\frac{e^{-\mu(\mathbf{X}_i)}\mu(\mathbf{X}_i)^y}{y!} & \text{if } y = 1, 2, \ldots \end{cases}$$

Here, we have denoted by $\mathbf{Z}_i$ the vector of explanatory variables acting on π and by $\mathbf{X}_i$ the vector of those acting on μ. These two vectors may share common components, coincide, or be distinct, depending on the modeler's choice.

REMARK.– Interpreting the effect of the explanatory variables can be complicated when they act on both π and μ at the same time. For this reason, many authors recommend avoiding using the same sets of explanatory variables in both $\mathbf{X}_i$ and $\mathbf{Z}_i$.

■

In this model, overdispersion must be understood in terms of the conditional distribution of Y_i given $\mathbf{X}_i$ and $\mathbf{Z}_i$:

$$\mathbb{E}(Y_i|\mathbf{X}_i, \mathbf{Z}_i) = (1 - \pi(\mathbf{Z}_i))\mu(\mathbf{X}_i)$$

and:

$$\text{var}(Y_i|\mathbf{X}_i, \mathbf{Z}_i) = (1 + \pi(\mathbf{Z}_i)\mu(\mathbf{X}_i))\mathbb{E}(Y_i|\mathbf{X}_i, \mathbf{Z}_i) \geq \mathbb{E}(Y_i|\mathbf{X}_i, \mathbf{Z}_i)$$

In Lambert (1992), $\pi(\mathbf{Z}_i)$ is modeled using logistic regression:

$$\pi(\mathbf{Z}_i) = \frac{e^{\gamma^\top \mathbf{Z}_i}}{1 + e^{\gamma^\top \mathbf{Z}_i}}$$

and:

$$\mu(\mathbf{X}_i) = e^{\beta^\top \mathbf{X}_i}$$

where β and γ are the unknown regression parameters to be estimated. For this, the maximum likelihood method can be used. Suppose that we have available a sample of independent observations $\{(Y_i, \mathbf{X}_i, \mathbf{Z}_i), i = 1, \ldots, n\}$. The likelihood is calculated as follows:

$$L_n(\beta,\gamma) = \prod_{i=1}^{n} \left(\pi(\mathbf{Z}_i) + (1-\pi(\mathbf{Z}_i))e^{-\mu(\mathbf{X}_i)}\right)^{1\{Y_i=0\}} \times \left((1-\pi(\mathbf{Z}_i))\frac{e^{-\mu(\mathbf{X}_i)}\mu(\mathbf{X}_i)^{Y_i}}{Y_i!}\right)^{1\{Y_i>0\}} \qquad [4.6]$$

The MLE of (β, γ) does not admit an explicit expression but it can be approximated by means of a Newton–Raphson type algorithm, like in the `zeroinfl` function from the R package `pscl` (Jackman 2020).

The MLE is consistent and asymptotically Gaussian. We will come back to this in section 4.2.3, in the general framework of the zero-inflated *generalized* Poisson regression model.

4.2.2. Semi-parametric ZIP models

In practice, $\pi(\mathbf{Z}_i)$ and $\mu(\mathbf{X}_i)$ are typically modeled parametrically (for simplicity of implementation and interpretation). Nevertheless, the parametric assumptions are more restrictive. *Semi-parametric* models, which are more flexible, have been proposed in the literature. For example, Lam et al. (2006) propose a ZIP(π_i, μ_i) model in which π_i and μ_i are given, respectively, by:

$$\pi_i = \frac{e^{\gamma^\top \mathbf{Z}_i}}{1 + e^{\gamma^\top \mathbf{Z}_i}}$$

and:

$$\mu_i = e^{\beta^\top \mathbf{X}_i + g(T_i)}$$

where $g(\cdot)$ is an unknown function, T_i is a quantitative explanatory variable and $\mathbf{Z}_i = (1, \mathbf{X}_i^\top, T_i)^\top$ (without loss of generality, Lam et al. (2006) assumes $T_i \in [0,1]$). The parameters of the model are β, γ and $g(\cdot)$.

The model therefore contains parametric unknowns – the vectors β and γ – and a nonparametric, or functional, unknown – the function $g(\cdot)$. For this reason, it is said to be semi-parametric.

In this model, the likelihood [4.6] becomes:

$$L_n(\beta,\gamma,g(\cdot)) = \prod_{i=1}^n \left(1+e^{\gamma^\top \mathbf{Z}_i}\right)^{-1}\left(e^{\gamma^\top \mathbf{Z}_i} + e^{-\exp(\beta^\top \mathbf{X}_i + g(T_i))}\right)^{1\{Y_i=0\}}$$
$$\times\left(\frac{e^{-\exp(\beta^\top \mathbf{X}_i+g(T_i))+Y_i(\beta^\top \mathbf{X}_i+g(T_i))}}{Y_i!}\right)^{1\{Y_i>0\}} \qquad [4.7]$$

Lam et al. (2006) propose estimating $g(\cdot)$ using a piecewise affine function on the interval $[0,1]$:

$$\hat{g}_m(t,\mathbf{a}) = \sum_{j=1}^m \left(\frac{a_j - a_{j-1}}{t_j - t_{j-1}}t - \frac{a_j t_{j-1} - a_{j-1}t_j}{t_j - t_{j-1}}\right) 1\{t_{j-1} \le t < t_j\}$$

where $0 = t_0 < t_1 < \ldots < t_m = 1$ denotes a partition of $[0,1]$, and $\mathbf{a} = (a_0,\ldots,a_m)^\top = (g(t_0),\ldots,g(t_m))^\top$ is an $(m+1)$-vector of unknown components. Estimating $g(\cdot)$ therefore reduces down to estimating a finite number of parameters, and we arrive back at a parametric estimation problem in which the parameters are β,γ and $\mathbf{a}$. We can use the maximum likelihood method. The likelihood to maximize is obtained by replacing $g(\cdot)$ by $\hat{g}_m(\cdot,\mathbf{a})$ in [4.7]. Once $\mathbf{a}$ has been estimated (we denote its MLE by $\hat{\mathbf{a}}_n$), we estimate $g(\cdot)$ as $\hat{g}_m(\cdot,\hat{\mathbf{a}}_n)$.

Lam et al. (2006) assume that $g(\cdot)$ is of class $\mathcal{C}^2$ and that $m = O(n^k)$ for some $0 < k < 1$. Under these conditions, $\hat{g}_m(\cdot,\hat{\mathbf{a}}_n)$ is consistent for $g(\cdot)$ (note that $\hat{g}_m(\cdot,\hat{\mathbf{a}}_n)$ depends on n via m: the larger n is, the larger m is, and thus the finer the partition).

Furthermore, the MLE's of β and γ are consistent and asymptotically Gaussian (we will not go into any further details here, but we will describe some asymptotic results below in a more general model).

In practice, Lam et al. (2006) recommends using a uniform partition $t_i = i/m$, $i = 0,\ldots,m$ and choosing m with the help of the AIC.

He et al. (2010) generalize this approach and propose a ZIP model in which both π_i and μ_i contain a nonparametric component:

$$\begin{cases} \mu_i = e^{\beta^\top \mathbf{X}_i + g(T_i)} \\ \pi_i = \frac{e^{\gamma^\top \mathbf{X}_i + h(T_i)}}{1+e^{\gamma^\top \mathbf{X}_i + h(T_i)}} \end{cases}$$

Like in Lam et al. (2006), $g(\cdot)$ and $h(\cdot)$ are approximated using piecewise affine functions. Up to notational adaption, the likelihood in the model proposed by He et al. (2010) is calculated analogously to the likelihood [4.7].

For a fixed n, this likelihood depends on a finite number of parameters which are β, γ, and the coefficients $\mathbf{a} = (g(t_0), \ldots, g(t_m))^\top$ and $\mathbf{b} = (h(t_0), \ldots, h(t_m))^\top$ in the approximations of $g(\cdot)$ and $h(\cdot)$ by piecewise affine functions. We denote by:

$$(\hat{\beta}_n, \hat{\gamma}_n, \hat{\mathbf{a}}_n, \hat{\mathbf{b}}_n) = \arg \max_{\beta,\gamma,\mathbf{a},\mathbf{b}} L_n(\beta, \gamma, \hat{g}_m(\cdot, \mathbf{a}), \hat{h}_m(\cdot, \mathbf{b}))$$

the MLE's of β, γ, $\mathbf{a}$ and $\mathbf{b}$. Also denote by $\theta = (\beta^\top, \gamma^\top, g(\cdot), h(\cdot))^\top$, θ_0 the true value of θ, and $\hat{\theta}_n = (\hat{\beta}_n^\top, \hat{\gamma}_n^\top, \hat{g}_m(\cdot, \hat{\mathbf{a}}_n), \hat{h}_m(\cdot, \hat{\mathbf{b}}_n))^\top$. Finally, set:

$$d(\theta_1, \theta_2) = \|\beta_1 - \beta_2\| + \|\gamma_1 - \gamma_2\| + \|g_1 - g_2\|_2 + \|h_1 - h_2\|_2$$

where $\|\cdot\|_2$ denotes the norm:

$$\|f\|_2 = \left(\int_0^1 |f(t)|^2 \, dt \right)^{\frac{1}{2}}$$

He et al. (2010) prove the (almost sure) convergence of $\hat{\theta}_n$.

THEOREM 4.1.– *Suppose that the explanatory variables $\mathbf{X}_i$ are bounded, $T_i \in [0,1]$, β_0 and γ_0 belong to the interiors of compact subsets of $\mathbb{R}^p$, $g_0(\cdot)$ and $h_0(\cdot)$ are of class C^r (for $r = 1$ or 2) and $m = O(n^k)$ for a given $0 < k < 1$. Then $d(\hat{\theta}_n, \theta_0) \xrightarrow[n\to\infty]{a.s.} 0$. Furthermore, $d(\hat{\theta}_n, \theta_0) = O_{\mathbb{P}}(\max\{n^{-(1-k)/2}, n^{-rk}\})$.*

In particular, if we take $k = 1/(2r+1)$, we then have $d(\hat{\theta}_n, \theta_0) = O_{\mathbb{P}}(n^{-r/(2r+1)})$, which is the optimal rate of convergence (He et al. 2010).

REMARK.– Recall that if $(X_n)_n$ denotes a sequence of real random variables, $X_n = O_{\mathbb{P}}(1)$ means that for every $\varepsilon > 0$, there exists $M > 0$ such that for each $n \geq 1$, $\mathbb{P}(|X_n| > M) \leq \varepsilon$. We say that the sequence $(X_n)_n$ is uniformly tight, or bounded in probability. More generally, we denote $X_n = O_{\mathbb{P}}(R_n)$ if there exists a sequence $(Y_n)_n$ such that $X_n = Y_n R_n$ and $Y_n = O_{\mathbb{P}}(1)$. ■

We adopt the notation from He et al. (2010) to state the asymptotic normality of $\hat{\beta}_n$ and $\hat{\gamma}_n$. We denote $\mathbf{W} = (Y, \mathbf{X}^\top, T)^\top$, $\xi(\theta, \mathbf{W}) = \beta^\top \mathbf{X} + g(T)$ and $\eta(\theta, \mathbf{W}) = \gamma^\top \mathbf{X} + h(T)$. Also denote by:

$$\begin{aligned} \ell(\theta, \mathbf{W}) &= 1\{Y = 0\} \ln(\pi + (1 - \pi)e^{-\mu}) \\ &\quad + 1\{Y > 0\}(\ln(1 - \pi) - \mu + Y \ln \mu) \end{aligned}$$

the contribution of an individual to the log-likelihood. Set:

$$
\begin{aligned}
D_1(\xi) &= \frac{\partial \ell(\theta, \mathbf{W})}{\partial \xi} \\
&= -1\{Y=0\}\frac{(1-\pi)e^{\xi - e^{\xi}}}{\pi + (1-\pi)e^{-e^{\xi}}} + 1\{Y>0\}(Y - e^{\xi}) \\
D_2(\eta) &= \frac{\partial \ell(\theta, \mathbf{W})}{\partial \eta} \\
&= 1\{Y=0\}\frac{e^{\eta}}{e^{\eta} + e^{-\mu}} - \frac{e^{\eta}}{1+e^{\eta}}
\end{aligned}
$$

and:

$$
J(\mathbf{W}) = \frac{D_2^2(\eta(\theta_0, \mathbf{W}))e^{\ell(\theta_0, \mathbf{W})}}{\mathbb{E}[D_2^2(\eta(\theta_0, \mathbf{W}))]}
$$

We denote also:

$$
\delta(\theta, \mathbf{W}) = \frac{D_1(\xi)}{D_2(\eta)} - \mathbb{E}_J\left(\frac{D_1(\xi)}{D_2(\eta)}\middle| T\right)
$$

where $\mathbb{E}_J$ denotes the mean taken with respect to the density J, and:

$$
H(\mathbf{W}) = \frac{D_2^2(\eta(\theta_0, \mathbf{W}))\delta^2(\theta_0, \mathbf{W})e^{\ell(\theta_0, \mathbf{W})}}{\mathbb{E}[D_2^2(\eta(\theta_0, \mathbf{W}))\delta^2(\theta_0, \mathbf{W})]}
$$

Lastly, denote:

$$
\ell_{\beta,\gamma}(\theta, \mathbf{W}) =
$$

$$
D_2(\eta)\begin{pmatrix} \frac{D_1(\xi)}{D_2(\eta)}\mathbf{X} - \delta\mathbb{E}_H\left(\frac{D_1(\xi)}{D_2(\eta)}\delta^{-1}\mathbf{X}\middle| T\right) - (1 - \delta\mathbb{E}_H(\delta^{-1}|T))\mathbb{E}_J\left(\frac{D_1(\xi)}{D_2(\eta)}\mathbf{X}\middle| T\right) \\ \mathbf{X} - \delta\mathbb{E}_H(\delta^{-1}\mathbf{X}|T) - (1 - \delta\mathbb{E}_H(\delta^{-1}|T))\mathbb{E}_J(\mathbf{X}|T) \end{pmatrix}
$$

and $\Sigma(\theta) = \mathbb{E}(\ell_{\beta,\gamma}(\theta, \mathbf{W})\ell_{\beta,\gamma}(\theta, \mathbf{W})^\top)$. He et al. (2010) proves the following theorem (we only mention the main regularity conditions).

THEOREM 4.2.– *Suppose that the explanatory variables $\mathbf{X}_i$ are bounded, $T_i \in [0,1]$, β_0 and γ_0 belong to the interiors of compact subsets of $\mathbb{R}^p$, $g_0(\cdot)$ and $h_0(\cdot)$ are of class C^2 and $m = O(n^k)$ for a given $0 < k < 1$. Then the MLE $\hat{\beta}_n$ and $\hat{\gamma}_n$ satisfy:*

$$
\sqrt{n}\left((\hat{\beta}_n - \beta_0)^\top, (\hat{\gamma}_n - \gamma_0)^\top\right)^\top \xrightarrow[n\to\infty]{\mathcal{L}} \mathcal{N}(0, \Sigma^{-1}(\theta_0))
$$

He et al. (2010) and Lam et al. (2006) discuss the estimation of the asymptotic variance of $(\hat{\beta}_n, \hat{\gamma}_n)$.

Note that a readily available R function to calculate $\hat{\beta}_n$ and $\hat{\gamma}_n$ does not exist, which limits the usage of semi-parametric ZIP models.

We have described an estimation method based upon the utilization of piecewise affine functions to estimate the functional components of the semi-parametric ZIP model. This is not the only possibility. For example, Wang et al. (2015) and Lu and Li (2016) have proposed to use splines (piecewise polynomial functions) to estimate the semi-parametric ZIP model defined by:

$$\begin{cases} \ln(\mu_i) = g_\mu(\beta_1^\top \mathbf{X}_{i,1}) + \gamma_1^\top \mathbf{Z}_{i,1} \\ \text{logit}(\pi_i) = g_\pi(\beta_2^\top \mathbf{X}_{i,2}) + \gamma_2^\top \mathbf{Z}_{i,2} \end{cases}$$

where $g_\mu(\cdot)$ and $g_\pi(\cdot)$ are unknown functions and $\mathbf{X}_{i,1}, \mathbf{X}_{i,2}, \mathbf{Z}_{i,1}, \mathbf{Z}_{i,2}$ are explanatory variables. Please refer to Wang et al. (2015) and Lu and Li (2016) for further details.

4.2.3. *Zero-inflated generalized Poisson model*

Overdispersion can have multiple causes, among which include excess zeros and unobserved heterogeneity. When these two causes exist simultaneously, the ZIP model is unsatisfactory because it only takes overdispersion caused by an excess of zeros into account (the distribution of the response variable in the sub-population at risk – the Poisson distribution – remains equidispersed).

To take the two cases of overdispersion into account simultaneously, Famoye and Singh (2006) have proposed replacing the Poisson distribution in the ZIP model with a generalized Poisson distribution.

4.2.3.1. *Generalized Poisson distribution*

Introduced by Consul and Jain (1973), the generalized Poisson distribution is a distribution with two parameters, which "augments" the Poisson distribution by introducing an overdispersion parameter. Several parameterizations exist, but the one that we will state here has the advantage of having a simple expression for $\mathbb{E}(Y)$.

DEFINITION 4.1.– *A random variable Y with values in $\mathbb{N}$ follows the generalized Poisson distribution $\mathcal{GP}(\mu, \varphi)$, with $\mu > 0$ and $\varphi \geq 1$, if:*

$$\mathbb{P}(Y = y) = \frac{\mu(\mu + (\varphi - 1)y)^{y-1}}{y!}\varphi^{-y}e^{-\frac{(\mu+(\varphi-1)y)}{\varphi}}, \quad y = 0, 1, 2, \ldots \quad [4.8]$$

The mean and the variance of the $\mathcal{GP}(\mu, \varphi)$ distribution are given by:

$$\mathbb{E}(Y) = \mu \quad \text{and} \quad \text{var}(Y) = \varphi^2 \mu$$

The coefficient of dispersion $\phi = \text{var}(Y)/\mathbb{E}(Y)$ equals:

$$\phi = \varphi^2$$

If $\varphi = 1$, then $\phi = 1$ and the $\mathcal{GP}(\mu, \varphi)$ distribution is equidispersed. In this case, we can easily check that [4.8] becomes:

$$\mathbb{P}(Y = y) = \frac{e^{-\mu}\mu^y}{y!}$$

and the generalized Poisson distribution in fact coincides with the Poisson one. If $\varphi > 1$, then the distribution is overdispersed.

REMARK.– It is possible to consider $\varphi < 1$ in [4.8]; the distribution is then underdispersed. In this case, its support is restricted to the set $\{0, 1, \dots, m\}$, where m is the largest positive integer such that $\mu + (\varphi - 1)m \geq 0$ (this constraint comes from the fact that $\mu + (\varphi - 1)y$ must be positive). This requires φ to be greater than $1 - \mu/m$. Due to these constraints, the generalized Poisson distribution is not very practical to use in the underdispersed case. So from here on, we will uniquely consider the case when $\varphi > 1$. ■

We obtain a generalized Poisson *regression* model by making μ and/or φ depend on explanatory variables (Consul and Famoye 1992). This model can then be used to construct a zero-inflated generalized Poisson regression (ZIGP) model. This model integrates the two causes of overdispersion: an excess of zeros and the overdispersion from the generalized Poisson distribution.

4.2.3.2. *The ZIGP model*

The ZIGP regression model (with $\varphi > 1$, for the overdispersed case) is defined by:

$$\mathbb{P}(Y_i = y) = \begin{cases} \pi_i + (1 - \pi_i)e^{-\frac{\mu_i}{\varphi_i}} & \text{if } y = 0 \\ (1 - \pi_i)\frac{\mu_i(\mu_i + (\varphi_i - 1)y)^{y-1}}{y!}\varphi_i^{-y}e^{-\frac{(\mu_i + (\varphi_i - 1)y)}{\varphi_i}} & \text{if } y = 1, 2, \dots \end{cases}$$

where π_i, μ_i and φ_i are functions of the explanatory variables. This model has been studied in detail by Erhardt (2006) and Czado et al. (2007). Czado and Min (2005) consider the particular case where π and φ are constants.

The mean and variance of Y_i in the ZIGP model are derived from the formulas [4.3] and [4.4]:

$$\mathbb{E}(Y_i) = (1 - \pi_i)\mu_i$$

and:

$$\text{var}(Y_i) = (\varphi_i^2 + \pi_i\mu_i)\mathbb{E}(Y_i)$$

The expression for the coefficient of dispersion:

$$\phi_i = \varphi_i^2 + \pi_i\mu_i$$

illustrates the two sources of the overdispersion, which increases with both π_i and φ_i.

In Erhardt (2006), the authors suggest modeling π_i, μ_i and φ_i by:

$$\begin{cases} \pi_i = \frac{e^{\gamma^\top \mathbf{Z}_i}}{1+e^{\gamma^\top \mathbf{Z}_i}} \\ \mu_i = e^{\beta^\top \mathbf{X}_i} \\ \varphi_i = 1 + e^{\alpha^\top \mathbf{W}_i} > 1 \end{cases}$$

where $\mathbf{X}_i, \mathbf{W}_i, \mathbf{Z}_i$ are vectors of explanatory variables (possibly having components in common) and α, β, γ are unknown parameters to be estimated.

We denote by $\theta = (\alpha^\top, \beta^\top, \gamma^\top)^\top$ the set of model parameters, and by q the dimension of θ. Suppose that we have available a sample of n independent observations of the variables $(Y_i, \mathbf{X}_i, \mathbf{W}_i, \mathbf{Z}_i)$. The likelihood of θ is calculated as follows:

$$L_n(\theta) = \prod_{i=1}^{n} \left(\pi_i + (1 - \pi_i)e^{-\frac{\mu_i}{\varphi_i}}\right)^{1\{Y_i=0\}}$$
$$\times \left((1 - \pi_i)\frac{\mu_i(\mu_i + (\varphi_i - 1)Y_i)^{Y_i - 1}}{Y_i!}\varphi_i^{-Y_i} e^{-\frac{(\mu_i + (\varphi_i - 1)Y_i)}{\varphi_i}}\right)^{1\{Y_i>0\}}$$

The MLE:

$$\hat{\theta}_n = \arg\max_{\theta} \ln L_n(\theta)$$

does not admit an explicit expression and must be approximated by means of an optimization algorithm. Erhardt (2006) provides an `R` script based on the `optim` function in its appendices.

4.2.3.3. *Asymptotic properties of the MLE*

As the ZIGP model is not a generalized linear model, the asymptotic results from Fahrmeir and Kaufmann (1985) therefore do not apply. Erhardt (2006) and Czado et al. (2007) have reproven the consistency and asymptotic normality of the MLE for the ZIGP model:

THEOREM 4.3.– *Suppose that the explanatory variables are bounded, the true value θ_0 of θ belongs to the interior of a compact subset of $\mathbb{R}^q$ and there exists a constant c such that for each $n \geq 1$, $n/\lambda_{\min}(\mathbf{F}_n(\theta_0)) \leq c$, where $\lambda_{\min}(\mathbf{F}_n(\theta))$ denotes the smallest eigenvalue of the matrix:*

$$\mathbf{F}_n(\theta) = -\mathbb{E}\left(\frac{\partial^2 \ln L_n(\theta)}{\partial\theta\partial\theta^\top}\right)$$

Then $\hat{\theta}_n \xrightarrow[n\to\infty]{\mathbb{P}} \theta_0$ *and* $\mathbf{F}_n^{1/2}(\theta_0)(\hat{\theta}_n - \theta_0) \xrightarrow[n\to\infty]{\mathcal{L}} \mathcal{N}(0, I_q)$.

Confidence intervals and hypothesis tests for the components of θ can be obtained in a similar way to that in section 2.3.2.

REMARK.– Up to model adaptions, the techniques used by Erhardt (2006) and Czado et al. (2007) in the ZIGP model can be used to prove the consistency and asymptotic normality of the MLE in the ZIP and $\mathcal{GP}$ models. ■

4.2.4. *A zero-inflation test*

In the example from section 4.1.1, an excess of zeros had been suggested by the histogram of the consultation numbers. Zero-inflation tests have been proposed in the literature. The one that we present here is a score test due to van den Broek (1995), and it has the advantage of being implemented in the `R` package `countreg` (Zeileis and Kleiber 2020). It tests for an excess of zeros in the Poisson model.

Under the null hypothesis, the Poisson model adjusts itself correctly to the data. The alternative hypothesis is that of the ZIP model, defined by:

$$\mathbb{P}(Y_i = y) = \begin{cases} \pi + (1-\pi)e^{-\mu_i} & \text{if } y = 0 \\ (1-\pi)\dfrac{e^{-\mu_i}\mu_i^y}{y!} & \text{if } y = 1, 2, \ldots \end{cases}$$

where $\mu_i = e^{\beta^\top \mathbf{x}_i}$ and π is a constant.

Jansakul and Hinde (2002) extend the test from van den Broek (1995) to the case where π depends on explanatory variables. Cao et al. (2014) consider a π which varies according to a qualitative explanatory variable (stratified population). Deng and Paul (2000, 2005) construct zero-inflation tests for GLMs (these tests include the one from van den Broek (1995) as a particular case for the Poisson model). Xiang et al. (2006) and Moghimbeigi et al. (2009) test for excess zeros in Poisson random effect models with correlated data (data grouped in clusters, hierarchical data). As these tests are not yet implemented in R, we will avoid going into them here in any further detail. Finally, note that Lee et al. 2009 proposes a zero-inflation test for a bivariate ZIP model (a model based upon the bivariate Poisson distribution, which we will not go into here).

Let us begin with the test from van den Broek (1995) and denote $\omega = \pi/(1-\pi)$. Testing for an excess of zeros in the Poisson model is equivalent to testing:

$$\mathcal{H}_0 : \omega = 0 \text{ against } \mathcal{H}_1 : \omega > 0$$

The test proposed by van den Broek (1995) is a score test, and it is constructed using the likelihood of (ω, β):

$$L_n(\beta,\omega) = \prod_{i=1}^{n} \left(\frac{\omega}{1+\omega} + \frac{e^{-\mu_i}}{1+\omega} \right)^{1\{Y_i=0\}} \left(\frac{1}{1+\omega} \frac{e^{-\mu_i}\mu_i^{Y_i}}{Y_i!} \right)^{1\{Y_i>0\}}$$

We denote by:

$$S_n(\beta,\omega) = \frac{\partial \ln L_n(\beta,\omega)}{\partial(\beta^\top,\omega)^\top} \quad \text{and} \quad J_n(\beta,\omega) = -\mathbb{E}\left(\frac{\partial^2 \ln L_n(\beta,\omega)}{\partial(\beta^\top,\omega)^\top \partial(\beta^\top,\omega)} \right)$$

the score and Fisher information matrix, respectively. Also we denote by $\tilde{\beta}$ the MLE of β obtained under $\mathcal{H}_0$, and set $\tilde{\mu}_i = e^{\tilde{\beta}^\top \mathbf{X}_i}$. van den Broek (1995) shows that the score test statistic, given by:

$$T_n(\tilde{\beta},0) = S_n^\top(\tilde{\beta},0) J_n^{-1}(\tilde{\beta},0) S_n(\tilde{\beta},0)$$

is equal to:

$$\frac{\left(\sum_{i=1}^{n} \frac{1\{Y_i=0\} - e^{-\tilde{\mu}_i}}{e^{-\tilde{\mu}_i}} \right)^2}{\left(\sum_{i=1}^{n} \frac{1-e^{-\tilde{\mu}_i}}{e^{-\tilde{\mu}_i}} \right) - n\bar{Y}_n}$$

under the condition that the linear predictor $\beta^\top \mathbf{X}_i$ possesses a constant, or intercept, term. The advantage of this score test is that it only requires an estimate of the model under $\mathcal{H}_0$, which here is the Poisson model.

REMARK.– The quantity $e^{-\tilde{\mu}_i}$ estimates the probability $\mathbb{P}(Y_i = 0) = e^{-\mu_i}$. Intuitively, $T_n(\tilde{\beta}, 0)$ compares the number of zeros observed in the sample to that expected under the Poisson model. ■

If $\mathcal{H}_0$ is true, then the asymptotic distribution of $T_n(\tilde{\beta}, 0)$ is the mixture $\frac{1}{2}\delta_0 + \frac{1}{2}\chi_1^2$ formed from a χ^2-distribution with one degree of freedom along with a Dirac measure at zero. This nonstandard distribution comes from the fact that the null hypothesis $\mathcal{H}_0$ lies on the boundary of the parameter space of ω. To test $\mathcal{H}_0$ at the asymptotic level α, it is necessary to take the critical value to be the quantile of order $1 - 2\alpha$ of χ_1^2.

Let us apply this test to the `docvisits` data set. The code:

```
mod_pois=glm(nbvisits~.,data=datadoc,family=poisson)
zitest(mod_pois)
```

returns the score test statistic and corresponding p-value:

```
        Zero inflation test

data:  mod_pois
S = 131.81, p-value < 2.2e-16
```

The result tells us to reject $\mathcal{H}_0$ (the hypothesis that the Poisson model is suitable). However, this does not imply that the ZIP model is appropriate. Other models may be more suitable, such as the ZIGP model or the zero-inflated negative binomial regression model (ZINB model), described in section 4.3.

The `zeroinfl` function from the `pscl` package (Jackman 2020) uses a quasi-Newton type algorithm to approximate the MLE in the ZIP model. As an example, below we will fit a ZIP model to the `nbvisits` variable (`docvisits` dataset). Recall that a function that is immediately available to estimate a ZIGP model does not exist in R. Nevertheless, it is not too complicated to program the log-likelihood and then apply an optimization algorithm to it (in fact, we have already done this in section 3.1.3).

The model that we will adjust is the following:

$$Y_i \sim \text{ZIP}(\pi_i, \mu_i), i = 1, \dots, n$$

where:

$$\begin{aligned}\mu_i = \exp(&\beta_1 + \beta_2\texttt{age}_i + \beta_3\texttt{health}_i + \beta_4\texttt{handicap}_i + \beta_5\texttt{hdegree}_i + \beta_6\texttt{married}_i \\ &+\beta_7\texttt{schooling}_i + \beta_8\texttt{hhincome}_i + \beta_9\texttt{children}_i + \beta_{10}\texttt{self}_i + \beta_{11}\texttt{civil}_i \\ &+\beta_{12}\texttt{bluec}_i + \beta_{13}\texttt{employed}_i + \beta_{14}\texttt{public}_i + \beta_{15}\texttt{addon}_i)\end{aligned}$$

and:

$$\text{logit}(\pi_i) = \gamma_1 + \gamma_2\texttt{age}_i + \gamma_3\texttt{health}_i + \gamma_4\texttt{handicap}_i + \gamma_5\texttt{hdegree}_i$$
$$+\gamma_6\texttt{married}_i + \gamma_7\texttt{schooling}_i + \gamma_8\texttt{hhincome}_i + \gamma_9\texttt{children}_i$$
$$+\gamma_{10}\texttt{self}_i + \gamma_{11}\texttt{civil}_i + \gamma_{12}\texttt{bluec}_i + \gamma_{13}\texttt{employed}_i + \gamma_{14}\texttt{public}_i$$
$$+\gamma_{15}\texttt{addon}_i$$

The syntax is the following:

```
datadoc=data.frame(age,health,handicap,hdegree,married,schooling,
    hhincome,children,self,civil,bluec,employed,public,addon)
m1=zeroinfl(nbvisits~.|.,data=datadoc,dist="poisson")
```

The . in `zeroinfl` indicates to R that each variable declared in `datadoc` must be used in π_i and μ_i. To use a subset of these variables, they can be simply listed and separated by the + symbol (variables declared before the | symbol are those used in the linear predictor of μ_i). The following output is obtained:

```
Count model coefficients (poisson with log link):
              Estimate Std. Error z value Pr(>|z|)
(Intercept)   2.129762   0.141184  15.085  < 2e-16 ***
age           0.010490   0.001544   6.794 1.09e-11 ***
health       -0.164014   0.005995 -27.357  < 2e-16 ***
handicap      0.354925   0.073384   4.837 1.32e-06 ***
hdegree      -0.004885   0.001256  -3.889 0.000101 ***
married      -0.148064   0.039897  -3.711 0.000206 ***
schooling    -0.001754   0.007229  -0.243 0.808276
hhincome      0.004186   0.007514   0.557 0.577460
children      0.077826   0.036762   2.117 0.034258 *
self         -0.184664   0.072072  -2.562 0.010401 *
civil        -0.121271   0.078980  -1.535 0.124668
bluec         0.076415   0.039395   1.940 0.052414 .
employed     -0.147991   0.044200  -3.348 0.000813 ***
public        0.124572   0.069299   1.798 0.072241 .
addon         0.256449   0.094568   2.712 0.006692 **

Zero-inflation model coefficients (binomial with logit link):
              Estimate Std. Error z value Pr(>|z|)
(Intercept) -2.294393   0.510495  -4.494 6.98e-06 ***
age         -0.003763   0.005892  -0.639 0.523026
health       0.287170   0.029225   9.826  < 2e-16 ***
handicap    -0.072481   0.438152  -0.165 0.868610
hdegree     -0.005216   0.008430  -0.619 0.536111
married     -0.273377   0.154293  -1.772 0.076428 .
schooling    0.007918   0.024489   0.323 0.746439
hhincome    -0.029586   0.027686  -1.069 0.285240
```

```
children      0.469391   0.133440    3.518 0.000435 ***
self          0.203449   0.213158    0.954 0.339857
civil         0.179254   0.229451    0.781 0.434668
bluec        -0.018382   0.140634   -0.131 0.896008
employed      0.080858   0.178414    0.453 0.650403
public       -0.038569   0.200288   -0.193 0.847297
addon         0.072519   0.385801    0.188 0.850899
---
Signif. codes:  0 '***' 0.001 '**' 0.01 '*' 0.05 '.' 0.1 ' ' 1

Number of iterations in BFGS optimization: 36
Log-likelihood: -4450 on 30 Df
```

The usual model selection criteria such as the AIC and BIC apply to zero-inflated models. Choosing which criteria to use depends on whether the desired objective is explanatory or predictive (for more on these subjects, the reader can refer to the works of Hastie et al. (2009) and James et al. (2014)).

For zero-inflated models, the user is mostly limited by the capabilities of R. For example, the stepAIC function from the MASS package (Venables and Ripley 2002) can perform automatic variable selection (backward, forward, stepwise) using either the AIC or BIC, but it either simultaneously adds or removes variables in the linear predictors of π_i and μ_i.

The be.zeroinfl function from the mpath package (Wang 2020) implements a backward algorithm, which drops the least significant predictor from the model at each step (namely, the one with the largest p-value from the Wald nullity test). The variable is only dropped from the linear predictor for which it is the least significant. The procedure terminates once every p-value is less than a fixed level α chosen by the user. The syntax is the following:

```
selection_m1=be.zeroinfl(m1,data=datadoc,dist="poisson",alpha
    =0.05)
summary(selection_m1)
```

The selected model is:

```
Count model coefficients (poisson with log link):
             Estimate Std. Error z value Pr(>|z|)
(Intercept)  2.049439   0.099367  20.625  < 2e-16 ***
age          0.010549   0.001540   6.850 7.39e-12 ***
health      -0.163323   0.005968 -27.366  < 2e-16 ***
handicap     0.355161   0.073240   4.849 1.24e-06 ***
hdegree     -0.004916   0.001255  -3.918 8.92e-05 ***
married     -0.148316   0.039616  -3.744 0.000181 ***
children     0.075838   0.036697   2.067 0.038772 *
self        -0.154943   0.068285  -2.269 0.023263 *
```

```
bluec          0.089674    0.036397    2.464 0.013748 *
employed      -0.159996    0.041415   -3.863 0.000112 ***
public         0.197936    0.052330    3.782 0.000155 ***
addon          0.262534    0.094452    2.780 0.005443 **

Zero-inflation model coefficients (binomial with logit link):
              Estimate Std. Error z value Pr(>|z|)
(Intercept) -2.410680   0.233937  -10.305  < 2e-16 ***
health       0.289553   0.028891   10.022  < 2e-16 ***
hdegree     -0.007325   0.003701   -1.979   0.0478 *
married     -0.344446   0.128821   -2.674   0.0075 **
children     0.525819   0.122325    4.299 1.72e-05 ***
---
Signif. codes:  0 '***' 0.001 '**' 0.01 '*' 0.05 '.' 0.1 ' ' 1
Number of iterations in BFGS optimization: 22
Log-likelihood: -4454 on 17 Df
```

The selection algorithm terminates after 14 steps. The log-likelihood, AIC and BIC at each step are given as outputs.

Here, the BIC has decreased at each step, and the AIC has increased at the last step.

```
BIC of zero-inflated model 9035.056
AIC of zero-inflated model 8941.519
step 14
         loglik      BIC      AIC
 [1,] -4449.984 9117.531 8957.967
 [2,] -4449.997 9110.056 8955.995
 [3,] -4450.016 9102.591 8954.032
 [4,] -4450.032 9095.121 8952.065
 [5,] -4450.060 9087.676 8950.121
 [6,] -4450.153 9080.358 8948.306
 [7,] -4450.244 9073.038 8946.487
 [8,] -4450.383 9065.813 8944.765
 [9,] -4450.630 9058.806 8943.260
[10,] -4451.119 9052.282 8942.238
[11,] -4451.708 9045.957 8941.416
[12,] -4452.335 9039.710 8940.670
[13,] -4453.759 9035.056 8941.519
```

The effect of the predictors selected in the `Zero-inflation model` part (π_i model) is interpreted as in a logistic model.

The effect of the predictors selected in the `Count model` part is interpreted as in a classical Poisson model, noting that this effect is conditional on belonging to the at-risk subpopulation (we will come back to this last point in section 4.6).

4.3. Zero-inflated negative binomial model

4.3.1. *Negative binomial model*

First, recall[2] that a random variable with values in $\mathbb{N}$ follows the negative binomial distribution NB2 if:

$$\mathbb{P}(Y_i = y) = \frac{\Gamma(y + \frac{1}{\kappa})}{y!\Gamma(\frac{1}{\kappa})} \left(\frac{\kappa \mu_i}{1 + \kappa \mu_i} \right)^y \left(\frac{1}{1 + \kappa \mu_i} \right)^{\frac{1}{\kappa}}, \quad y = 0, 1, 2, \ldots$$

where $\kappa > 0$. Also recall that:

$$\mathbb{E}(Y_i) = \mu_i \quad \text{and} \quad \text{var}(Y_i) = \mu_i(1 + \kappa \mu_i)$$

The NB2 distribution takes its name from the fact that the variance is a quadratic function of the mean (the "2" here refers to the power of μ_i in the variance) (Cameron and Trivedi 1998; Hilbe 2011). This distribution is overdispersed, and its coefficient of dispersion equals:

$$\phi = 1 + \kappa \mu_i$$

The κ coefficient can be interpreted as a dispersion parameter, and the Poisson distribution, which is equidispersed, can be seen as a particular case of the NB2 distribution when $\kappa \to 0$. Indeed, remember that the NB2 distribution is the marginal distribution of Y when $Y|U \sim \mathcal{P}(\mu U)$ and $U \sim G(1, 1/\kappa)$ (see section 1.5.2). However, if $U \sim G(1, 1/\kappa)$, we get: $\mathbb{E}(U) = 1$ and $\text{var}(U) = \kappa$. When $\kappa \to 0$, U becomes the constant variable 1.

This observation suggests that testing the overdispersion of a sample can be done by testing a Poisson model against a negative binomial model, that is by testing:

$$\mathcal{H}_0 : \kappa = 0 \quad \text{against} \quad \mathcal{H}_1 : \kappa > 0$$

in the NB2 model. In the case of a test between nested models, the likelihood ratio test is often used.

REMARK.– In the negative binomial model, the log link function is generally used (i.e. we set $\ln(\mu_i) = \beta^\top \mathbf{X}_i$) rather than the canonical link function, which imposes the constraint $\beta^\top \mathbf{X}_i < 0$. The parameters β and κ are estimated using the maximum likelihood method (in `R`, by using the `glm.nb` function from the `MASS` package

2 See equation [1.3], in Chapter 1.

(Venables and Ripley 2002)). Readers interested in further developments on the negative binomial distribution can consult (Cameron and Trivedi 1998; Hilbe 2011). ■

The likelihood ratio statistic to test $\mathcal{H}_0$ against $\mathcal{H}_1$ can be written as:

$$LRT_n = 2(\ell_{n,\mathcal{H}_1}(\hat{\beta}_n, \hat{\kappa}_n) - \ell_{n,\mathcal{H}_0}(\hat{\beta}_n))$$

where $\ell_{n,\mathcal{H}_1}(\hat{\beta}_n, \hat{\kappa}_n)$ is the log-likelihood of the NB2 model (namely, under the hypothesis $\mathcal{H}_1$) and $\ell_{n,\mathcal{H}_0}(\hat{\beta}_n)$ is the log-likelihood of the Poisson model under $\mathcal{H}_0$.

Under $\mathcal{H}_0$, LRT_n is asymptotically distributed as the mixture $\frac{1}{2}\delta_0 + \frac{1}{2}\chi_1^2$ of χ_1^2 and Dirac measure at zero (again, this is due to the fact that the null hypothesis lies on the boundary of the parameter space). This test can be implemented in `R` using the `odTest` function from the `pscl` package (Jackman 2020).

4.3.2. *ZINB model*

Based on the NB2 distribution, a zero-inflated negative binomial regression model can be constructed by setting:

$$\mathbb{P}(Y_i = y) = \begin{cases} \pi_i + (1-\pi_i)\left(1+\kappa\mu_i\right)^{-\frac{1}{\kappa}} & \text{if } y = 0 \\ (1-\pi_i)\frac{\Gamma(y+\frac{1}{\kappa})}{y!\Gamma(\frac{1}{\kappa})}\left(\frac{\kappa\mu_i}{1+\kappa\mu_i}\right)^y\left(\frac{1}{1+\kappa\mu_i}\right)^{\frac{1}{\kappa}} & \text{if } y = 1, 2, \ldots \end{cases} \quad [4.9]$$

Like the ZIGP model, the ZINB model takes two sources of overdispersion into account: an excess of zeros and the over-dispersion arising from the negative binomial model.

The mean and variance of Y_i are derived again from the formulas [4.3] and [4.4]:

$$\mathbb{E}(Y_i) = (1-\pi_i)\mu_i$$

and:

$$\text{var}(Y_i) = (1 + \pi_i\mu_i + \kappa\mu_i)\mathbb{E}(Y_i)$$

The coefficient of dispersion equals:

$$\phi_i = 1 + \pi_i\mu_i + \kappa\mu_i$$

We see that there are two sources of overdispersion: an excess of zeros (associated with the probability π_i) and the dispersion parameter κ.

The ZINB model [4.9] is implemented by the `zeroinfl` function from the `pscl` package (Jackman 2020) (with $\mu_i = \exp(\beta^\top \mathbf{X}_i)$ and a logistic model for π_i). The likelihood is calculated in a similar way as that for the ZIP and ZIGP models:

$$L_n(\beta,\gamma,\kappa) = \prod_{i=1}^{n} \left(\pi_i + (1-\pi_i)\left(1+\kappa\mu_i\right)^{-\frac{1}{\kappa}}\right)^{1\{Y_i=0\}}$$
$$\times \left((1-\pi_i)\frac{\Gamma(Y_i+\frac{1}{\kappa})}{Y_i!\Gamma(\frac{1}{\kappa})}\left(\frac{\kappa\mu_i}{1+\kappa\mu_i}\right)^{Y_i}\left(\frac{1}{1+\kappa\mu_i}\right)^{\frac{1}{\kappa}}\right)^{1\{Y_i>0\}} \quad [4.10]$$

and a quasi-Newton algorithm is used to calculate the MLEs. The code below estimates a ZINB model based on the `docvisits` data set before performing a backward variable selection:

```
m2=zeroinfl(nbvisits~.|.,data=datadoc,dist="negbin")
selection_m2=be.zeroinfl(m2,data=datadoc,dist="negbin",alpha
    =0.05)
summary(selection_m2)
```

The results are the following[3]:

```
Count model coefficients (negbin with log link):
              Estimate Std. Error z value Pr(>|z|)
(Intercept)   1.884232   0.180747  10.425  < 2e-16 ***
age           0.010361   0.002898   3.575  0.00035 ***
health       -0.188032   0.014291 -13.158  < 2e-16 ***
handicap      0.258160   0.087697   2.944  0.00324 **
married      -0.176722   0.078785  -2.243  0.02489 *
self         -0.276661   0.120230  -2.301  0.02139 *
public        0.278351   0.091851   3.030  0.00244 **
Log(theta)    0.239150   0.090996   2.628  0.00859 **

Zero-inflation model coefficients (binomial with logit link):
             Estimate Std. Error z value Pr(>|z|)
(Intercept) -3.42137     0.42530  -8.045 8.65e-16 ***
health       0.33629     0.04825   6.970 3.16e-12 ***
married     -0.58981     0.21355  -2.762  0.00575 **
children     0.79566     0.19873   4.004 6.23e-05 ***
---
Signif. codes:  0 '***' 0.001 '**' 0.01 '*' 0.05 '.' 0.1 ' ' 1

Theta = 1.2702
Number of iterations in BFGS optimization: 18
Log-likelihood: -3650 on 12 Df
```

3 In the output, `theta` corresponds to $1/\kappa$.

The coefficients are to be interpreted as in the ZIP model (in the ZINB model too, the effect of the predictors selected in `Count model` should be understood conditionally on belonging to the at-risk sub-population).

There exist other parameterizations of the negative binomial distribution, and hence of the ZINB model. For example, Ridout et al. (2001) and Yang et al. (2009) consider the ZINB model defined by:

$$\mathbb{P}(Y_i = y) = \begin{cases} \pi_i + (1-\pi_i)\left(1+\kappa\mu_i^c\right)^{-\mu_i^{1-c}/\kappa} & \text{if } y = 0 \\ (1-\pi_i)\frac{\Gamma(y+\mu_i^{1-c}/\kappa)}{y!\Gamma(\mu_i^{1-c}/\kappa)}\left(1+\mu_i^{-c}/\kappa\right)^{-y}\left(1+\kappa\mu_i^c\right)^{-\mu_i^{1-c}/\kappa} & \\ & \text{if } y = 1, 2, \ldots \end{cases}$$

where $c \geq 0$ (we denote this model by ZINB-c). For this parameterization, the mean and variance of Y_i are given by:

$$\mathbb{E}(Y_i) = (1-\pi_i)\mu_i$$

and:

$$\text{var}(Y_i) = (1 + \pi_i\mu_i + \kappa\mu_i^c)\mathbb{E}(Y_i)$$

When $c = 1$, the ZINB-c model reduces to the model [4.9]. When $c = 0$, the variance of the negative binomial distribution underlying the ZINB model equals $\text{var}(Y_i) = (1+\kappa)\mathbb{E}(Y_i)$, and is therefore a linear function of the mean. This negative binomial distribution is called the NB1 distribution. The NB1 and NB2 distributions are the two most commonly used negative binomial distributions. When $\kappa \to 0$, the ZINB-c model reduces to the ZIP model.

4.3.3. *The ZIP model versus the ZINB model*

In practice, how do we choose between using a ZIP model and a ZINB one? A ZINB model will be appropriate if an additional source of overdispersion is added to the excess of zeros. Multiple tests have been proposed in the literature.

Ridout et al. (2001) construct a score test for the ZIP model against the ZINB-c one. The hypotheses are the following:

$$\mathcal{H}_0 : \kappa = 0 \quad \text{against} \quad \mathcal{H}_1 : \kappa > 0$$

The proposed statistic can be written as:

$$T_c = \frac{1}{2}\sum_{i=1}^{n} \hat{\mu}_i^{c-1}\left((Y_i - \hat{\mu}_i)^2 - Y_i - 1\{Y_i = 0\}\hat{\mu}_i^2\frac{\hat{\pi}_i}{\hat{p}_{0,i}}\right)\sqrt{\hat{J}^{\kappa\kappa}}, \quad c = 0, 1$$

where $\hat{\mu}_i$, $\hat{\pi}_i$ and $\hat{p}_{0,i}$ are the estimates of μ_i, π_i and $\mathbb{P}(Y_i = 0)$ obtained under $\mathcal{H}_0$, and where $\hat{J}^{\kappa\kappa}$ is the element of the inverse of the Fisher information matrix corresponding to κ. T_0 and T_1 allow for the ZIP model to be tested against the ZINB-1 and ZINB-2 ones, respectively. Under $\mathcal{H}_0$ (i.e. under the ZIP model), T_c asymptotically follows the standard normal distribution. When the sample size is too small for the normal approximation to be of good quality, Jung et al. (2005) propose estimating the critical values by the means of bootstrap.

The Wald, score and likelihood ratio tests for the ZIP model against the ZINB and ZIGP ones have similarly been proposed in Yang et al. (2009). Xiang et al. (2007) propose a score test for the ZIP model against the ZINB one when the observations are correlated (clustered or repeated data).

These tests have not yet been implemented in R. We can instead compare the ZIP, ZINB and ZIGP models by means of either the AIC or BIC (Hilbe 2014).

For the `docvisits` data set, the BIC of the ZIP and ZINB models after automatic variable selection are obtained as:

```
> AIC(selection_m1,k=log(n)) # ZIP
[1] 9035.056
> AIC(selection_m2,k=log(n)) # ZINB
[1] 7390.455
```

which leads us to prefer (based upon goodness of fit) the ZINB model, which is also the more parsimonious one.

4.4. Zero-inflated binomial model

The zero-inflated binomial (ZIB) model was introduced by Hall (2000). It was constructed on the same principle as the ZIP and ZINB models. In the ZIB(k, p, π) model, the probabilities p_y of the model [4.2] come from the binomial distribution $\mathcal{B}(k, p)$. The model is written as:

$$\mathbb{P}(Y = y) = \begin{cases} \pi + (1 - \pi)(1 - p)^k & \text{if } y = 0 \\ \\ (1 - \pi)C_k^y p^y (1 - p)^{k-y} & \text{if } y = 1, 2, \ldots, k \end{cases}$$

We also denote:

$$Y \sim \pi\delta_0 + (1 - \pi)\mathcal{B}(k, p)$$

or also:

$$Y \sim \begin{cases} 0 & \text{with probability } \pi \\ \mathcal{B}(k,p) & \text{with probability } 1-\pi \end{cases}$$

Figure 4.3 represents the frequency distributions of the ZIB$(12, 0.5, 0.4)$ and $\mathcal{B}(12, 0.5)$ distributions. To obtain it, the `dzibinom` function from the `R` package `VGAM` (Yee 2010, 2015) can be used:

```
barplot(rbind(dzibinom(0:12,12,0.5,0.4),dbinom(0:12,12,0.5)),
    beside=TRUE,col=c("blue","white"),names.arg=as.character
    (0:12))
```

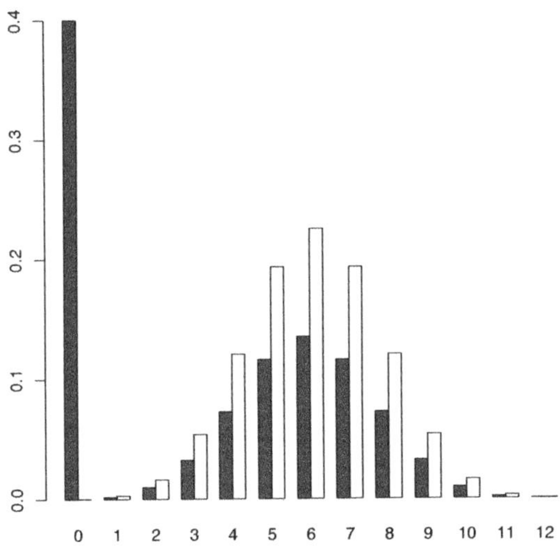

Figure 4.3. *Frequency distributions of the ZIB$(12, 0.5, 0.4)$ (blue) and $\mathcal{B}(12, 0.5)$ (white) distributions. For a color version of this figure, see www.iste.co.uk/dupuy/linearmodels.zip*

The mean and variance of the ZIB(k, p, π) distribution are derived from formulas [4.3] and [4.4], with $Y^* \sim \mathcal{B}(k, p)$:

$$\mathbb{E}(Y) = (1-\pi)kp$$

and:

$$\begin{aligned} \text{var}(Y) &= (1-\pi)\text{var}(Y^*) + \pi(1-\pi)(\mathbb{E}Y^*)^2 \\ &= (1-\pi)kp(1-p) + \pi(1-\pi)(kp)^2 \\ &= (1-\pi)kp(1-p+kp\pi) \end{aligned}$$

The coefficient of dispersion therefore equals $\phi = 1 - p + kp\pi$ and the ZIB model is either underdispersed (if $k\pi < 1$) or overdispersed (if $k\pi > 1$).

If π and/or p depend on any explanatory variables, we obtain a ZIB regression model. The logistic model is generally used for p and π. Set:

$$p_i = \frac{e^{\beta^\top \mathbf{X}_i}}{1 + e^{\beta^\top \mathbf{X}_i}} \quad \text{and} \quad \pi_i = \frac{e^{\gamma^\top \mathbf{W}_i}}{1 + e^{\gamma^\top \mathbf{W}_i}}$$

and suppose that we have available an independent sample $\{(Y_i, \mathbf{X}_i, \mathbf{W}_i), i = 1, \ldots, n\}$, where $Y_i \sim \text{ZIB}(k_i, p_i, \pi_i)$. The likelihood of $\theta = (\beta, \gamma)$ can be written as:

$$\begin{aligned} L_n(\theta) &= \prod_{i=1}^{n} \left(\pi_i + (1 - \pi_i)(1 - p_i)^{k_i}\right)^{1\{Y_i=0\}} \\ &\times \left((1 - \pi_i) C_{k_i}^{Y_i} p_i^{Y_i} (1 - p_i)^{k_i - Y_i}\right)^{1\{Y_i>0\}} \\ &= \prod_{i=1}^{n} (1 + e^{\gamma^\top \mathbf{W}_i})^{-1} \prod_{i=1}^{n} (e^{\gamma^\top \mathbf{W}_i} + (1 + e^{\beta^\top \mathbf{X}_i})^{-k_i})^{1\{Y_i=0\}} \\ &\times \prod_{i=1}^{n} \left(C_{k_i}^{Y_i} \frac{e^{Y_i \beta^\top \mathbf{X}_i}}{(1 + e^{\beta^\top \mathbf{X}_i})^{k_i}}\right)^{1\{Y_i>0\}} \end{aligned} \qquad [4.11]$$

The MLE $\hat{\theta}_n$ does not admit an explicit expression and must be approximated numerically (Hall (2000) uses the EM algorithm, whereas Diallo et al. (2017) use the Newton–Raphson algorithm). It is consistent and asymptotically Gaussian, and a consistent estimator of its asymptotic variance–covariance matrix is given by $(-\frac{1}{n} \frac{\partial^2 \ln L_n(\hat{\theta}_n)}{\partial \theta \partial \theta^\top})^{-1}$ (see Diallo et al. (2017)).

REMARK.– The particular case where $k_i = 1$ for each $i = 1, \ldots, n$ requires particular attention, due to the problem of model identifiability. This issue can be solved by making appropriate assumptions (see Diop et al. (2011) and Dupuy (2018). ■

The ZIB model has given rise to a variety of developments, which we do not go further into here: Hall (2000) has adapted it for correlated data, and Deng and Zhang (2015) and Tian et al. (2015) have proposed the EIB model (for *endpoint-inflated binomial model*) to take into account a simultaneous excess of the values on the support boundary of the binomial distribution. In the EIB model, the distribution of Y_i is given by:

$$Y_i \sim \begin{cases} 0 & \text{with probability } \pi_{i,0} \\ k_i & \text{with probability } \pi_{i,1} \\ \mathcal{B}(k_i, p_i) & \text{with probability } 1 - \pi_{i,0} - \pi_{i,1} \end{cases}$$

Dupuy (2017) has established the asymptotic properties of the MLE in this model.

4.5. Censored and missing data: examples of problems

In this section, we describe some problems involving censored and missing data in zero-inflated models.

4.5.1. *Censored ZIP model*

Section 3.1.2 was dedicated to the Poisson regression model with a right-censored response variable. In this section, we are interested in the same problem but in the framework of the ZIP model. The context is as follows:

Consider the model:

$$\mathbb{P}(Y_i = y) = \begin{cases} \pi(\mathbf{Z}_i) + (1 - \pi(\mathbf{Z}_i))e^{-\mu(\mathbf{X}_i)} & \text{if } y = 0 \\ (1 - \pi(\mathbf{Z}_i))\dfrac{e^{-\mu(\mathbf{X}_i)}\mu(\mathbf{X}_i)^y}{y!} & \text{if } y = 1, 2, \ldots \end{cases}$$

where:

$$\mu(\mathbf{X}_i) = e^{\beta^\top \mathbf{X}_i} \quad \text{and} \quad \pi(\mathbf{Z}_i) = \frac{e^{\gamma^\top \mathbf{Z}_i}}{1 + e^{\gamma^\top \mathbf{Z}_i}}$$

where $\mathbf{X}_i \in \mathbb{R}^p$ and $\mathbf{Z}_i \in \mathbb{R}^q$ are vectors of explanatory variables (which can be distinct or have components in common), and where β, γ are regression parameters to be estimated. In the following, set $\psi = (\beta^\top, \gamma^\top)^\top$, and denote by k the dimension of ψ and by ψ_0 its true value.

Suppose that we have available an independent sample:

$$\{(Y_i^*, \delta_i, \mathbf{X}_i, \mathbf{Z}_i), i = 1, \ldots, n\}$$

with the same notation as before: C_i is a censoring variable (here, strictly positive), $Y_i^* = \min(Y_i, C_i)$, and $\delta_i = 1\{Y_i < C_i\}$ is the censoring indicator. Suppose that the censoring is noninformative (so that its probability distribution does not depend on ψ) and independent of Y_i conditionally on $\mathbf{X}_i$ and $\mathbf{Z}_i$.

Under these hypotheses, the likelihood of ψ can be calculated in an analogous way to that in section 3.1.2 (we denote $J_i = 1\{Y_i^* = 0\}$):

$$
\begin{aligned}
L_n(\psi) &= \prod_{i=1}^{n} \mathbb{P}(Y_i = y_i^*|\mathbf{X}_i, \mathbf{Z}_i)^{\delta_i} \mathbb{P}(Y_i \geq y_i^*|\mathbf{X}_i, \mathbf{Z}_i)^{1-\delta_i} \\
&= \prod_{i=1}^{n} \left\{\mathbb{P}(Y_i = y_i^*|\mathbf{X}_i, \mathbf{Z}_i)^{1-J_i} \mathbb{P}(Y_i = 0|\mathbf{X}_i, \mathbf{Z}_i)^{J_i}\right\}^{\delta_i} \\
&\times \left\{\mathbb{P}(Y_i \geq y_i^*|\mathbf{X}_i, \mathbf{Z}_i)\right\}^{(1-\delta_i)(1-J_i)}
\end{aligned}
$$

To pass from the first line to the second, we have used the fact that:

$$
\mathbb{P}(Y_i \geq y_i^*|\mathbf{X}_i, \mathbf{Z}_i)^{1-\delta_i} = \left\{\mathbb{P}(Y_i \geq y_i^*|\mathbf{X}_i, \mathbf{Z}_i)\right\}^{(1-\delta_i)(1-J_i)}
$$

which comes from the equality: $(1 - \delta_i)J_i = 0$. Indeed:

– if $J_i = 0$, the result is immediate;

– if $J_i = 1$, then $Y_i^* = 0$. However by hypothesis, C_i is strictly positive, so necessarily we have that $Y_i = 0$ and $Y_i < C_i$. Consequently, $\delta_i = 1$ and $(1 - \delta_i)J_i = 0$.

In its "expanded" form, the log-likelihood $\ell_n(\psi) = \ln L_n(\psi)$ can be written as:

$$
\begin{aligned}
\ell_n(\psi) &= \sum_{i=1}^{n} \delta_i J_i \ln\left(e^{\gamma^\top \mathbf{Z}_i} + e^{-\exp(\beta^\top \mathbf{X}_i)}\right) \\
&+ \sum_{i=1}^{n} \delta_i (1 - J_i)\left(Y_i^* \beta^\top \mathbf{X}_i - e^{\beta^\top \mathbf{X}_i} - \ln(Y_i^*!)\right) \\
&+ \sum_{i=1}^{n} (1 - \delta_i)(1 - J_i) \ln\left(1 - \sum_{k=0}^{Y_i^*-1} \frac{e^{-\exp(\beta^\top \mathbf{X}_i) + k\beta^\top \mathbf{X}_i}}{k!}\right) \\
&- \sum_{i=1}^{n} \ln\left(1 + e^{\gamma^\top \mathbf{Z}_i}\right)
\end{aligned}
$$

The MLE $\hat{\psi}_n = (\hat{\beta}_n^\top, \hat{\gamma}_n^\top)^\top$ can be obtained by solving the system $\partial \ell_n(\psi)/\partial\psi = 0$ (in Nguyen and Dupuy (2021), the `maxLik` package developed by Henningsen and Toomet (2011) is used to approximate $\hat{\psi}_n$).

The following theorem states the consistency and asymptotic normality of $\hat{\psi}_n$ (see Nguyen and Dupuy (2021)). Set:

$$
\mathbf{F}_n(\psi) = -\mathbb{E}\left(\frac{\partial^2 \ell_n(\psi)}{\partial\psi\partial\psi^\top}\right)
$$

and denote by $\lambda_{\min}(\mathbf{F}_n(\psi))$ the smallest eigenvalue of $\mathbf{F}_n(\psi)$.

THEOREM 4.4.– *Suppose that the explanatory variables* $\mathbf{X}_i$ *and* $\mathbf{Z}_i$ *are bounded,* ψ_0 *belongs to the interior of a compact subset of* $\mathbb{R}^k$*, there exists a constant c such that for each* $n \geq 1$, $n/\lambda_{\min}(\mathbf{F}_n(\psi_0)) \leq c$ *and for each* $i = 1, 2, \ldots$*, the variable* C_i *is strictly positive, bounded, noninformative and independent of* Y_i *conditionally on* $\mathbf{X}_i$ *and* $\mathbf{Z}_i$*. Then* $\hat{\psi}_n \xrightarrow[n\to\infty]{\mathbb{P}} \psi_0$ *and:*

$$\mathbf{F}_n^{1/2}(\psi_0)(\hat{\psi}_n - \psi_0) \xrightarrow[n\to\infty]{\mathcal{L}} \mathcal{N}(0, I_k)$$

Confidence intervals and hypothesis tests for the components of ψ can be obtained by estimating the asymptotic variance of $\hat{\psi}_n$ by $(-\frac{1}{n}\frac{\partial^2 \ell_n(\hat{\psi}_n)}{\partial\psi\partial\psi^\top})^{-1}$.

4.5.2. *Missing covariables in the ZIB model*

Section 3.2 was dedicated to a missing data problem in two GLMs. The missing data – the censoring indicator – was linked to the response variable. In this section, we are interested in a problem with missing covariables. The expression "missing covariables" refers to the situation in which certain explanatory variables are not observed in some of the individuals in the sample.

Missing covariables problems in regression have given rise to a large number of works: see, for example, Robins et al. (1994); Schafer and Yucel (2002); Liang et al. (2004); Yang et al. (2005); Guo et al. (2014) for linear models, Ibrahim (1990); Horton and Laird (1999); Ibrahim et al. (1999, 2005); Sinha et al. (2010); Davis et al. (2015) for GLMs; Paik (1997); Paik and Tsai (1997); Chen and Little (1999); Herring and Ibrahim (2001); Luo et al. (2009); White and Royston (2009); Song and Wang (2013); Hao et al. (2014); Qiu (2017) for duration models, and Chen and Fu (2011); Lukusa et al. (2016); Diallo et al. (2019); Lee et al. (2020); Lukusa and Phoa (2020); Lee et al. (2021) for zero-inflated models. Our aim is not to provide an exhaustive review of this literature here. As an example, let us describe how the IPW and multiple-imputation methods can be applied to a problem with missing covariables in the ZIB and ZIP models.

The context is the following. Consider the ZIB model:

$$Y_i \sim \text{ZIB}(k_i, p_i, \pi_i), \quad i = 1, \ldots, n$$

where $\text{logit}(p_i) = \beta^\top \mathbf{X}_i$, $\text{logit}(\pi_i) = \gamma^\top \mathbf{W}_i$ and $k_i \geq 2$. The components of $\mathbf{X}$ and $\mathbf{W}$ may either be categorical or continuous. Suppose that some of these components are missing for certain individuals (for the others, $\mathbf{X}$ and $\mathbf{W}$ are completely observed). Furthermore, suppose that the components susceptible to be missing are the same for each individual.

To formalize ideas, if individual i has missing data, let us decompose $\mathbf{X}_i$ and $\mathbf{W}_i$ into the form:

$$\mathbf{X}_i = (\mathbf{X}_i^{(\text{obs}),\top}, \mathbf{X}_i^{(\text{miss}),\top})^\top, \quad \mathbf{W}_i = (\mathbf{W}_i^{(\text{obs}),\top}, \mathbf{W}_i^{(\text{miss}),\top})^\top$$

where $\{\mathbf{X}_i^{(\text{obs})}, \mathbf{W}_i^{(\text{obs})}\}$ and $\{\mathbf{X}_i^{(\text{miss})}, \mathbf{W}_i^{(\text{miss})}\}$ denote the observed and missing components of $\{\mathbf{X}_i, \mathbf{W}_i\}$, respectively. We denote by:

$$\mathbf{S}_i = (Y_i, \mathbf{X}_i^{(\text{obs}),\top}, \mathbf{W}_i^{(\text{obs}),\top})^\top$$

the vector of observed variables and by ξ_i the missing data indicator, defined by:

$$\xi_i = \begin{cases} 1 & \text{if } \mathbf{X}_i \text{ and } \mathbf{W}_i \text{ are completely observed} \\ 0 & \text{if some components of } \mathbf{X}_i \text{ and } \mathbf{W}_i \text{ are missing} \end{cases}$$

Lastly, suppose that the missing data is MAR, so that:

$$\mathbb{P}(\xi_i = 1 | \mathbf{S}_i, \mathbf{X}_i^{(\text{miss})}, \mathbf{W}_i^{(\text{miss})}) = \mathbb{P}(\xi_i = 1 | \mathbf{S}_i)$$

The available data for each individual i is of the form:

$$\mathcal{O}_i = (Y_i, \mathbf{X}_i, \mathbf{W}_i, \xi_i = 1) \quad \text{or} \quad \mathcal{O}_i = (Y_i, \mathbf{X}_i^{(\text{obs})}, \mathbf{W}_i^{(\text{obs})}, \xi_i = 0)$$

REMARK.– If we wanted to introduce a constant term in $\beta^\top \mathbf{X}_i$ and $\gamma^\top \mathbf{W}_i$, we could set $X_{i1} = 1$ and $W_{i1} = 1$. Of course, X_{i1} and W_{i1} feature in $\mathbf{X}_i^{(\text{obs})}$ and $\mathbf{W}_i^{(\text{obs})}$. On the other hand, the vector $\mathbf{S}_i$ contains the constant 1 only once. To avoid overburdening the notation, we will nevertheless set $\mathbf{S}_i = (Y_i, \mathbf{X}_i^{(\text{obs}),\top}, \mathbf{W}_i^{(\text{obs}),\top})^\top$, all while keeping in mind that either X_{i1} or W_{i1} has been removed. ■

In the absence of missing data, the likelihood in the ZIB model is given by [4.11]. From this, we obtain the log-likelihood:

$$\begin{aligned} \ln L_n(\theta) &= -\sum_{i=1}^{n} \ln(1 + e^{\gamma^\top \mathbf{W}_i}) + \sum_{i=1}^{n} 1\{Y_i = 0\} \ln(e^{\gamma^\top \mathbf{W}_i} + (1 + e^{\beta^\top \mathbf{X}_i})^{-k_i}) \\ &+ \sum_{i=1}^{n} 1\{Y_i > 0\} \left(\ln C_{k_i}^{Y_i} + Y_i \beta^\top \mathbf{X}_i - k_i \ln(1 + e^{\beta^\top \mathbf{X}_i}) \right) \\ &:= \sum_{i=1}^{n} \ell_i(\theta) \end{aligned}$$

The MLE of $\theta = (\beta, \gamma)$ is obtained by solving the system $\partial \ln L_n(\theta)/\partial\theta = 0$, namely:

$$\sum_{i=1}^{n} \dot{\ell}_i(\theta) = 0 \qquad [4.12]$$

where $\dot{\ell}_i(\theta) = \partial \ell_i(\theta)/\partial\theta$.

In the presence of missing data, Diallo et al. (2019) use the IPW estimation method. It considers only complete cases, that are weighted by the inverse of their selection probabilities. The estimating equation [4.12] becomes:

$$\sum_{i=1}^{n} \frac{\xi_i}{\mathbb{P}(\xi_i = 1|\mathbf{S}_i)} \dot{\ell}_i(\theta) = 0$$

In practice, the probabilities $\mathbb{P}(\xi_i = 1|\mathbf{S}_i)$ are unknown. Let us assume that they are given by a parametric model $r(\mathbf{S}_i, \alpha)$, where r is a known function (e.g. logistic and probit) and $\alpha \in \mathbb{R}^d$ is an unknown parameter. Denote the MLE of α by $\hat{\alpha}_n$, which is obtained by maximizing the likelihood:

$$\prod_{i=1}^{n} \{r(\mathbf{S}_i, \alpha)\}^{\xi_i} \{1 - r(\mathbf{S}_i, \alpha)\}^{1-\xi_i}$$

The IPW estimator of θ (denoted by $\hat{\theta}_n$) is finally obtained by solving:

$$\sum_{i=1}^{n} \frac{\xi_i}{r(\mathbf{S}_i, \hat{\alpha}_n)} \dot{\ell}_i(\theta) = 0$$

Denote:

$$A(\theta) = -\mathbb{E}\left(\frac{\partial^2 \ell_i(\theta)}{\partial\theta\partial\theta^\top}\right)$$

$$B(\theta, \alpha) = -\mathbb{E}\left((1 - r(\mathbf{S}_i, \alpha))\dot{\ell}_i(\theta)\mathbf{S}_i^\top\right)$$

$$J(\theta, \alpha) = \mathbb{E}\left(\frac{\dot{\ell}_i(\theta)\dot{\ell}_i(\theta)^\top}{r(\mathbf{S}_i, \alpha)}\right)$$

$$\Sigma(\alpha) = \mathbb{E}\left[\mathbf{S}_i\mathbf{S}_i^\top r(\mathbf{S}_i, \alpha)(1 - r(\mathbf{S}_i, \alpha))\right]$$

The following theorem states the asymptotic properties of $\hat{\theta}_n$ (the proof is given in Diallo et al. (2019)).

THEOREM 4.5.– *Suppose that* $\mathbf{X}_i$ *and* $\mathbf{W}_i$ *are bounded and that the true values* β_0, γ_0 *and* α_0 *belong to the interiors of compact subsets of* $\mathbb{R}^p, \mathbb{R}^q$ *and* $\mathbb{R}^d$*, respectively. Then* $\hat{\theta}_n \xrightarrow[n\to\infty]{\mathbb{P}} \theta_0$ *and:*

$$\sqrt{n}(\hat{\theta}_n - \theta_0) \xrightarrow[n\to\infty]{\mathcal{L}} \mathcal{N}(0, \Theta)$$

where:

$$\Theta = A^{-1}(\theta_0)\{J(\theta_0, \alpha_0) - B(\theta_0, \alpha_0)\Sigma^{-1}(\alpha_0)B(\theta_0, \alpha_0)^\top\}A^{-1}(\theta_0)$$

If $\mathbb{P}(\xi = 1|\mathbf{S}) = 1$, the matrix Θ reduces to $A^{-1}(\theta_0)$, the asymptotic variance–covariance matrix of the MLE in the ZIB model without missing data.

Set:

$$A_n(\theta, \alpha) = -\frac{1}{n}\sum_{i=1}^{n} \frac{\xi_i}{r(\mathbf{S}_i, \alpha)} \frac{\partial^2 \ell_i(\theta)}{\partial\theta\partial\theta^\top}$$

$$B_n(\theta, \alpha) = -\frac{1}{n}\sum_{i=1}^{n} \xi_i \frac{1 - r(\mathbf{S}_i, \alpha)}{r(\mathbf{S}_i, \alpha)} \dot{\ell}_i(\theta)\mathbf{S}_i^\top$$

$$J_n(\theta, \alpha) = \frac{1}{n}\sum_{i=1}^{n} \xi_i \frac{\dot{\ell}_i(\theta)\dot{\ell}_i(\theta)^\top}{r^2(\mathbf{S}_i, \alpha)}$$

$$\Sigma_n(\alpha) = \frac{1}{n}\sum_{i=1}^{n} \mathbf{S}_i\mathbf{S}_i^\top r(\mathbf{S}_i, \alpha)(1 - r(\mathbf{S}_i, \alpha))$$

A consistent estimator of Θ is:

$$A_n^{-1}(\hat{\theta}_n, \hat{\alpha}_n)\left\{J_n(\hat{\theta}_n, \hat{\alpha}_n) - B_n(\hat{\theta}_n, \hat{\alpha}_n)\Sigma_n^{-1}(\hat{\alpha}_n)B_n(\hat{\theta}_n, \hat{\alpha}_n)^\top\right\}A_n^{-1}(\hat{\theta}_n, \hat{\alpha}_n)$$

The analogous problem in the ZIP model has been studied by Lukusa et al. (2016) and Lee et al. (2020) when $\mathbf{X}_i^{(\text{obs})}$ and $\mathbf{W}_i^{(\text{obs})}$ are categorical variables (section 4.5.3.1), and by Lukusa and Phoa (2020) in the more general case when $\mathbf{X}_i^{(\text{obs})}$ and $\mathbf{W}_i^{(\text{obs})}$ have both continuous and categorical components (section 4.5.3.2).

4.5.3. *Missing covariables in the ZIP model*

4.5.3.1. *Case with categorical observed covariables*

Here, the model is the following:

$$Y_i \sim \text{ZIP}(\mu_i, \pi_i), \quad i = 1, \ldots, n$$

where $\ln(\mu_i) = \beta^\top \mathbf{X}_i$ and $\text{logit}(\pi_i) = \gamma^\top \mathbf{W}_i$. Without missing data, the likelihood of $\theta = (\beta^\top, \gamma^\top)^\top$ is given by [4.6]. From this, we obtain the log-likelihood:

$$\begin{aligned}\ln L_n(\theta) &= -\sum_{i=1}^{n} \ln(1 + e^{\gamma^\top \mathbf{W}_i}) + \sum_{i=1}^{n} 1\{Y_i = 0\} \ln\left(e^{\gamma^\top \mathbf{W}_i} + e^{-e^{\beta^\top \mathbf{X}_i}}\right) \\ &+ \sum_{i=1}^{n} 1\{Y_i > 0\} \left(Y_i \beta^\top \mathbf{X}_i - e^{\beta^\top \mathbf{X}_i} - \ln(Y_i!)\right) \\ &:= \sum_{i=1}^{n} \ell_i(\theta)\end{aligned}$$

The MLE is obtained by solving the score equation[4]:

$$\sum_{i=1}^{n} \dot{\ell}_i(\theta) = 0$$

where $\dot{\ell}_i(\theta) = \partial \ell_i(\theta)/\partial\theta$.

In Lukusa et al. (2016), the variables $\mathbf{X}_i^{(\text{obs})}$ and $\mathbf{W}_i^{(\text{obs})}$ are assumed to be categorical. We denote by:

$$\mathbf{V}_i = (\mathbf{X}_i^{(\text{obs}),\top}, \mathbf{W}_i^{(\text{obs}),\top})^\top$$

the vector of observed variables ($\mathbf{V}_i$ contains the constant 1 only once). The data are assumed to be MAR:

$$\mathbb{P}(\xi_i = 1 | Y_i, \mathbf{V}_i, \mathbf{X}_i^{(\text{miss})}, \mathbf{W}_i^{(\text{miss})}) = \mathbb{P}(\xi_i = 1 | Y_i, \mathbf{V}_i)$$

4.5.3.1.1. IPW estimator

Let $r(Y_i, \mathbf{V}_i) = \mathbb{P}(\xi_i = 1 | Y_i, \mathbf{V}_i)$. The IPW estimator is obtained by solving the same equation from the previous section:

$$\sum_{i=1}^{n} \frac{\xi_i}{r(Y_i, \mathbf{V}_i)} \dot{\ell}_i(\theta) = 0$$

4 In this section and the following one, for the sake of convenience, we will use the same notation $\ell_i(\theta)$ and $\dot{\ell}_i(\theta)$ from section 4.5.2. Depending on the context, $\ell_i(\theta)$ and $\dot{\ell}_i(\theta)$ therefore denote the likelihood and its derivative, respectively, in the ZIB or ZIP models.

As we have mentioned several times before, the selection probabilities are unknown in general. As the variables Y_i and $\mathbf{V}_i$ are discrete, Lukusa et al. (2016) propose estimating $r(Y_i, \mathbf{V}_i)$ non-parametrically as:

$$\hat{r}(Y_i, \mathbf{V}_i) = \frac{\sum_{j=1}^{n} \xi_j 1\{Y_j = Y_i\} 1\{\mathbf{V}_j = \mathbf{V}_i\}}{\sum_{j=1}^{n} 1\{Y_j = Y_i\} 1\{\mathbf{V}_j = \mathbf{V}_i\}}$$

The IPW estimator of θ is therefore the solution to the equation:

$$\sum_{i=1}^{n} \frac{\xi_i}{\hat{r}(Y_i, \mathbf{V}_i)} \dot{\ell}_i(\theta) = 0$$

Set:

$$\begin{aligned}
A(\theta) &= -\mathbb{E}\left(\frac{\partial^2 \ell_i(\theta)}{\partial\theta\partial\theta^\top}\right) \\
J(\theta, r) &= \mathbb{E}\left(\frac{\dot{\ell}_i(\theta)\dot{\ell}_i(\theta)^\top}{r(Y_i, \mathbf{V}_i)}\right) \\
\dot{\ell}_i^*(\theta) &= \mathbb{E}[\dot{\ell}_i(\theta) | Y_i, \mathbf{V}_i], \quad i = 1, \dots, n \\
C^*(\theta) &= \mathbb{E}(\dot{\ell}_i^*(\theta)\dot{\ell}_i^*(\theta)^\top) \\
J^*(\theta, r) &= \mathbb{E}\left(\frac{\dot{\ell}_i^*(\theta)\dot{\ell}_i^*(\theta)^\top}{r(Y_i, \mathbf{V}_i)}\right)
\end{aligned} \qquad [4.13]$$

Under certain regularity conditions that we do not include here (see Lukusa et al. (2016)), Lukusa et al. (2016) prove the following theorem:

THEOREM 4.6.– *The IPW estimator satisfies* $\hat{\theta}_n \xrightarrow[n\to\infty]{\mathbb{P}} \theta_0$ *and:*

$$\sqrt{n}(\hat{\theta}_n - \theta_0) \xrightarrow[n\to\infty]{\mathcal{L}} \mathcal{N}(0, \Theta)$$

where $\Theta = A^{-1}(\theta_0)\{J(\theta_0, r) - [J^*(\theta_0, r) - C^*(\theta_0)]\}A^{-1}(\theta_0)$.

Here again, if $\mathbb{P}(\xi = 1 | Y, \mathbf{V}) = 1$, then the matrix Θ reduces to $A^{-1}(\theta_0)$, the asymptotic variance–covariance matrix of the MLE in the ZIP model in the absence of missing data.

Let us construct the empirical versions of $A(\theta), J(\theta, r), \dot{\ell}_i^*(\theta), C^*(\theta)$ and $J^*(\theta, r)$:

$$A_n(\theta, r) = -\frac{1}{n}\sum_{i=1}^{n} \frac{\xi_i}{r(Y_i, \mathbf{V}_i)} \frac{\partial^2 \ell_i(\theta)}{\partial\theta\partial\theta^\top}$$

$$J_n(\theta, r) = \frac{1}{n}\sum_{i=1}^{n} \frac{\xi_i}{r^2(Y_i, \mathbf{V}_i)} \dot{\ell}_i(\theta)\dot{\ell}_i(\theta)^\top$$

$$\widehat{\dot{\ell}_i^*}(\theta) = \frac{\sum_{j=1}^{n} \xi_j \dot{\ell}_j(\theta) 1\{Y_j = Y_i, \mathbf{V}_j = \mathbf{V}_i\}}{\sum_{j=1}^{n} \xi_j 1\{Y_j = Y_i, \mathbf{V}_j = \mathbf{V}_i\}}, \quad i = 1, \ldots, n$$

$$C_n^*(\theta) = \frac{1}{n}\sum_{i=1}^{n} \widehat{\dot{\ell}_i^*}(\theta)\widehat{\dot{\ell}_i^*}(\theta)^\top$$

and:

$$J_n^*(\theta, r) = \frac{1}{n}\sum_{i=1}^{n} \frac{\widehat{\dot{\ell}_i^*}(\theta)\widehat{\dot{\ell}_i^*}(\theta)^\top}{r(Y_i, \mathbf{V}_i)}$$

A consistent estimator of Θ is given by:

$$A_n^{-1}(\hat{\theta}_n, \hat{r})\{J_n(\hat{\theta}_n, \hat{r}) - [J_n^*(\hat{\theta}_n, \hat{r}) - C_n^*(\hat{\theta}_n)]\}A_n^{-1}(\hat{\theta}_n, \hat{r})$$

(see Lukusa et al. (2016)).

4.5.3.1.2. Multiple imputation

Still assuming that $\mathbf{X}_i^{(\mathrm{obs})}$ and $\mathbf{W}_i^{(\mathrm{obs})}$ are categorical, Lee et al. (2020) propose to estimate θ using multiple imputation. To simplify notation, suppose as in Lee et al. (2020) that a single explanatory variable is missing (e.g. the jth component of $\mathbf{X}$).

Multiple imputation consists of completing the sample by replacing any missing data with values taken randomly according to the conditional distribution of the missing variable given the observed variables.

Lee et al. (2020) therefore estimate the conditional distribution of X_{ij} given $(Y_i, \mathbf{V}_i)$ by using the conditional empirical cumulative distribution function:

$$\widehat{F}(x|Y_i, \mathbf{V}_i) = \sum_{\ell=1}^{n} \left\{ \frac{\xi_\ell 1\{Y_\ell = Y_i\} 1\{\mathbf{V}_\ell = \mathbf{V}_i\}}{\sum_{k=1}^{n} \xi_k 1\{Y_k = Y_i\} 1\{\mathbf{V}_k = \mathbf{V}_i\}} \right\} 1\{X_{\ell j} \leq x\} \quad [4.14]$$

The missing data X_{ij} are replaced by values $\tilde{X}_{ij}$ simulated from [4.14]. The process is repeated M times to obtained M completed samples. For each one, an estimator $\hat{\theta}_n^{MI,(m)}$ of θ is obtained by maximizing the likelihood [4.6] of the ZIP model. A final estimator of θ is then obtained by averaging:

$$\hat{\theta}_n^{MI} = \frac{1}{M}\sum_{m=1}^{M} \hat{\theta}_n^{MI,(m)}$$

Lee et al. (2020) show that $\hat{\theta}_n^{MI}$ is consistent and asymptotically Gaussian. Its asymptotic variance is the same as that of the IPW estimator (theorem 4.6).

4.5.3.2. *Case with continuous observed covariables*

Let us use the notation from section 4.5.3.1 again and set $\mathbf{S}_i = (Y_i, \mathbf{V}_i^\top)^\top$. When $\mathbf{V}_i = (\mathbf{X}_i^{(\text{obs}),\top}, \mathbf{W}_i^{(\text{obs}),\top})^\top$ contains continuous components, Lukusa and Phoa (2020) propose estimating the selection probabilities $\mathbb{P}(\xi_i = 1|Y_i, \mathbf{V}_i)$:

– either parametrically, by assuming that there exists a model $r(\mathbf{S}_i, \alpha) = \mathbb{P}(\xi_i = 1|Y_i, \mathbf{V}_i)$ known up to some parameter α;

– or non-parametrically, by using kernel estimation.

In the first case, we begin by estimating α by maximizing the likelihood:

$$\prod_{i=1}^{n}\{r(\mathbf{S}_i, \alpha)\}^{\xi_i}\{1 - r(\mathbf{S}_i, \alpha)\}^{1-\xi_i}$$

Then the selection probabilities are estimated using $r(\mathbf{S}_i, \hat{\alpha}_n)$. In the second case, Lukusa and Phoa (2020) propose estimating $r(Y_i, \mathbf{V}_i) := \mathbb{P}(\xi_i = 1|Y_i, \mathbf{V}_i)$ directly as:

$$\hat{r}(Y_i, \mathbf{V}_i) = \frac{\sum_{j=1}^{n} \xi_j 1\{Y_j = Y_i\}\mathbf{K}_{\mathcal{H}}(\mathbf{V}_j - \mathbf{V}_i)}{\sum_{j=1}^{n} 1\{Y_j = Y_i\}\mathbf{K}_{\mathcal{H}}(\mathbf{V}_j - \mathbf{V}_i)}$$

where $\mathcal{H}$ is a positive–definite smoothing matrix, $\mathbf{K}$ is a kernel function (a probability density) and $\mathbf{K}_{\mathcal{H}}(u) = (\det(\mathcal{H}))^{1/2}\mathbf{K}(\mathcal{H}^{-1/2}u)$. The IPW estimator of θ is obtained by solving:

$$\sum_{i=1}^{n} \frac{\xi_i}{r(\mathbf{S}_i, \hat{\alpha}_n)}\dot{\ell}_i(\theta) = 0 \qquad [4.15]$$

in the parametric case, and:

$$\sum_{i=1}^{n} \frac{\xi_i}{\hat{r}(Y_i, \mathbf{V}_i)}\dot{\ell}_i(\theta) = 0 \qquad [4.16]$$

in the nonparametric case.

We denote by $\hat{\theta}_n^{(1)}$ and $\hat{\theta}_n^{(2)}$ the IPW estimators obtained from [4.15] and [4.16], respectively. Their asymptotic properties are described in the following two theorems (these results are established under certain regularity conditions stated in Lukusa and Phoa (2020), and are not stated here).

For theorem 4.7, let us reuse the notation $A(\theta)$, $J(\theta,\alpha)$, $B(\theta,\alpha)$ and $\Sigma(\alpha)$ introduced in section 4.5.2 (albeit with $\ell_i(\theta)$ and $\dot{\ell}_i(\theta)$ calculated using the ZIP model). For theorem 4.8, the notation from [4.14] is also reused.

THEOREM 4.7.– *The estimator $\hat{\theta}_n^{(1)}$ satisfies $\hat{\theta}_n^{(1)} \xrightarrow[n\to\infty]{\mathbb{P}} \theta_0$ and:*

$$\sqrt{n}(\hat{\theta}_n^{(1)} - \theta_0) \xrightarrow[n\to\infty]{\mathcal{L}} \mathcal{N}(0, \Theta^{(1)})$$

where $\Theta^{(1)} = A^{-1}(\theta_0)\{J(\theta_0,\alpha_0) - B(\theta_0,\alpha_0)\Sigma^{-1}(\alpha_0)B(\theta_0,\alpha_0)^\top\}A^{-1}(\theta_0)$.

THEOREM 4.8.– *The estimator $\hat{\theta}_n^{(2)}$ satisfies $\hat{\theta}_n^{(2)} \xrightarrow[n\to\infty]{\mathbb{P}} \theta_0$ and:*

$$\sqrt{n}(\hat{\theta}_n^{(2)} - \theta_0) \xrightarrow[n\to\infty]{\mathcal{L}} \mathcal{N}(0, \Theta^{(2)})$$

where $\Theta^{(2)} = A^{-1}(\theta_0)\{J(\theta_0,r) - [J^*(\theta_0,r) - C^*(\theta_0)]\}A^{-1}(\theta_0)$.

Consistent estimators of $\Theta^{(1)}$ and $\Theta^{(2)}$ are:

$$A_n^{-1}(\hat{\theta}_n^{(1)},\hat{\alpha}_n) \times \left\{J_n(\hat{\theta}_n^{(1)},\hat{\alpha}_n) - B_n(\hat{\theta}_n^{(1)},\hat{\alpha}_n)\Sigma_n^{-1}(\hat{\alpha}_n)B_n(\hat{\theta}_n^{(1)},\hat{\alpha}_n)^\top\right\} A_n^{-1}(\hat{\theta}_n^{(1)},\hat{\alpha}_n)$$

and:

$$A_n^{-1}(\hat{\theta}_n^{(2)},\hat{r})\{J_n(\hat{\theta}_n^{(2)},\hat{r}) - [J_n^*(\hat{\theta}_n^{(2)},\hat{r}) - C_n^*(\hat{\theta}_n^{(2)})]\}A_n^{-1}(\hat{\theta}_n^{(2)},\hat{r})$$

with the same notation introduced beforehand.

4.6. Marginal zero-inflated models

4.6.1. *Introduction*

The ZIP, ZIGP and ZINB regression models are mixture models. They are formed from two sub-models: (i) a model for the probability of belonging to the at-risk subpopulation and (ii) a count model (Poisson, negative binomial, etc.) for the response variable of the at-risk subpopulation (in the subpopulation not at risk, the response is always equal to 0). The parameters of the count model quantify the effect which the explanatory variables have on the *conditional* mean of the count, given that the individual is at risk. Sometimes however, it can be interesting to interpret the effect that the explanatory variables have on the *marginal* mean of the response.

To make things precise, let S_i denote the variable that equals 1 if individual i is at risk, and 0 otherwise. This variable is not observed. In zero-inflated models, the count model applies to the conditional mean $\mu_i = \mathbb{E}(Y_i|\mathbf{X}_i, S_i = 1)$, which is to say the mean of Y_i given that individual i is at risk, and given the explanatory variables $\mathbf{X}_i$. For example, in the ZIP and ZINB models, we set $\mu_i = \exp(\beta^\top \mathbf{X}_i)$. But, according to the question at hand, it can also be interesting to evaluate the effect that the explanatory variables have on the *marginal* mean, $\mathbb{E}(Y_i|\mathbf{X}_i)$.

REMARK.– Even though it is called the marginal mean, $\mathbb{E}(Y_i|\mathbf{X}_i)$ is actually conditional (it is the mean of Y_i given $\mathbf{X}_i$). Nevertheless, in the context of marginal zero-inflated models, the term "conditional" refers to conditioning by $\{S_i = 1\}$. Without this conditioning, the mean of Y_i is said to be marginal. ■

In the `docvisits` data set, μ_i represents the average number of consultations of an individual who continues to see a doctor. For its part, the mean $\mathbb{E}(Y_i|\mathbf{X}_i)$ represents the average number of consultations of an individual taken at random from the total population, and no longer just from the at-risk subpopulation.

In the following, denote $\nu_i = \mathbb{E}(Y_i|\mathbf{X}_i)$. Of course, ν_i and μ_i are linked. Let $\mathbb{P}(S_i = 1|\mathbf{X}_i) = 1 - \pi_i$ denote the probability that individual i is at risk. Then we have:

$$
\begin{aligned}
\nu_i &= \sum_{y=0}^{+\infty} y\mathbb{P}(Y_i = y|\mathbf{X}_i) \\
&= \sum_{y=1}^{+\infty} y \left[\mathbb{P}(Y_i = y|\mathbf{X}_i, S_i = 1)(1-\pi_i) + \underbrace{\mathbb{P}(Y_i = y|\mathbf{X}_i, S_i = 0)}_{=0} \pi_i \right] \\
&= \sum_{y=1}^{+\infty} y\mathbb{P}(Y_i = y|\mathbf{X}_i, S_i = 1)(1-\pi_i) \\
&= (1-\pi_i)\sum_{y=0}^{+\infty} y\mathbb{P}(Y_i = y|\mathbf{X}_i, S_i = 1) \\
&= (1-\pi_i)\mathbb{E}(Y_i|\mathbf{X}_i, S_i = 1) \\
&= (1-\pi_i)\mu_i
\end{aligned}
$$

Note that:

$$\mathbb{E}(Y_i|\mathbf{X}_i) \leq \mathbb{E}(Y_i|\mathbf{X}_i, S_i = 1)$$

Intuitively, it is logical that the mean of Y_i will be greater for the at-risk subpopulation than for the general population, which additionally includes individuals who are not at risk, and for whom $Y_i = 0$.

Take the example of the ZIP model. If we set:

$$\pi_i = \frac{e^{\gamma^\top \mathbf{X}_i}}{1 + e^{\gamma^\top \mathbf{X}_i}} \quad \text{and} \quad \mu_i = e^{\beta^\top \mathbf{X}_i} \qquad [4.17]$$

then:

$$\begin{aligned} \nu_i &= \mathbb{E}(Y_i|\mathbf{X}_i) \\ &= \frac{e^{\beta^\top \mathbf{X}_i}}{1 + e^{\gamma^\top \mathbf{X}_i}} \end{aligned}$$

In the Poisson model $Y_i \sim \mathcal{P}(e^{\beta^\top \mathbf{X}_i})$, recall that we can interpret the coefficients β_j from the ratio:

$$\frac{\mathbb{E}(Y_i|\mathbf{X}_{i,(-j)} = \mathbf{x}_{i,(-j)}, X_{ij} = x + 1)}{\mathbb{E}(Y_i|\mathbf{X}_{i,(-j)} = \mathbf{x}_{i,(-j)}, X_{ij} = x)} \qquad [4.18]$$

where $\mathbf{X}_{i,(-j)}$ denotes the vector $\mathbf{X}_i$ with its jth component X_{ij} removed. This ratio equals $\exp(\beta_j)$. Therefore, if X_{ij} increases by one unit, all other things being equal, then the mean of Y_i will be multiplied by a factor of $\exp(\beta_j)$.

In the ZIP model, this interpretation remains valid when considering the effect that the regressors have on $\mu_i = \mathbb{E}(Y_i|\mathbf{X}_i, S_i = 1)$. On the other hand, the effect of the X_{ij} on the marginal mean $\mathbb{E}(Y_i|\mathbf{X}_i)$ becomes difficult to interpret. To see for ourselves, we calculate the ratio [4.18] in the ZIP model [4.17]. We denote by $\gamma_{(-j)}$ the vector γ with its jth component removed. Then we have:

$$\begin{aligned} &\frac{\mathbb{E}(Y_i|\mathbf{X}_{i,(-j)} = \mathbf{x}_{i,(-j)}, X_{ij} = x + 1)}{\mathbb{E}(Y_i|\mathbf{X}_{i,(-j)} = \mathbf{x}_{i,(-j)}, X_{ij} = x)} \\ &\quad = \exp(\beta_j)\frac{1 + \exp(\gamma_{(-j)}\mathbf{x}_{i,(-j)} + \gamma_j x)}{1 + \exp(\gamma_{(-j)}\mathbf{x}_{i,(-j)} + \gamma_j(x+1))} \end{aligned}$$

This ratio depends on x and γ, except in the particular case when $\gamma_j = 0$. It is therefore not possible to simply interpret the effect that the explanatory variables have on the marginal mean of the ZIP model. This remark also applies to the ZIGP and ZINB models. Nevertheless, if we wish to provide such interpretations, then it would be necessary to directly model the marginal mean, leading to the formulation of *marginal* zero-inflated models.

4.6.2. *MZIP and MZINB models*

Long et al. (2014) have introduced the marginal zero-inflated Poisson (MZIP) model. In the previous section, we saw that:

$$\nu_i = (1 - \pi_i)\mu_i$$

The ZIP model is defined using π_i and μ_i. The MZIP model is instead defined using π_i and ν_i. For example, Long et al. (2014) set:

$$\pi_i = \frac{e^{\gamma^\top \mathbf{Z}_i}}{1 + e^{\gamma^\top \mathbf{Z}_i}} \qquad [4.19]$$

and:

$$\nu_i = e^{\beta^\top \mathbf{X}_i} \qquad [4.20]$$

(in their notation, the authors distinguish between the explanatory variables which act on π_i and those which act on ν_i). In the MZIP model, the effect of the X_{ij} on the marginal mean ν_i can be interpreted via the ratio [4.18], as can be done in the Poisson model.

We can easily deduce μ_i from ν_i and π_i:

$$\begin{aligned}\mu_i &= \frac{\nu_i}{(1 - \pi_i)} \\ &= e^{\beta^\top \mathbf{X}_i}(1 + e^{\gamma^\top \mathbf{Z}_i})\end{aligned}$$

The likelihood of (β, γ) in the MZIP model is therefore obtained from the likelihood [4.6] of the ZIP model:

$$\begin{aligned}L_n(\beta,\gamma) &= \prod_{i=1}^{n} \left(\pi_i + (1-\pi_i)e^{-\mu_i}\right)^{1\{Y_i=0\}} \left((1-\pi_i)\frac{e^{-\mu_i}\mu_i^{Y_i}}{Y_i!}\right)^{1\{Y_i>0\}} \\ &= \prod_{i=1}^{n}(1 + e^{\gamma^\top \mathbf{Z}_i})^{-1}(e^{\gamma^\top \mathbf{Z}_i} + e^{-(1+e^{\gamma^\top \mathbf{Z}_i})e^{\beta^\top \mathbf{X}_i}})^{1\{Y_i=0\}} \\ &\times \prod_{i=1}^{n}\left(\frac{e^{-(1+e^{\gamma^\top \mathbf{Z}_i})e^{\beta^\top \mathbf{X}_i}+Y_i\beta^\top \mathbf{X}_i}(1+e^{\gamma^\top \mathbf{Z}_i})^{Y_i}}{Y_i!}\right)^{1\{Y_i>0\}}\end{aligned}$$

Preisser et al. (2016) adopt the same principle to construct a marginal zero-inflated negative binomial (MZINB) model. As in the MZIP model, the MZINB one is defined using π_i and ν_i. Preisser et al. (2016) use the models [4.19] and [4.20]. The likelihood of (β, γ) in the MZINB model is obtained from the likelihood [4.10] of the ZINB model:

$$
\begin{aligned}
L_n(\beta, \gamma, \kappa) &= \prod_{i=1}^{n} \left(\pi_i + (1-\pi_i)(1+\kappa\mu_i)^{-\frac{1}{\kappa}} \right)^{1\{Y_i=0\}} \\
&\times \left((1-\pi_i) \frac{\Gamma(Y_i + \frac{1}{\kappa})}{Y_i!\Gamma(\frac{1}{\kappa})} \left(\frac{\kappa\mu_i}{1+\kappa\mu_i} \right)^{Y_i} \left(\frac{1}{1+\kappa\mu_i} \right)^{\frac{1}{\kappa}} \right)^{1\{Y_i>0\}} \\
&= \prod_{i=1}^{n} (1+e^{\gamma^\top \mathbf{Z}_i})^{-1} \left(e^{\gamma^\top \mathbf{Z}_i} + [1+\kappa e^{\beta^\top \mathbf{X}_i}(1+e^{\gamma^\top \mathbf{Z}_i})]^{-\frac{1}{\kappa}} \right)^{1\{Y_i=0\}} \\
&\times \prod_{i=1}^{n} \left\{ \frac{\Gamma(Y_i + \frac{1}{\kappa})}{Y_i!\Gamma(\frac{1}{\kappa})} \left(\frac{\kappa e^{\beta^\top \mathbf{X}_i}(1+e^{\gamma^\top \mathbf{Z}_i})}{1+\kappa e^{\beta^\top \mathbf{X}_i}(1+e^{\gamma^\top \mathbf{Z}_i})} \right)^{Y_i} \right. \\
&\times \left. \left(1+\kappa e^{\beta^\top \mathbf{X}_i}(1+e^{\gamma^\top \mathbf{Z}_i})\right)^{-\frac{1}{\kappa}} \right\}^{1\{Y_i>0\}}
\end{aligned}
$$

In the MZIP and MZINB models, the MLE must be approximated numerically. Long et al. (2014) and Preisser et al. (2016) use a quasi-Newton algorithm. In these two articles, the reader will find numerical studies of the properties of the MLE. A score test of the MZIP model against the MZINB one – similar to the score test of the ZIP model against the ZINB one – is stated in Inan et al. (2018).

4.7. Exercises

Exercise 1 – Zero-inflated model

Let Y^* be a random count. Set $p_y = \mathbb{P}(Y^* = y)$ for $y = 0, 1, 2 \ldots$. Let $X \sim \mathcal{B}(1-\pi)$ be independent of Y^*. Set $Y = XY^*$.

1) Show that:

$$
\mathbb{P}(Y = y) = \begin{cases} \pi + (1-\pi)p_0 & \text{if } y = 0 \\ (1-\pi)p_y & \text{if } y = 1, 2, \ldots \end{cases}
$$

2) Starting from the definition of Y as $Y = XY^*$, we derive the formulas:

$$\mathbb{E}(Y) = (1-\pi)\mathbb{E}(Y^*) \quad [4.21]$$

and:

$$\text{var}(Y) = (1-\pi)\text{var}(Y^*) + \pi(1-\pi)(\mathbb{E}(Y^*))^2 \quad [4.22]$$

3) Recall that the moment generating function of a random variable Z is the function $M_Z(t) = \mathbb{E}(e^{tZ})$, $t \in \mathbb{R}$. Also recall that if Z admits a second-order moment, then $\mathbb{E}(Z) = M_Z^{(1)}(0)$ and $\text{var}(Z) = M_Z^{(2)}(0) - (M_Z^{(1)}(0))^2$, where $M_Z^{(k)}(t) = \partial^k M_Z(t)/\partial t^k$.

a) Show that:

$$M_Y(t) = \pi + (1-\pi)M_{Y^*}(t)$$

HINT.– Use the equality $\mathbb{E}(e^{tXY^*}) = \mathbb{E}(\mathbb{E}(e^{tXY^*}|Y^*))$.

b) Obtain [4.21] and [4.22] by using the derivatives of $M_Y(t)$.

4) Calculate the coefficient of dispersion $\phi = \text{var}(Y)/\mathbb{E}(Y)$ of Y as a function of the coefficient of dispersion ϕ^* of Y^*. Comment on the result.

Exercise 2 – MLE in the ZIP model

Let $Y_1, \ldots, Y_n$ be an i.i.d. sample of the ZIP model [4.5]:

$$\mathbb{P}(Y_i = y) = \begin{cases} \pi + (1-\pi)e^{-\mu} & \text{if } y = 0 \\ (1-\pi)\frac{e^{-\mu}\mu^y}{y!} & \text{if } y = 1, 2, \ldots \end{cases}$$

Denote by $(\hat{\pi}, \hat{\mu})$ the MLE of (π, μ) and by $\hat{p}_0 = \hat{\pi} + (1-\hat{\pi})e^{-\hat{\mu}}$ the estimator of $\mathbb{P}(Y_i = 0)$ obtained from $(\hat{\pi}, \hat{\mu})$. Show that:

$$\hat{p}_0 = \frac{1}{n}\sum_{i=1}^{n} 1\{Y_i = 0\}$$

HINT.– Denote by L_n the likelihood of (π, μ). Use the fact that $(\hat{\pi}, \hat{\mu})$ satisfies the equation $\partial \ln L_n(\hat{\pi}, \hat{\mu})/\partial\pi = 0$.

Exercise 3 – MLE in the ZIB model

Let $Y_1, \ldots, Y_n$ be an i.i.d. sample of the ZIB model, defined by:

$$\mathbb{P}(Y_i = y) = \begin{cases} \pi + (1-\pi)(1-p)^k & \text{if } y = 0 \\ (1-\pi)C_k^y p^y (1-p)^{k-y} & \text{if } y = 1, 2, \ldots, k \end{cases}$$

Denote by $(\hat{\pi}, \hat{p})$ the MLE of (π, p) and $\hat{p}_0 = \hat{\pi} + (1-\hat{\pi})(1-\hat{p})^k$. Show that:

$$\hat{p}_0 = \frac{1}{n}\sum_{i=1}^{n} 1\{Y_i = 0\}$$

Exercise 4 – Hurdle models

Consider the ZIP model:

$$\mathbb{P}(Y = y) = \begin{cases} \pi + (1-\pi)e^{-\mu} & \text{if } y = 0 \\ (1-\pi)\frac{e^{-\mu}\mu^y}{y!} & \text{if } y = 1, 2, \ldots \end{cases}$$

1) Set $\omega = \pi + (1-\pi)e^{-\mu}$. Show that we can rewrite the model in the form:

$$\mathbb{P}(Y = y) = \begin{cases} \omega & \text{if } y = 0 \\ (1-\omega)g(y) & \text{if } y = 1, 2, \ldots \end{cases} \qquad [4.23]$$

where:

$$g(y) = \frac{\mu^y e^{-\mu}}{y!(1-e^{-\mu})}$$

Check that g is the density of the truncated Poisson distribution at zero (i.e. if $U \sim \mathcal{P}(\mu)$, then $g(y) = \mathbb{P}(U = y | U > 0)$, $y = 1, 2, \ldots$).

REMARK.– The model [4.23] is called the Poisson-hurdle model. More generally, a hurdle model is defined by (i) the probability ω of observing 0 and (ii) a discrete distribution (either the Poisson distribution or some other one) truncated at zero (Agresti 2015). ■

2) The Poisson-hurdle model can not only model zero-inflation relative to the Poisson distribution, but also zero-deflation (relative to the same distribution). Let $U \sim \mathcal{P}(\mu)$ and denote by Y a random variable of the Poisson-hurdle distribution. Under what condition placed on ω and μ does the inequality $\mathbb{P}(Y = 0) > \mathbb{P}(U = 0)$ hold (zero-inflation)? Under what condition does $\mathbb{P}(Y = 0) < \mathbb{P}(U = 0)$ hold (zero-deflation)?

3) Let Y^* be a random variable with density g and let $X \sim \mathcal{B}(1-\omega)$ be independent of Y^*. Set $Y = XY^*$.

a) Show that Y follows the hurdle model [4.23].

b) Calculate $\mathbb{E}(Y^*), \mathbb{E}(Y^{*2})$, and $\text{var}(Y^*)$. From this, deduce $\mathbb{E}(Y)$ and $\text{var}(Y)$.

c) Calculate the coefficient of dispersion $\phi^* = \text{var}(Y^*)/\mathbb{E}(Y^*)$ of Y^*. Calculate the coefficient of dispersion ϕ of Y and express it as a function of ϕ^*. Comment on this result.

4) A Poisson-hurdle regression model for Y_i can be constructed from equation [4.23] by setting:

$$\text{logit}(\omega_i) = \beta_1^\top \mathbf{X}_{1i} \quad \text{and} \quad \ln(\mu_i) = \beta_2^\top \mathbf{X}_{2i}$$

where $\mathbf{X}_{1i}$ and $\mathbf{X}_{2i}$ are vectors of explanatory variables (either distinct or having components in common) and where β_1, β_2 are parameters. Suppose we have available an independent sample $\{(Y_i, \mathbf{X}_{1i}, \mathbf{X}_{2i}), i = 1, \ldots, n\}$. Calculate the likelihood of (β_1, β_2). Show that it factors into a product $L_1(\beta_1) \times L_2(\beta_2)$ of two terms, with one factor depending only on β_1, and the other on β_2. What does this mean when it comes to estimating β_1 and β_2?

5) Consider the hurdle model:

$$\mathbb{P}(Y_i = y) = \begin{cases} \omega & \text{if } y = 0 \\ (1-\omega)\frac{\mu_i^y e^{-\mu_i}}{y!(1-e^{-\mu_i})} & \text{if } y = 1, 2, \ldots \end{cases}$$

where $\omega \in (0,1)$ and $\ln(\mu_i) = \beta^\top \mathbf{X}_i$. Suppose we have available an independent sample $\{(Y_i, \mathbf{X}_i), i = 1, \ldots, n\}$. Write down the likelihood of (ω, β), and then calculate the likelihood equations. Show that the MLE of ω is $\hat{\omega} = n^{-1} \sum_{i=1}^n 1\{Y_i = 0\}$.

REMARK.– In R, hurdle models can be estimated using the `hurdle` function from the `pscl` package (Jackman 2020). ■

References

Agresti, A. (2015). *Foundations of Linear and Generalized Linear Models*. John Wiley & Sons, New York.

Andersen, P.K., Borgan, Ø., Gill, R.D., Keiding, N. (1993). *Statistical Models Based on Counting Processes*. Springer-Verlag, New York.

Antoniadis, A., Berruyer, J., Carmona, R. (1992). *Régression non linéaire et applications*. Economica, Paris.

Azaïs, J.-M. and Bardet, J.-M. (2012). *Le modèle linéaire par l'exemple. Régression, analyse de la variance et plans d'expérience illustrés par R et SAS*. Dunod, Paris.

Bernhardt, P.W., Wang, H.J., Zhang, D. (2015). Statistical methods for generalized linear models with covariates subject to detection limits. *Statistics in Biosciences*, 7(1), 68–89.

Boucher, J.-P. and Denuit, M. (2008). Credibility premiums for the zero-inflated Poisson model and new hunger for bonus interpretation. *Insurance: Mathematics and Economics*, 42(2), 727–735.

Boucher, J.-P., Denuit, M., Guillen, M. (2009). Number of accidents or number of claims? An approach with zero-inflated Poisson models for panel data. *The Journal of Risk and Insurance*, 76(4), 821–846.

Bousselmi, B., Dupuy, J.-F., Karoui, A. (2021). Censored count data regression with missing censoring information. *Electronic Journal of Statistics*, 15(2), 4343–4383.

van den Broek, J. (1995). A score test for zero inflation in a Poisson distribution. *Biometrics*, 51, 738–743.

Cameron, A.C. and Trivedi, P.K. (1998). *Regression Analysis of Count Data*. Cambridge University Press, Cambridge.

Cao, G., Hsu, W.-W., Todem, D. (2014). A score-type test for heterogeneity in zero-inflated models in a stratified population. *Statistics in Medicine*, 33(12), 2103–2114.

Caudill, S. and Mixon, F. (1995). Modeling household fertility decisions: Estimation and testing of censored regression models for count data. *Empirical Economics*, 20, 183–196.

Chen, X.-D. and Fu, Y.-Z. (2011). Model selection for zero-inflated regression with missing covariates. *Computational Statistics & Data Analysis*, 55(1), 765–773.

Chen, H.Y. and Little, R.J.A. (1999). Proportional hazards regression with missing covariates. *Journal of the American Statistical Association*, 94(447), 896–908.

Chen, T., Zhang, H., Zhang, B. (2019). A semiparametric marginalized zero-inflated model for analyzing healthcare utilization panel data with missingness. *Journal of Applied Statistics*, 46(16), 2862–2883.

Coly, S., Yao, A.-F., Abrial, D., Charras-Garrido, M. (2016). Distributions to model overdispersed count data. *Journal de la Société Française de Statistique*, 157(2), 39–63.

Consul, P.C. and Famoye, F. (1992). Generalized Poisson regression model. *Communications in Statistics – Theory and Methods*, 21(1), 89–109.

Consul, P.C. and Jain, G.C. (1973). A generalization of the Poisson distribution. *Technometrics*, 15(4), 791–799.

Cornillon, P.-A. and Matzner-Løber, E. (2007). *Régression : théorie et applications*. Springer, Berlin.

Czado, C. and Min, A. (2005). Consistency and asymptotic normality of the maximum likelihood estimator in a zero-inflated generalized Poisson regression. Technical Report 423, Institut für Statistik der Ludwig-Maximilians-Universität München, Munich.

Czado, C., Erhardt, V., Min, A., Wagner, S. (2007). Zero-inflated generalized Poisson models with regression effects on the mean, dispersion and zero-inflation level applied to patent outsourcing rates. *Statistical Modelling*, 7(2), 125–153.

Davis, K.A., Sinha, S.K., Park, C.G. (2015). Constrained inference for generalized linear models with incomplete covariate data. *Journal of Statistical Computation and Simulation*, 85(4), 693–710.

Dempster, A.P., Laird, N.M., Rubin, D.B. (1977). Maximum likelihood from incomplete data via the EM algorithm. *Journal of the Royal Statistical Society. Series B*, 39(1), 1–38.

Deng, D. and Paul, S.R. (2000). Score tests for zero inflation in generalized linear models. *The Canadian Journal of Statistics*, 28(3), 563–570.

Deng, D. and Paul, S.R. (2005). Score tests for zero-inflation and over-dispersion in generalized linear models. *Statistica Sinica*, 15(1), 257–276.

Deng, D. and Zhang, Y. (2015). Score tests for both extra zeros and extra ones in binomial mixed regression models. *Communications in Statistics – Theory and Methods*, 44(14), 2881–2897.

Diallo, A.O., Diop, A., Dupuy, J.-F. (2017). Asymptotic properties of the maximum-likelihood estimator in zero-inflated binomial regression. *Communications in Statistics – Theory and Methods*, 46(20), 9930–9948.

Diallo, A.O., Diop, A., Dupuy, J.-F. (2018). Analysis of multinomial counts with joint zero-inflation, with an application to health economics. *Journal of Statistical Planning and Inference*, 194, 85–105.

Diallo, A.O., Diop, A., Dupuy, J.-F. (2019). Estimation in zero-inflated binomial regression with missing covariates. *Statistics*, 53(4), 839–865.

Diop, A., Diop, A., Dupuy, J.-F. (2011). Maximum likelihood estimation in the logistic regression model with a cure fraction. *Electronic Journal of Statistics*, 5, 460–483.

Dobson, A.J. (1990). *An Introduction to Generalized Linear Models*. Chapman & Hall, London.

Droesbeke, J.-J., Lejeune, M., Saporta, G. (2005). *Modèles statistiques pour données qualitatives*. Editions Technip, Paris.

Dunn, P.K. and Smyth, G.K. (2018). *Generalized Linear Models with Examples in R*. Springer, New York.

Dupuy, J.-F. (2017). Inference in a generalized endpoint-inflated binomial regression model. *Statistics*, 51(4), 888–903.

Dupuy, J.-F. (2018). *Statistical Methods for Overdispersed Count Data*. ISTE Press, London, and Elsevier, Oxford.

Dupuy, J.-F. (2020). Censored gamma regression with uncertain censoring status. *Mathematical Methods of Statistics*, 29, 172–196.

Erhardt, V. (2006). Verallgemeinerte Poisson und Nullenüberschuss- Regressionsmodelle mit regressiertem Erwartungswert, Dispersions- und Nullenüberschuss-Parameter und eine Anwendung zur Patentmodellierung. PhD Thesis, Technische Universität München, Munich.

Fahrmeir, L. and Kaufmann, H. (1985). Consistency and asymptotic normality of the maximum likelihood estimator in generalized linear models. *The Annals of Statistics*, 13(1), 342–368.

Famoye, F. and Singh, K.P. (2006). Zero-inflated generalized Poisson model with an application to domestic violence data. *Journal of Data Science*, 4, 117–130.

Famoye, F. and Wang, W. (2004). Censored generalized Poisson regression model. *Computational Statistics & Data Analysis*, 46(3), 547–560.

Faraway, J.J. (2016). *Extending the Linear Model with R: Generalized Linear, Mixed Effects and Nonparametric Regression Models*. CRC Press, Boca Raton.

Fleming, T.R. and Harrington, D.P. (1991). *Counting Processes and Survival Analysis*. Wiley-InterScience, New York.

Foutz, R.V. (1977). On the unique consistent solution to the likelihood equations. *Journal of the American Statistical Association*, 72(357), 147–148.

Gourieroux, C. and Monfort, A. (1981). Asymptotic properties of the maximum likelihood estimator in dichotomous logit models. *Journal of Econometrics*, 17(1), 83–97.

Guo, X., Xu, W., Zhu, L. (2014). Multi-index regression models with missing covariates at random. *Journal of Multivariate Analysis*, 123, 345–363.

Guyon, X. (2001). *Statistique et économétrie : du modèle linéaire... aux modèles non-linéaires*. Ellipses, Paris.

Hall, D.B. (2000). Zero-inflated Poisson and binomial regression with random effects: A case study. *Biometrics*, 56, 1030–1039.

Hao, M., Song, X., Sun, L. (2014). Reweighting estimators for the additive hazards model with missing covariates. *The Canadian Journal of Statistics*, 42(2), 285–307.

Hardin, J.W. and Hilbe, J.M. (2018). *Generalized Linear Models and Extensions*. Stata Press, College Station.

Hastie, T., Tibshirani, R., Friedman, J. (2009). *The Elements of Statistical Learning: Data Mining, Inference, and Prediction*. Springer, Berlin.

He, X., Xue, H., Shi, N. Z. (2010). Sieve maximum likelihood estimation for doubly semiparametric zero-inflated Poisson models. *Journal of Multivariate Analysis*, 101(9), 2026–2038.

Henningsen, A. and Toomet, O. (2011). maxLik: A package for maximum likelihood estimation in R. *Computational Statistics*, 26(3), 443–458. doi: 10.1007/s00180-010-0217-1.

Herring, A.H. and Ibrahim, J.G. (2001). Likelihood-based methods for missing covariates in the Cox proportional hazards model. *Journal of the American Statistical Association*, 96(453), 292–302.

Hilbe, J.M. (2011). *Negative Binomial Regression*. Cambridge University Press, Cambridge.

Hilbe, J.M. (2014). *Modeling Count Data*. Cambridge University Press, Cambridge.

Horton, N.J. and Laird, N.M. (1999). Maximum likelihood analysis of generalized linear models with missing covariates. *Statistical Methods in Medical Research*, 8(1), 37–50.

Hu, M.C., Pavlicova, M., Nunes, E.V. (2011). Zero-inflated and hurdle models of count data with extra zeros: Examples from an HIV-risk reduction intervention trial. *The American Journal of Drug and Alcohol Abuse*, 37(5), 367–375.

Ibrahim, J.G. (1990). Incomplete data in generalized linear models. *Journal of the American Statistical Association*, 85(411), 765–769.

Ibrahim, J.G., Lipsitz, S.R., Chen, M.-H. (1999). Missing covariates in generalized linear models when the missing data mechanism is non-ignorable. *Journal of the Royal Statistical Society. Series B, Statistical Methodology*, 61(1), 173–190.

Ibrahim, J.G., Chen, M.-H., Lipsitz, S.R., Herring, A.H. (2005). Missing-data methods for generalized linear models: A comparative review. *Journal of the American Statistical Association*, 100(469), 332–346.

Imbert, A. and Vialaneix, N. (2018). Décrire, prendre en compte, imputer et évaluer les valeurs manquantes dans les études statistiques : une revue des approches existantes. *Journal de la Société Française de Statistique*, 159(2), 1–55.

Inan, G., Preisser, J., Das, K. (2018). A score test for testing a marginalized zero-inflated Poisson regression model against a marginalized zero-inflated negative binomial regression model. *Journal of Agricultural, Biological and Environmental Statistics*, 23, 113–128.

Jackman, S. (2020). pscl: Classes and Methods for R Developed in the Political Science Computational Laboratory. R package version 1.5.5. United States Studies Centre, University of Sydney [Online]. Available at: https://github.com/atahk/pscl/.

James, G., Witten, D., Hastie, T., Tibshirani, R. (2014). *An Introduction to Statistical Learning: With Applications in R*. Springer, New York.

Jansakul, N. and Hinde, J. (2002). Score tests for zero-inflated Poisson models. *Computational Statistics & Data Analysis*, 40(1), 75–96.

Jochmann, M. (2017). zic: Bayesian Inference for Zero-Inflated Count Models. R package version 0.9.1 [Online]. Available at: https://CRAN.R-project.org/package=zic.

de Jong, P. and Heller, G.Z. (2008). *Generalized Linear Models for Insurance Data*. Cambridge University Press, Cambridge.

Jung, B.C., Jhun, M., Lee, J.W. (2005). Bootstrap tests for overdispersion in a zero-inflated Poisson regression model. *Biometrics*, 61(2), 626–628.

Kaplan, E.L. and Meier, P. (1958). Nonparametric estimation from incomplete observations. *Journal of the American Statistical Association*, 53(282), 457–481.

Karlis, D., Papatla, P., Roy, S. (2016). Finite mixtures of censored Poisson regression models. *Statistica Neerlandica*, 70(2), 100–122.

Kenward, M.G. and Carpenter, J. (2007). Multiple imputation: Current perspectives. *Statistical Methods in Medical Research*, 16(3), 199–218.

Klein, J.P. and Moeschberger, M.L. (2013). *Survival Analysis: Techniques for Censored and Truncated Data*. Springer, New York.

Lam, K.F., Xue, H., Cheung, Y.B. (2006). Semiparametric analysis of zero-inflated count data. *Biometrics*, 62(4), 996–1003.

Lambert, D. (1992). Zero-inflated Poisson regression, with an application to defects in manufacturing. *Technometrics*, 34(1), 1–14.

Lee, J., Jung, B.C., Jin, S.H. (2009). Tests for zero inflation in a bivariate zero-inflated Poisson model. *Statistica Neerlandica*, 63(4), 400–417.

Lee, W.-C., Sinha, S., Arbuckle, T., Fisher, M. (2018). Estimation in generalized linear models under censored covariates with an application to MIREC data. *Statistics in Medicine*, 37, 4539–4556.

Lee, S.M., Lukusa, T.M., Li, C.-S. (2020). Estimation of a zero-inflated Poisson regression model with missing covariates via nonparametric multiple imputation methods. *Computational Statistics*, 35, 725–754.

Lee, S.-M., Pho, K.-H., Li, C.-S. (2021). Validation likelihood estimation method for a zero-inflated Bernoulli regression model with missing covariates. *Journal of Statistical Planning and Inference*, 214, 105–127.

Liang, H., Wang, S., Robins, J.M., Carroll, R.J. (2004). Estimation in partially linear models with missing covariates. *Journal of the American Statistical Association*, 99(466), 357–367.

Little, R. and Rubin, D. (2002). *Statistical Analysis with Missing Data*. John Wiley & Sons, New York.

Long, D.L., Preisser, J.S., Herring, A.H., Golin, C.E. (2014). A marginalized zero-inflated Poisson regression model with overall exposure effects. *Statistics in Medicine*, 33(29), 5151–5165.

Long, D.L., Preisser, J.S., Herring, A.H., Golin, C.E. (2015). A marginalized zero-inflated Poisson regression model with random effects. *Journal of the Royal Statistical Society. Series C, Applied Statistics*, 64(5), 815–830.

Lu, M. and Li, C.-S. (2016). Spline-based semiparametric estimation of a zero-inflated Poisson regression single-index model. *Annals of the Institute of Statistical Mathematics*, 68, 1111–1134.

Lukusa, M.T. and Phoa, F.K.H. (2020). A note on the weighting-type estimations of the zero-inflated Poisson regression model with missing data in covariates. *Statistics & Probability Letters*, 158, 108654.

Lukusa, T.M., Lee, S.M., Li, C.S. (2016). Semiparametric estimation of a zero-inflated Poisson regression model with missing covariates. *Metrika*, 79(4), 457–483.

Luo, X., Tsai, W.Y., Xu, Q. (2009). Pseudo-partial likelihood estimators for the Cox regression model with missing covariates. *Biometrika*, 96(3), 617–633.

May, R.C., Ibrahim, J.G., Chu, H. (2011). Maximum likelihood estimation in generalized linear models with multiple covariates subject to detection limits. *Statistics in Medicine*, 30(20), 2551–2561.

McCullagh, P. and Nelder, J.A. (1989). *Generalized Linear Models*, 2nd edition. Chapman & Hall, London.

Moghimbeigi, A., Eshraghian, M.R., Mohammad, K., McArdle, B. (2009). A score test for zero-inflation in multilevel count data. *Computational Statistics & Data Analysis*, 53(4), 1239–1248.

Mullahy, J. (1986). Specification and testing of some modified count data models. *Journal of Econometrics*, 33(3), 341–365.

Nelder, J.A. and Wedderburn, R.W.M. (1972). Generalized linear models. *Journal of the Royal Statistical Society. Series A, General*, 135, 370–384.

Nguyen, V.T. and Dupuy, J.-F. (2021). Asymptotic results in censored zero-inflated Poisson regression. *Communications in Statistics – Theory and Methods*, 50(12), 2759–2779.

Paik, M.C. (1997). Multiple imputation for the Cox proportional hazards model with missing covariates. *Lifetime Data Analysis*, 3(3), 289–298.

Paik, M.C. and Tsai, W.-Y. (1997). On using the Cox proportional hazards model with missing covariates. *Biometrika*, 84(3), 579–593.

Pizer, S. D. and Prentice, J.C. (2011). Time is money: Outpatient waiting times and health insurance choices of elderly veterans in the United States. *Journal of Health Economics*, 30(4), 626–636.

Preisser, J.S., Das, K., Long, D.L., Divaris, K. (2016). Marginalized zero-inflated negative binomial regression with application to dental caries. *Statistics in Medicine*, 35(10), 1722–1735.

Qiu, Z. (2017). Statistical inference under imputation for proportional hazard model with missing covariates. *Communications in Statistics – Theory and Methods*, 46(23), 11575–11590.

R Core Team (2020). R: A language and environment for statistical computing. R Foundation for Statistical Computing, Vienna [Online]. Available at: https://www.R-project.org/.

Ridout, M., Hinde, J., Demétrio, C.G.B. (2001). A score test for testing a zero-inflated Poisson regression model against zero-inflated negative binomial alternatives. *Biometrics*, 57(1), 219–223.

Riphahn, R.T., Wambach, A., Million, A. (2003). Incentive effects in the demand for health care: A bivariate panel count data estimation. *Journal of Applied Econometrics*, 18(4), 387–405.

Robins, J.M., Rotnitzky, A., Zhao, L.P. (1994). Estimation of regression coefficients when some regressors are not always observed. *Journal of the American Statistical Association*, 89(427), 846–866.

Rubin, D.B. (1987). *Multiple Imputation for Nonresponse in Surveys*. John Wiley & Sons, New York.

Sari, N. (2009). Physical inactivity and its impact on healthcare utilization. *Health Economics*, 18(8), 885–901.

Sarma, S. and Simpson, W. (2006). A microeconometric analysis of Canadian health care utilization. *Health Economics*, 15(3), 219–239.

Schafer, J.L. (1999). Multiple imputation: A primer. *Statistical Methods in Medical Research*, 8(1), 3–15.

Schafer, J.L. and Yucel, R.M. (2002). Computational strategies for multivariate linear mixed-effects models with missing values. *Journal of Computational and Graphical Statistics*, 11(2), 437–457.

Scharfstein, D.O., Rotnitzky, A., Robins, J.M. (1999). Adjusting for nonignorable drop-out using semiparametric nonresponse models. *Journal of the American Statistical Association*, 94(448), 1096–1120.

Seaman, S.R. and White, I.R. (2013). Review of inverse probability weighting for dealing with missing data. *Statistical Methods in Medical Research*, 22(3), 278–295.

Shmueli, G., Minka, T.P., Kadane, J.B., Borle, S., Boatwright, P. (2005). A useful distribution for fitting discrete data: Revival of the Conway–Maxwell–Poisson distribution. *Journal of the Royal Statistical Society. Series C, Applied Statistics*, 54(1), 127–142.

Sinha, S.K. (2008). Robust methods for generalized linear models with nonignorable missing covariates. *The Canadian Journal of Statistics*, 36(2), 277–299.

Sinha, S.K., Laird, N.M., Fitzmaurice, G.M. (2010). Multivariate logistic regression with incomplete covariate and auxiliary information. *Journal of Multivariate Analysis*, 101(10), 2389–2397.

Song, X. and Wang, C.-Y. (2013). Time-varying coefficient proportional hazards model with missing covariates. *Statistics in Medicine*, 32(12), 2013–2030.

Staub, K.E. and Winkelmann, R. (2013). Consistent estimation of zero-inflated count models. *Health Economics*, 22(6), 673–686.

Sundberg, R. (2019). *Statistical Modelling by Exponential Families*. Cambridge University Press, Cambridge.

Terza, J.V. (1985). A Tobit-type estimator for the censored Poisson regression model. *Economics Letters*, 18(4), 361–365.

Therneau, T. and Grambsch, P. (2013). *Modeling Survival Data: Extending the Cox Model*. Springer, New York.

Tian, G.-L., Ma, H., Zhou, Y., Deng, D. (2015). Generalized endpoint-inflated binomial model. *Computational Statistics & Data Analysis*, 89, 97–114.

Tross, S., Feaster, D.J., Thorens, G., Duan, R., Gomez, Z., Pavlicova, M., Hu, M.C., Kyle, T., Erickson, S., Spector, A. et al. (2015). Substance use, depression and sociodemographic determinants of HIV sexual risk behavior in outpatient substance abuse treatment patients. *Journal of Addiction Medicine*, 9(6), 457–463.

Tsiatis, A.A. (2006). *Semiparametric Theory and Missing Data*. Springer, New York.

Tsimikas, J.V., Bantis, L.E., Georgiou, S.D. (2012). Inference in generalized linear regression models with a censored covariate. *Computational Statistics & Data Analysis*, 56(6), 1854–1868.

van der Vaart, A.W. (1998). *Asymptotic Statistics*. Cambridge University Press, Cambridge.

Venables, W.N. and Ripley, B.D. (2002). *Modern Applied Statistics with S*. Springer, New York.

Wang, Z. (2020). mpath: Regularized Linear Models. R package version 0.4-2.17 [Online]. Available at: https://CRAN.R-project.org/package=mpath.

Wang, X., Zhang, J., Yu, L., Yin, G. (2015). Generalized partially linear single-index model for zero-inflated count data. *Statistics in Medicine*, 34(5), 876–886.

White, H. (1982). Maximum likelihood estimation of misspecified models. *Econometrica*, 50(1), 1–25.

White, I.R. and Royston, P. (2009). Imputing missing covariate values for the Cox model. *Statistics in Medicine*, 28(15), 1982–1998.

Xiang, L., Lee, A.H., Yau, K.K.W., McLachlan, G.J. (2006). A score test for zero-inflation in correlated count data. *Statistics in Medicine*, 25(10), 1660–1671.

Xiang, L., Lee, A.H., Yau, K.K.W., McLachlan, G.J. (2007). A score test for overdispersion in zero-inflated Poisson mixed regression model. *Statistics in Medicine*, 26(7), 1608–1622.

Yang, X., Belin, T.R., Boscardin, W.J. (2005). Imputation and variable selection in linear regression models with missing covariates. *Biometrics*, 61(2), 498–506.

Yang, Z., Hardin, J.W., Addy, C.L. (2009). Testing overdispersion in the zero-inflated Poisson model. *Journal of Statistical Planning and Inference*, 139(9), 3340–3353.

Yee, T.W. (2010). The VGAM package for categorical data analysis. *Journal of Statistical Software*, 32(10), 1–34.

Yee, T.W. (2015). *Vector Generalized Linear and Additive Models: With an Implementation in R*. Springer, New York.

Yeh, H.W., Gajewski, B., Mukhopadhyay, P., Behbod, F. (2012). The zero-truncated Poisson with right censoring: An application to translational breast cancer research. *Statistics in Biopharmaceutical Research*, 4(3), 252–263.

Yen, S.T., Tang, C.-H., Su, S.-J.B. (2001). Demand for traditional medicine in Taiwan: A mixed Gaussian Poisson model approach. *Health Economics*, 10(3), 221–232.

Yip, K.C. and Yau, K.K. (2005). On modeling claim frequency data in general insurance with extra zeros. *Insurance: Mathematics and Economics*, 36(2), 153–163.

Zeileis, A. and Hothorn, T. (2002). Diagnostic checking in regression relationships. *R News*, 2(3), 7–10 [Online]. Available at: https://CRAN.R-project.org/doc/Rnews/.

Zeileis, A. and Kleiber, C. (2020). Countreg: Count Data Regression. R package version 0.2-1 [Online]. Available at: http://R-Forge.R-project.org/projects/countreg/.

Zhang, P., Pitt, D., Wu, X. (2022). A new multivariate zero-inflated hurdle model with applications in automobile insurance. *ASTIN Bulletin*, 52(2), 393–416.

Zhao, J. and Shao, J. (2015). Semiparametric pseudo-likelihoods in generalized linear models with nonignorable missing data. *Journal of the American Statistical Association*, 110(512), 1577–1590.

Index

Other titles from

iSTE

in

Mathematics and Statistics

2025

GAIVORONSKI Alexei A., KNOPOV Pavel S., NORKIN Vladimir I., ZASLAVSKYI Volodymyr A.
Stochastic Modeling and Optimization Methods for Critical Infrastructure Protection 1: Stochastic Modeling
Stochastic Modeling and Optimization Methods for Critical Infrastructure Protection 2: Methods and Tools

2024

BOURLÈS Henri
System Theory – A Modern Approach 1: Linear Ordinary and Functional Differential Equations
(New Mathematical Methods, Systems and Applications Set – Volume 1)

MAKAROV Volodymyr, MAYKO Nataliya
Traditional Functional-Discrete Methods for the Problems of Mathematical Physics: New Aspects

2023

AIT BEN HASSI El Mustapha
The Theory of Distributions: Introduction

KOROLIOUK Dmitri, SAMOILENKO Igor
Asymptotic and Analytic Methods in Stochastic Evolutionary Systems

PARROCHIA Daniel
Graphs, Orders, Infinites and Philosophy

2022

CHAKRAVARTHY Srinivas R.
Introduction to Matrix-Analytic Methods in Queues 1: Analytical and Simulation Approach – Basics
Introduction to Matrix-Analytic Methods in Queues 2: Analytical and Simulation Approach – Queues and Simulation

LESFARI Ahmed
Integrable Systems

RADCHENKI Vadym M.
General Stochastic Measures: Integration, Path Properties and Equations

DE SAPORTA Benoîte, ZILI Mounir
Martingales and Financial Mathematics in Discrete Time

SIMON Jacques
Distributions
(Analysis for PDEs Set – Volume 3)

2021

KOROLIOUK Dmitri, SAMOILENKO Igor
Random Evolutionary Systems: Asymptotic Properties and Large Deviations

MOKLYACHUK Mikhail
Convex Optimization: Introductory Course

POGORUI Anatoliy, SWISHCHUK Anatoliy, RODRÍGUEZ-DAGNINO Ramón M.
Random Motions in Markov and Semi-Markov Random Environments 1: Homogeneous Random Motions and their Applications
Random Motions in Markov and Semi-Markov Random Environments 2: High-dimensional Random Motions and Financial Applications

PROVENZI Edoardo
From Euclidean to Hilbert Spaces: Introduction to Functional Analysis and its Applications

2020

BARBU Vlad Stefan, VERGNE Nicolas
Statistical Topics and Stochastic Models for Dependent Data with Applications

CHABANYUK Yaroslav, NIKITIN Anatolii, KHIMKA Uliana
Asymptotic Analyses for Complex Evolutionary Systems with Markov and Semi-Markov Switching Using Approximation Schemes

KOROLIOUK Dmitri
Dynamics of Statistical Experiments

MANOU-ABI Solym Mawaki, DABO-NIANG Sophie, SALONE Jean-Jacques
Mathematical Modeling of Random and Deterministic Phenomena

SIMON Jacques
Continuous Functions
(Analysis for PDEs Set – Volume 23)

2019

BANNA Oksana, MISHURA Yuliya, RALCHENKO Kostiantyn, SHKLYAR Sergiy
Fractional Brownian Motion: Approximations and Projections

GANA Kamel, BROC Guillaume
Structural Equation Modeling with lavaan

KUKUSH Alexander
Gaussian Measures in Hilbert Space: Construction and Properties

LUZ Maksym, MOKLYACHUK Mikhail
Estimation of Stochastic Processes with Stationary Increments and Cointegrated Sequences

MICHELITSCH Thomas, PÉREZ RIASCOS Alejandro, COLLET Bernard, NOWAKOWSKI Andrzej, NICOLLEAU Franck
Fractional Dynamics on Networks and Lattices

VOTSI Irene, LIMNIOS Nikolaos, PAPADIMITRIOU Eleftheria, TSAKLIDIS George
Earthquake Statistical Analysis through Multi-state Modeling
(Statistical Methods for Earthquakes Set – Volume 2)

2018

AZAÏS Romain, BOUGUET Florian
Statistical Inference for Piecewise-deterministic Markov Processes

IBRAHIMI Mohammed
Mergers & Acquisitions: Theory, Strategy, Finance

PARROCHIA Daniel
Mathematics and Philosophy

2017

CARONI Chysseis
First Hitting Time Regression Models: Lifetime Data Analysis Based on Underlying Stochastic Processes
(Mathematical Models and Methods in Reliability Set – Volume 4)

CELANT Giorgio, BRONIATOWSKI Michel
Interpolation and Extrapolation Optimal Designs 2: Finite Dimensional General Models

CONSOLE Rodolfo, MURRU Maura, FALCONE Giuseppe
Earthquake Occurrence: Short- and Long-term Models and their Validation
(Statistical Methods for Earthquakes Set – Volume 1)

D'AMICO Guglielmo, DI BIASE Giuseppe, JANSSEN Jacques, MANCA Raimondo
Semi-Markov Migration Models for Credit Risk
(Stochastic Models for Insurance Set – Volume 1)

GONZÁLEZ VELASCO Miguel, del PUERTO GARCÍA Inés, YANEV George P.
Controlled Branching Processes
(Branching Processes, Branching Random Walks and Branching Particle Fields Set – Volume 2)

HARLAMOV Boris
Stochastic Analysis of Risk and Management
(Stochastic Models in Survival Analysis and Reliability Set – Volume 2)

KERSTING Götz, VATUTIN Vladimir
Discrete Time Branching Processes in Random Environment
(Branching Processes, Branching Random Walks and Branching Particle Fields Set – Volume 1)

MISHURA Yuliya, SHEVCHENKO Georgiy
Theory and Statistical Applications of Stochastic Processes

NIKULIN Mikhail, CHIMITOVA Ekaterina
Chi-squared Goodness-of-fit Tests for Censored Data
(Stochastic Models in Survival Analysis and Reliability Set – Volume 3)

SIMON Jacques
Banach, Fréchet, Hilbert and Neumann Spaces
(Analysis for PDEs Set – Volume 1)

2016

CELANT Giorgio, BRONIATOWSKI Michel
Interpolation and Extrapolation Optimal Designs 1: Polynomial Regression and Approximation Theory

CHIASSERINI Carla Fabiana, GRIBAUDO Marco, MANINI Daniele
Analytical Modeling of Wireless Communication Systems
(Stochastic Models in Computer Science and Telecommunication Networks Set – Volume 1)

GOUDON Thierry
Mathematics for Modeling and Scientific Computing

KAHLE Waltraud, MERCIER Sophie, PAROISSIN Christian
Degradation Processes in Reliability
(Mathematial Models and Methods in Reliability Set – Volume 3)

KERN Michel
Numerical Methods for Inverse Problems

RYKOV Vladimir
Reliability of Engineering Systems and Technological Risks
(Stochastic Models in Survival Analysis and Reliability Set – Volume 1)

2015

DEVOLDER Pierre, JANSSEN Jacques, MANCA Raimondo
Basic Stochastic Processes

LE GAT Yves
Recurrent Event Modeling Based on the Yule Process
(Mathematical Models and Methods in Reliability Set – Volume 2)

DE SAPORTA Benoîte, DUFOUR François, ZHANG Huilong
Numerical Methods for Simulation and Optimization of Piecewise Deterministic Markov Processes

2014

COOKE Roger M., NIEBOER Daan, MISIEWICZ Jolanta
Fat-tailed Distributions: Data, Diagnostics and Dependence
(Mathematical Models and Methods in Reliability Set – Volume 1)

MACKEVIČIUS Vigirdas
Integral and Measure: From Rather Simple to Rather Complex

PASCHOS Vangelis Th
Combinatorial Optimization – 3-volume series – 2nd edition
Concepts of Combinatorial Optimization / Concepts and Fundamentals – Volume 1
Paradigms of Combinatorial Optimization – Volume 2
Applications of Combinatorial Optimization – Volume 3

2013

COUALLIER Vincent, GERVILLE-RÉACHE Léo, HUBER Catherine, LIMNIOS Nikolaos, MESBAH Mounir
Statistical Models and Methods for Reliability and Survival Analysis

JANSSEN Jacques, MANCA Oronzio, MANCA Raimondo
Applied Diffusion Processes from Engineering to Finance

SERICOLA Bruno
Markov Chains: Theory, Algorithms and Applications

2012

BOSQ Denis
Mathematical Statistics and Stochastic Processes

CHRISTENSEN Karl Bang, KREINER Svend, MESBAH Mounir
Rasch Models in Health

DECREUSEFOND Laurent, MOYAL Pascal
Stochastic Modeling and Analysis of Telecom Networks

DEVOLDER Pierre, JANSSEN Jacques, MANCA Raimondo
Stochastic Methods for Pension Funds

2011

MACKEVIČIUS Vigirdas
Introduction to Stochastic Analysis: Integrals and Differential Equations

MAHJOUB Ridha
Recent Progress in Combinatorial Optimization – ISCO2010

RAYNAUD Hervé, ARROW Kenneth
Managerial Logic

2010

BAGDONAVIČIUS Vilijandas, KRUOPIS Julius, NIKULIN Mikhail
Nonparametric Tests for Censored Data

IOSIFESCU Marius, LIMNIOS Nikoloas, OPRISAN Gheorghe
Introduction to Stochastic Models

VASSILIOU P.C.G.
Discrete-time Asset Pricing Models in Applied Stochastic Finance

2008

ANISIMOV Vladimir
Switching Processes in Queuing Models

FICHE Georges, HÉBUTERNE Gérard
Mathematics for Engineers

HUBER Catherine, LIMNIOS Nikolaos, MESBAH Mounir, NIKULIN Mikhail
Mathematical Methods in Survival Analysis, Reliability and Quality of Life

JANSSEN Jacques, MANCA Raimondo, VOLPE Ernesto
Mathematical Finance

2007

HARLAMOV Boris
Continuous Semi-Markov Processes

2006

CLERC Maurice
Particle Swarm Optimization

Printed and bound by CPI Group (UK) Ltd, Croydon, CR0 4YY
13/09/2026
14961039-0001